GO!
with Microsoft®

Excel 2010
Brief

Shelley Gaskin and Alicia Vargas

Prentice Hall

Boston   Columbus   Indianapolis   New York   San Francisco   Upper Saddle River
Amsterdam   Cape Town   Dubai   London   Madrid   Milan   Munich   Paris   Montreal   Toronto
Delhi   Mexico City   Sao Paulo   Sydney   Hong Kong   Seoul   Singapore   Taipei   Tokyo

Associate VP/Executive Acquisitions Editor, Print:
  Stephanie Wall
Editorial Project Manager: Laura Burgess
Editor in Chief: Michael Payne
Product Development Manager: Eileen Bien Calabro
Development Editor: Ginny Munroe
Editorial Assistant: Nicole Sam
Director of Marketing: Kate Valentine
Marketing Manager: Tori Olson Alves
Marketing Coordinator: Susan Osterlitz
Marketing Assistant: Darshika Vyas
Senior Managing Editor: Cynthia Zonneveld
Associate Managing Editor: Camille Trentacoste
Production Project Manager: Mike Lackey
Operations Director: Alexis Heydt
Operations Specialist: Natacha Moore

Senior Art Director: Jonathan Boylan
Cover Photo: © Ben Durrant
Text and Cover Designer: Blair Brown
Manager, Cover Visual Research & Permissions:
  Karen Sanatar
Manager, Rights and Permissions: Zina Arabia
AVP/Director of Online Programs, Media: Richard Keaveny
AVP/Director of Product Development, Media: Lisa Strite
Media Project Manager, Editorial: Alana Coles
Media Project Manager, Production: John Cassar
Full-Service Project Management: PreMediaGlobal
Composition: PreMediaGlobal
Printer/Binder: Quebecor World Book Services
Cover Printer: Lehigh-Phoenix Color
Text Font: Bookman Light

Credits and acknowledgments borrowed from other sources and reproduced, with permission, in this textbook appear on appropriate page within text.

Microsoft® and Windows® are registered trademarks of the Microsoft Corporation in the U.S.A. and other countries. Screen shots and icons reprinted with permission from the Microsoft Corporation. This book is not sponsored or endorsed by or affiliated with the Microsoft Corporation.

10 9 8 7 6 5 4 3 2 1

Prentice Hall
is an imprint of

www.pearsonhighered.com

ISBN 10: 0-13-509771-1
ISBN 13: 978-0-13-509771-7

Brief Contents

Contents

Excel

Chapter 3   Analyzing Data with Pie Charts, Line Charts, and What-If Analysis Tools 177

GO! System Contributors

We thank the following people for their hard work and support in making the *GO!* System all that it is!

Instructor Resource Authors

Adickes, Erich	Parkland College	Holland, Susan	Southeast Community College-Nebraska
Baray, Carrie	Ivy Tech Community College		
Clausen, Jane	Western Iowa Tech Community College	Landenberger, Toni	Southeast Community College-Nebraska
Crossley, Connie	Cincinnati State Technical and Community College	McMahon, Richard	University of Houston—Downtown
		Miller, Sandra	Wenatchee Valley College
Emrich, Stefanie	Metropolitan Community College of Omaha, Nebraska	Niebur, Katherine	Dakota County Technical College
		Nowakowski, Anthony	Buffalo State
Faix, Dennis	Harrisburg Area Community College	Pierce, Tonya	Ivy Tech Community College
Hadden, Karen	Western Iowa Tech Community College	Roselli, Diane	Harrisburg Area Community College
		St. John, Steve	Tulsa Community College
Hammerle, Patricia	Indiana University/Purdue University at Indianapolis	Sterr, Jody	Blackhawk Technical College
		Thompson, Joyce	Lehigh Carbon Community College
Hines, James	Tidewater Community College	Tucker, William	Austin Community College

Technical Editors

Matthew Bisi	Barbara Edington	Joyce Nielsen	Jan Snyder
Mary Corcoran	Sarah Evans	Janet Pickard	Mara Zebest
Lori Damanti	Adam Layne	Sean Portnoy	

Student Reviewers

Albinda, Sarah Evangeline	Phoenix College	Innis, Tim	Tulsa Community College
Allen, John	Asheville-Buncombe Tech Community College	Jarboe, Aaron	Central Washington University
		Key, Penny	Greenville Technical College
Alexander, Steven	St. Johns River Community College	Klein, Colleen	Northern Michigan University
Alexander, Melissa	Tulsa Community College	Lloyd, Kasey	Ivy Tech Bloomington
Bolz, Stephanie	Northern Michigan University	Moeller, Jeffrey	Northern Michigan University
Berner, Ashley	Central Washington University	Mullen, Sharita	Tidewater Community College
Boomer, Michelle	Northern Michigan University	Nelson, Cody	Texas Tech University
Busse, Brennan	Northern Michigan University	Nicholson, Regina	Athens Tech College
Butkey, Maura	Central Washington University	Niehaus, Kristina	Northern Michigan University
Cates, Concita	Phoenix College	Nisa, Zaibun	Santa Rosa Community College
Charles, Marvin	Harrisburg Area Community College	Nunez, Nohelia	Santa Rosa Community College
		Oak, Samantha	Central Washington University
Christensen, Kaylie	Northern Michigan University	Oberly, Sara	Harrisburg Area Community College Lancaster
Clark, Glen D. III	Harrisburg Area Community College		
		Oertii, Monica	Central Washington University
Cobble, Jan N.	Greenville Technical College	Palenshus, Juliet	Central Washington University
Connally, Brianna	Central Washington University	Pohl, Amanda	Northern Michigan University
Davis, Brandon	Northern Michigan University	Presnell, Randy	Central Washington University
Davis, Christen	Central Washington University	Reed, Kailee	Texas Tech University
De Jesus Garcia, Maria	Phoenix College	Ritner, April	Northern Michigan University
Den Boer, Lance	Central Washington University	Roberts, Corey	Tulsa Community College
Dix, Jessica	Central Washington University	Rodgers, Spencer	Texas Tech University
Moeller, Jeffrey	Northern Michigan University	Rodriguez, Flavia	Northwestern State University
Downs, Elizabeth	Central Washington University	Rogers, A.	Tidewater Community College
Elser, Julie	Harrisburg Area Community College	Rossi, Jessica Ann	Central Washington University
		Rothbauer, Taylor	Trident Technical College
Erickson, Mike	Ball State University	Rozelle, Lauren	Texas Tech University
Frye, Alicia	Phoenix College	Schmadeke, Kimberly	Kirkwood Community College
Gadomski, Amanda	Northern Michigan University	Shafapay, Natasha	Central Washington University
Gassert, Jennifer	Harrisburg Area Community College	Shanahan, Megan	Northern Michigan University
		Sullivan, Alexandra Nicole	Greenville Technical College
Gross, Mary Jo	Kirkwood Community College	Teska, Erika	Hawaii Pacific University
Gyselinck, Craig	Central Washington University	Torrenti, Natalie	Harrisburg Area Community College
Harrison, Margo	Central Washington University		
Hatt, Patrick	Harrisburg Area Community College	Traub, Amy	Northern Michigan University
Heacox, Kate	Central Washington University	Underwood, Katie	Central Washington University
Hedgman, Shaina	Tidewater College	Walters, Kim	Central Washington University
Hill, Cheretta	Northwestern State University	Warren, Jennifer L.	Greenville Technical College
Hochstedler, Bethany	Harrisburg Area Community College Lancaster	Wilson, Kelsie	Central Washington University
		Wilson, Amanda	Green River Community College
Homer, Jean	Greenville Technical College	Wylie, Jimmy	Texas Tech University

Contributors continued

Series Reviewers

Abraham, Reni	Houston Community College	Cannon, Kim	Greenville Technical College
Addison, Paul	Ivy Tech Community College	Carreon, Cleda	Indiana University—Purdue University, Indianapolis
Agatston, Ann	Agatston Consulting Technical College	Carriker, Sandra	North Shore Community College
Akuna, Valeria, Ph.D.	Estrella Mountain Community College	Casey, Patricia	Trident Technical College
Alexander, Melody	Ball Sate University	Cates, Wally	Central New Mexico Community College
Alejandro, Manuel	Southwest Texas Junior College	Chaffin, Catherine	Shawnee State University
Alger, David	Tidewater Community College Chesapeake Campus	Chauvin, Marg	Palm Beach Community College, Boca Raton
Allen, Jackie	Rowan-Cabarrus Community College	Challa, Chandrashekar	Virginia State University
Ali, Farha	Lander University	Chamlou, Afsaneh	NOVA Alexandria
Amici, Penny	Harrisburg Area Community College	Chapman, Pam	Wabaunsee Community College
Anderson, Patty A.	Lake City Community College	Christensen, Dan	Iowa Western Community College
Andrews, Wilma	Virginia Commonwealth College, Nebraska University	Clay, Betty	Southeastern Oklahoma State University
Anik, Mazhar	Tiffin University	Collins, Linda D.	Mesa Community College
Armstrong, Gary	Shippensburg University	Cone, Bill	Northern Arizona University
Arnold, Linda L.	Harrisburg Area Community College	Conroy-Link, Janet	Holy Family College
Ashby, Tom	Oklahoma City Community College	Conway, Ronald	Bowling Green State University
		Cornforth, Carol G.	WVNCC
Atkins, Bonnie	Delaware Technical Community College	Cosgrove, Janet	Northwestern CT Community
Aukland, Cherie	Thomas Nelson Community College	Courtney, Kevin	Hillsborough Community College
		Coverdale, John	Riverside Community College
Bachand, LaDonna	Santa Rosa Community College	Cox, Rollie	Madison Area Technical College
Bagui, Sikha	University of West Florida	Crawford, Hiram	Olive Harvey College
Beecroft, Anita	Kwantlen University College	Crawford, Sonia	Central New Mexico Community College
Bell, Paula	Lock Haven College	Crawford, Thomasina	Miami-Dade College, Kendall Campus
Belton, Linda	Springfield Tech. Community College	Credico, Grace	Lethbridge Community College
Bennett, Judith	Sam Houston State University	Crenshaw, Richard	Miami Dade Community College, North
Bhatia, Sai	Riverside Community College	Crespo, Beverly	Mt. San Antonio College
Bishop, Frances	DeVry Institute—Alpharetta (ATL)	Crooks, Steven	Texas Tech University
Blaszkiewicz, Holly	Ivy Tech Community College/Region 1	Crossley, Connie	Cincinnati State Technical Community College
Boito, Nancy	HACC Central Pennsylvania's Community College	Curik, Mary	Central New Mexico Community College
Borger-Boglin, Grietje L.	San Antonio College/Northeast Lakeview College	De Arazoza, Ralph	Miami Dade Community College
		Danno, John	DeVry University/Keller Graduate School
Branigan, Dave	DeVry University	Davis, Phillip	Del Mar College
Bray, Patricia	Allegany College of Maryland	Davis, Richard	Trinity Valley Community College
Britt, Brenda K.	Fayetteville Technical Community College	Davis, Sandra	Baker College of Allen Park
		Dees, Stephanie D.	Wharton County Junior College
Brotherton, Cathy	Riverside Community College	DeHerrera, Laurie	Pikes Peak Community College
Brown, Judy	Western Illinois University	Delk, Dr. K. Kay	Seminole Community College
Buehler, Lesley	Ohlone College	Denton, Bree	Texas Tech University
Buell, C	Central Oregon Community College	Dix, Jeanette	Ivy Tech Community College
		Dooly, Veronica P.	Asheville-Buncombe Technical Community College
Burns, Christine	Central New Mexico Community College	Doroshow, Mike	Eastfield College
Byars, Pat	Brookhaven College	Douglas, Gretchen	SUNYCortland
Byrd, Julie	Ivy Tech Community College	Dove, Carol	Community College of Allegheny
Byrd, Lynn	Delta State University, Cleveland, Mississippi	Dozier, Susan	Tidewater Community College, Virginia Beach Campus
Cacace, Richard N.	Pensacola Junior College	Driskel, Loretta	Niagara Community College
Cadenhead, Charles	Brookhaven College	Duckwiler, Carol	Wabaunsee Community College
Calhoun, Ric	Gordon College	Duhon, David	Baker College
Cameron, Eric	Passaic Community College	Duncan, Mimi	University of Missouri-St. Louis
Canine, Jill	Ivy Tech Community College of Indiana	Duthie, Judy	Green River Community College
Cannamore, Madie	Kennedy King	Duvall, Annette	Central New Mexico Community College

Ecklund, Paula	Duke University
Eilers, Albert	Cincinnati State Technical and Community College
Eng, Bernice	Brookdale Community College
Epperson, Arlin	Columbia College
Evans, Billie	Vance-Granville Community College
Evans, Jean	Brevard Community College
Feuerbach, Lisa	Ivy Tech East Chicago
Finley, Jean	ABTCC
Fisher, Fred	Florida State University
Foster, Nancy	Baker College
Foster-Shriver, Penny L.	Anne Arundel Community College
Foster-Turpen, Linda	CNM
Foszcz, Russ	McHenry County College
Fry, Susan	Boise State University
Fustos, Janos	Metro State
Gallup, Jeanette	Blinn College
Gelb, Janet	Grossmont College
Gentry, Barb	Parkland College
Gerace, Karin	St. Angela Merici School
Gerace, Tom	Tulane University
Ghajar, Homa	Oklahoma State University
Gifford, Steve	Northwest Iowa Community College
Glazer, Ellen	Broward Community College
Gordon, Robert	Hofstra University
Gramlich, Steven	Pasco-Hernando Community College
Graviett, Nancy M.	St. Charles Community College, St. Peters, Missouri
Greene, Rich	Community College of Allegheny County
Gregoryk, Kerry	Virginia Commonwealth State
Griggs, Debra	Bellevue Community College
Grimm, Carol	Palm Beach Community College
Guthrie, Rose	Fox Valley Technical College
Hahn, Norm	Thomas Nelson Community College
Haley-Hunter, Deb	Bluefield State College
Hall, Linnea	Northwest Mississippi Community College
Hammerschlag, Dr. Bill	Brookhaven College
Hansen, Michelle	Davenport University
Hayden, Nancy	Indiana University—Purdue University, Indianapolis
Hayes, Theresa	Broward Community College
Headrick, Betsy	Chattanooga State
Helfand, Terri	Chaffey College
Helms, Liz	Columbus State Community College
Hernandez, Leticia	TCI College of Technology
Hibbert, Marilyn	Salt Lake Community College
Hinds, Cheryl	Norfolk State University
Hines, James	Tidewater Community College
Hoffman, Joan	Milwaukee Area Technical College
Hogan, Pat	Cape Fear Community College
Holland, Susan	Southeast Community College
Holliday, Mardi	Community College of Philadelphia
Hollingsworth, Mary Carole	Georgia Perimeter College
Hopson, Bonnie	Athens Technical College
Horvath, Carrie	Albertus Magnus College
Horwitz, Steve	Community College of Philadelphia
Hotta, Barbara	Leeward Community College
Howard, Bunny	St. Johns River Community
Howard, Chris	DeVry University
Huckabay, Jamie	Austin Community College
Hudgins, Susan	East Central University
Hulett, Michelle J.	Missouri State University
Humphrey, John	Asheville Buncombe Technical Community College
Hunt, Darla A.	Morehead State University, Morehead, Kentucky
Hunt, Laura	Tulsa Community College
Ivey, Joan M.	Lanier Technical College
Jacob, Sherry	Jefferson Community College
Jacobs, Duane	Salt Lake Community College
Jauken, Barb	Southeastern Community
Jerry, Gina	Santa Monica College
Johnson, Deborah S.	Edison State College
Johnson, Kathy	Wright College
Johnson, Mary	Kingwood College
Johnson, Mary	Mt. San Antonio College
Jones, Stacey	Benedict College
Jones, Warren	University of Alabama, Birmingham
Jordan, Cheryl	San Juan College
Kapoor, Bhushan	California State University, Fullerton
Kasai, Susumu	Salt Lake Community College
Kates, Hazel	Miami Dade Community College, Kendall
Keen, Debby	University of Kentucky
Keeter, Sandy	Seminole Community College
Kern-Blystone, Dorothy Jean	Bowling Green State
Kerwin, Annette	College of DuPage
Keskin, Ilknur	The University of South Dakota
Kinney, Mark B.	Baker College
Kirk, Colleen	Mercy College
Kisling, Eric	East Carolina University
Kleckner, Michelle	Elon University
Kliston, Linda	Broward Community College, North Campus
Knuth, Toni	Baker College of Auburn Hills
Kochis, Dennis	Suffolk County Community College
Kominek, Kurt	Northeast State Technical Community College
Kramer, Ed	Northern Virginia Community College
Kretz, Daniel	Fox Valley Technical College
Laird, Jeff	Northeast State Community College
Lamoureaux, Jackie	Central New Mexico Community College
Lange, David	Grand Valley State
LaPointe, Deb	Central New Mexico Community College
Larsen, Jacqueline Anne	A-B Tech
Larson, Donna	Louisville Technical Institute
Laspina, Kathy	Vance-Granville Community College
Le Grand, Dr. Kate	Broward Community College
Lenhart, Sheryl	Terra Community College
Leonard, Yvonne	Coastal Carolina Community College
Letavec, Chris	University of Cincinnati
Lewis, Daphne L, Ed.D.	Wayland Baptist University
Lewis, Julie	Baker College-Allen Park
Liefert, Jane	Everett Community College

Lindaman, Linda	Black Hawk Community College	Meredith, Mary	University of Louisiana at Lafayette
Lindberg, Martha	Minnesota State University	Mermelstein, Lisa	Baruch College
Lightner, Renee	Broward Community College	Metos, Linda	Salt Lake Community College
Lindberg, Martha	Minnesota State University	Meurer, Daniel	University of Cincinnati
Linge, Richard	Arizona Western College	Meyer, Colleen	Cincinnati State Technical and Community College
Logan, Mary G.	Delgado Community College		
Loizeaux, Barbara	Westchester Community College	Meyer, Marian	Central New Mexico Community College
Lombardi, John	South University		
Lopez, Don	Clovis-State Center Community College District	Miller, Cindy	Ivy Tech Community College, Lafayette, Indiana
Lopez, Lisa	Spartanburg Community College	Mills, Robert E.	Tidewater Community College, Portsmouth Campus
Lord, Alexandria	Asheville Buncombe Tech		
Lovering, LeAnne	Augusta Technical College	Mitchell, Susan	Davenport University
Lowe, Rita	Harold Washington College	Mohle, Dennis	Fresno Community College
Low, Willy Hui	Joliet Junior College	Molki, Saeed	South Texas College
Lucas, Vickie	Broward Community College	Monk, Ellen	University of Delaware
Luna, Debbie	El Paso Community College	Moore, Rodney	Holland College
Luoma, Jean	Davenport University	Morris, Mike	Southeastern Oklahoma State University
Luse, Steven P.	Horry Georgetown Technical College		
		Morris, Nancy	Hudson Valley Community College
Lynam, Linda	Central Missouri State University		
Lyon, Lynne	Durham College	Moseler, Dan	Harrisburg Area Community College
Lyon, Pat Rajski	Tomball College		
Macarty, Matthew	University of New Hampshire	Nabors, Brent	Reedley College, Clovis Center
MacKinnon, Ruth	Georgia Southern University	Nadas, Erika	Wright College
Macon, Lisa	Valencia Community College, West Campus	Nadelman, Cindi	New England College
		Nademlynsky, Lisa	Johnson & Wales University
Machuca, Wayne	College of the Sequoias	Nagengast, Joseph	Florida Career College
Mack, Sherri	Butler County Community College	Nason, Scott	Rowan Cabarrus Community College
Madison, Dana	Clarion University		
Maguire, Trish	Eastern New Mexico University	Ncube, Cathy	University of West Florida
Malkan, Rajiv	Montgomery College	Newsome, Eloise	Northern Virginia Community College Woodbridge
Manning, David	Northern Kentucky University		
Marcus, Jacquie	Niagara Community College	Nicholls, Doreen	Mohawk Valley Community College
Marghitu, Daniela	Auburn University		
Marks, Suzanne	Bellevue Community College	Nicholson, John R.	Johnson County Community College
Marquez, Juanita	El Centro College		
Marquez, Juan	Mesa Community College	Nielson, Phil	Salt Lake Community College
Martin, Carol	Harrisburg Area Community College	Nunan, Karen L.	Northeast State Technical Community College
Martin, Paul C.	Harrisburg Area Community College	O'Neal, Lois Ann	Rogers State University
		Odegard, Teri	Edmonds Community College
Martyn, Margie	Baldwin-Wallace College	Ogle, Gregory	North Community College
Marucco, Toni	Lincoln Land Community College	Orr, Dr. Claudia	Northern Michigan University South
Mason, Lynn	Lubbock Christian University		
Matutis, Audrone	Houston Community College	Orsburn, Glen	Fox Valley Technical College
Matkin, Marie	University of Lethbridge	Otieno, Derek	DeVry University
Maurel, Trina	Odessa College	Otton, Diana Hill	Chesapeake College
May, Karen	Blinn College	Oxendale, Lucia	West Virginia Institute of Technology
McCain, Evelynn	Boise State University		
McCannon, Melinda	Gordon College		
McCarthy, Marguerite	Northwestern Business College	Paiano, Frank	Southwestern College
McCaskill, Matt L.	Brevard Community College	Pannell, Dr. Elizabeth	Collin College
McClellan, Carolyn	Tidewater Community College	Patrick, Tanya	Clackamas Community College
McClure, Darlean	College of Sequoias	Paul, Anindya	Daytona State College
McCrory, Sue A.	Missouri State University	Peairs, Deb	Clark State Community College
McCue, Stacy	Harrisburg Area Community College	Perez, Kimberly	Tidewater Community College
		Porter, Joyce	Weber State University
McEntire-Orbach, Teresa	Middlesex County College	Prince, Lisa	Missouri State University-Springfield Campus
McKinley, Lee	Georgia Perimeter College		
McLeod, Todd	Fresno City College	Proietti, Kathleen	Northern Essex Community College
McManus, Illyana	Grossmont College		
McPherson, Dori	Schoolcraft College	Puopolo, Mike	Bunker Hill Community College
Meck, Kari	HACC	Pusins, Delores	HCCC
Meiklejohn, Nancy	Pikes Peak Community College	Putnam, Darlene	Thomas Nelson Community College
Menking, Rick	Hardin-Simmons University		

Raghuraman, Ram — Joliet Junior College
Rani, Chigurupati — BMCC/CUNY
Reasoner, Ted Allen — Indiana University—Purdue
Reeves, Karen — High Point University
Remillard, Debbie — New Hampshire Technical Institute
Rhue, Shelly — DeVry University
Richards, Karen — Maplewoods Community College
Richardson, Mary — Albany Technical College
Rodgers, Gwen — Southern Nazarene University
Rodie, Karla — Pikes Peak Community College
Roselli, Diane Maie — Harrisburg Area Community College
Ross, Dianne — University of Louisiana in Lafayette
Rousseau, Mary — Broward Community College, South
Rovetto, Ann — Horry-Georgetown Technical College
Rusin, Iwona — Baker College
Sahabi, Ahmad — Baker College of Clinton Township
Samson, Dolly — Hawaii Pacific University
Sams, Todd — University of Cincinnati
Sandoval, Everett — Reedley College
Santiago, Diana — Central New Mexico Community College
Sardone, Nancy — Seton Hall University
Scafide, Jean — Mississippi Gulf Coast Community College
Scheeren, Judy — Westmoreland County Community College
Scheiwe, Adolph — Joliet Junior College
Schneider, Sol — Sam Houston State University
Schweitzer, John — Central New Mexico Community College
Scroggins, Michael — Southwest Missouri State University
Sedlacek, Brenda — Tidewater Community College
Sell, Kelly — Anne Arundel Community College
Sever, Suzanne — Northwest Arkansas Community College
Sewell, John — Florida Career College
Sheridan, Rick — California State University-Chico
Silvers, Pamela — Asheville Buncombe Tech
Sindt, Robert G. — Johnson County Community College
Singer, Noah — Tulsa Community College
Singer, Steven A. — University of Hawai'i, Kapi'olani Community College
Sinha, Atin — Albany State University
Skolnick, Martin — Florida Atlantic University
Smith, Kristi — Allegany College of Maryland
Smith, Patrick — Marshall Community and Technical College
Smith, Stella A. — Georgia Gwinnett College
Smith, T. Michael — Austin Community College
Smith, Tammy — Tompkins Cortland Community Collge
Smolenski, Bob — Delaware County Community College
Smolenski, Robert — Delaware Community College
Southwell, Donald — Delta College
Spangler, Candice — Columbus State
Spangler, Candice — Columbus State Community College
Stark, Diane — Phoenix College
Stedham, Vicki — St. Petersburg College, Clearwater
Stefanelli, Greg — Carroll Community College
Steiner, Ester — New Mexico State University
Stenlund, Neal — Northern Virginia Community College, Alexandria
St. John, Steve — Tulsa Community College
Sterling, Janet — Houston Community College
Stoughton, Catherine — Laramie County Community College
Sullivan, Angela — Joliet Junior College

Sullivan, Denise — Westchester Community College
Sullivan, Joseph — Joliet Junior College
Swart, John — Louisiana Tech University
Szurek, Joseph — University of Pittsburgh at Greensburg
Taff, Ann — Tulsa Community College
Taggart, James — Atlantic Cape Community College
Tarver, Mary Beth — Northwestern State University
Taylor, Michael — Seattle Central Community College
Terrell, Robert L. — Carson-Newman College
Terry, Dariel — Northern Virginia Community College
Thangiah, Sam — Slippery Rock University
Thayer, Paul — Austin Community College
Thompson, Joyce — Lehigh Carbon Community College
Thompson-Sellers, Ingrid — Georgia Perimeter College
Tomasi, Erik — Baruch College
Toreson, Karen — Shoreline Community College
Townsend, Cynthia — Baker College
Trifiletti, John J. — Florida Community College at Jacksonville
Trivedi, Charulata — Quinsigamond Community College, Woodbridge
Tucker, William — Austin Community College
Turgeon, Cheryl — Asnuntuck Community College
Turpen, Linda — Central New Mexico Community College
Upshaw, Susan — Del Mar College
Unruh, Angela — Central Washington University
Vanderhoof, Dr. Glenna — Missouri State University-Springfield Campus
Vargas, Tony — El Paso Community College
Vicars, Mitzi — Hampton University
Villarreal, Kathleen — Fresno
Vitrano, Mary Ellen — Palm Beach Community College
Vlaich-Lee, Michelle — Greenville Technical College
Volker, Bonita — Tidewater Community College
Waddell, Karen — Butler Community College
Wahila, Lori (Mindy) — Tompkins Cortland Community College
Wallace, Melissa — Lanier Technical College
Walters, Gary B. — Central New Mexico Community College
Waswick, Kim — Southeast Community College, Nebraska
Wavle, Sharon M. — Tompkins Cortland Community College
Webb, Nancy — City College of San Francisco
Webb, Rebecca — Northwest Arkansas Community College
Weber, Sandy — Gateway Technical College
Weissman, Jonathan — Finger Lakes Community College
Wells, Barbara E. — Central Carolina Technical College
Wells, Lorna — Salt Lake Community College
Welsh, Jean — Lansing Community College Nebraska
White, Bruce — Quinnipiac University
Willer, Ann — Solano Community College
Williams, Mark — Lane Community College
Williams, Ronald D. — Central Piedmont Community College
Wilms, Dr. G. Jan — Union University
Wilson, Kit — Red River College
Wilson, MaryLou — Piedmont Technical College
Wilson, Roger — Fairmont State University
Wimberly, Leanne — International Academy of Design and Technology

Winters, Floyd	Manatee Community College	Yip, Thomas	Passaic Community College
Worthington, Paula	Northern Virginia Community College	Zavala, Ben	Webster Tech
		Zaboski, Maureen	University of Scranton
Wright, Darrell	Shelton State Community College	Zlotow, Mary Ann	College of DuPage
Wright, Julie	Baker College	Zudeck, Steve	Broward Community College, North
Yauney, Annette	Herkimer County Community College	Zullo, Matthew D.	Wake Technical Community College

About the Authors

Shelley Gaskin, Series Editor, is a professor in the Business and Computer Technology Division at Pasadena City College in Pasadena, California. She holds a bachelor's degree in Business Administration from Robert Morris College (Pennsylvania), a master's degree in Business from Northern Illinois University, and a doctorate in Adult and Community Education from Ball State University. Before joining Pasadena City College, she spent 12 years in the computer industry where she was a systems analyst, sales representative, and Director of Customer Education with Unisys Corporation. She also worked for Ernst & Young on the development of large systems applications for their clients. She has written and developed training materials for custom systems applications in both the public and private sector, and has written and edited numerous computer application textbooks.

This book is dedicated to my students, who inspire me every day.

Alicia Vargas is a faculty member in Business Information Technology at Pasadena City College. She holds a master's and a bachelor's degree in business education from California State University, Los Angeles, and has authored several textbooks and training manuals on Microsoft Word, Microsoft Excel, and Microsoft PowerPoint.

This book is dedicated with all my love to my husband Vic, who makes everything possible; and to my children Victor, Phil, and Emmy, who are an unending source of inspiration and who make everything worthwhile.

Teach the Course You Want in Less Time

A Microsoft® Office textbook designed for student success!

■ **Project-Based** – Students learn by creating projects that they will use in the real world.

■ **Microsoft Procedural Syntax** – Steps are written to put students in the right place at the right time.

■ **Teachable Moment** – Expository text is woven into the steps—at the moment students need to know it—not chunked together in a block of text that will go unread.

■ **Sequential Pagination** – Students have actual page numbers instead of confusing letters and abbreviations.

Student Outcomes and Learning Objectives – Objectives are clustered around projects that result in student outcomes.

Project Activities – A project summary stated clearly and quickly.

Project Files – Clearly shows students which files are needed for the project and the names they will use to save their documents.

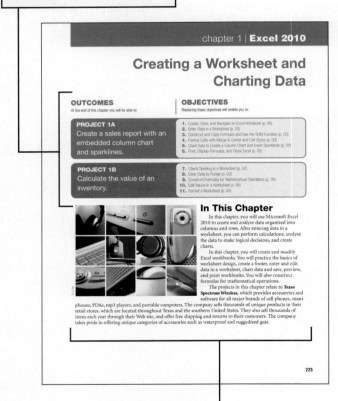

Scenario – Each chapter opens with a story that sets the stage for the projects the student will create.

Project Results – Shows students how their final outcome will appear.

Key Feature

Microsoft Procedural Syntax – Steps are written to put the student in the right place at the right time.

Color Coding – Color variations between the two projects in each chapter make it easy to identify which project students are working on.

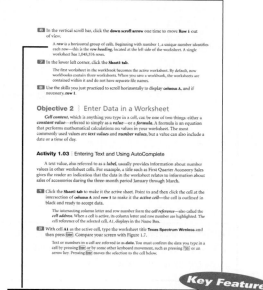

Key Feature

Sequential Pagination – Students are given actual page numbers to navigate through the textbook instead of confusing letters and abbreviations.

Key Feature

Teachable Moment – Expository text is woven into the steps—at the moment students need to know it—not chunked together in a block of text that will go unread.

End-of-Chapter

Content-Based Assessments – Assessments with defined solutions.

Objective List - Every project includes a listing of covered objectives from Projects A and B.

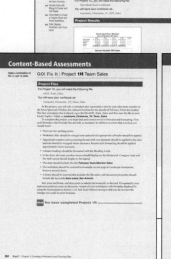

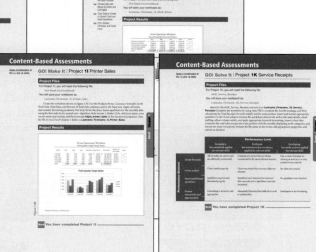

End-of-Chapter

Outcomes-Based Assessments – Assessments with open-ended solutions.

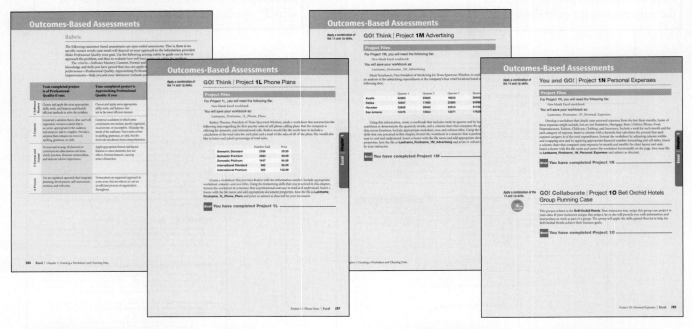

Task-Specific Rubric – A matrix specific to the **GO! Solve It** projects that states the criteria and standards for grading these defined-solution projects.

Outcomes Rubric – A matrix specific to the **GO! Think** projects that states the criteria and standards for grading these open-ended assessments.

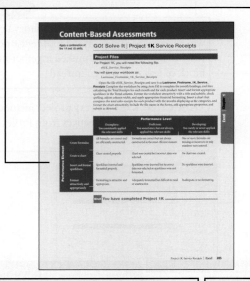

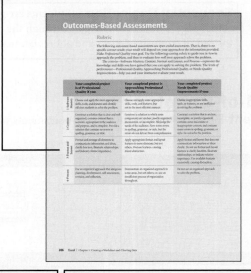

Student CD – All student data files readily available on a CD that comes with the book.

Podcasts – Videos that teach some of the more difficult topics when working with Microsoft applications.

Student Videos – A visual and audio walk-through of every A and B project in the book (see sample images on following page).

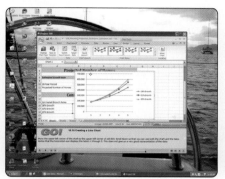

Student Videos! – Each chapter comes with two videos that include audio, demonstrating the objectives and activities taught in the chapter.

All Instructor materials available on the IRCD

Instructor Materials

Annotated Instructor Edition - An instructor tool includes a full copy of the student textbook annotated with teaching tips, discussion topics, and other useful pieces for teaching each chapter.

Assignment Sheets – Lists all the assignments for the chapter. Just add in the course information, due dates, and points. Providing these to students ensures they will know what is due and when.

Scripted Lectures – Classroom lectures prepared for you.

Annotated Solution Files – Coupled with the assignment tags, these create a grading and scoring system that makes grading so much easier for you.

PowerPoint Lectures – PowerPoint presentations for each chapter.

Scoring Rubrics – Can be used either by students to check their work or by you as a quick check-off for the items that need to be corrected.

Syllabus Templates - For 8-week, 12-week, and 16-week courses.

Test Bank – Includes a variety of test questions for each chapter.

Companion Website – Online content such as the Online Study Guide, Glossary, and Student Data Files are all at **www.pearsonhighered.com/go**.

Using the Common Features of Microsoft Office 2010

OUTCOMES
At the end of this chapter you will be able to:

OBJECTIVES
Mastering these objectives will enable you to:

PROJECT 1A
Create, save, and print a Microsoft Office 2010 file.

1. Use Windows Explorer to Locate Files and Folders (p. 3)
2. Locate and Start a Microsoft Office 2010 Program (p. 6)
3. Enter and Edit Text in an Office 2010 Program (p. 9)
4. Perform Commands from a Dialog Box (p. 11)
5. Create a Folder, Save a File, and Close a Program (p. 13)
6. Add Document Properties and Print a File (p. 18)

PROJECT 1B
Use the Ribbon and dialog boxes to perform common commands in a Microsoft Office 2010 file.

7. Open an Existing File and Save It with a New Name (p. 22)
8. Explore Options for an Application (p. 25)
9. Perform Commands from the Ribbon (p. 26)
10. Apply Formatting in Office Programs (p. 32)
11. Use the Microsoft Office 2010 Help System (p. 43)
12. Compress Files (p. 44)

olly/Shutterstock

In This Chapter

In this chapter, you will use Windows Explorer to navigate the Windows folder structure, create a folder, and save files in Microsoft Office 2010 programs. You will also practice using the features of Microsoft Office 2010 that are common across the major programs that comprise the Microsoft Office 2010 suite. These common features include creating, saving, and printing files.

Common features also include the new Paste Preview and Microsoft Office Backstage view. You will apply formatting, perform commands, and compress files. You will see that creating professional-quality documents is easy and quick in Microsoft Office 2010, and that finding your way around is fast and efficient.

The projects in this chapter relate to **Oceana Palm Grill**, which is a chain of 25 casual, full-service restaurants based in Austin, Texas. The Oceana Palm Grill owners plan an aggressive expansion program. To expand by 15 additional restaurants in North Carolina and Florida by 2018, the company must attract new investors, develop new menus, and recruit new employees, all while adhering to the company's quality guidelines and maintaining its reputation for excellent service. To succeed, the company plans to build on its past success and maintain its quality elements.

Project 1A PowerPoint File

Project Activities

In Activities 1.01 through 1.06, you will create a PowerPoint file, save it in a folder that you create by using Windows Explorer, and then print the file or submit it electronically as directed by your instructor. Your completed PowerPoint slide will look similar to Figure 1.1.

Project Files

For Project 1A, you will need the following file:

New blank PowerPoint presentation

You will save your file as:

Lastname_Firstname_1A_Menu_Plan

Project Results

Oceana Palm Grill Menu Plan

Prepared by Firstname Lastname

For Laura Hernandez

Figure 1.1
Project 1A Menu Plan

Objective 1 | Use Windows Explorer to Locate Files and Folders

A *file* is a collection of information stored on a computer under a single name, for example, a Word document or a PowerPoint presentation. Every file is stored in a *folder*—a container in which you store files—or a *subfolder*, which is a folder within a folder. Your Windows operating system stores and organizes your files and folders, which is a primary task of an operating system.

You *navigate*—explore within the organizing structure of Windows—to create, save, and find your files and folders by using the *Windows Explorer* program. Windows Explorer displays the files and folders on your computer, and is at work anytime you are viewing the contents of files and folders in a *window*. A window is a rectangular area on a computer screen in which programs and content appear; a window can be moved, resized, minimized, or closed.

Activity 1.01 | Using Windows Explorer to Locate Files and Folders

1 Turn on your computer and display the Windows *desktop*—the opening screen in Windows that simulates your work area.

> **Note | Comparing Your Screen with the Figures in This Textbook**
>
> Your screen will match the figures shown in this textbook if you set your screen resolution to 1024 × 768. At other resolutions, your screen will closely resemble, but not match, the figures shown. To view your screen's resolution, on the Windows 7 desktop, right-click in a blank area, and then click Screen resolution. In Windows Vista, right-click a blank area, click Personalize, and then click Display Settings. In Windows XP, right-click the desktop, click Properties, and then click the Settings tab.

2 In your CD/DVD tray, insert the **Student CD** that accompanies this textbook. Wait a few moments for an **AutoPlay** window to display. Compare your screen with Figure 1.2.

> *AutoPlay* is a Windows feature that lets you choose which program to use to start different kinds of media, such as music CDs, or CDs and DVDs containing photos; it displays when you plug in or insert media or storage devices.

> **Note | If You Do Not Have the Student CD**
>
> If you do not have the Student CD, consult the inside back flap of this textbook for instructions on how to download the files from the Pearson Web site.

Figure 1.2

AutoPlay window
Close button
Windows desktop (yours may vary in color and arrangement)

3 In the upper right corner of the **AutoPlay** window, move your mouse over—*point* to—the **Close** button ![close button], and then *click*—press the left button on your mouse pointing device one time.

4 On the left side of the **Windows taskbar**, click the **Start** button 🔵 to display the **Start menu**. Compare your screen with Figure 1.3.

The *Windows taskbar* is the area along the lower edge of the desktop that contains the *Start button* and an area to display buttons for open programs. The Start button displays the *Start menu*, which provides a list of choices and is the main gateway to your computer's programs, folders, and settings.

Figure 1.3

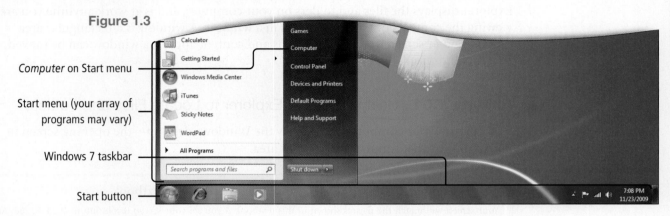

Computer on Start menu
Start menu (your array of programs may vary)
Windows 7 taskbar
Start button

5 On the right side of the **Start menu**, click **Computer** to see the disk drives and other hardware connected to your computer. Compare your screen with Figure 1.4, and then take a moment to study the table in Figure 1.5.

The *folder window* for *Computer* displays. A folder window displays the contents of the current folder, *library*, or device, and contains helpful parts so that you can navigate within Windows.

In Windows 7, a library is a collection of items, such as files and folders, assembled from *various locations*; the locations might be on your computer, an external hard drive, removable media, or someone else's computer.

The difference between a folder and a library is that a library can include files stored in *different locations*—any disk drive, folder, or other place that you can store files and folders.

Figure 1.4

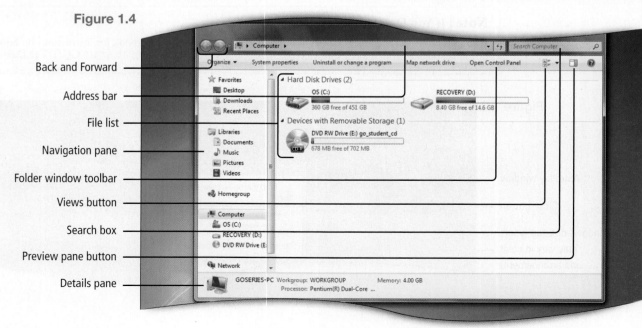

Back and Forward
Address bar
File list
Navigation pane
Folder window toolbar
Views button
Search box
Preview pane button
Details pane

Window Part	Use to:
Address bar	Navigate to a different folder or library, or go back to a previous one.
Back and Forward buttons	Navigate to other folders or libraries you have already opened without closing the current window. These buttons work in conjunction with the address bar; that is, after you use the address bar to change folders, you can use the Back button to return to the previous folder.
Details pane	Display the most common file properties—information about a file, such as the author, the date you last changed the file, and any descriptive *tags*, which are custom file properties that you create to help find and organize your files.
File list	Display the contents of the current folder or library. In Computer, the file list displays the disk drives.
Folder window for *Computer*	Display the contents of the current folder, library, or device. The Folder window contains helpful features so that you can navigate within Windows.
Folder window toolbar	Perform common tasks, such as changing the view of your files and folders or burning files to a CD. The buttons available change to display only relevant tasks.
Navigation pane	Navigate to, open, and display favorites, libraries, folders, saved searches, and an expandable list of drives.
Preview pane button	Display (if you have chosen to open this pane) the contents of most files without opening them in a program. To open the preview pane, click the Preview pane button on the toolbar to turn it on and off.
Search box	Look for an item in the current folder or library by typing a word or phrase in the search box.
Views button	Choose how to view the contents of the current location.

Figure 1.5

6 On the toolbar of the **Computer** folder window, click the **Views button arrow** 📇 ▾ — the small arrow to the right of the Views button—to display a list of views that you can apply to the file list. If necessary, on the list, click **Tiles**.

> The Views button is a *split button*; clicking the main part of the button performs a *command* and clicking the arrow opens a menu or list. A command is an instruction to a computer program that causes an action to be carried out.

> When you open a folder or a library, you can change how the files display in the file list. For example, you might prefer to see large or small *icons*—pictures that represent a program, a file, a folder, or some other object—or an arrangement that lets you see various types of information about each file. Each time you click the Views button, the window changes, cycling through several views—additional view options are available by clicking the Views button arrow.

Another Way

Point to the CD/DVD drive, right-click, and then click Open.

7 In the **file list**, under **Devices with Removable Storage**, point to your **CD/DVD Drive**, and then *double-click*—click the left mouse button two times in rapid succession—to display the list of folders on the CD. Compare your screen with Figure 1.6.

> When double-clicking, keep your hand steady between clicks; this is more important than the speed of the two clicks.

Figure 1.6

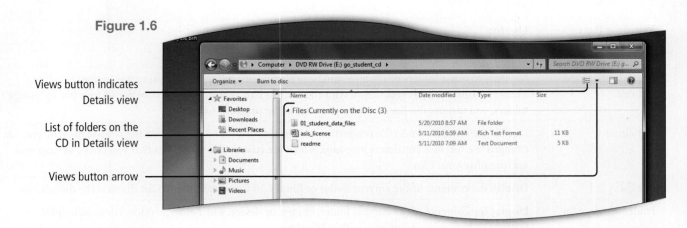

Views button indicates Details view

List of folders on the CD in Details view

Views button arrow

8 In the **file list**, point to the folder **01_student_data_files** and double-click to display the list of subfolders in the folder. Double-click to open the folder **01_common_features**. Compare your screen with Figure 1.7.

The Student Resource CD includes files that you will use to complete the projects in this textbook. If you prefer, you can also copy the **01_student_data_files** folder to a location on your computer's hard drive or to a removable device such as a *USB flash drive*, which is a small storage device that plugs into a computer USB port. Your instructor might direct you to other locations where these files are located; for example, on your learning management system.

Figure 1.7

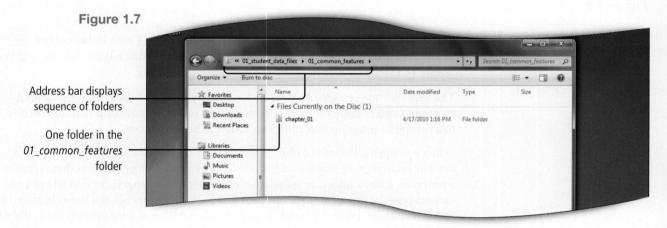

Address bar displays sequence of folders

One folder in the *01_common_features* folder

9 In the upper right corner of the **Computer** window, click the **Close** button to redisplay your desktop.

Objective 2 | Locate and Start a Microsoft Office 2010 Program

Microsoft Office 2010 includes programs, servers, and services for individuals, small organizations, and large enterprises. A *program*, also referred to as an *application*, is a set of instructions used by a computer to perform a task, such as word processing or accounting.

Activity 1.02 | Locating and Starting a Microsoft Office 2010 Program

1 On the **Windows taskbar**, click the **Start** button to display the **Start** menu.

2 From the displayed **Start** menu, locate the group of **Microsoft Office 2010** programs on your computer—the Office program icons from which you can start the program may be located on your Start menu, in a Microsoft Office folder on the **All Programs** list, on your desktop, or any combination of these locations; the location will vary depending on how your computer is configured.

> **All Programs** is an area of the Start menu that displays all the available programs on your computer system.

3 Examine Figure 1.8, and notice the programs that are included in the Microsoft Office Professional Plus 2010 group of programs. (Your group of programs may vary.)

> **Microsoft Word** is a word processing program, with which you create and share documents by using its writing tools.

> **Microsoft Excel** is a spreadsheet program, with which you calculate and analyze numbers and create charts.

> **Microsoft Access** is a database program, with which you can collect, track, and report data.

> **Microsoft PowerPoint** is a presentation program, with which you can communicate information with high-impact graphics and video.

> Additional popular Office programs include **Microsoft Outlook** to manage e-mail and organizational activities, **Microsoft Publisher** to create desktop publishing documents such as brochures, and **Microsoft OneNote** to manage notes that you make at meetings or in classes and to share notes with others on the Web.

> The Professional Plus version of Office 2010 also includes **Microsoft SharePoint Workspace** to share information with others in a team environment and **Microsoft InfoPath Designer and Filler** to create forms and gather data.

Figure 1.8

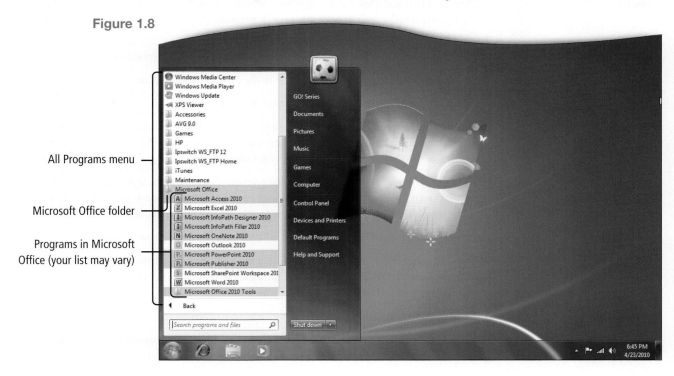

All Programs menu

Microsoft Office folder

Programs in Microsoft Office (your list may vary)

4 Click to open the program **Microsoft PowerPoint 2010**. Compare your screen with Figure 1.9, and then take a moment to study the description of these screen elements in the table in Figure 1.10.

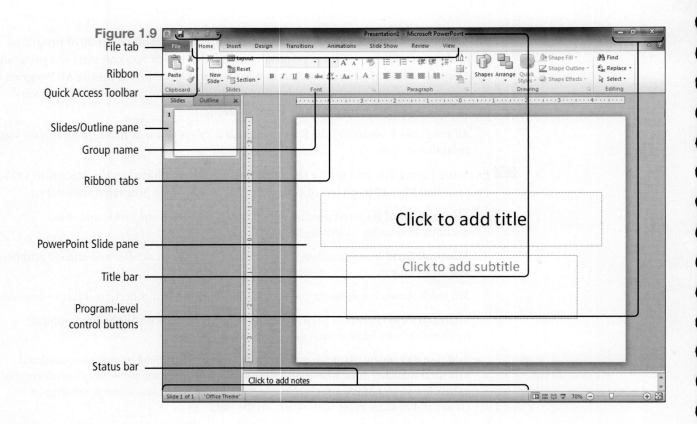

Figure 1.9

File tab
Ribbon
Quick Access Toolbar

Slides/Outline pane
Group name

Ribbon tabs

PowerPoint Slide pane

Title bar

Program-level
control buttons

Status bar

Screen Element	Description
File tab	Displays Microsoft Office Backstage view, which is a centralized space for all of your file management tasks such as opening, saving, printing, publishing, or sharing a file—all the things you can do *with* a file.
Group names	Indicate the name of the groups of related commands on the displayed tab.
PowerPoint Slide pane	Displays a large image of the active slide in the PowerPoint program.
Program-level control buttons	Minimizes, restores, or closes the program window.
Quick Access Toolbar	Displays buttons to perform frequently used commands and resources with a single click. The default commands include Save, Undo, and Redo. You can add and delete buttons to customize the Quick Access Toolbar for your convenience.
Ribbon	Displays a group of task-oriented tabs that contain the commands, styles, and resources you need to work in an Office 2010 program. The look of your Ribbon depends on your screen resolution. A high resolution will display more individual items and button names on the Ribbon.
Ribbon tabs	Display the names of the task-oriented tabs relevant to the open program.
Slides/Outline pane	Displays either thumbnails of the slides in a PowerPoint presentation (Slides tab) or the outline of the presentation's content (Outline tab). In each Office 2010 program, different panes display in different ways to assist you.
Status bar	Displays file information on the left and View and Zoom on the right.
Title bar	Displays the name of the file and the name of the program. The program window control buttons—Minimize, Maximize/Restore Down, and Close—are grouped on the right side of the title bar.

Figure 1.10

Objective 3 | Enter and Edit Text in an Office 2010 Program

All of the programs in Office 2010 require some typed text. Your keyboard is still the primary method of entering information into your computer. Techniques to *edit*—make changes to—text are similar among all of the Office 2010 programs.

Activity 1.03 | Entering and Editing Text in an Office 2010 Program

1 In the middle of the PowerPoint Slide pane, point to the text *Click to add title* to display the ⊡ pointer, and then click one time.

The *insertion point*—a blinking vertical line that indicates where text or graphics will be inserted—displays.

In Office 2010 programs, the mouse *pointer*—any symbol that displays on your screen in response to moving your mouse device—displays in different shapes depending on the task you are performing and the area of the screen to which you are pointing.

2 Type **Oceana Grille Info** and notice how the insertion point moves to the right as you type. Point slightly to the right of the letter *e* in *Grille* and click to place the insertion point there. Compare your screen with Figure 1.11.

Figure 1.11

Insertion point ——

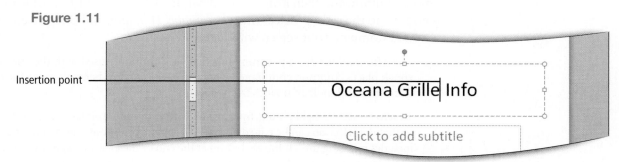

3 On your keyboard, locate and press the [Backspace] key to delete the letter *e*.

Pressing [Backspace] removes a character to the left of the insertion point.

4 Point slightly to the left of the *I* in *Info* and click one time to place the insertion point there. Type **Menu** and then press [Spacebar] one time. Compare your screen with Figure 1.12.

By *default*, when you type text in an Office program, existing text moves to the right to make space for new typing. Default refers to the current selection or setting that is automatically used by a program unless you specify otherwise.

Figure 1.12

Menu inserted ——

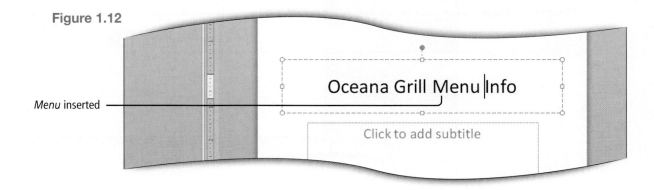

5 Press ⟨Del⟩ four times to delete *Info* and then type **Plan**

> Pressing ⟨Del⟩ removes—deletes—a character to the right of the insertion point.

6 With your insertion point blinking after the word *Plan*, on your keyboard, hold down the ⟨Ctrl⟩ key. While holding down ⟨Ctrl⟩, press ⟨←⟩ three times to move the insertion point to the beginning of the word *Grill*.

> This is a *keyboard shortcut*—a key or combination of keys that performs a task that would otherwise require a mouse. This keyboard shortcut moves the insertion point to the beginning of the previous word.

> A keyboard shortcut is commonly indicated as ⟨Ctrl⟩ + ⟨←⟩ (or some other combination of keys) to indicate that you hold down the first key while pressing the second key. A keyboard shortcut can also include three keys, in which case you hold down the first two and then press the third. For example, ⟨Ctrl⟩ + ⟨Shift⟩ + ⟨←⟩ selects one word to the left.

7 With the insertion point blinking at the beginning of the word *Grill*, type **Palm** and press ⟨Spacebar⟩.

8 Click anywhere in the text *Click to add subtitle*. With the insertion point blinking, type the following and include the spelling error: **Prepered by Annabel Dunham**

9 With your mouse, point slightly to the left of the *A* in *Annabel*, hold down the left mouse button, and then *drag*—hold down the left mouse button while moving your mouse—to the right to select the text *Annabel Dunham*, and then release the mouse button. Compare your screen with Figure 1.13.

> The *Mini toolbar* displays commands that are commonly used with the selected object, which places common commands close to your pointer. When you move the pointer away from the Mini toolbar, it fades from view.

> To *select* refers to highlighting, by dragging with your mouse, areas of text or data or graphics so that the selection can be edited, formatted, copied, or moved. The action of dragging includes releasing the left mouse button at the end of the area you want to select. The Office programs recognize a selected area as one unit, to which you can make changes. Selecting text may require some practice. If you are not satisfied with your result, click anywhere outside of the selection, and then begin again.

Figure 1.13

Mini toolbar displays

Annabel Dunham selected

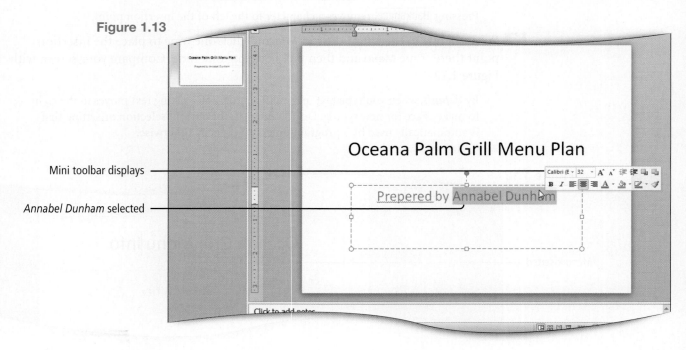

Oceana Palm Grill Menu Plan

Prepered by Annabel Dunham

10 With the text *Annabel Dunham* selected, type your own firstname and lastname.

In any Windows-based program, such as the Microsoft Office 2010 programs, selected text is deleted and then replaced when you begin to type new text. You will save time by developing good techniques to select and then edit or replace selected text, which is easier than pressing the [Del] key numerous times to delete text that you do not want.

11 Notice that the misspelled word *Prepered* displays with a wavy red underline; additionally, all or part of your name might display with a wavy red underline.

Office 2010 has a dictionary of words against which all entered text is checked. In Word and PowerPoint, words that are *not* in the dictionary display a wavy red line, indicating a possible misspelled word or a proper name or an unusual word—none of which are in the Office 2010 dictionary.

In Excel and Access, you can initiate a check of the spelling, but wavy red underlines do not display.

12 Point to *Prepered* and then ***right-click***—click your right mouse button one time.

The Mini toolbar and a ***shortcut menu*** display. A shortcut menu displays commands and options relevant to the selected text or object—known as ***context-sensitive commands*** because they relate to the item you right-clicked.

Here, the shortcut menu displays commands related to the misspelled word. You can click the suggested correct spelling *Prepared*, click Ignore All to ignore the misspelling, add the word to the Office dictionary, or click Spelling to display a ***dialog box***. A dialog box is a small window that contains options for completing a task. Whenever you see a command followed by an ***ellipsis*** (…), which is a set of three dots indicating incompleteness, clicking the command will always display a dialog box.

13 On the displayed shortcut menu, click **Prepared** to correct the misspelled word. If necessary, point to any parts of your name that display a wavy red underline, right-click, and then on the shortcut menu, click Ignore All so that Office will no longer mark your name with a wavy underline in this file.

More Knowledge | Adding to the Office Dictionary

The main dictionary contains the most common words, but does not include all proper names, technical terms, or acronyms. You can add words, acronyms, and proper names to the Office dictionary by clicking Add to Dictionary when they are flagged, and you might want to do so for your own name and other proper names and terms that you type often.

Objective 4 | Perform Commands from a Dialog Box

In a dialog box, you make decisions about an individual object or topic. A dialog box also offers a way to adjust a number of settings at one time.

Activity 1.04 | Performing Commands from a Dialog Box

1 Point anywhere in the blank area above the title *Oceana Palm Grill Menu Plan* to display the ⌖ pointer.

2 Right-click to display a shortcut menu. Notice the command *Format Background* followed by an ellipsis (...). Compare your screen with Figure 1.14.

Recall that a command followed by an ellipsis indicates that a dialog box will display if you click the command.

Figure 1.14

Shortcut menu ─────

Ellipsis following command ─────

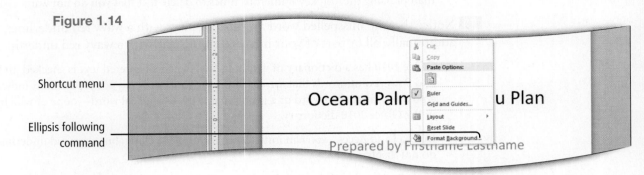

3 Click **Format Background** to display the **Format Background** dialog box, and then compare your screen with Figure 1.15.

Figure 1.15

Fill selected ─────

Format Background dialog box ─────

Options related to the background fill ─────

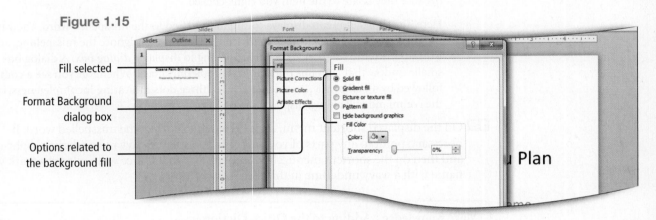

4 On the left, if necessary, click **Fill** to display the **Fill** options.

Fill is the inside color of an object. Here, the dialog box displays the option group names on the left; some dialog boxes provide a set of tabs across the top from which you can display different sets of options.

5 On the right, under **Fill**, click the **Gradient fill** option button.

The dialog box displays additional settings related to the gradient fill option. An *option button* is a round button that enables you to make one choice among two or more options. In a gradient fill, one color fades into another.

6 Click the **Preset colors arrow**—the arrow in the box to the right of the text *Preset colors*—and then in the gallery, in the second row, point to the fifth fill color to display the ScreenTip *Fog*.

A *gallery* is an Office feature that displays a list of potential results. A *ScreenTip* displays useful information about mouse actions, such as pointing to screen elements or dragging.

7 Click **Fog**, and then notice that the fill color is applied to your slide. Click the **Type arrow**, and then click **Rectangular** to change the pattern of the fill color. Compare your screen with Figure 1.16.

Figure 1.16

Gradient fill option
button selected

Rectangular displays

Close button

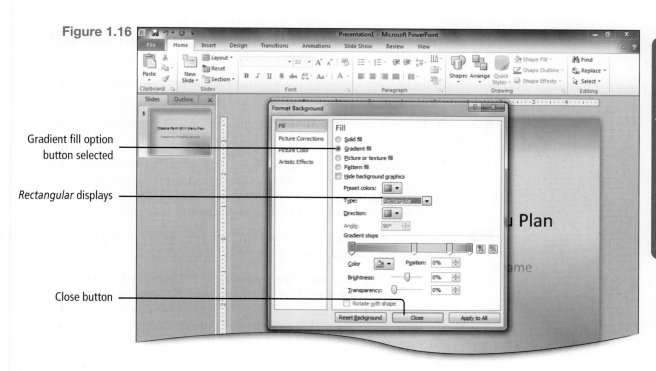

8 At the bottom of the dialog box, click **Close**.

As you progress in your study of Microsoft Office, you will practice using many dialog boxes and applying dramatic effects such as this to your Word documents, Excel spreadsheets, Access databases, and PowerPoint slides.

Objective 5 | Create a Folder, Save a File, and Close a Program

A *location* is any disk drive, folder, or other place in which you can store files and folders. Where you store your files depends on how and where you use your data. For example, for your classes, you might decide to store primarily on a removable USB flash drive so that you can carry your files to different locations and access your files on different computers.

If you do most of your work on a single computer, for example your home desktop system or your laptop computer that you take with you to school or work, store your files in one of the Libraries—Documents, Music, Pictures, or Videos—provided by your Windows operating system.

Although the Windows operating system helps you to create and maintain a logical folder structure, take the time to name your files and folders in a consistent manner.

Activity 1.05 | Creating a Folder, Saving a File, and Closing a Program

A PowerPoint presentation is an example of a file. Office 2010 programs use a common dialog box provided by the Windows operating system to assist you in saving files. In this activity, you will create a folder on a USB flash drive in which to store files. If you prefer to store on your hard drive, you can use similar steps to store files in your My Documents folder in your Documents library.

1 Insert a USB flash drive into your computer, and if necessary, **Close** ⬛ the **AutoPlay** dialog box. If you are not using a USB flash drive, go to Step 2.

> As the first step in saving a file, determine where you want to save the file, and if necessary, insert a storage device.

2 At the top of your screen, in the title bar, notice that *Presentation1 – Microsoft PowerPoint* displays.

> Most Office 2010 programs open with a new unsaved file with a default name— *Presentation1*, *Document1*, and so on. As you create your file, your work is temporarily stored in the computer's memory until you initiate a Save command, at which time you must choose a file name and location in which to save your file.

3 In the upper left corner of your screen, click the **File tab** to display **Microsoft Office Backstage** view. Compare your screen with Figure 1.17.

> Microsoft Office *Backstage view* is a centralized space for tasks related to *file* management; that is why the tab is labeled *File*. File management tasks include, for example, opening, saving, printing, publishing, or sharing a file. The *Backstage tabs*—*Info*, *Recent*, *New*, *Print*, *Save & Send*, and *Help*—display along the left side. The tabs group file-related tasks together.

> Above the Backstage tabs, *Quick Commands*—*Save*, *Save As*, *Open*, and *Close*—display for quick access to these commands. When you click any of these commands, Backstage view closes and either a dialog box displays or the active file closes.

> Here, the *Info tab* displays information—*info*—about the current file. In the center panel, various file management tasks are available in groups. For example, if you click the Protect Presentation button, a list of options that you can set for this file that relate to who can open or edit the presentation displays.

> On the Info tab, in the right panel, you can also examine the *document properties*. Document properties, also known as *metadata*, are details about a file that describe or identify it, such as the title, author name, subject, and keywords that identify the document's topic or contents. On the Info page, a thumbnail image of the current file displays in the upper right corner, which you can click to close Backstage view and return to the document.

More Knowledge | Deciding Where to Store Your Files

Where should you store your files? In the libraries created by Windows 7 (Documents, Pictures, and so on)? On a removable device like a flash drive or external hard drive? In Windows 7, it is easy to find your files, especially if you use the libraries. Regardless of where you save a file, Windows 7 will make it easy to find the file again, even if you are not certain where it might be.

In Windows 7, storing all of your files within a library makes sense. If you perform most of your work on your desktop system or your laptop that travels with you, you can store your files in the libraries created by Windows 7 for your user account—Documents, Pictures, Music, and so on. Within these libraries, you can create folders and subfolders to organize your data. These libraries are a good choice for storing your files because:

- From the Windows Explorer button on the taskbar, your libraries are always just one click away.
- The libraries are designed for their contents; for example, the Pictures folder displays small images of your digital photos.
- You can add new locations to a library; for example, an external hard drive, or a network drive. Locations added to a library behave just like they are on your hard drive.
- Other users of your computer cannot access your libraries.
- The libraries are the default location for opening and saving files within an application, so you will find that you can open and save files with fewer navigation clicks.

Figure 1.17

Save command
Information about the file you are working on
Info tab selected
Backstage tabs, Info tab active
Groups
Indicates unsaved file with default name
Document Properties
Screen thumbnail

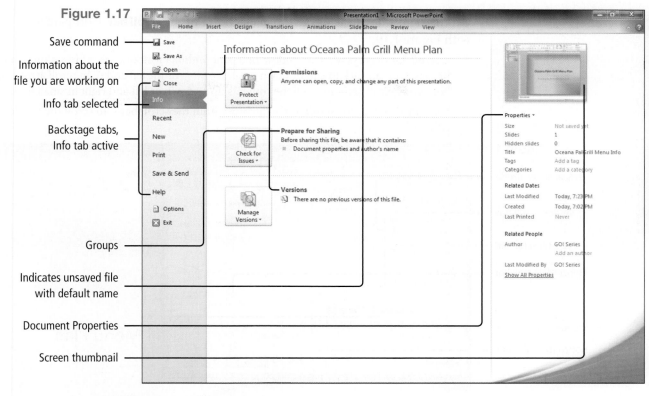

4 Above the **Backstage tabs**, click **Save** to display the **Save As** dialog box.

Backstage view closes and the Save As dialog box, which includes a folder window and an area at the bottom to name the file and set the file type, displays.

When you are saving something for the first time, for example a new PowerPoint presentation, the Save and Save As commands are identical. That is, the Save As dialog box will display if you click Save or if you click Save As.

Note | Saving Your File

After you have named a file and saved it in your desired location, the Save command saves any changes you make to the file without displaying any dialog box. The Save As command will display the Save As dialog box and let you name and save a new file based on the current one—in a location that you choose. After you name and save the new document, the original document closes, and the new document—based on the original one—displays.

---

5 In the **Save As** dialog box, on the left, locate the **navigation pane**; compare your screen with Figure 1.18.

By default, the Save command opens the Documents library unless your default file location has been changed.

Figure 1.18

Save As dialog box
Address bar
Default save location
Navigation pane
File list (yours will vary)
File name box
Save as type defaults to *PowerPoint Presentation*

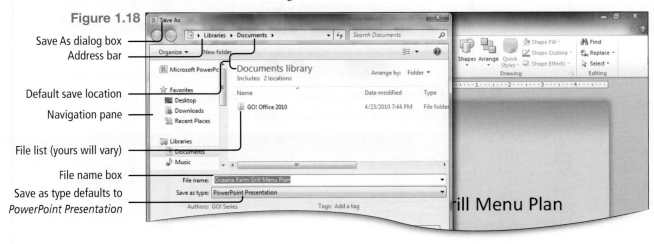

6 On the right side of the **navigation pane**, point to the **scroll bar**. Compare your screen with Figure 1.19.

> A *scroll bar* displays when a window, or a pane within a window, has information that is not in view. You can click the up or down scroll arrows—or the left and right scroll arrows in a horizontal scroll bar—to scroll the contents up or down or left and right in small increments.
>
> You can also drag the *scroll box*—the box within the scroll bar—to scroll the window in either direction.

Figure 1.19

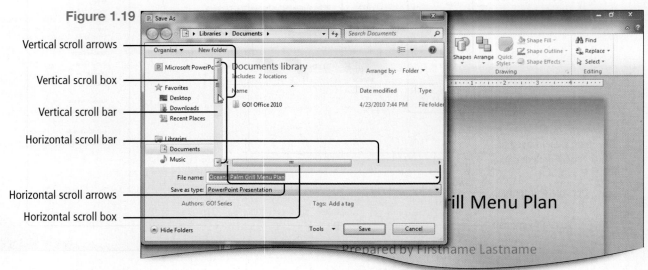

Vertical scroll arrows
Vertical scroll box
Vertical scroll bar
Horizontal scroll bar
Horizontal scroll arrows
Horizontal scroll box

7 Click the **down scroll arrow** as necessary so that you can view the lower portion of the **navigation pane**, and then click the icon for your USB flash drive. Compare your screen with Figure 1.20. (If you prefer to store on your computer's hard drive instead of a USB flash drive, in the navigation pane, click Documents.)

Figure 1.20

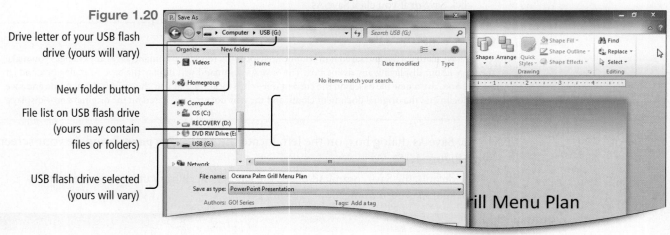

Drive letter of your USB flash drive (yours will vary)
New folder button
File list on USB flash drive (yours may contain files or folders)
USB flash drive selected (yours will vary)

8 On the toolbar, click the **New folder** button.

> In the file list, a new folder is created, and the text *New folder* is selected.

9 Type **Common Features Chapter 1** and press Enter. Compare your screen with Figure 1.21.

> In Windows-based programs, the Enter key confirms an action.

Figure 1.21

New folder

10 In the **file list**, double-click the name of your new folder to open it and display its name in the **address bar**.

11 In the lower portion of the dialog box, click in the **File name** box to select the existing text. Notice that Office inserts the text at the beginning of the presentation as a suggested file name.

12 On your keyboard, locate the ⎯ key. Notice that the Shift of this key produces the underscore character. With the text still selected, type **Lastname_Firstname_1A_ Menu_Plan** Compare your screen with Figure 1.22.

> You can use spaces in file names, however some individuals prefer not to use spaces. Some programs, especially when transferring files over the Internet, may not work well with spaces in file names. In general, however, unless you encounter a problem, it is OK to use spaces. In this textbook, underscores are used instead of spaces in file names.

Figure 1.22

File name box indicates your file name

Save as type box indicates *PowerPoint Presentation*

Save button

13 In the lower right corner, click **Save**; or press Enter. See Figure 1.23.

> Your new file name displays in the title bar, indicating that the file has been saved to a location that you have specified.

Figure 1.23

File name in title bar

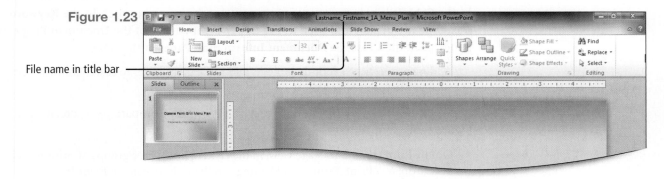

14 In the text that begins *Prepared by*, click to position the insertion point at the end of your name, and then press Enter to move to a new line. Type **For Laura Hernandez**

15 Click the **File tab** to display **Backstage** view. At the top of the center panel, notice that the path where your file is stored displays. Above the Backstage tabs, click **Close** to close the file. In the message box, click **Save** to save the changes you made and close the file. Leave PowerPoint open.

> PowerPoint displays a message asking if you want to save the changes you have made. Because you have made additional changes to the file since your last Save operation, an Office program will always prompt you to save so that you do not lose any new data.

Objective 6 | Add Document Properties and Print a File

The process of printing a file is similar in all of the Office applications. There are differences in the types of options you can select. For example, in PowerPoint, you have the option of printing the full slide, with each slide printing on a full sheet of paper, or of printing handouts with small pictures of slides on a page.

Activity 1.06 | Adding Document Properties and Printing a File

> **Alert!** | **Are You Printing or Submitting Your Files Electronically?**
>
> If you are submitting your files electronically only, or have no printer attached, you can still complete this activity. Complete Steps 1-9, and then submit your file electronically as directed by your instructor.

1 In the upper left corner, click the **File tab** to display **Backstage** view. Notice that the **Recent tab** displays.

> Because no file was open in PowerPoint, Office applies predictive logic to determine that your most likely action will be to open a PowerPoint presentation that you worked on recently. Thus, the Recent tab displays a list of PowerPoint presentations that were recently open on your system.

2 At the top of the **Recent Presentations** list, click your **Lastname_Firstname_1A_ Menu_Plan** file to open it.

3 Click the **File tab** to redisplay **Backstage** view. On the right, under the screen thumbnail, click **Properties**, and then click **Show Document Panel**. In the **Author** box, delete the existing text, and then type your firstname and lastname. Notice that in PowerPoint, some variation of the slide title is automatically inserted in the Title box. In the **Subject** box, type your Course name and section number. In the **Keywords** box, type **menu plan** and then in the upper right corner of the **Document Properties** panel, click the **Close the Document Information Panel** button [×].

> Adding properties to your documents will make them easier to search for in systems such as Microsoft SharePoint.

Another Way

Press Ctrl + P or Ctrl + F2 to display the Print tab in Backstage view.

4 Redisplay **Backstage** view, and then click the **Print tab**. Compare your screen with Figure 1.24.

> On the Print tab in Backstage view, in the center panel, three groups of printing-related tasks display—Print, Printer, and Settings. In the right panel, the *Print Preview* displays, which is a view of a document as it will appear on the paper when you print it.

> At the bottom of the Print Preview area, on the left, the number of pages and arrows with which you can move among the pages in Print Preview display. On the right, *Zoom* settings enable you to shrink or enlarge the Print Preview. Zoom is the action of increasing or decreasing the viewing area of the screen.

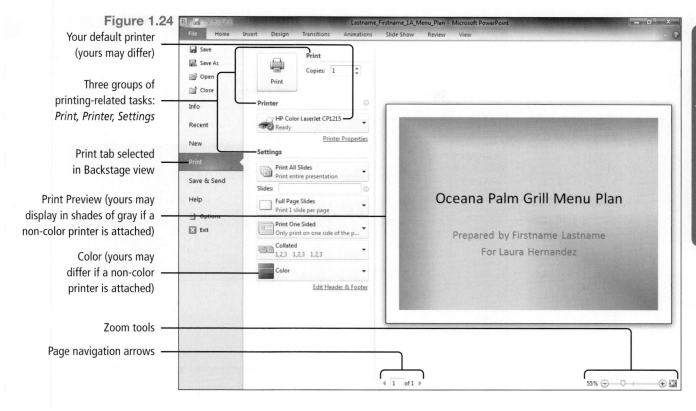

Figure 1.24

Your default printer (yours may differ)

Three groups of printing-related tasks: *Print, Printer, Settings*

Print tab selected in Backstage view

Print Preview (yours may display in shades of gray if a non-color printer is attached)

Color (yours may differ if a non-color printer is attached)

Zoom tools

Page navigation arrows

5 Locate the **Settings group**, and notice that the default setting is to **Print All Slides** and to print **Full Page Slides**—each slide on a full sheet of paper.

6 Point to **Full Page Slides**, notice that the button glows orange, and then click the button to display a gallery of print arrangements. Compare your screen with Figure 1.25.

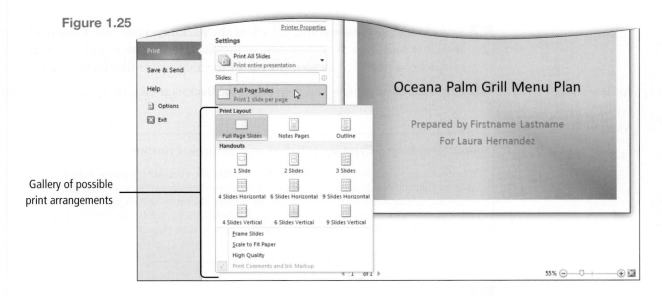

Figure 1.25

Gallery of possible print arrangements

7 In the displayed gallery, under **Handouts**, click **1 Slide**, and then compare your screen with Figure 1.26.

The Print Preview changes to show how your slide will print on the paper in this arrangement.

Figure 1.26

Handouts selected

Print Preview displays
the 1 slide printed as
handouts setting

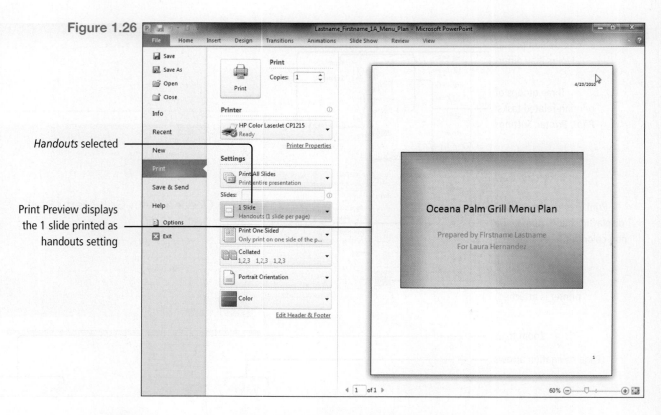

8 To submit your file electronically, skip this step and move to Step 9. To print your slide, be sure your system is connected to a printer, and then in the **Print group**, click the **Print** button. On the Quick Access Toolbar, click **Save** 🖫, and then move to Step 10.

> The handout will print on your default printer—on a black and white printer, the colors will print in shades of gray. Backstage view closes and your file redisplays in the PowerPoint window.

9 To submit your file electronically, above the **Backstage tabs**, click **Close** to close the file and close **Backstage** view, click **Save** in the displayed message, and then follow the instructions provided by your instructor to submit your file electronically.

Another Way
In the upper right corner of your PowerPoint window, click the red Close button.

10 Display **Backstage** view, and then below the **Backstage tabs**, click **Exit** to close your file and close PowerPoint.

More Knowledge | Creating a PDF as an Electronic Printout

From Backstage view, you can save an Office file as a *PDF file*. *Portable Document Format* (PDF) creates an image of your file that preserves the look of your file, but that cannot be easily changed. This is a popular format for sending documents electronically, because the document will display on most computers. From Backstage view, click Save & Send, and then in the File Types group, click Create PDF/XPS Document. Then in the third panel, click the Create PDF/XPS button, navigate to your chapter folder, and then in the lower right corner, click Publish.

End **You have completed Project 1A**

Project 1B Word File

myitlab
Project 1B Training

Project Activities

In Activities 1.07 through 1.16, you will open, edit, save, and then compress a Word file. Your completed document will look similar to Figure 1.27.

Project Files

For Project 1B, you will need the following file:

cf01B_Cheese_Promotion

You will save your Word document as:

Lastname_Firstname_1B_Cheese_Promotion

Project Results

Memo

TO:	Laura Mabry Hernandez, General Manager
FROM:	Donna Jackson, Executive Chef
DATE:	December 17, 2014
SUBJECT:	Cheese Specials on Tuesdays

To increase restaurant traffic between 4:00 p.m. and 6:00 p.m., I am proposing a trial cheese event in one of the restaurants, probably Orlando. I would like to try a weekly event on Tuesday evenings where the focus is on a good selection of cheese.

I envision two possibilities: a selection of cheese plates or a cheese bar—or both. The cheeses would have to be matched with compatible fruit and bread or crackers. They could be used as appetizers, or for desserts, as is common in Europe. The cheese plates should be varied and diverse, using a mixture of hard and soft, sharp and mild, unusual and familiar.

I am excited about this new promotion. If done properly, I think it could increase restaurant traffic in the hours when individuals want to relax with a small snack instead of a heavy dinner.

The promotion will require that our employees become familiar with the types and characteristics of both foreign and domestic cheeses. Let's meet to discuss the details and the training requirements, and to create a flyer that begins something like this:

Oceana Palm Grill Tuesday Cheese Tastings

Lastname_Firstname_1B_Cheese_Promotion

Figure 1.27
Project 1B Cheese Promotion

Objective 7 | Open an Existing File and Save It with a New Name

In any Office program, use the Open command to display the *Open dialog box*, from which you can navigate to and then open an existing file that was created in that same program.

The Open dialog box, along with the Save and Save As dialog boxes, are referred to as *common dialog boxes*. These dialog boxes, which are provided by the Windows programming interface, display in all of the Office programs in the same manner. Thus, the Open, Save, and Save As dialog boxes will all look and perform the same in each Office program.

Activity 1.07 | Opening an Existing File and Saving it with a New Name

In this activity, you will display the Open dialog box, open an existing Word document, and then save it in your storage location with a new name.

1 Determine the location of the student data files that accompany this textbook, and be sure you can access these files.

> For example:
>
> If you are accessing the files from the Student CD that came with this textbook, insert the CD now.
>
> If you copied the files from the Student CD or from the Pearson Web site to a USB flash drive that you are using for this course, insert the flash drive in your computer now.
>
> If you copied the files to the hard drive of your computer, for example in your Documents library, be sure you can locate the files on the hard drive.

2 Determine the location of your **Common Features Chapter 1** folder you created in Activity 1.05, in which you will store your work from this chapter, and then be sure you can access that folder.

> For example:
>
> If you created your chapter folder on a USB flash drive, insert the flash drive in your computer now. This can be the same flash drive where you have stored the student data files; just be sure to use the chapter folder you created.
>
> If you created your chapter folder in the Documents library on your computer, be sure you can locate the folder. Otherwise, create a new folder at the computer at which you are working, or on a USB flash drive.

3 Using the technique you practiced in Activity 1.02, locate and then start the **Microsoft Word 2010** program on your system.

> **Another Way**
>
> In the Word (or other program) window, press [Ctrl] + [F12] to display the Open dialog box.

4 On the Ribbon, click the **File tab** to display **Backstage** view, and then click **Open** to display the **Open** dialog box.

5 In the **navigation pane** on the left, use the scroll bar to scroll as necessary, and then click the location of your student data files to display the location's contents in the **file list**. Compare your screen with Figure 1.28.

> For example:
>
> If you are accessing the files from the Student CD that came with your book, under Computer, click the CD/DVD.
>
> If you are accessing the files from a USB flash drive, under Computer, click the flash drive name.
>
> If you are accessing the files from the Documents library of your computer, under Libraries, click Documents.

Figure 1.28

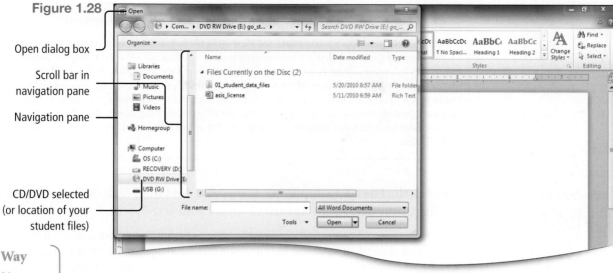

Open dialog box

Scroll bar in navigation pane

Navigation pane

CD/DVD selected (or location of your student files)

Another Way

Point to a folder name, right-click, and then from the shortcut menu, click Open.

6 Point to the folder **01_student_data_files** and double-click to open the folder. Point to the subfolder **01_common_features**, double-click, and then compare your screen with Figure 1.29.

Figure 1.29

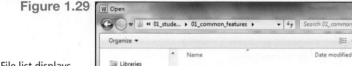

File list displays the contents of the *01_common_features* folder

Another Way

Click one time to select the file, and then press Enter or click the Open button in the lower right corner of the dialog box.

7 In the **file list**, point to the **chapter_01** subfolder and double-click to open it. In the **file list**, point to Word file **cf01B_Cheese_Promotion** and then double-click to open and display the file in the Word window. On the Ribbon, on the **Home tab**, in the **Paragraph group**, if necessary, click the **Show/Hide** button ¶ so that it is active—glowing orange. Compare your screen with Figure 1.30.

On the title bar at the top of the screen, the file name displays. If you opened the document from the Student CD, (*Read-Only*) will display. If you opened the document from another source to which the files were copied, (*Read-Only*) might not display. **Read-Only** is a property assigned to a file that prevents the file from being modified or deleted; it indicates that you cannot save any changes to the displayed document unless you first save it with a new name.

Figure 1.30

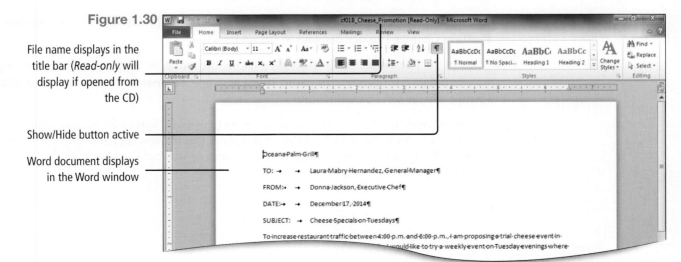

File name displays in the title bar (*Read-only* will display if opened from the CD)

Show/Hide button active

Word document displays in the Word window

Another Way

Press [F12] to display the Save As dialog box.

→ **8** Click the **File tab** to display **Backstage** view, and then click the **Save As** command to display the **Save As** dialog box. Compare your screen with Figure 1.31.

The Save As command displays the Save As dialog box where you can name and save a *new* document based on the currently displayed document. After you name and save the new document, the original document closes, and the new document—based on the original one—displays.

Figure 1.31

Save As dialog box

Navigation pane

Current file name selected

Default type is *Word Document*

9 In the **navigation pane**, click the location in which you are storing your projects for this chapter—the location where you created your **Common Features Chapter 1** folder; for example, your USB flash drive or the Documents library.

10 In the **file list**, double-click the necessary folders and subfolders until your **Common Features Chapter 1** folder displays in the **address bar**.

11 Click in the **File name** box to select the existing file name, or drag to select the existing text, and then using your own name, type **Lastname_Firstname_1B_Cheese_Promotion** Compare your screen with Figure 1.32.

As you type, the file name from your 1A project might display briefly. Because your 1A project file is stored in this location and you began the new file name with the same text, Office predicts that you might want the same or similar file name. As you type new characters, the suggestion is removed.

Figure 1.32

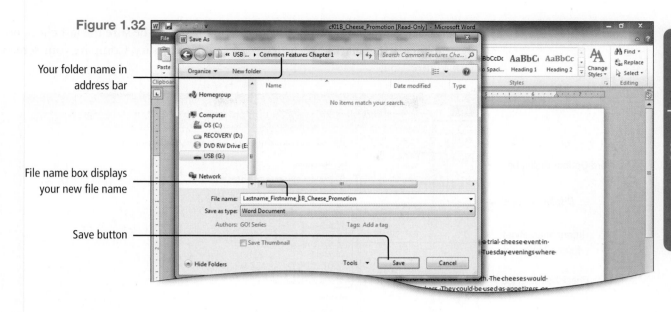

Your folder name in
address bar

File name box displays
your new file name

Save button

12 In the lower right corner of the **Save As** dialog box, click **Save**; or press Enter. Compare your screen with Figure 1.33.

> The original document closes, and your new document, based on the original, displays with the name in the title bar.

Figure 1.33

New document
name in title bar

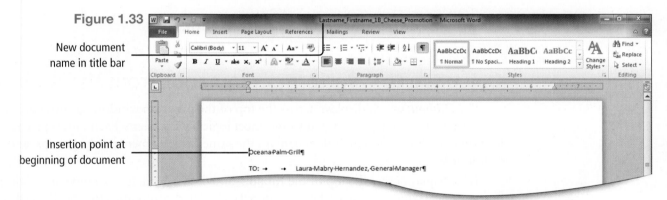

Insertion point at
beginning of document

Objective 8 | Explore Options for an Application

Within each Office application, you can open an *Options dialog box* where you can select program settings and other options and preferences. For example, you can set preferences for viewing and editing files.

Activity 1.08 | Viewing Application Options

1 Click the **File tab** to display **Backstage** view. Under the **Help tab**, click **Options**.

2 In the displayed **Word Options** dialog box, on the left, click **Display**, and then on the right, locate the information under **Always show these formatting marks on the screen**.

> When you press Enter, Spacebar, or Tab on your keyboard, characters display to represent these keystrokes. These screen characters do not print, and are referred to as *formatting marks* or *nonprinting characters*.

3 Under **Always show these formatting marks on the screen**, be sure the last check box, **Show all formatting marks**, is selected—select it if necessary. Compare your screen with Figure 1.34.

Figure 1.34

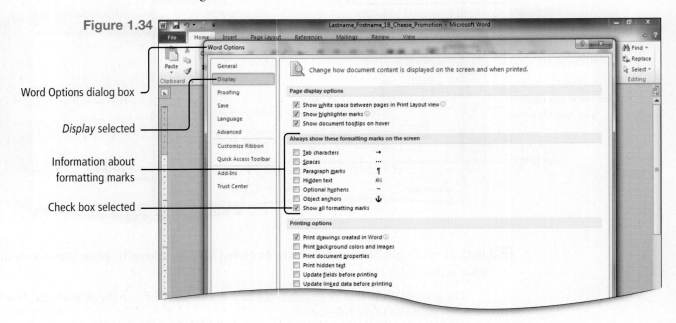

Word Options dialog box

Display selected

Information about formatting marks

Check box selected

4 In the lower right corner of the dialog box, click **OK**.

Objective 9 | Perform Commands from the Ribbon

The **Ribbon**, which displays across the top of the program window, groups commands and features in a manner that you would most logically use them. Each Office program's Ribbon is slightly different, but all contain the same three elements: **tabs**, **groups**, and **commands**.

Tabs display across the top of the Ribbon, and each tab relates to a type of activity; for example, laying out a page. Groups are sets of related commands for specific tasks. Commands—instructions to computer programs—are arranged in groups, and might display as a button, a menu, or a box in which you type information.

You can also minimize the Ribbon so only the tab names display. In the minimized Ribbon view, when you click a tab the Ribbon expands to show the groups and commands, and then when you click a command, the Ribbon returns to its minimized view. Most Office users, however, prefer to leave the complete Ribbon in view at all times.

Activity 1.09 | Performing Commands from the Ribbon

1 Take a moment to examine the document on your screen.

This document is a memo from the Executive Chef to the General Manager regarding a new restaurant promotion.

2 On the Ribbon, click the **View tab**. In the **Show group**, if necessary, click to place a check mark in the **Ruler** check box, and then compare your screen with Figure 1.35.

When working in Word, display the rulers so that you can see how margin settings affect your document and how text aligns. Additionally, if you set a tab stop or an indent, its location is visible on the ruler.

Figure 1.35

Quick Access Toolbar
Ruler selected
Button to minimize Ribbon

Rulers

3 On the Ribbon, click the **Home tab**. In the **Paragraph group**, if necessary, click the **Show/Hide** button ¶ so that it glows orange and formatting marks display in your document. Point to the button to display information about the button, and then compare your screen with Figure 1.36.

When the Show/Hide button is active—glowing orange—formatting marks display. Because formatting marks guide your eye in a document—like a map and road signs guide you along a highway—these marks will display throughout this instruction. Many expert Word users keep these marks displayed while creating documents.

Figure 1.36
Show/Hide button glows orange
Paragraph group
ScreenTip for Show/Hide button
Paragraph mark
Tab mark

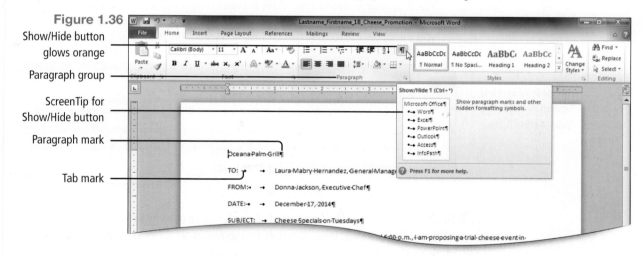

4 In the upper left corner of your screen, above the Ribbon, locate the **Quick Access Toolbar**.

The *Quick Access Toolbar* contains commands that you use frequently. By default, only the commands Save, Undo, and Redo display, but you can add and delete commands to suit your needs. Possibly the computer at which you are working already has additional commands added to the Quick Access Toolbar.

5 At the end of the Quick Access Toolbar, click the **Customize Quick Access Toolbar** button ▾.

6 Compare your screen with Figure 1.37.

A list of commands that Office users commonly add to their Quick Access Toolbar displays, including *Open*, *E-mail*, and *Print Preview and Print*. Commands already on the Quick Access Toolbar display a check mark. Commands that you add to the Quick Access Toolbar are always just one click away.

Here you can also display the More Commands dialog box, from which you can select any command from any tab to add to the Quick Access Toolbar.

Figure 1.37

Customize Quick
Access Toolbar

Popular commands to add

Existing commands
checked

Displays *More
Commands* dialog box

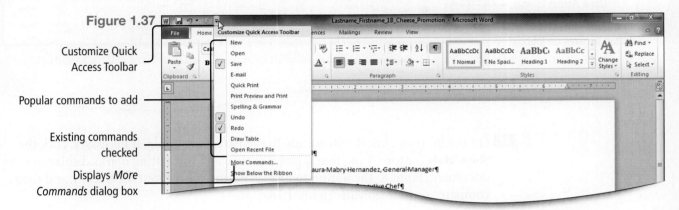

Another Way

Right-click any command on the Ribbon, and then on the shortcut menu, click Add to Quick Access Toolbar.

7 On the displayed list, click **Print Preview and Print**, and then notice that the icon is added to the **Quick Access Toolbar**. Compare your screen with Figure 1.38.

The icon that represents the Print Preview command displays on the Quick Access Toolbar. Because this is a command that you will use frequently while building Office documents, you might decide to have this command remain on your Quick Access Toolbar.

Figure 1.38

Icon for Print Preview
command added to
Quick Access Toolbar

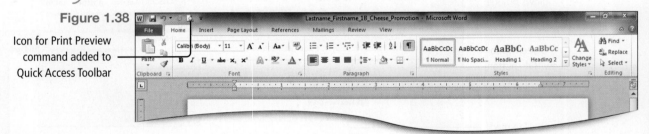

8 In the first line of the document, be sure your insertion point is blinking to the left of the *O* in *Oceana*. Press Enter one time to insert a blank paragraph, and then click to the left of the new paragraph mark (¶) in the new line.

The *paragraph symbol* is a formatting mark that displays each time you press Enter.

9 On the Ribbon, click the **Insert tab**. In the **Illustrations group**, point to the **Clip Art** button to display its ScreenTip.

Many buttons on the Ribbon have this type of *enhanced ScreenTip*, which displays more descriptive text than a normal ScreenTip.

10 Click the **Clip Art** button.

The Clip Art *task pane* displays. A task pane is a window within a Microsoft Office application that enables you to enter options for completing a command.

11 In the **Clip Art** task pane, click in the **Search for** box, delete any existing text, and then type **cheese grapes** Under **Results should be:**, click the arrow at the right, if necessary click to *clear* the check mark for **All media types** so that no check boxes are selected, and then click the check box for **Illustrations**. Compare your screen with Figure 1.39.

Figure 1.39

Search term

Blank paragraph

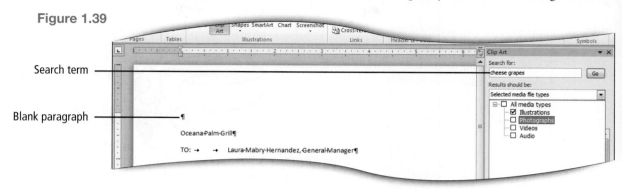

12 Click the **Results should be arrow** again to close the list, and then if necessary, click to place a check mark in the **Include Office.com content** check box.

> By selecting this check box, the search for clip art images will include those from Microsoft's online collections of clip art at www.office.com.

13 At the top of the **Clip Art** task pane, click **Go**. Wait a moment for clips to display, and then locate the clip indicated in Figure 1.40.

Figure 1.40

Check box selected

Locate this image

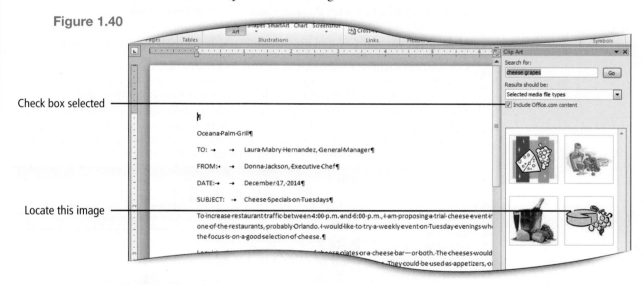

14 Click the image indicated in Figure 1.40 one time to insert it at the insertion point, and then in the upper right corner of the **Clip Art** task pane, click the **Close** ☒ button.

Alert! | If You Cannot Locate the Image

If the image shown in Figure 1.40 is unavailable, select a different cheese image that is appropriate.

---

15 With the image selected—surrounded by a border—on the Ribbon, click the **Home tab**, and then in the **Paragraph group**, click the **Center** button ☰. Click anywhere outside of the bordered picture to *deselect*—cancel the selection. Compare your screen with Figure 1.41.

Figure 1.41

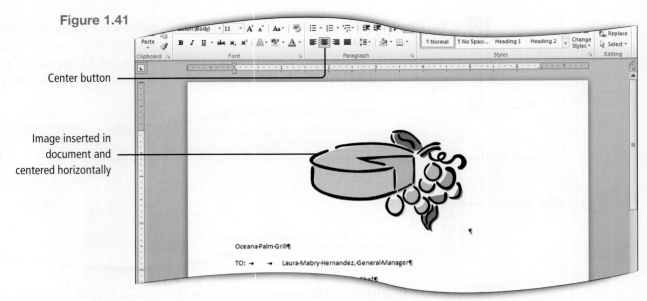

Center button

Image inserted in document and centered horizontally

Oceana·Palm·Grill¶

TO: → → Laura·Mabry·Hernandez,·General·Manager¶

16 Point to the inserted clip art image, and then watch the last tab of the Ribbon as you click the image one time to select it.

> The *Picture Tools* display and an additional tab—the *Format* tab—is added to the Ribbon. The Ribbon adapts to your work and will display additional tabs—referred to as *contextual tabs*—when you need them.

17 On the Ribbon, under **Picture Tools**, click the **Format tab**.

Alert! | The Size of Groups on the Ribbon Varies with Screen Resolution

Your monitor's screen resolution might be set higher than the resolution used to capture the figures in this book. In Figure 1.42 below, the resolution is set to 1024 × 768, which is used for all of the figures in this book. Compare that with Figure 1.43 below, where the screen resolution is set to 1280 × 1024.

At a higher resolution, the Ribbon expands some groups to show more commands than are available with a single click, such as those in the Picture Styles group. Or, the group expands to add descriptive text to some buttons, such as those in the Arrange group. Regardless of your screen resolution, all Office commands are available to you. In higher resolutions, you will have a more robust view of the commands.

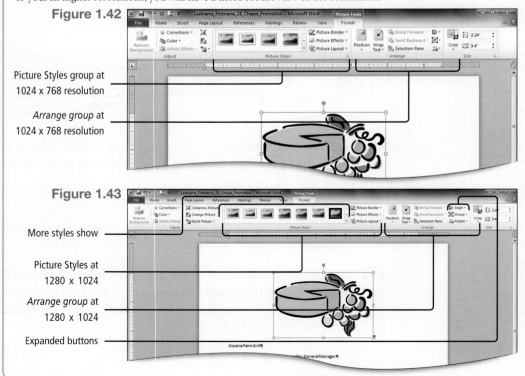

Figure 1.42

Picture Styles group at 1024 x 768 resolution

Arrange group at 1024 x 768 resolution

Figure 1.43

More styles show

Picture Styles at 1280 x 1024

Arrange group at 1280 x 1024

Expanded buttons

---

18 In the **Picture Styles group**, point to the first style to display the ScreenTip *Simple Frame, White*, and notice that the image displays with a white frame.

19 Watch the image as you point to the second picture style, and then to the third, and then to the fourth.

This is *Live Preview*, a technology that shows the result of applying an editing or formatting change as you point to possible results—*before* you actually apply it.

20 In the **Picture Styles group**, click the fourth style—**Drop Shadow Rectangle**—and then click anywhere outside of the image to deselect it. Notice that the Picture Tools no longer display on the Ribbon. Compare your screen with Figure 1.44.

Contextual tabs display only when you need them.

Figure 1.44

Picture Tools no longer display on the Ribbon

Drop Shadow Rectangle picture style applied to image

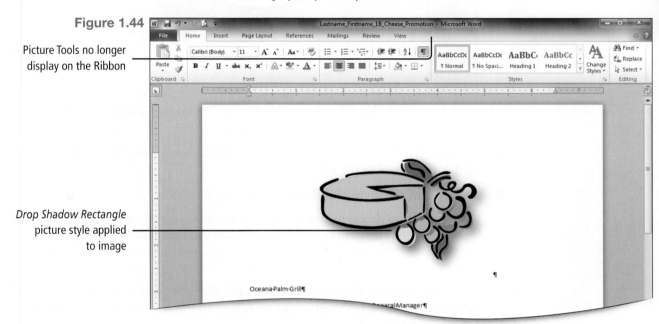

21 In the upper left corner of your screen, on the Quick Access Toolbar, click the **Save** button ⊟ to save the changes you have made.

Activity 1.10 | Minimizing and Using the Keyboard to Control the Ribbon

Instead of a mouse, some individuals prefer to navigate the Ribbon by using keys on the keyboard. You can activate keyboard control of the Ribbon by pressing the ⌗Alt⌗ key. You can also minimize the Ribbon to maximize your available screen space.

1 On your keyboard, press the ⌗Alt⌗ key, and then on the Ribbon, notice that small labels display. Press ⌗N⌗ to activate the commands on the **Insert tab**, and then compare your screen with Figure 1.45.

Each label represents a *KeyTip*—an indication of the key that you can press to activate the command. For example, on the Insert tab, you can press ⌗F⌗ to activate the Clip Art task pane.

Figure 1.45

KeyTips indicate that keyboard control of the Ribbon is active

Oceana·Palm·Grill¶

TO: →   →   Laura·Mabry·Hernandez,·General·Manager¶

2 Press [Esc] to redisplay the KeyTips for the tabs. Then, press [Alt] again to turn off keyboard control of the Ribbon.

3 Point to any tab on the Ribbon and right-click to display a shortcut menu.

> Here you can choose to display the Quick Access Toolbar below the Ribbon or minimize the Ribbon to maximize screen space. You can also customize the Ribbon by adding, removing, renaming, or reordering tabs, groups, and commands on the Ribbon, although this is not recommended until you become an expert Office user.

Another Way

Double-click the active tab; or, click the Minimize the Ribbon button at the right end of the Ribbon.

4 Click **Minimize the Ribbon**. Notice that only the Ribbon tabs display. Click the **Home tab** to display the commands. Click anywhere in the document, and notice that the Ribbon reverts to its minimized view.

Another Way

Double-click any tab to redisplay the full Ribbon.

5 Right-click any Ribbon tab, and then click **Minimize the Ribbon** again to turn the minimize feature off.

> Most expert Office users prefer to have the full Ribbon display at all times.

6 Point to any tab on the Ribbon, and then on your mouse device, roll the mouse wheel. Notice that different tabs become active as your roll the mouse wheel.

> You can make a tab active by using this technique, instead of clicking the tab.

Objective 10 | Apply Formatting in Office Programs

Formatting is the process of establishing the overall appearance of text, graphics, and pages in an Office file—for example, in a Word document.

Activity 1.11 | Formatting and Viewing Pages

In this activity, you will practice common formatting techniques used in Office applications.

1 On the Ribbon, click the **Insert tab**, and then in the **Header & Footer group**, click the **Footer** button.

Another Way

On the Design tab, in
the Insert group, click
Quick Parts, click Field,
and then under Field
names, click FileName.

2 At the top of the displayed gallery, under **Built-In**, click **Blank**. At the bottom of your
document, with *Type text* highlighted in blue, using your own name type the file
name of this document **Lastname_Firstname_1B_Cheese_Promotion** and then
compare your screen with Figure 1.46.

> Header & Footer Tools are added to the Ribbon. A ***footer*** is a reserved area for text or
> graphics that displays at the bottom of each page in a document. Likewise, a ***header*** is
> a reserved area for text or graphics that displays at the top of each page in a document.
> When the footer (or header) area is active, the document area is inactive (dimmed).

Figure 1.46

Design tab added

Header & Footer
Tools active

Document area inactive
(dimmed) when
footer area is active

*Close Header and
Footer* button

Your file name

Footer area displays

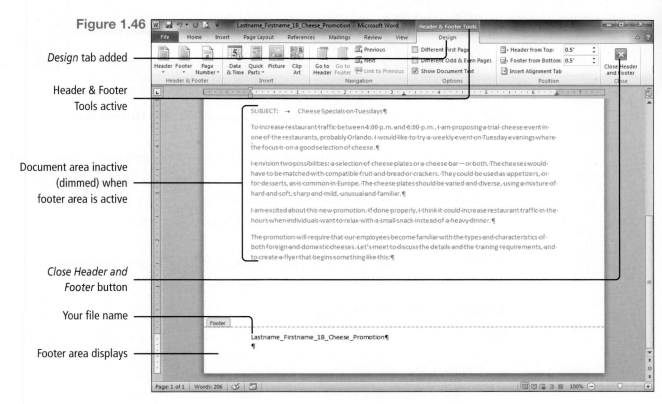

3 On the Ribbon, on the **Design tab**, in the **Close group**, click the **Close Header and
Footer** button.

4 On the Ribbon, click the **Page Layout tab**. In the **Page Setup group**, click the **Orientation**
button, and notice that two orientations display—*Portrait* and *Landscape*. Click
Landscape.

> In ***portrait orientation***, the paper is taller than it is wide. In ***landscape orientation***, the
> paper is wider than it is tall.

5 In the lower right corner of the screen, locate the **Zoom control** buttons
.

> To ***zoom*** means to increase or decrease the viewing area. You can zoom in to look closely
> at a section of a document, and then zoom out to see an entire page on the screen. You can
> also zoom to view multiple pages on the screen.

6 Drag the **Zoom slider** to the left until you have zoomed to
approximately *60%*. Compare your screen with Figure 1.47.

Figure 1.47

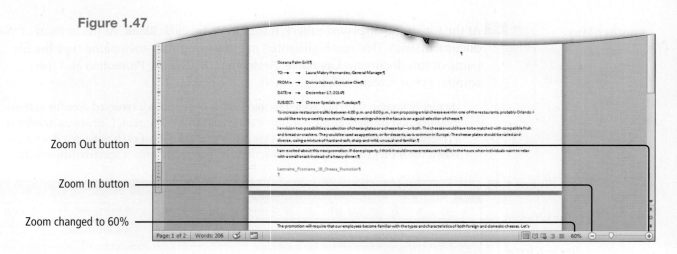

Zoom Out button

Zoom In button

Zoom changed to 60%

7 On the **Page Layout tab**, in the **Page Setup group**, click the **Orientation** button, and then click **Portrait**.

> Portrait orientation is commonly used for business documents such as letters and memos.

8 In the lower right corner of your screen, click the **Zoom In** button ⊕ as many times as necessary to return to the **100%** zoom setting.

> Use the zoom feature to adjust the view of your document for editing and for your viewing comfort.

9 On the Quick Access Toolbar, click the **Save** button 🖫 to save the changes you have made to your document.

Activity 1.12 | Formatting Text

1 To the left of *Oceana Palm Grill*, point in the margin area to display the 🔏 pointer and click one time to select the entire paragraph. Compare your screen with Figure 1.48.

> Use this technique to select complete paragraphs from the margin area. Additionally, with this technique you can drag downward to select multiple-line paragraphs—which is faster and more efficient than dragging through text.

Figure 1.48

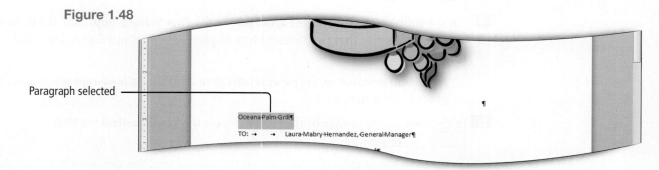

Paragraph selected

2 On the Ribbon, click the **Home tab**, and then in the **Paragraph group**, click the **Center** button ≡ to center the paragraph.

> *Alignment* refers to the placement of paragraph text relative to the left and right margins. *Center alignment* refers to text that is centered horizontally between the left and right margins. You can also align text at the left margin, which is the default alignment for text in Word, or at the right margin.

3 On the **Home tab**, in the **Font group**, click the **Font button arrow** `Calibri (Body) ▾`. At the top of the list, point to **Cambria**, and as you do so, notice that the selected text previews in the Cambria font.

A *font* is a set of characters with the same design and shape. The default font in a Word document is Calibri, which is a *sans serif* font—a font design with no lines or extensions on the ends of characters.

The Cambria font is a *serif* font—a font design that includes small line extensions on the ends of the letters to guide the eye in reading from left to right.

The list of fonts displays as a gallery showing potential results. For example, in the Font gallery, you can see the actual design and format of each font as it would look if applied to text.

4 Point to several other fonts and observe the effect on the selected text. Then, at the top of the **Font** gallery, under **Theme Fonts**, click **Cambria**.

A *theme* is a predesigned set of colors, fonts, lines, and fill effects that look good together and that can be applied to your entire document or to specific items.

A theme combines two sets of fonts—one for text and one for headings. In the default Office theme, Cambria is the suggested font for headings.

5 With the paragraph *Oceana Palm Grill* still selected, on the **Home tab**, in the **Font group**, click the **Font Size button arrow** `11 ▾`, point to **36**, and then notice how Live Preview displays the text in the font size to which you are pointing. Compare your screen with Figure 1.49.

Figure 1.49

Font Size button

Font button

Font Size list

Pointing to 36 pt font size

Oceana Palm Grill centered, Cambria font applied

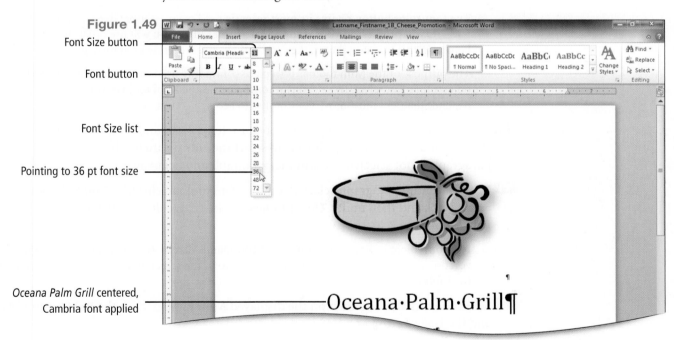

6 On the displayed list of font sizes, click **20**.

Fonts are measured in *points*, with one point equal to 1/72 of an inch. A higher point size indicates a larger font size. Headings and titles are often formatted by using a larger font size. The word *point* is abbreviated as *pt*.

7 With *Oceana Palm Grill* still selected, on the **Home tab**, in the **Font group**, click the **Font Color button arrow** `A ▾`. Under **Theme Colors**, in the seventh column, click the last color—**Olive Green, Accent 3, Darker 50%**. Click anywhere to deselect the text.

8 To the left of *TO:*, point in the left margin area to display the 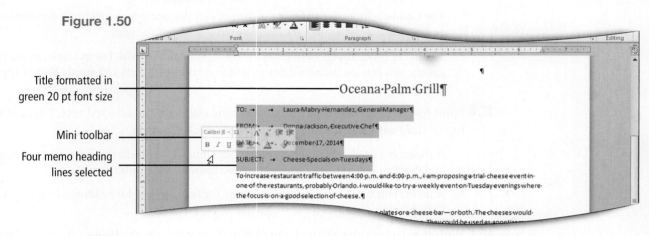 pointer, hold down the left mouse button, and then drag down to select the four memo headings. Compare your screen with Figure 1.50.

> Use this technique to select complete paragraphs from the margin area—dragging downward to select multiple-line paragraphs—which is faster and more efficient than dragging through text.

Figure 1.50

Title formatted in green 20 pt font size

Mini toolbar

Four memo heading lines selected

9 With the four paragraphs selected, on the Mini toolbar, click the **Font Color** button [A▾], which now displays a dark green bar instead of a red bar.

> The font color button retains its most recently used color—Olive Green, Accent 3, Darker 50%. As you progress in your study of Microsoft Office, you will use other buttons that behave in this manner; that is, they retain their most recently used format.

> The purpose of the Mini toolbar is to place commonly used commands close to text or objects that you select. By selecting a command on the Mini toolbar, you reduce the distance that you must move your mouse to access a command.

10 Click anywhere in the paragraph that begins *To increase*, and then *triple-click*—click the left mouse button three times—to select the entire paragraph. If the entire paragraph is not selected, click in the paragraph and begin again.

11 With the entire paragraph selected, on the Mini toolbar, click the **Font Color button arrow** [A▾], and then under **Theme Colors**, in the sixth column, click the first color—**Red, Accent 2**.

> It is convenient to have commonly used commands display on the Mini toolbar so that you do not have to move your mouse to the top of the screen to access the command from the Ribbon.

12 Select the text *TO:* and then on the displayed Mini toolbar, click the **Bold** button [B] and the **Italic** button [I].

> *Font styles* include bold, italic, and underline. Font styles emphasize text and are a visual cue to draw the reader's eye to important text.

13 On the displayed Mini toolbar, click the **Italic** button [I] again to turn off the Italic formatting. Notice that the Italic button no longer glows orange.

> A button that behaves in this manner is referred to as a *toggle button*, which means it can be turned on by clicking it once, and then turned off by clicking it again.

14 With *TO:* still selected, on the Mini toolbar, click the **Format Painter** button ✅. Then, move your mouse under the word *Laura*, and notice the ⬛I mouse pointer. Compare your screen with Figure 1.51.

> You can use the *Format Painter* to copy the formatting of specific text or of a paragraph and then apply it in other locations in your document.
>
> The pointer takes the shape of a paintbrush, and contains the formatting information from the paragraph where the insertion point is positioned. Information about the Format Painter and how to turn it off displays in the status bar.

Figure 1.51

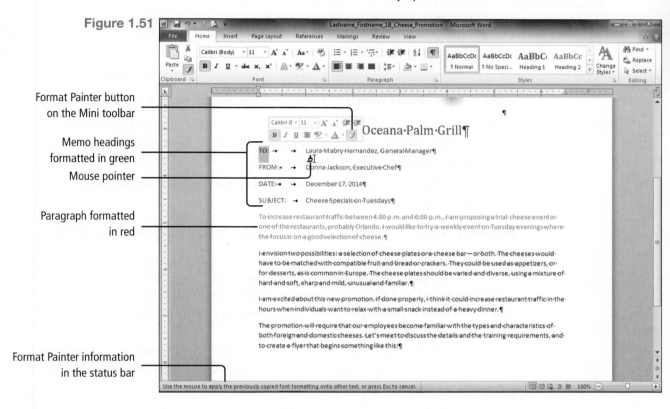

Format Painter button on the Mini toolbar

Memo headings formatted in green

Mouse pointer

Paragraph formatted in red

Format Painter information in the status bar

15 With the ⬛I pointer, drag to select the text *FROM:* and notice that the Bold formatting is applied. Then, point to the selected text *FROM:* and on the Mini toolbar, *double-click* the **Format Painter** button ✅.

16 Select the text *DATE:* to copy the Bold formatting, and notice that the pointer retains the ⬛I shape.

> When you *double-click* the Format Painter button, the Format Painter feature remains active until you either click the Format Painter button again, or press ⎋Esc to cancel it—as indicated on the status bar.

17 With Format Painter still active, select the text *SUBJECT:*, and then on the Ribbon, on the **Home tab**, in the **Clipboard group**, notice that the **Format Painter** button ✅ is glowing orange, indicating that it is active. Compare your screen with Figure 1.52.

Figure 1.52

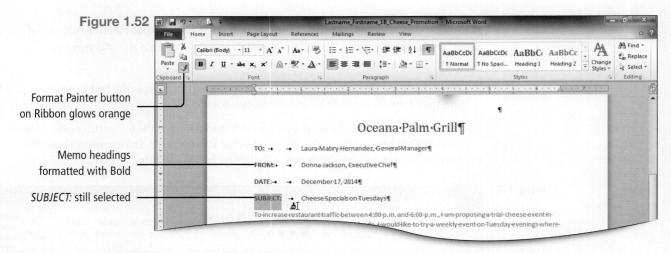

Format Painter button on Ribbon glows orange

Memo headings formatted with Bold

SUBJECT: still selected

18 Click the **Format Painter** button on the Ribbon to turn the command off.

19 In the paragraph that begins *To increase*, triple-click again to select the entire paragraph. On the displayed Mini toolbar, click the **Bold** button B and the **Italic** button I. Click anywhere to deselect.

20 On the Quick Access Toolbar, click the **Save** button to save the changes you have made to your document.

Activity 1.13 | Using the Office Clipboard to Cut, Copy, and Paste

The **Office Clipboard** is a temporary storage area that holds text or graphics that you select and then cut or copy. When you *copy* text or graphics, a copy is placed on the Office Clipboard and the original text or graphic remains in place. When you *cut* text or graphics, a copy is placed on the Office Clipboard, and the original text or graphic is removed—cut—from the document.

After cutting or copying, the contents of the Office Clipboard are available for you to *paste*—insert—in a new location in the current document, or into another Office file.

1 Hold down Ctrl and press Home to move to the beginning of your document, and then take a moment to study the table in Figure 1.53, which describes similar keyboard shortcuts with which you can navigate quickly in a document.

To Move	Press
To the beginning of a document	Ctrl + Home
To the end of a document	Ctrl + End
To the beginning of a line	Home
To the end of a line	End
To the beginning of the previous word	Ctrl + ←
To the beginning of the next word	Ctrl + →
To the beginning of the current word (if insertion point is in the middle of a word)	Ctrl + ←
To the beginning of a paragraph	Ctrl + ↑
To the beginning of the next paragraph	Ctrl + ↓
To the beginning of the current paragraph (if insertion point is in the middle of a paragraph)	Ctrl + ↑
Up one screen	PgUp
Down one screen	PageDown

Figure 1.53

2 To the left of *Oceana Palm Grill*, point in the left margin area to display the pointer, and then click one time to select the entire paragraph. On the **Home tab**, in the **Clipboard group**, click the **Copy** button.

Because anything that you select and then copy—or cut—is placed on the Office Clipboard, the Copy command and the Cut command display in the Clipboard group of commands on the Ribbon.

There is no visible indication that your copied selection has been placed on the Office Clipboard.

3 On the **Home tab**, in the **Clipboard group**, to the right of the group name *Clipboard*, click the **Dialog Box Launcher** button, and then compare your screen with Figure 1.54.

The Clipboard task pane displays with your copied text. In any Ribbon group, the ***Dialog Box Launcher*** displays either a dialog box or a task pane related to the group of commands.

It is not necessary to display the Office Clipboard in this manner, although sometimes it is useful to do so. The Office Clipboard can hold 24 items.

Figure 1.54

Copy button

Dialog Box Launcher in Clipboard group

Clipboard task pane displays

Selected text on the Office Clipboard

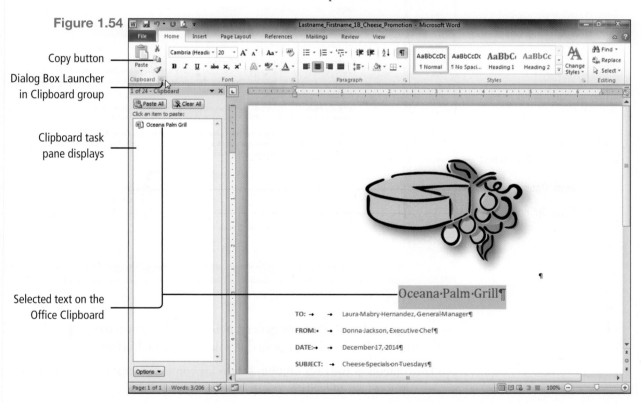

4 In the upper right corner of the **Clipboard** task pane, click the **Close** button.

5 Press Ctrl + End to move to the end of your document. Press Enter one time to create a new blank paragraph. On the **Home tab**, in the **Clipboard group**, point to the **Paste** button, and then click the *upper* portion of this split button.

The Paste command pastes the most recently copied item on the Office Clipboard at the insertion point location. If you click the lower portion of the Paste button, a gallery of Paste Options displays.

6 Click the **Paste Options** button 📋 that displays below the pasted text as shown in Figure 1.55.

> Here you can view and apply various formatting options for pasting your copied or cut text. Typically you will click Paste on the Ribbon and paste the item in its original format. If you want some other format for the pasted item, you can do so from the *Paste Options gallery.*
>
> The Paste Options gallery provides a Live Preview of the various options for changing the format of the pasted item with a single click. The Paste Options gallery is available in three places: on the Ribbon by clicking the lower portion of the Paste button—the Paste button arrow; from the Paste Options button that displays below the pasted item following the paste operation; or, on the shortcut menu if you right-click the pasted item.

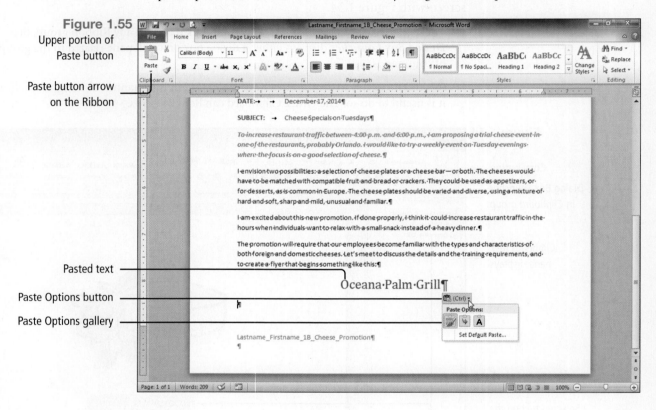

Figure 1.55
Upper portion of Paste button
Paste button arrow on the Ribbon
Pasted text
Paste Options button
Paste Options gallery

7 In the displayed **Paste Options** gallery, *point* to each option to see the Live Preview of the format that would be applied if you clicked the button.

> The contents of the Paste Options gallery are contextual; that is, they change based on what you copied and where you are pasting.

8 Press Esc to close the gallery; the button will remain displayed until you take some other screen action.

Another Way
On the Home tab, in the Clipboard group, click the Cut button; or, use the keyboard shortcut Ctrl + X.

9 Press Ctrl + Home to move to the top of the document, and then click the **cheese image** one time to select it. While pointing to the selected image, right-click, and then on the shortcut menu, click **Cut**.

> Recall that the Cut command cuts—removes—the selection from the document and places it on the Office Clipboard.

10 Press `Del` one time to remove the blank paragraph from the top of the document, and then press `Ctrl` + `End` to move to the end of the document.

11 With the insertion point blinking in the blank paragraph at the end of the document, right-click, and notice that the **Paste Options** gallery displays on the shortcut menu. Compare your screen with Figure 1.56.

Figure 1.56

Paste Options on
shortcut menu

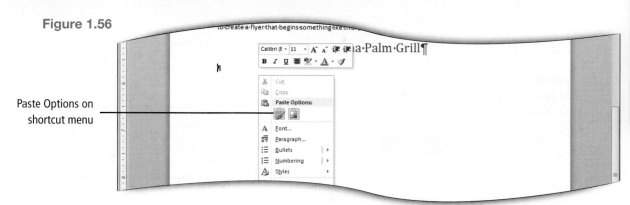

12 On the shortcut menu, under **Paste Options**, click the first button—**Keep Source Formatting** .

13 Click the picture to select it. On the **Home tab**, in the **Paragraph group**, click the **Center** button .

14 Above the cheese picture, click to position the insertion point at the end of the word *Grill*, press `Spacebar` one time, and then type **Tuesday Cheese Tastings** Compare your screen with Figure 1.57.

Figure 1.57

Heading

Picture inserted
and centered

Activity 1.14 | Viewing Print Preview and Printing a Word Document

1 Press `Ctrl` + `Home` to move to the top of your document. Select the text *Oceana Palm Grill*, and then replace the selected text by typing **Memo**

2 Display **Backstage** view, on the right, click **Properties**, and then click **Show Document Panel**. Replace the existing author name with your first and last name. In the **Subject** box, type your course name and section number, and then in the **Keywords** box, type **cheese promotion** and then **Close** the **Document Information Panel**.

Another Way
Press Ctrl + F2 to display Print Preview.

3 On the Quick Access Toolbar, click **Save** 🖫 to save the changes you have made to your document.

4 On the Quick Access Toolbar, click the **Print Preview** button 🔍 that you added. Compare your screen with Figure 1.58.

Figure 1.58

Memo typed

If no printer is attached to your system, OneNote is the default printer

Print tab active in Backstage view

Print Preview (if you have a non-color printer as your default printer, the preview may display in shades of gray)

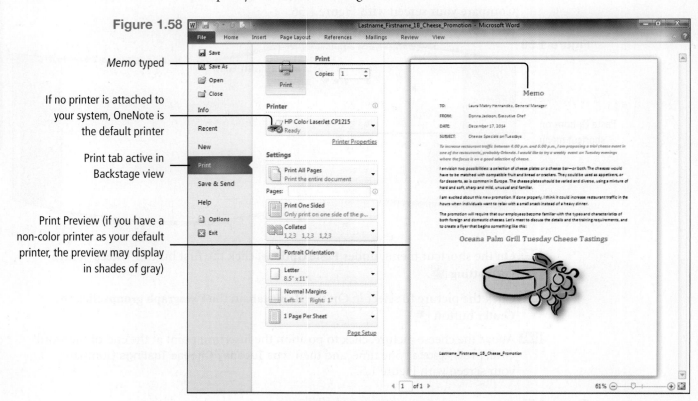

5 Examine the **Print Preview**. Under **Settings**, notice that in **Backstage** view, several of the same commands that are available on the Page Layout tab of the Ribbon also display.

For convenience, common adjustments to Page Layout display here, so that you can make last-minute adjustments without closing Backstage view.

6 If you need to make any corrections, click the Home tab to return to the document and make any necessary changes.

It is good practice to examine the Print Preview before printing or submitting your work electronically. Then, make any necessary corrections, re-save, and redisplay Print Preview.

7 If you are directed to do so, click Print to print the document; or, above the Info tab, click Close, and then submit your file electronically according to the directions provided by your instructor.

If you click the Print button, Backstage view closes and the Word window redisplays.

8 On the Quick Access Toolbar, point to the **Print Preview icon** 🔍 you placed there, right-click, and then click **Remove from Quick Access Toolbar**.

If you are working on your own computer and you want to do so, you can leave the icon on the toolbar; in a lab setting, you should return the software to its original settings.

9 At the right end of the title bar, click the program **Close** button ![X].

10 If a message displays asking if you want the text on the Clipboard to be available after you quit Word, click **No**.

This message most often displays if you have copied some type of image to the Clipboard. If you click Yes, the items on the Clipboard will remain for you to use.

Objective 11 | Use the Microsoft Office 2010 Help System

Within each Office program, the Help feature provides information about all of the program's features and displays step-by-step instructions for performing many tasks.

Activity 1.15 | Using the Microsoft Office 2010 Help System in Excel

In this activity, you will use the Microsoft Help feature to find information about formatting numbers in Excel.

> **Another Way**
> Press F1 to display Help.

1 **Start** the **Microsoft Excel 2010** program. In the upper right corner of your screen, click the **Microsoft Excel Help** button ![?].

2 In the **Excel Help** window, click in the white box in upper left corner, type **formatting numbers** and then click **Search** or press Enter.

3 On the list of results, click **Display numbers as currency**. Compare your screen with Figure 1.59.

Figure 1.59

Excel Help window —
Search term —
Print button —
Search button —

Help information —

Excel Help button —

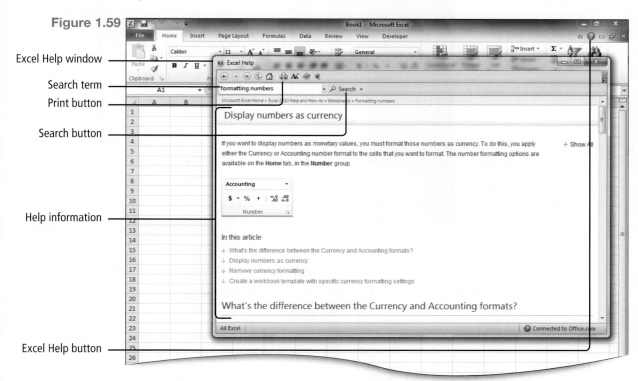

4 If you want to do so, on the toolbar at the top of the **Excel Help** window, click the Print ![printer] button to print a copy of this information for your reference.

5 On the title bar of the Excel Help window, click the **Close** button ![x]. On the right side of the Microsoft Excel title bar, click the **Close** button ![x] to close Excel.

Objective 12 | Compress Files

A *compressed file* is a file that has been reduced in size. Compressed files take up less storage space and can be transferred to other computers faster than uncompressed files. You can also combine a group of files into one compressed folder, which makes it easier to share a group of files.

Activity 1.16 | Compressing Files

In this activity, you will combine the two files you created in this chapter into one compressed file.

1 On the Windows taskbar, click the **Start** button ![start], and then on the right, click **Computer**.

2 On the left, in the **navigation pane**, click the location of your two files from this chapter—your USB flash drive or other location—and display the folder window for your **Common Features Chapter 1** folder. Compare your screen with Figure 1.60.

Figure 1.60

Address bar displays path

Your chapter files in file list (your name displays)

Folder window for your chapter folder

Location selected in navigation pane (your location may vary)

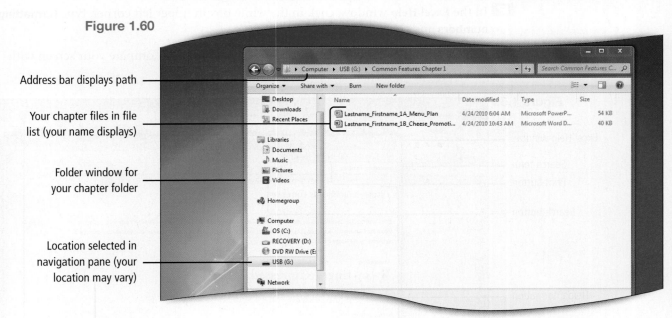

3 In the **file list**, click your **Lastname_Firstname_1A_Menu_Plan** file one time to select it.

4 Hold down Ctrl, and then click your **Lastname_Firstname_1B_Cheese_Promotion** file to select both files. Release Ctrl.

In any Windows-based program, holding down Ctrl while selecting enables you to select multiple items.

5 Point anywhere over the two selected files and right-click. On the shortcut menu, point to **Send to**, and then compare your screen with Figure 1.61.

Figure 1.61

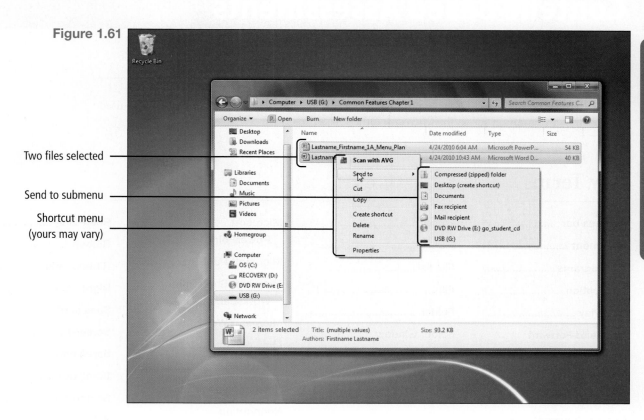

Two files selected

Send to submenu

Shortcut menu
(yours may vary)

6 On the shortcut submenu, click **Compressed (zipped) folder**.

Windows creates a compressed folder containing a *copy* of each of the selected files. The folder name is the name of the file or folder to which you were pointing, and is selected—highlighted in blue—so that you can rename it.

7 Using your own name, type **Lastname_Firstname_Common_Features_Ch1** and press Enter.

The compressed folder is now ready to attach to an e-mail or share in some other electronic format.

8 **Close** ☒ the folder window. If directed to do so by your instructor, submit your compressed folder electronically.

More Knowledge | Extracting Compressed Files

Extract means to decompress, or pull out, files from a compressed form. When you extract a file, an uncompressed copy is placed in the folder that you specify. The original file remains in the compressed folder.

End You have completed Project 1B ———————————————————

Content-Based Assessments

Summary

In this chapter, you used Windows Explorer to navigate the Windows file structure. You also used features that are common across the Microsoft Office 2010 programs.

Key Terms

Matching

Match each term in the second column with its correct definition in the first column by writing the letter of the term on the blank line in front of the correct definition.

A Address bar

B Command

C File

D Folder

E Folder window

F Icons

G Keyboard shortcut

H Library

I Microsoft Excel

J Program

K Ribbon

L Start menu

M Subfolder

N Title bar

O Windows Explorer

_____ 1.   A collection of information stored on a computer under a single name.

_____ 2.   A container in which you store files.

_____ 3.   A folder within a folder.

_____ 4.   The program that displays the files and folders on your computer.

_____ 5.   The Windows menu that is the main gateway to your computer.

_____ 6.   In Windows 7, a window that displays the contents of the current folder, library, or device, and contains helpful parts so that you can navigate.

_____ 7.   In Windows, a collection of items, such as files and folders, assembled from various locations that might be on your computer.

_____ 8.   The bar at the top of a folder window with which you can navigate to a different folder or library, or go back to a previous one.

_____ 9.   An instruction to a computer program that carries out an action.

_____ 10. Small pictures that represent a program, a file, a folder, or an object.

_____ 11. A set of instructions that a computer uses to perform a specific task.

_____ 12. A spreadsheet program used to calculate numbers and create charts.

_____ 13. The user interface that groups commands on tabs at the top of the program window.

_____ 14. A bar at the top of the program window displaying the current file and program name.

_____ 15. One or more keys pressed to perform a task that would otherwise require a mouse.

Multiple Choice

Circle the correct answer.

1. A small toolbar with frequently used commands that displays when selecting text or objects is the:
    A. Quick Access Toolbar   B. Mini toolbar   C. Document toolbar

2. In Office 2010, a centralized space for file management tasks is:
    A. a task pane   B. a dialog box   C. Backstage view

3. The commands Save, Save As, Open, and Close in Backstage view are located:
    A. above the Backstage tabs   B. below the   C. under the screen thumbnail
                                     Backstage tabs

4. The tab in Backstage view that displays information about the current file is the:
    A. Recent tab   B. Info tab   C. Options tab

5. Details about a file, including the title, author name, subject, and keywords are known as:
    A. document properties   B. formatting marks   C. KeyTips

6. An Office feature that displays a list of potential results is:
    A. Live Preview   B. a contextual tab   C. a gallery

7. A type of formatting emphasis applied to text such as bold, italic, and underline, is called:

   A. a font style   B. a KeyTip   C. a tag

8. A technology showing the result of applying formatting as you point to possible results is called:

   A. Live Preview   B. Backstage view   C. gallery view

9. A temporary storage area that holds text or graphics that you select and then cut or copy is the:

   A. paste options gallery   B. ribbon   C. Office clipboard

10. A file that has been reduced in size is:

    A. a compressed file   B. an extracted file   C. a PDF file

Creating a Worksheet and Charting Data

OUTCOMES
At the end of this chapter you will be able to:

OBJECTIVES
Mastering these objectives will enable you to:

PROJECT 1A
Create a sales report with an embedded column chart and sparklines.

1. Create, Save, and Navigate an Excel Workbook (p. 51)
2. Enter Data in a Worksheet (p. 54)
3. Construct and Copy Formulas and Use the SUM Function (p. 60)
4. Format Cells with Merge & Center and Cell Styles (p. 64)
5. Chart Data to Create a Column Chart and Insert Sparklines (p. 66)
6. Print, Display Formulas, and Close Excel (p. 71)

PROJECT 1B
Calculate the value of an inventory.

7. Check Spelling in a Worksheet (p. 77)
8. Enter Data by Range (p. 79)
9. Construct Formulas for Mathematical Operations (p. 80)
10. Edit Values in a Worksheet (p. 85)
11. Format a Worksheet (p. 86)

kwest/Shutterstock

In This Chapter

In this chapter, you will use Microsoft Excel 2010 to create and analyze data organized into columns and rows. After entering data in a worksheet, you can perform calculations, analyze the data to make logical decisions, and create charts.

In this chapter, you will create and modify Excel workbooks. You will practice the basics of worksheet design, create a footer, enter and edit data in a worksheet, chart data, and then save, preview, and print workbooks. You will also construct formulas for mathematical operations.

The projects in this chapter relate to **Texas Spectrum Wireless**, which provides accessories and software for all major brands of cell phones, smart phones, PDAs, mp3 players, and portable computers. The company sells thousands of unique products in their retail stores, which are located throughout Texas and the southern United States. They also sell thousands of items each year through their Web site, and offer free shipping and returns to their customers. The company takes pride in offering unique categories of accessories such as waterproof and ruggedized gear.

Project 1A Sales Report with Embedded Column Chart and Sparklines

myitlab
Project 1A Training

Project Activities

In Activities 1.01 through 1.16, you will create an Excel worksheet for Roslyn Thomas, the President of Texas Spectrum Wireless. The worksheet displays the first quarter sales of wireless accessories for the current year, and includes a chart to visually represent the data. Your completed worksheet will look similar to Figure 1.1.

Project Files

For Project 1A, you will need the following file:

New blank Excel workbook

You will save your workbook as:

Lastname_Firstname_1A_Quarterly_Sales

Project Results

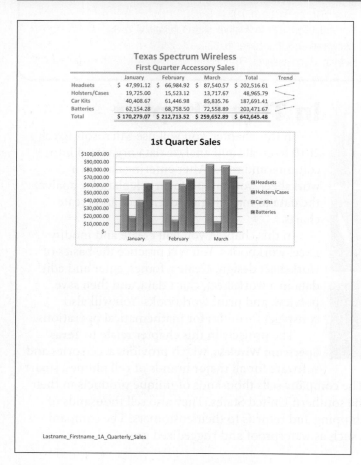

Lastname_Firstname_1A_Quarterly_Sales

Figure 1.1
Project 1A Quarterly Sales

Objective 1 | Create, Save, and Navigate an Excel Workbook

On startup, Excel displays a new blank *workbook*—the Excel document that stores your data—which contains one or more pages called a *worksheet*. A worksheet—or *spreadsheet*—is stored in a workbook, and is formatted as a pattern of uniformly spaced horizontal rows and vertical columns. The intersection of a column and a row forms a box referred to as a *cell*.

Activity 1.01 | Starting Excel and Naming and Saving a Workbook

1 **Start** Excel. In the lower right corner of the window, if necessary, click the Normal button 🔳, and then to the right, locate the zoom—magnification—level.

> Your zoom level should be 100%, although some figures in this textbook may be shown at a higher zoom level.

Another Way

Use the keyboard shortcut F12 to display the Save As dialog box.

2 In the upper left corner of your screen, click the **File tab** to display **Backstage** view, click **Save As**, and then in the **Save As** dialog box, navigate to the location where you will store your workbooks for this chapter.

3 In your storage location, create a new folder named **Excel Chapter 1** Open the new folder to display its folder window, and then in the **File name** box, notice that *Book1* displays as the default file name.

4 In the **File name** box, click *Book1* to select it, and then using your own name, type **Lastname_Firstname_1A_Quarterly_Sales** being sure to include the underscore (Shift + -) instead of spaces between words. Compare your screen with Figure 1.2.

Figure 1.2

Path to your new *Excel Chapter 1* folder in address bar (yours may vary)

File name with your name and underscores between words

Save button

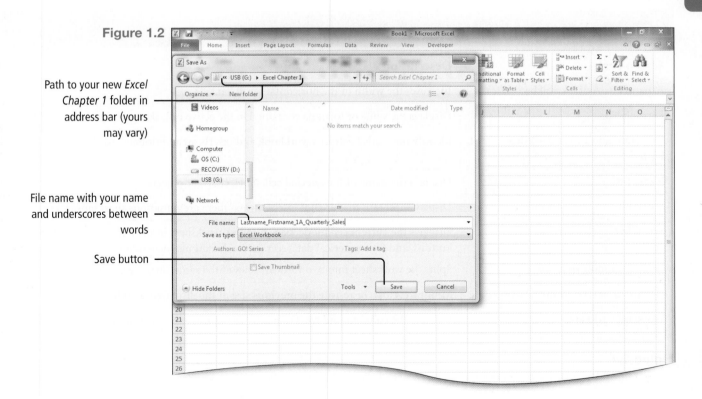

Excel | Chapter 1

5 Click **Save**. Compare your screen with Figure 1.3, and then take a moment to study the Excel window parts in the table in Figure 1.4.

Figure 1.3

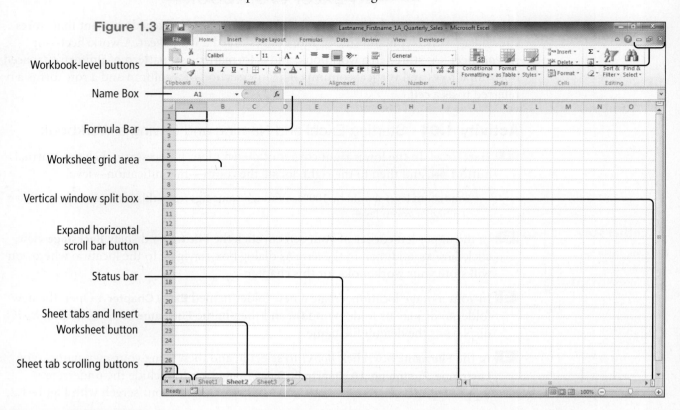

Workbook-level buttons

Name Box

Formula Bar

Worksheet grid area

Vertical window split box

Expand horizontal scroll bar button

Status bar

Sheet tabs and Insert Worksheet button

Sheet tab scrolling buttons

Parts of the Excel Window

Screen Part	Description
Expand horizontal scroll bar button	Increases the width of the horizontal scroll bar.
Formula Bar	Displays the value or formula contained in the active cell; also permits entry or editing.
Sheet tabs and Insert Worksheet button	Identify the worksheets in a workbook and inserts an additional worksheet.
Name Box	Displays the name of the selected cell, table, chart, or object.
Sheet tab scrolling buttons	Display sheet tabs that are not in view when there are numerous sheet tabs.
Status bar	Displays the current cell mode, page number, worksheet information, view and zoom buttons, and for numerical data, common calculations such as Sum and Average.
Vertical window split box	Splits the worksheet into two vertical views of the same worksheet.
Workbook-level buttons	Minimize, close, or restore the previous size of the displayed workbook.
Worksheet grid area	Displays the columns and rows that intersect to form the worksheet's cells.

Figure 1.4

Activity 1.02 | Navigating a Worksheet and a Workbook

1 Take a moment to study Figure 1.5 and the table in Figure 1.6 to become familiar with the Excel workbook window.

Figure 1.5

Expand Formula Bar button
Lettered column headings
Select All box
Numbered row headings
Excel pointer
Horizontal window split box

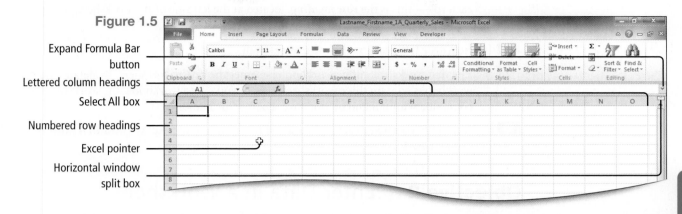

Excel Workbook Window Elements

Workbook Window Element	Description
Excel pointer	Displays the pointer in Excel.
Expand Formula Bar button	Increases the height of the Formula Bar to display lengthy cell content.
Horizontal window split box	Splits the worksheet into two horizontal views of the same worksheet.
Lettered column headings	Indicate the column letter.
Numbered row headings	Indicate the row number.
Select All box	Selects all the cells in a worksheet.

Figure 1.6

2 In the lower right corner of the screen, in the horizontal scroll bar, click the **right scroll arrow** one time to shift **column A** out of view.

> A *column* is a vertical group of cells in a worksheet. Beginning with the first letter of the alphabet, *A*, a unique letter identifies each column—this is called the *column heading*. Clicking one of the horizontal scroll bar arrows shifts the window either left or right one column at a time.

3 Point to the **right scroll arrow**, and then hold down the left mouse button until the columns begin to scroll rapidly to the right; release the mouse button when you begin to see pairs of letters as the column headings.

4 Slowly drag the horizontal scroll box to the left, and notice that just above the scroll box, ScreenTips with the column letters display as you drag. Drag the horizontal scroll box left or right—or click the left or right scroll arrow—as necessary to position **column Z** near the center of your screen.

> Column headings after column Z use two letters starting with AA, AB, and so on through ZZ. After that, columns begin with three letters beginning with AAA. This pattern provides 16,384 columns. The last column is XFD.

5 In the lower left portion of your screen, click the **Sheet2 tab**.

> The second worksheet displays and is the active sheet. Column A displays at the left.

6 In the vertical scroll bar, click the **down scroll arrow** one time to move **Row 1** out of view.

> A *row* is a horizontal group of cells. Beginning with number 1, a unique number identifies each row—this is the *row heading*, located at the left side of the worksheet. A single worksheet has 1,048,576 rows.

7 In the lower left corner, click the **Sheet1 tab**.

> The first worksheet in the workbook becomes the active worksheet. By default, new workbooks contain three worksheets. When you save a workbook, the worksheets are contained within it and do not have separate file names.

8 Use the skills you just practiced to scroll horizontally to display **column A**, and if necessary, **row 1**.

Objective 2 | Enter Data in a Worksheet

Cell content, which is anything you type in a cell, can be one of two things: either a *constant value*—referred to simply as a *value*—or a *formula*. A formula is an equation that performs mathematical calculations on values in your worksheet. The most commonly used values are *text values* and *number values*, but a value can also include a date or a time of day.

Activity 1.03 | Entering Text and Using AutoComplete

A text value, also referred to as a *label*, usually provides information about number values in other worksheet cells. For example, a title such as First Quarter Accessory Sales gives the reader an indication that the data in the worksheet relates to information about sales of accessories during the three-month period January through March.

1 Click the **Sheet1 tab** to make it the active sheet. Point to and then click the cell at the intersection of **column A** and **row 1** to make it the *active cell*—the cell is outlined in black and ready to accept data.

> The intersecting column letter and row number form the *cell reference*—also called the *cell address*. When a cell is active, its column letter and row number are highlighted. The cell reference of the selected cell, *A1*, displays in the Name Box.

2 With cell **A1** as the active cell, type the worksheet title **Texas Spectrum Wireless** and then press Enter. Compare your screen with Figure 1.7.

> Text or numbers in a cell are referred to as *data*. You must confirm the data you type in a cell by pressing Enter or by some other keyboard movement, such as pressing Tab or an arrow key. Pressing Enter moves the selection to the cell below.

Figure 1.7

Name Box displays active cell—A2

Column heading and row heading of the active cell highlighted

Worksheet title entered

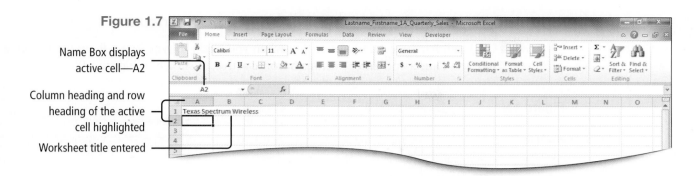

3 In cell **A1**, notice that the text does not fit; the text spills over and displays in cells **B1** and **C1** to the right.

If text is too long for a cell and cells to the right are empty, the text will display. If the cells to the right contain other data, only the text that will fit in the cell displays.

4 In cell **A2**, type the worksheet subtitle **First Quarter Accessory Sales** and then press Enter. Compare your screen with Figure 1.8.

Figure 1.8

Name Box displays *A3* (cell reference of active cell)

Column heading and row heading of selected cell highlighted

Worksheet subtitle typed

Excel pointer

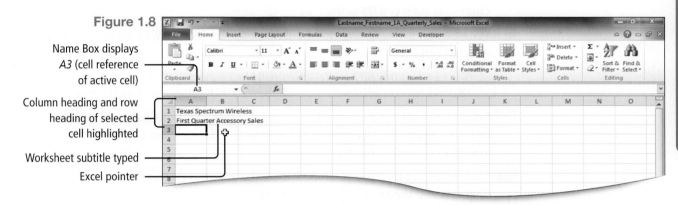

5 Press Enter again to make cell **A4** the active cell. In cell **A4**, type **Headsets** which will form the first row title, and then press Enter.

The text characters that you typed align at the left edge of the cell—referred to as *left alignment*—and cell A5 becomes the active cell. Left alignment is the default for text values.

6 In cell **A5**, type **H** and notice the text from the previous cell displays.

If the first characters you type in a cell match an existing entry in the column, Excel fills in the remaining characters for you. This feature, called *AutoComplete*, assists only with alphabetic values.

7 Continue typing the remainder of the row title **olsters/Cases** and press Enter.

The AutoComplete suggestion is removed when the entry you are typing differs from the previous value.

Another Way

Use the keyboard shortcut Ctrl + S to Save changes to your workbook.

8 In cell **A6**, type **Car Kits** and press Enter. In cell **A7**, type **Batteries** and press Enter. In cell **A8**, type **Total** and press Enter. On the Quick Access Toolbar, click **Save** .

Activity 1.04 | Using Auto Fill and Keyboard Shortcuts

1 Click cell **B3**. Type **J** and notice that when you begin to type in a cell, on the **Formula Bar**, the **Cancel** and **Enter** buttons become active, as shown in Figure 1.9.

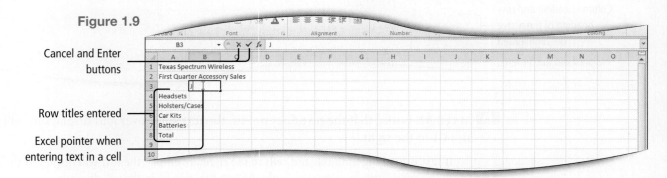

Figure 1.9

Cancel and Enter buttons

Row titles entered

Excel pointer when entering text in a cell

2 Continue to type **anuary** On the **Formula Bar**, notice that values you type in a cell also display there. Then, on the **Formula Bar**, click the **Enter** button ✔ to confirm the entry and keep cell **B3** active.

3 With cell **B3** active, locate the small black square in the lower right corner of the selected cell.

> You can drag this *fill handle*—the small black square in the lower right corner of a selected cell—to adjacent cells to fill the cells with values based on the first cell.

4 Point to the **fill handle** until the ⊞ pointer displays, hold down the left mouse button, drag to the right to cell **D3**, and as you drag, notice the ScreenTips *February* and *March*. Release the mouse button.

5 Under the text that you just filled, click the **Auto Fill Options** button ⊞▼ that displays, and then compare your screen with Figure 1.10.

> *Auto Fill* generates and extends a *series* of values into adjacent cells based on the value of other cells. A series is a group of things that come one after another in succession; for example, *January, February, March.*

> The Auto Fill Options button displays options to fill the data; options vary depending on the content and program from which you are filling, and the format of the data you are filling.

> *Fill Series* is selected, indicating the action that was taken. Because the options are related to the current task, the button is referred to as being *context sensitive.*

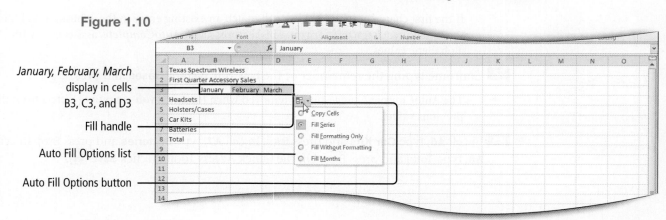

Figure 1.10

January, February, March display in cells B3, C3, and D3

Fill handle

Auto Fill Options list

Auto Fill Options button

6 Click in any cell to cancel the display of the Auto Fill Options list.

> The list no longer displays; the button will display until you perform some other screen action.

7 Press Ctrl + Home, which is the keyboard shortcut to make cell **A1** active.

8 On the Quick Access Toolbar, click **Save** 🖫 to save the changes you have made to your workbook, and then take a moment to study the table in Figure 1.11 to become familiar with additional keyboard shortcuts with which you can navigate the Excel worksheet.

Keyboard Shortcuts to Navigate the Excel Window

To Move the Location of the Active Cell:	Press:
Up, down, right, or left one cell	↑, ↓, →, ←
Down one cell	Enter
Up one cell	Shift + Enter
Up one full screen	Page Up
Down one full screen	PageDown
To column A of the current row	Home
To the last cell in the last column of the active area (the rectangle formed by all the rows and columns in a worksheet that contain entries)	Ctrl + End
To cell A1	Ctrl + Home
Right one cell	Tab
Left one cell	Shift + Tab

Figure 1.11

Activity 1.05 | Aligning Text and Adjusting the Size of Columns

1 In the **column heading area**, point to the vertical line between **column A** and **column B** to display the ⊞ pointer, press and hold down the left mouse button, and then compare your screen with Figure 1.12.

A ScreenTip displays information about the width of the column. The default width of a column is 64 *pixels*. A pixel, short for *picture element*, is a point of light measured in dots per square inch. Sixty-four pixels equal 8.43 characters, which is the average number of digits that will fit in a cell using the default font. The default font in Excel is Calibri and the default font size is 11.

Figure 1.12

Column heading area ———

Mouse pointer ———

ScreenTip ———

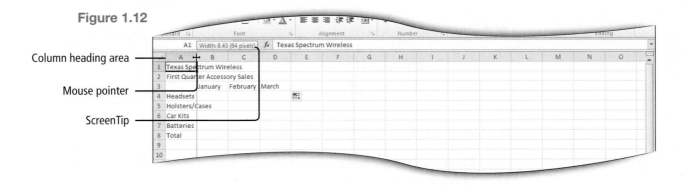

2 Drag to the right, and when the number of pixels indicated in the ScreenTip reaches **100 pixels**, release the mouse button. If you are not satisfied with your result, click Undo ⤺ on the Quick Access Toolbar and begin again.

> This width accommodates the longest row title in cells A4 through A8—*Holsters/Cases*. The worksheet title and subtitle in cells A1 and A2 span more than one column and still do not fit in column A.

3 Point to cell **B3** and then drag across to select cells **B3**, **C3**, and **D3**. Compare your screen with Figure 1.13; if you are not satisfied with your result, click anywhere and begin again.

> The three cells, B3 through D3, are selected and form a *range*—two or more cells on a worksheet that are adjacent (next to each other) or nonadjacent (not next to each other). This range of cells is referred to as *B3:D3*. When you see a colon (:) between two cell references, the range includes all the cells between the two cell references.
>
> A range of cells that is selected in this manner is indicated by a dark border, and Excel treats the range as a single unit so you can make the same changes to more than one cell at a time. The selected cells in the range are highlighted except for the first cell in the range, which displays in the Name Box.

Figure 1.13

First cell in selected range—B3—displays in Name Box

Column A widened to 100 pixels

Range B3:D3 selected

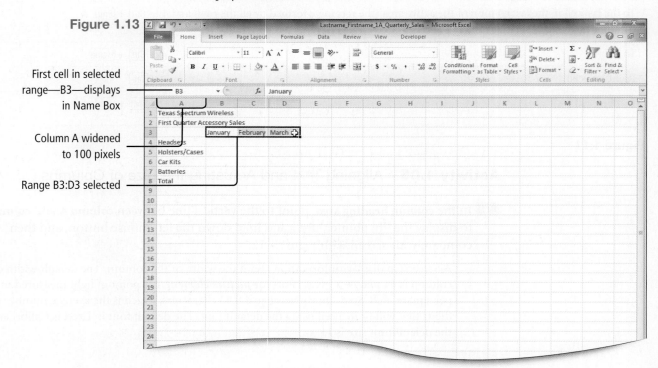

4 With the range **B3:D3** selected, point anywhere over the selected range, right-click, and then on the Mini toolbar, click the **Center** button ▤. On the Quick Access Toolbar, click **Save** 🖫.

> The column titles *January*, *February*, *March* align in the center of each cell.

Activity 1.06 | Entering Numbers

To type number values, use either the number keys across the top of your keyboard or the numeric keypad if you have one—laptop computers may not have a numeric keypad.

1 Under *January*, click cell **B4**, type **47991.12** and then on the **Formula Bar**, click the **Enter** button ✓ to maintain cell **B4** as the active cell. Compare your screen with Figure 1.14.

> By default, *number* values align at the right edge of the cell. The default ***number format***—a specific way in which Excel displays numbers—is the ***general format***. In the default general format, whatever you type in the cell will display, with the exception of trailing zeros to the right of a decimal point. For example, in the number 237.50 the *0* following the *5* is a trailing zero.

> Data that displays in a cell is the ***displayed value***. Data that displays in the Formula Bar is the ***underlying value***. The number of digits or characters that display in a cell—the displayed value—depends on the width of the column. Calculations on numbers will always be based on the underlying value, not the displayed value.

Figure 1.14

Underlying value in the Formula Bar

Displayed value in the cell

General indicated as the Number format

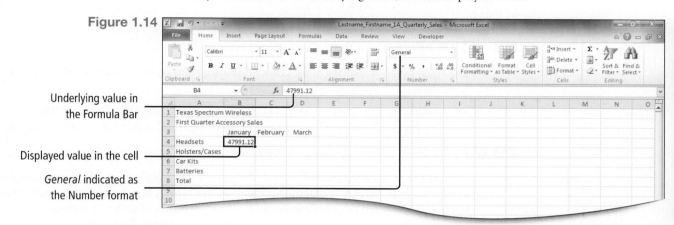

2 Press [Tab] to make cell **C4** active. Then, enter the remaining sales numbers as shown by using the following technique: Press [Tab] to confirm your entry and move across the row, and then press [Enter] at the end of a row to move to the next row.

	January	February	March
Headsets	47991.12	66984.92	87540.57
Holsters/Cases	19725	15523.12	13717.67
Car Kits	40408.67	61446.98	85835.76
Batteries	62154.28	68758.50	72558.89

3 Compare the numbers you entered with Figure 1.15 and then **Save** 📄 your workbook.

> In the default general format, trailing zeros to the right of a decimal point will not display. For example, when you type *68758.50*, the cell displays 68758.5 instead.

Figure 1.15

Values entered for each category in each month

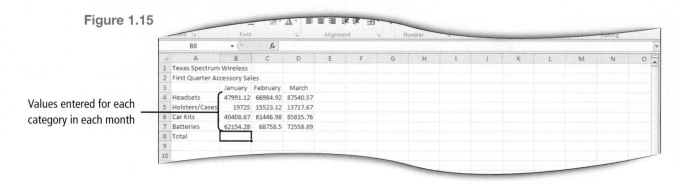

Objective 3 | Construct and Copy Formulas and Use the SUM Function

A cell contains either a constant value (text or numbers) or a formula. A formula is an equation that performs mathematical calculations on values in other cells, and then places the result in the cell containing the formula. You can create formulas or use a *function*—a prewritten formula that looks at one or more values, performs an operation, and then returns a value.

Activity 1.07 | Constructing a Formula and Using the SUM Function

In this activity, you will practice three different ways to sum a group of numbers in Excel.

1 Click cell **B8** to make it the active cell and type **=**

The equal sign (=) displays in the cell with the insertion point blinking, ready to accept more data.

All formulas begin with the = sign, which signals Excel to begin a calculation. The Formula Bar displays the = sign, and the Formula Bar Cancel and Enter buttons display.

2 At the insertion point, type **b4** and then compare your screen with Figure 1.16.

A list of Excel functions that begin with the letter *B* may briefly display—as you progress in your study of Excel, you will use functions of this type. A blue border with small corner boxes surrounds cell B4, which indicates that the cell is part of an active formula. The color used in the box matches the color of the cell reference in the formula.

Figure 1.16

Cell B4 outlined in blue to show it is part of an active formula

Cell B8 displays the beginning of the formula, with *b4* in blue to match outlined cell

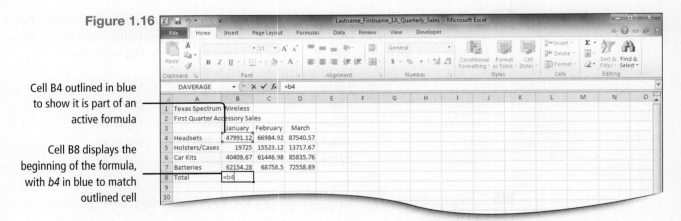

3 At the insertion point, type **+** and then type **b5**

A border of another color surrounds cell B5, and the color matches the color of the cell reference in the active formula. When typing cell references, it is not necessary to use uppercase letters.

4 At the insertion point, type **+b6+b7** and then press Enter.

The result of the formula calculation—*170279.1*—displays in the cell. Recall that in the default General format, trailing zeros do not display.

5 Click cell **B8** again, look at the **Formula Bar**, and then compare your screen with Figure 1.17.

> The formula adds the values in cells B4 through B7, and the result displays in cell B8. In this manner, you can construct a formula by typing. Although cell B8 displays the *result* of the formula, the formula itself displays in the Formula Bar. This is referred to as the *underlying formula*.

> Always view the Formula Bar to be sure of the exact content of a cell—*a displayed number may actually be a formula.*

Figure 1.17

Formula displays in Formula Bar

Total of values in cells B4:B7 displays in cell B8

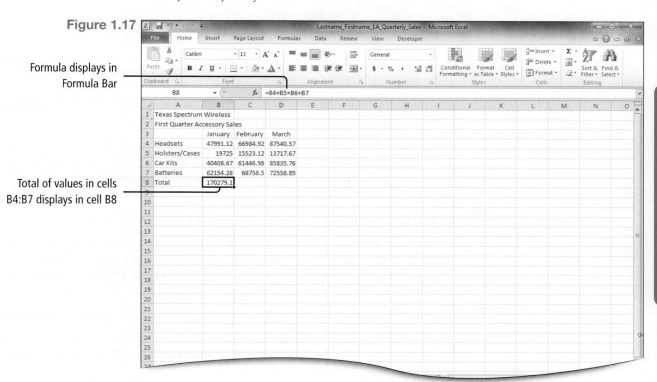

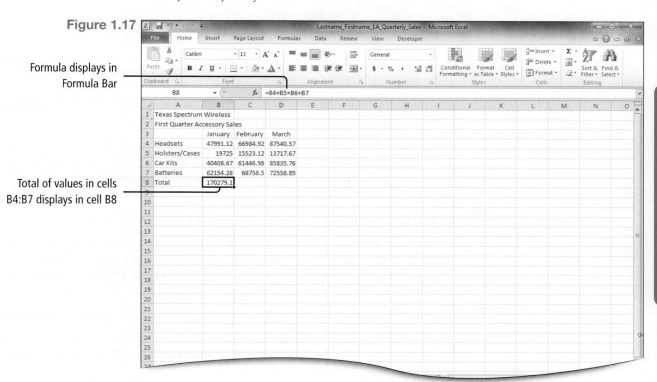

6 Click cell **C8** and type **=** to signal the beginning of a formula. Then, point to cell **C4** and click one time.

> The reference to the cell C4 is added to the active formula. A moving border surrounds the referenced cell, and the border color and the color of the cell reference in the formula are color coded to match.

7 At the insertion point, type **+** and then click cell **C5**. Repeat this process to complete the formula to add cells **C4** through **C7**, and then press [Enter].

> The result of the formula calculation—*212713.5*—displays in the cell. This method of constructing a formula is the *point and click method*.

Another Way

Use the keyboard short-cut [Alt] + [=]; or, on the Formulas tab, in the Function Library group, click the AutoSum button.

8 Click cell **D8**. On the **Home tab**, in the **Editing group**, click the **Sum** button [Σ], and then compare your screen with Figure 1.18.

> *SUM* is an Excel function—a prewritten formula. A moving border surrounds the range D4:D7 and *=SUM(D4:D7)* displays in cell D8.

> The = sign signals the beginning of a formula, *SUM* indicates the type of calculation that will take place (addition), and *(D4:D7)* indicates the range of cells on which the sum calculation will be performed. A ScreenTip provides additional information about the action.

Excel | Chapter 1

Figure 1.18

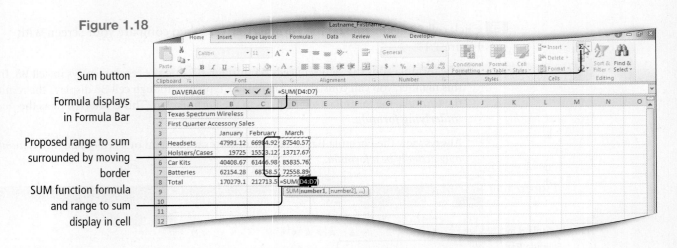

Sum button

Formula displays
in Formula Bar

Proposed range to sum
surrounded by moving
border

SUM function formula
and range to sum
display in cell

---

9 Look at the **Formula Bar**, and notice that the formula also displays there. Then, look again at the cells surrounded by the moving border.

> When you activate the Sum function, Excel first looks *above* the active cell for a range of cells to sum. If no range is above the active cell, Excel will look to the *left* for a range of cells to sum. If the proposed range is not what you want to calculate, you can select a different group of cells.

10 Press [Enter] to construct a formula by using the prewritten SUM function.

> Your total is *259652.9*. Because the Sum function is frequently used, it has its own button in the Editing group on the Home tab of the Ribbon. A larger version of the button also displays on the Formulas tab in the Function Library group. This button is also referred to as *AutoSum*.

11 Notice that the totals in the range **B8:D8** display only *one* decimal place. Click **Save** 💾.

> Number values that are too long to fit in the cell do *not* spill over into the unoccupied cell to the right in the same manner as text values. Rather, Excel rounds the number to fit the space.

> *Rounding* is a procedure that determines which digit at the right of the number will be the last digit displayed and then increases it by one if the next digit to its right is 5, 6, 7, 8, or 9.

Activity 1.08 | Copying a Formula by Using the Fill Handle

You have practiced three ways to create a formula—by typing, by using the point-and-click technique, and by using a Function button from the Ribbon. You can also copy formulas. When you copy a formula from one cell to another, Excel adjusts the cell references to fit the new location of the formula.

1 Click cell **E3**, type **Total** and then press [Enter].

> The text in cell E3 is centered because the centered format continues from the adjacent cell.

2 With cell **E4** as the active cell, hold down [Alt], and then press [=]. Compare your screen with Figure 1.19.

> [Alt] + [=] is the keyboard shortcut for the Sum function. Recall that Excel first looks above the selected cell for a proposed range of cells to sum, and if no data is detected, Excel looks to the left and proposes a range of cells to sum.

Figure 1.19

Sum function formula displays in Formula Bar

Sum function formula displays in cell

Proposed range to sum outlined with moving border

3 On the **Formula Bar**, click the **Enter** button ✓ to display the result and keep cell **E4** active.

> The total dollar amount of *Headsets* sold in the quarter is *202516.6*. In cells E5:E8, you can see that you need a formula similar to the one in E4, but formulas that refer to the cells in row 5, row 6, and so on.

4 With cell **E4** active, point to the fill handle in the lower right corner of the cell until the ⊞ pointer displays. Then, drag down through cell **E8**; if you are not satisfied with your result, on the Quick Access Toolbar, click Undo 🔄 and begin again. Compare your screen with Figure 1.20.

Figure 1.20

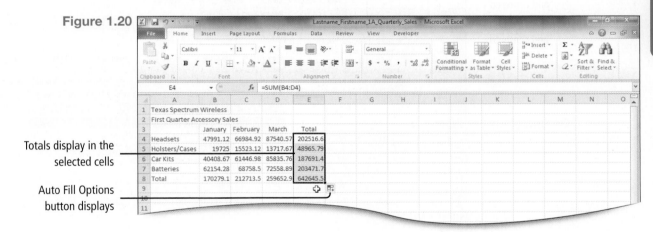

Totals display in the selected cells

Auto Fill Options button displays

5 Click cell **E5**, look at the **Formula Bar**, and notice the formula *=SUM(B5:D5)*. Click cell **E6**, look at the **Formula Bar**, and then notice the formula *=SUM(B6:D6)*.

> In each row, Excel copied the formula but adjusted the cell references *relative to* the row number. This is called a ***relative cell reference***—a cell reference based on the relative position of the cell that contains the formula and the cells referred to.

> The calculation is the same, but it is performed on the cells in that particular row. Use this method to insert numerous formulas into spreadsheets quickly.

6 Click cell **F3,** type **Trend** and then press Enter. **Save** 💾 your workbook.

Objective 4 | Format Cells with Merge & Center and Cell Styles

Format—change the appearance of—cells to make your worksheet attractive and easy to read.

Activity 1.09 | Using Merge & Center and Applying Cell Styles

Another Way

Select the range, right-click over the selection, and then on the Mini toolbar, click the Merge & Center button.

1 Select the range **A1:F1**, and then in the **Alignment group**, click the **Merge & Center** button. Then, select the range **A2:F2** and click the **Merge & Center** button.

The *Merge & Center* command joins selected cells into one larger cell and centers the contents in the new cell; individual cells in the range B1:F1 and B2:F2 can no longer be selected—they are merged into cell A1 and A2 respectively.

2 Click cell **A1**. In the **Styles group**, click the **Cell Styles** button, and then compare your screen with Figure 1.21.

A *cell style* is a defined set of formatting characteristics, such as font, font size, font color, cell borders, and cell shading.

Figure 1.21

Cell Styles button
Cell A1 merged and centered
Cell A2 merged and centered
Cell Styles gallery

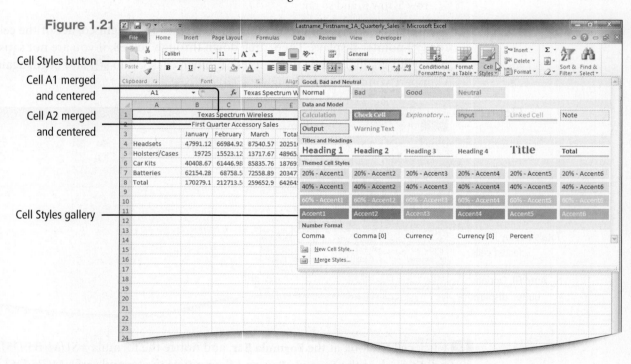

3 In the displayed gallery, under **Titles and Headings**, click **Title** and notice that the row height adjusts to accommodate this larger font size.

4 Click cell **A2**, display the **Cell Styles** gallery, and then under **Titles and Headings**, click **Heading 1**.

Use cell styles to maintain a consistent look in a worksheet and across worksheets in a workbook.

5 Select the range **B3:F3**, hold down [Ctrl], and then select the range **A4:A8** to select the column titles and the row titles.

Use this technique to select two or more ranges that are nonadjacent—not next to each other.

6 Display the **Cell Styles** gallery, click **Heading 4** to apply this cell style to the column titles and row titles, and then **Save** 🔲 your workbook.

Another Way

In the Name Box type b4:e4,b8:e8 and then press Enter.

Activity 1.10 | Formatting Financial Numbers

1 Select the range **B4:E4**, hold down Ctrl, and then select the range **B8:E8**.

This range is referred to as *b4:e4,b8:e8* with a comma separating the references to the two nonadjacent ranges.

Another Way

Display the Cell Styles gallery, and under Number Format, click Currency.

2 On the **Home tab**, in the **Number group**, click the **Accounting Number Format** button ⓢ ˅. Compare your screen with Figure 1.22.

The *Accounting Number Format* applies a thousand comma separator where appropriate, inserts a fixed U.S. dollar sign aligned at the left edge of the cell, applies two decimal places, and leaves a small amount of space at the right edge of the cell to accommodate a parenthesis when negative numbers are present. Excel widens the columns to accommodate the formatted numbers.

Figure 1.22

Accounting Number Format button

Nonadjacent ranges selected with Accounting Number Format applied

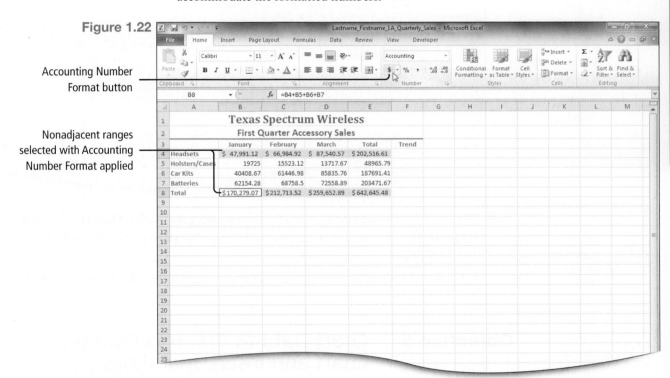

3 Select the range **B5:E7**, and then in the **Number group**, click the **Comma Style** button ＇.

The *Comma Style* inserts thousand comma separators where appropriate and applies two decimal places. Comma Style also leaves space at the right to accommodate a parenthesis when negative numbers are present.

When preparing worksheets with financial information, the first row of dollar amounts and the total row of dollar amounts are formatted in the Accounting Number Format; that is, with thousand comma separators, dollar signs, two decimal places, and space at the right to accommodate a parenthesis for negative numbers, if any. Rows that are *not* the first row or the total row should be formatted with the Comma Style.

4 Select the range **B8:E8**. From the **Styles group**, display the **Cell Styles** gallery, and then under **Titles and Headings**, click **Total**. Click any blank cell to cancel the selection, and then compare your screen with Figure 1.23.

> This is a common way to apply borders to financial information. The single border indicates that calculations were performed on the numbers above, and the double border indicates that the information is complete. Sometimes financial documents do not display values with cents; rather, the values are rounded up. You can do this by selecting the cells, and then clicking the Decrease Decimal button two times.

Figure 1.23

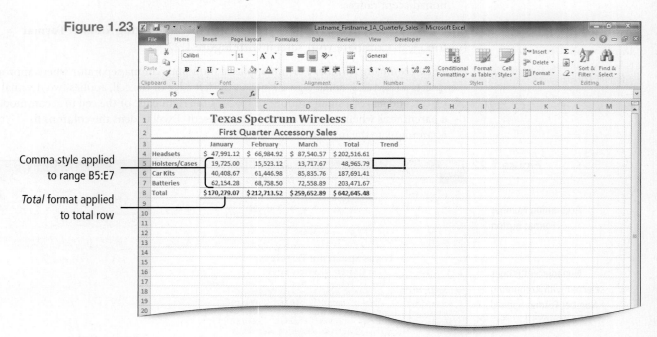

Comma style applied to range B5:E7

Total format applied to total row

5 Click the **Page Layout tab**, and then in the **Themes group**, click **Themes**. Click the **Composite** theme, and notice that the cell styles change to match the new theme. Click **Save**.

> Recall that a theme is a predefined set of colors, fonts, lines, and fill effects that look good together.

Objective 5 | Chart Data to Create a Column Chart and Insert Sparklines

A ***chart*** is a graphic representation of data in a worksheet. Data presented as a chart is easier to understand than a table of numbers. ***Sparklines*** are tiny charts embedded in a cell and give a visual trend summary alongside your data. A sparkline makes a pattern more obvious to the eye.

Activity 1.11 | Charting Data in a Column Chart

In this activity, you will create a ***column chart*** showing the monthly sales of accessories by category during the first quarter. A column chart is useful for illustrating comparisons among related numbers. The chart will enable the company president, Rosalyn Thomas, to see a pattern of overall monthly sales.

1 Select the range **A3:D7**. Click the **Insert tab**, and then in the **Charts group**, click **Column** to display a gallery of Column chart types.

> When charting data, typically you should *not* include totals—include only the data you want to compare. By using different *chart types*, you can display data in a way that is meaningful to the reader—common examples are column charts, pie charts, and line charts.

2 On the gallery of column chart types, under **2-D Column**, point to the first chart to display the ScreenTip *Clustered Column*, and then click to select it. Compare your screen with Figure 1.24.

> A column chart displays in the worksheet, and the charted data is bordered by colored lines. Because the chart object is selected—surrounded by a border and displaying sizing handles—contextual tools named *Chart Tools* display and add contextual tabs next to the standard tabs on the Ribbon.

Figure 1.24

Chart Tools display three additional tabs—*Design, Layout, Format*

Border and sizing handles indicate chart is selected

Charted data range bordered by colored lines (green = legend, blue = columns, purple = category labels)

Clustered column chart displays in worksheet

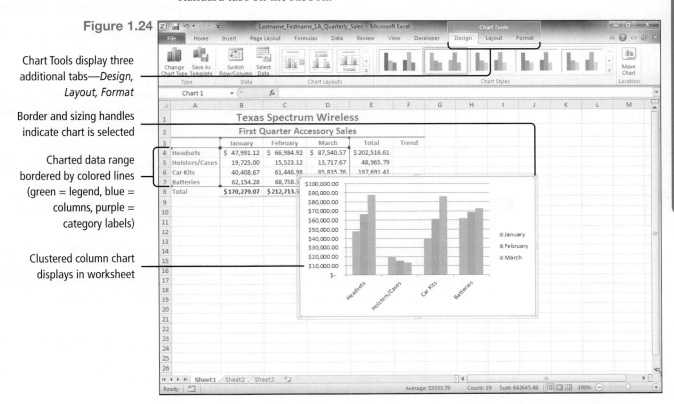

3 Point to the top border of the chart to display the pointer, and then drag the upper left corner of the chart just inside the upper left corner of cell **A10**, approximately as shown in Figure 1.25.

> Based on the data you selected in your worksheet, Excel constructs a column chart and adds *category labels*—the labels that display along the bottom of the chart to identify the category of data. This area is referred to as the *category axis* or the *x-axis*. Excel uses the row titles as the category names.

> On the left, Excel includes a numerical scale on which the charted data is based; this is the *value axis* or the *y-axis*. On the right, a *legend*, which identifies the patterns or colors that are assigned to the categories in the chart, displays.

Figure 1.25

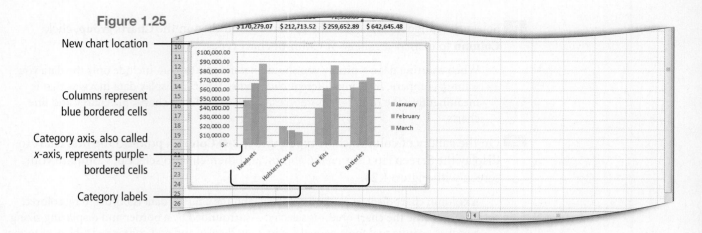

New chart location

Columns represent
blue bordered cells

Category axis, also called
x-axis, represents purple-
bordered cells

Category labels

4 On the Ribbon, locate the contextual tabs under **Chart Tools—Design**, **Layout**, and **Format**.

When a chart is selected, Chart Tools become available and three tabs provide commands for working with the chart.

5 Locate the group of cells bordered in blue.

Each of the twelve cells bordered in blue is referred to as a ***data point***—a value that originates in a worksheet cell. Each data point is represented in the chart by a ***data marker***—a column, bar, area, dot, pie slice, or other symbol in a chart that represents a single data point.

Related data points form a ***data series***; for example, there is a data series for *January*, for *February*, and for *March*. Each data series has a unique color or pattern represented in the chart legend.

6 On the **Design tab** of the Ribbon, in the **Data group**, click the **Switch Row/Column** button, and then compare your chart with Figure 1.26.

In this manner, you can easily change the categories of data from the row titles, which is the default, to the column titles. Whether you use row or column titles as your category names depends on how you want to view your charted data. Here, the president wants to see monthly sales and the breakdown of product categories within each month.

Figure 1.26

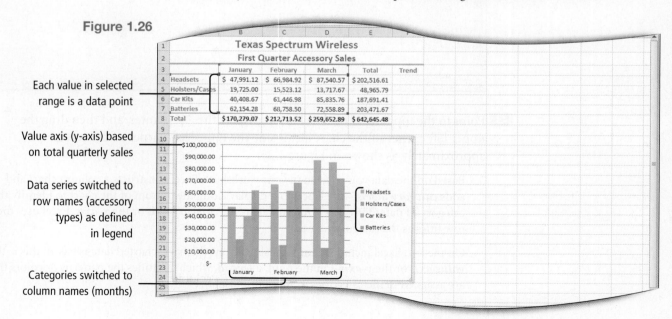

Each value in selected
range is a data point

Value axis (y-axis) based
on total quarterly sales

Data series switched to
row names (accessory
types) as defined
in legend

Categories switched to
column names (months)

7 On the **Design tab**, in the **Chart Layouts group**, locate and click the **More** button ⊡. Compare your screen with Figure 1.27.

> In the *Chart Layouts gallery*, you can select a predesigned *chart layout*—a combination of chart elements, which can include a title, legend, labels for the columns, and the table of charted cells.

Figure 1.27

Chart Layouts gallery

More buttons in Chart Styles group

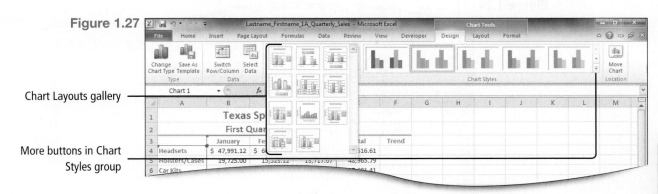

8 Click several different layouts to see the effect on your chart, and then using the ScreenTips as your guide, locate and click **Layout 1**.

9 In the chart, click anywhere in the text *Chart Title* to select the title box, watch the **Formula Bar** as you type **1st Quarter Sales** and then press [Enter] to display the new chart title.

10 Click in a white area just slightly *inside* the chart border to deselect the chart title. On the **Design tab**, in the **Chart Styles group**, click the **More** button ⊡. Compare your screen with Figure 1.28.

> The *Chart Styles gallery* displays an array of pre-defined *chart styles*—the overall visual look of the chart in terms of its colors, backgrounds, and graphic effects such as flat or beveled columns.

Figure 1.28

Chart Styles gallery

Title added to chart

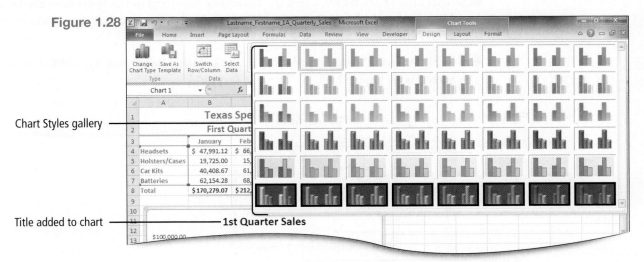

11 Using the ScreenTips as your guide, locate and click **Style 26**.

> This style uses a white background, formats the columns with theme colors, and applies a beveled effect. With this clear visual representation of the data, the president can see the sales of all product categories in each month, and can see that the sale of headsets and car kits has risen quite markedly during the quarter.

Excel | Chapter 1

12 Click any cell to deselect the chart, and notice that the *Chart Tools* no longer display in the Ribbon. Click **Save** 🖫, and then compare your screen with Figure 1.29.

Contextual tabs display when an object is selected, and then are removed from view when the object is deselected.

Figure 1.29

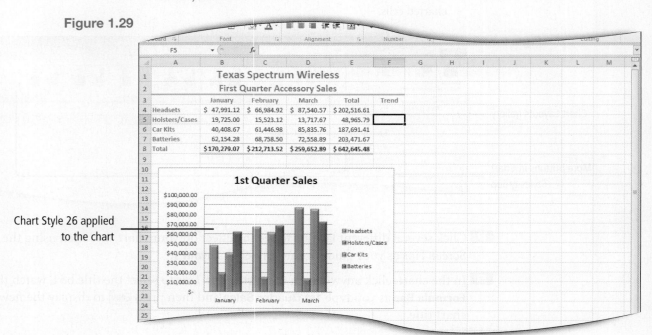

Chart Style 26 applied to the chart

Activity 1.12 | Creating and Formatting Sparklines

By creating sparklines, you provide a context for your numbers. Your readers will be able to see the relationship between a sparkline and its underlying data quickly.

Another Way
In the worksheet, select the range F4:F7 to insert it into the Location Range box.

1 Select the range **B4:D7**. Click the **Insert tab**, and then in the **Sparklines group**, click **Line**. In the displayed **Create Sparklines** dialog box, notice that the selected range *B4:D7* displays.

2 With the insertion point blinking in the **Location Range** box, type **f4:f7** Compare your screen with Figure 1.30.

Figure 1.30

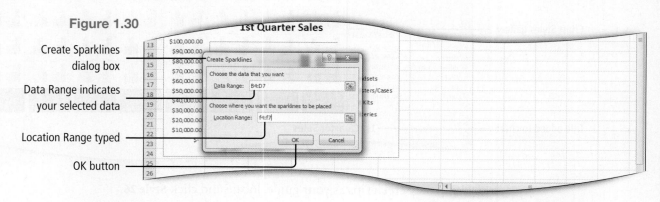

Create Sparklines dialog box

Data Range indicates your selected data

Location Range typed

OK button

3 Click **OK** to insert the trend lines in the range F4:F7, and then on the **Design tab**, in the **Show group**, click the **Markers** check box to select it.

Alongside each row of data, the sparkline provides a quick visual trend summary for sales of each accessory item over the three-month period. For example, you can see instantly that of the four items, only Holsters/Cases had declining sales for the period.

4 In the **Style group**, click the **More** button ⊡. In the second row, click the fourth style—**Sparkline Style Accent 4, Darker 25%**. Click cell **A1** to deselect the range. Click **Save** 🖫. Compare your screen with Figure 1.31.

Use markers, colors, and styles in this manner to further enhance your sparklines.

Figure 1.31

Sparklines inserted and formatted

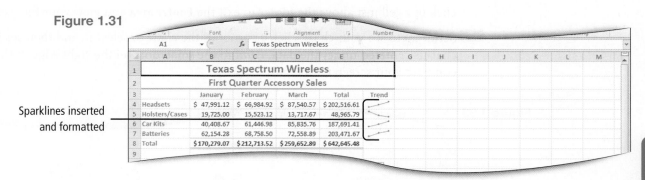

Objective 6 │ Print, Display Formulas, and Close Excel

Use *Page Layout view* and the commands on the Page Layout tab to prepare for printing.

Activity 1.13 │ Changing Views, Creating a Footer, and Using Print Preview

For each Excel project in this textbook, you will create a footer containing your name and the project name.

1 Be sure the chart is *not* selected. Click the **Insert tab**, and then in the **Text group**, click the **Header & Footer** button to switch to Page Layout view and open the **Header area**. Compare your screen with Figure 1.32.

In Page Layout view, you can see the edges of the paper of multiple pages, the margins, and the rulers. You can also insert a header or footer by typing in the areas indicated and use the Header & Footer Tools.

Figure 1.32

Go to Footer button

Rulers

Header area with three sections open; center section selected

Margin

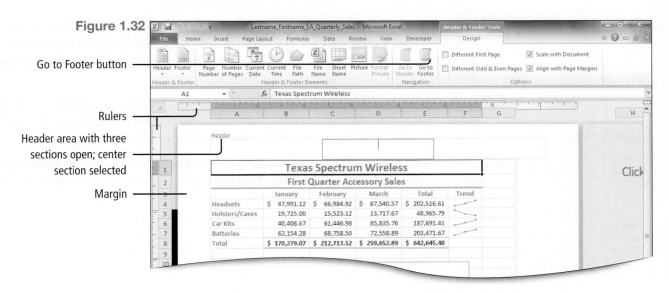

2 On the **Design tab**, in the **Navigation group**, click **Go to Footer** to open the **Footer area**, and then click just above the word *Footer* to place the insertion point in the **left section** of the **Footer area**.

3 In the **Header & Footer Elements group**, click the **File Name** button to add the name of your file to the footer—&*[File]* displays in the left section of the **Footer area**. Then, click in a cell just above the footer to exit the **Footer area** and view your file name.

4 Scroll up to see your chart, click a corner of the chart to select it, and then see if the chart is centered under the data. *Point* to the small dots on the right edge of the chart; compare your screen with Figure 1.33.

Figure 1.33

Horizontal resize pointer

Border indicates
chart is selected

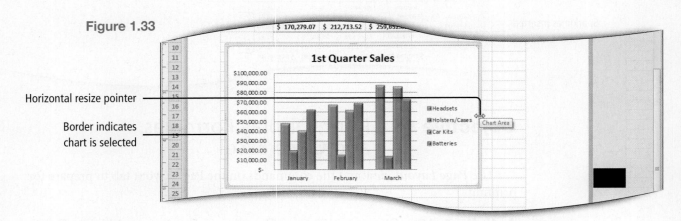

5 Drag the ↔ pointer to the right so that the right border of the chart is just inside the right border of **column F**. Be sure the left and right borders of the chart are just slightly **inside** the left border of **column A** and the right border of **column F**—adjust as necessary.

6 Click any cell to deselect the chart. Click the **Page Layout tab**, in the **Page Setup group**, click the **Margins** button, and then at the bottom of the **Margins** gallery, click **Custom Margins**. In the **Page Setup** dialog box, under **Center on page**, select the **Horizontally** check box.

> This action will center the data and chart horizontally on the page, as shown in the Preview area.

7 In the lower right corner of the **Page Setup** dialog box, click **OK**. In the upper left corner of your screen, click the **File tab** to display **Backstage** view. On the **Info tab**, on the right under the screen thumbnail, click **Properties**, and then click **Show Document Panel**.

8 In the **Author** box, replace the existing text with your firstname and lastname. In the **Subject** box, type your course name and section number. In the **Keywords** box type **accessory sales** and then **Close** [×] the **Document Information Panel**.

Another Way
Press Ctrl + F2 to
view the Print Preview.

--→ **9** Click the **File tab** to redisplay **Backstage** view, and then on the left, click the **Print tab** to view the Print commands and the **Print Preview**. Compare your screen with Figure 1.34.

Figure 1.34

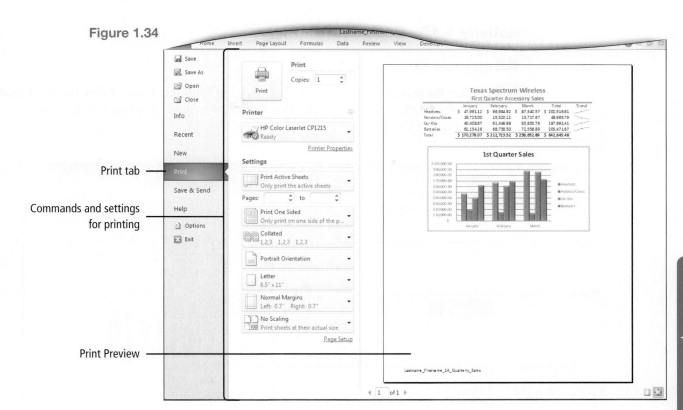

10 Note any adjustments that need to be made, and then on the Ribbon, click the **Home tab** to close Backstage view and return to the worksheet. In the lower right corner of your screen, click the **Normal** button ▦ to return to the Normal view, and then press [Ctrl] + [Home] to return to cell **A1**.

The *Normal view* maximizes the number of cells visible on your screen and keeps the column letters and row numbers closer. The vertical dotted line between columns indicates that as currently arranged, only the columns to the left of the dotted line will print on the first page. The exact position of the vertical line may depend on your default printer setting.

11 Make any necessary adjustments, and then **Save** 🖫 your workbook.

Activity 1.14 | Deleting Unused Sheets in a Workbook

A new Excel workbook contains three blank worksheets. It is not necessary to delete unused sheets, but doing so saves storage space and removes any doubt that additional information is in the workbook.

1 At the bottom of your worksheet, click the **Sheet2 tab** to display the second worksheet in the workbook and make it active.

> **Another Way**
>
> On the Home tab, in the Cells group, click the Delete button arrow, and then click Delete Sheet.

2 Hold down [Ctrl], and then click the **Sheet3 tab**. Release [Ctrl], and then with both sheets selected (the tab background is white), point to either of the selected sheet tabs, right-click, and then on the shortcut menu, click **Delete**.

Excel deletes the two unused sheets from your workbook. If you attempt to delete a worksheet with data, Excel will display a warning and permit you to cancel the deletion. *Sheet tabs* are labels along the lower border of the Excel window that identify each worksheet.

Activity 1.15 | Printing a Worksheet

1 Click **Save** 🖫.

2 Display **Backstage** view and on the left click the Print tab. Under **Print**, be sure **Copies** indicates *1*. Under **Settings**, verify that *Print Active Sheets* displays. Compare your screen with Figure 1.35.

Figure 1.35

Copies indicates *1*

Print Active Sheets

Print Preview

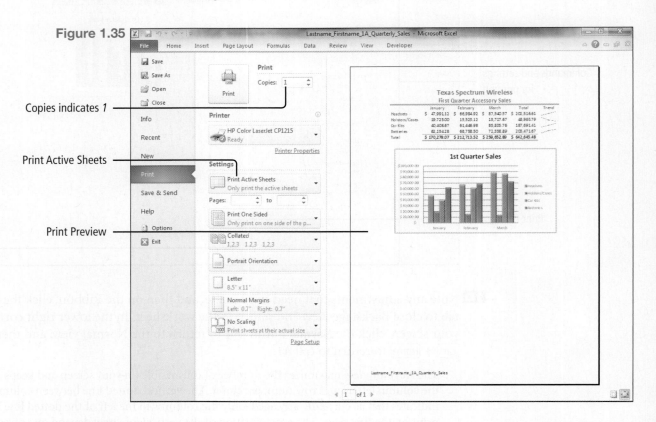

3 To print on paper, be sure that a printer is available to your system, and then in the **Print group**, click the **Print** button. To create an electronic printout, on the Backstage tabs, click the **Save & Send tab**, under **File Types** click **Create PDF/XPS Document**, and then on the right, click **Create PDF/XPS**. In the **Publish as PDF or XPS** dialog box, navigate to your storage location, and then click the **Publish** button to create the PDF file. Close the Adobe window.

Activity 1.16 | Displaying, Printing, and Hiding Formulas

When you type a formula in a cell, the cell displays the *results* of the formula calculation. Recall that this value is called the displayed value. You can view and print the underlying formulas in the cells. When you do so, a formula often takes more horizontal space to display than the result of the calculation.

1 If necessary, redisplay your worksheet. Because you will make some temporary changes to your workbook, on the Quick Access Toolbar, click **Save** 🖫 to be sure your work is saved up to this point.

Another Way
Hold down Ctrl, and then press ` (usually located below Esc).

2 On the **Formulas tab**, in the **Formula Auditing group**, click the **Show Formulas** button. Then, in the **column heading area**, point to the **column A** heading to display the ↓ pointer, hold down the left mouse button, and then drag to the right to select columns **A:F**. Compare your screen with Figure 1.36.

Figure 1.36

Dotted line shows page break

Underlying formulas displayed

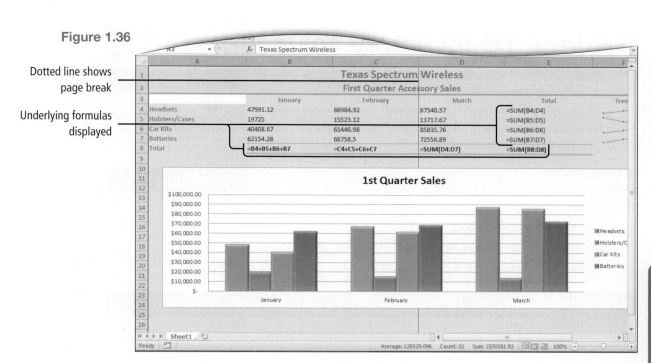

Note | Turning the Display of Formulas On and Off

The Show Formulas button is a toggle button. Clicking it once turns the display of formulas on—the button will glow orange. Clicking the button again turns the display of formulas off.

3 Point to the column heading boundary between any two of the selected columns to display the ⊞ pointer, and then double-click to AutoFit the selected columns.

AutoFit adjusts the width of a column to fit the cell content of the *widest* cell in the column.

Another Way

In the Scale to Fit group, click the Dialog Box Launcher button to display the Page tab of the Page Setup dialog box. Then, under Scaling, click the Fit to option button.

4 On the **Page Layout tab**, in the **Page Setup group**, click **Orientation**, and then click **Landscape**. In the **Scale to Fit** group, click the **Width arrow**, and then click **1 page** to scale the data to fit onto one page.

Scaling shrinks the width (or height) of the printed worksheet to fit a maximum number of pages, and is convenient for printing formulas. Although it is not always the case, formulas frequently take up more space than the actual data.

Another Way

In the Page Setup group, click the Dialog Box Launcher button to display the Page tab of the Page Setup dialog box. Then, under Orientation, click the Landscape option button.

5 In the **Page Setup group**, click the **Dialog Box Launcher** button 🔲. In the **Page Setup** dialog box, click the **Margins tab**, and then under **Center on page**, if necessary, click to select the **Horizontally** check box.

6 Click **OK** to close the dialog box. Check to be sure your chart is centered below the data and the left and right edges are slightly inside column A and column F—drag a chart edge and then deselect the chart if necessary. Display the **Print Preview**, and then submit your worksheet with formulas displayed, either printed or electronically, as directed by your instructor.

7 Click the **File tab** to display **Backstage** view, click **Close**, and when prompted, click **Don't Save** so that you do *not* save the changes you made—displaying formulas, changing column widths and orientation, and scaling—to print your formulas.

8 In the upper right corner of your screen, click the **Close** button 🔀 to exit Excel.

End **You have completed Project 1A** ―――――――――

Project 1B Inventory Valuation

myitlab
Project 1B Training

Project Activities

In Activities 1.17 through 1.24, you will create a workbook for Josette Lovrick, Operations Manager, which calculates the retail value of an inventory of car convenience products. Your completed worksheet will look similar to Figure 1.37.

Project Files

For Project 1B, you will need the following file:

New blank Excel workbook

You will save your workbook as:

Lastname_Firstname_1B_Car_Products

Project Results

Texas Spectrum Wireless
Car Products Inventory Valuation
As of December 31

	Warehouse Location	Quantity in Stock	Retail Price	Total Retail Value	Percent of Total Retail Value
Antenna Signal Booster	Dallas	1,126	$ 19.99	$ 22,508.74	8.27%
Car Power Port Adapter	Dallas	3,546	19.49	69,111.54	25.39%
Repeater Antenna	Houston	1,035	39.99	41,389.65	15.21%
SIM Card Reader and Writer	Houston	2,875	16.90	48,587.50	17.85%
Sticky Dash Pad	Houston	3,254	11.99	39,015.46	14.33%
Window Mount GPS Holder	Dallas	2,458	20.99	51,593.42	18.95%
Total Retail Value for All Products				$ 272,206.31	

Lastname_Firstname_1B_Car_Products

Figure 1.37
Project 1B Car Products

Objective 7 | Check Spelling in a Worksheet

In Excel, the spelling checker performs similarly to the other Microsoft Office programs.

Activity 1.17 | Checking Spelling in a Worksheet

1 **Start** Excel and display a new blank workbook. In cell **A1**, type **Texas Spectrum Wireless** and press [Enter]. In cell **A2**, type **Car Products Inventory** and press [Enter].

2 On the Ribbon, click the **File tab** to display **Backstage** view, click **Save As**, and then in the **Save As** dialog box, navigate to your **Excel Chapter 1** folder. As the **File name**, type **Lastname_Firstname_1B_Car_Products** and then click **Save**.

3 Press [Tab] to move to cell **B3**, type **Quantity** and press [Tab]. In cell **C3**, type **Average Cost** and press [Tab]. In cell **D3**, type **Retail Price** and press [Tab].

4 Click cell **C3**, and then look at the **Formula Bar**. Notice that in the cell, the displayed value is cut off; however, in the **Formula Bar**, the entire text value—the underlying value—displays. Compare your screen with Figure 1.38.

> Text that is too long to fit in a cell spills over to cells on the right only if they are empty. If the cell to the right contains data, the text in the cell to the left is truncated. The entire value continues to exist, but is not completely visible.

Figure 1.38

Entire contents of C3 display in Formula Bar

Cell C3 active, text cut off

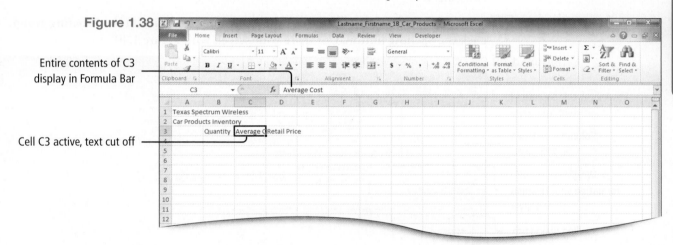

5 Click cell **E3**, type **Total Retail Value** and press [Tab]. In cell **F3**, type **Percent of Total Retail Value** and press [Enter].

6 Click cell **A4**. *Without* correcting the spelling error, type **Antena Signal Booster** Press [Enter]. In the range **A5:A10**, type the remaining row titles shown below. Then compare your screen with Figure 1.39.

> **Car Power Port Adapter**
>
> **Repeater Antenna**
>
> **SIM Card Reader and Writer**
>
> **Sticky Dash Pad**
>
> **Window Mount GPS Holder**
>
> **Total Retail Value for All Products**

Figure 1.39

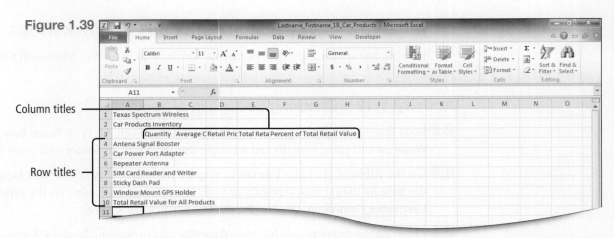

Column titles

Row titles

7 In the **column heading area**, point to the right boundary of **column A** to display the ⬌ pointer, and then drag to the right to widen **column A** to **215** pixels.

8 Select the range **A1:F1**, **Merge & Center** 🔲 the text, and then from the **Cell Styles** gallery, apply the **Title** style.

9 Select the range **A2:F2**, **Merge & Center** 🔲 the text, and then from the **Cell Styles** gallery, apply the **Heading 1** style. Press Ctrl + Home to move to the top of your worksheet.

> **Another Way**
> Press F7, which is the keyboard shortcut for the Spelling command.

10 With cell **A1** as the active cell, click the **Review tab**, and then in the **Proofing group**, click the **Spelling** button. Compare your screen with Figure 1.40.

Figure 1.40

Worksheet title formatted with Title style

Column A widened to 215 pixels

Worksheet subtitle formatted with Heading 1 style

Spelling dialog box

Word indicated as *Not in Dictionary*

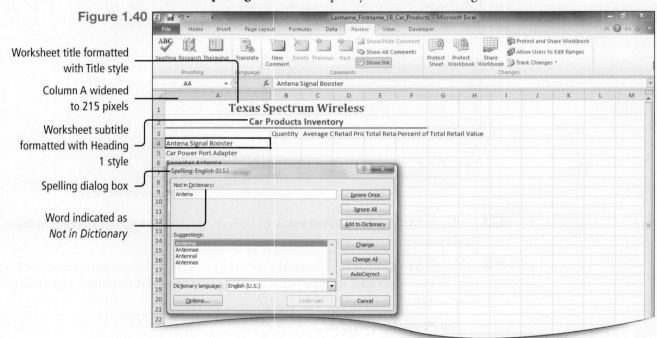

Alert! | Does a Message Display Asking if You Want to Continue Checking at the Beginning of the Sheet?

If a message displays asking if you want to continue checking at the beginning of the sheet, click Yes. The Spelling command begins its checking process with the currently selected cell and moves to the right and down. Thus, if your active cell was a cell after A4, this message may display.

---

11 In the **Spelling** dialog box, under **Not in Dictionary**, notice the word *Antena*.

The spelling tool does not have this word in its dictionary. Under *Suggestions*, Excel provides a list of suggested spellings.

12 Under **Suggestions**, click **Antenna**, and then click the **Change** button.

> *Antena*, a typing error, is changed to *Antenna*. A message box displays *The spelling check is complete for the entire sheet*—unless you have additional unrecognized words. Because the spelling check begins its checking process starting with the currently selected cell, it is good practice to return to cell A1 before starting the Spelling command.

13 Correct any other errors you may have made. When the message displays, *The spelling check is complete for the entire sheet*, click **OK**. **Save** 🖫 your workbook.

Objective 8 | Enter Data by Range

You can enter data by first selecting a range of cells. This is a time-saving technique, especially if you use the numeric keypad to enter the numbers.

Activity 1.18 | Entering Data by Range

1 Select the range **B4:D9**, type **1126** and then press ⏎Enter.

> The value displays in cell B4, and cell B5 becomes the active cell.

2 With cell **B5** active in the range, and pressing ⏎Enter after each entry, type the following, and then compare your screen with Figure 1.41:

> **4226**
> **1035**
> **2875**
> **3254**
> **2458**

> After you enter the last value and press ⏎Enter, the active cell moves to the top of the next column within the selected range. Although it is not required to enter data in this manner, you can see that selecting the range before you enter data saves time because it confines the movement of the active cell to the selected range.

Figure 1.41

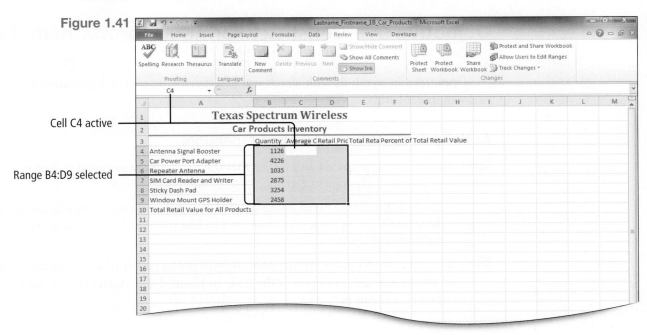

Cell C4 active

Range B4:D9 selected

3 With the selected range still active, from the following table, beginning in cell **C4** and pressing Enter after each entry, enter the data for the **Average Cost** column and then the **Retail Price** column. If you prefer, deselect the range to enter the values—typing in a selected range is optional.

Average Cost	Retail Price
9.75	19.99
9.25	19.49
16.90	39.99
9.55	16.90
4.20	12.99
10.45	20.99

Recall that the default number format for cells is the *General* number format, in which numbers display exactly as you type them and trailing zeros do not display, even if you type them.

4 Click any blank cell, and then compare your screen with Figure 1.42. Correct any errors you may have made while entering data, and then click **Save** 🖫.

Figure 1.42

Data entered

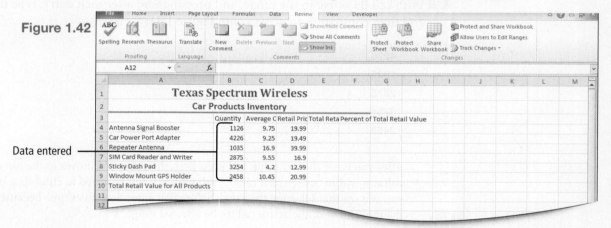

Objective 9 | Construct Formulas for Mathematical Operations

Operators are symbols with which you can specify the type of calculation you want to perform in a formula.

Activity 1.19 | Using Arithmetic Operators

1 Click cell **E4**, type **=b4*d4** and notice that the two cells are outlined as part of an active formula. Then press Enter.

The *Total Retail Value* of all *Antenna Signal Booster* items in inventory—*22508.74*—equals the *Quantity* (1,126) times the *Retail Price* (selling price) of 19.99. In Excel, the asterisk (*) indicates multiplication.

2 Take a moment to study the symbols you will use to perform basic mathematical operations in Excel, as shown in the table in Figure 1.43, which are referred to as *arithmetic operators*.

Symbols Used in Excel for Arithmetic Operators	
Operator Symbol	**Operation**
+	Addition
-	Subtraction (also negation)
*	Multiplication
/	Division
%	Percent
^	Exponentiation

Figure 1.43

Excel | Chapter 1

3 Click cell **E4**.

> You can see that in cells E5:E9, you need a formula similar to the one in E4, but one that refers to the cells in row 5, row 6, and so forth. Recall that you can copy formulas and the cell references will change *relative to* the row number.

4 With cell **E4** selected, position your pointer over the fill handle in the lower right corner of the cell until the ⊞ pointer displays. Then, drag down through cell **E9** to copy the formula.

Another Way

Select the range, display the Cell Styles gallery, and then under Number Format, click Comma [0].

5 Select the range **B4:B9**, and then on the **Home tab**, in the **Number group**, click the **Comma Style** button ⸴ . Then, in the **Number group**, click the **Decrease Decimal** button ⸴ two times to remove the decimal places from these values.

> Comma Style formats a number with two decimal places; because these are whole numbers referring to quantities, no decimal places are necessary.

6 Select the range **E4:E9**, and then at the bottom of your screen, in the status bar, notice the displayed values for **Average**, **Count**, and **Sum**—*48118.91833, 6* and *288713.51*.

> When you select numerical data, three calculations display in the status bar by default— Average, Count, and Sum. Here, Excel indicates that if you averaged the selected values, the result would be *48118.91833*, there are 6 cells in the selection that contain values, and that if you added the values the result would be 288713.51.

7 Click cell **E10**, in the **Editing group**, click the **Sum** button Σ, notice that Excel selects a range to sum, and then press Enter to display the total *288713.5*.

8 Select the range **C5:E9** and apply the **Comma Style** ⸴ ; notice that Excel widens column E.

9 Select the range **C4:E4**, hold down Ctrl, and then click cell **E10**. Release Ctrl and then apply the **Accounting Number Format** $ ˅ . Notice that Excel widens the columns as necessary.

Project 1B: Inventory Valuation | **Excel**   **81**

10 Click cell **E10**, and then from the **Cell Styles** gallery, apply the **Total** style. Click any blank cell, and then compare your screen with Figure 1.44.

Figure 1.44

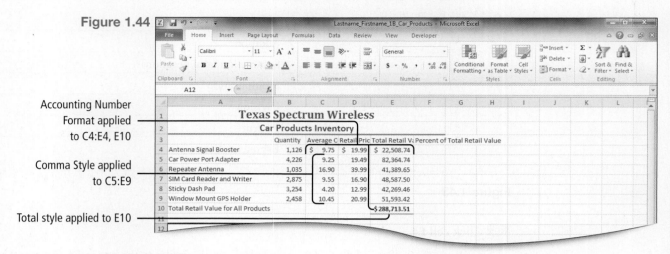

Accounting Number
Format applied
to C4:E4, E10

Comma Style applied
to C5:E9

Total style applied to E10

11 Save 💾 your workbook.

> **More Knowledge | Multiple Status Bar Calculations**
>
> You can display a total of six calculations on the status bar. To add additional calculations—Minimum, Maximum, and Numerical Count (the number of selected cells that contain a number value)—right-click on the status bar, and then click the additional calculations that you want to display.

Activity 1.20 | Copying Formulas Containing Absolute Cell References

In a formula, a relative cell reference refers to a cell by its position *in relation to* the cell that contains the formula. An ***absolute cell reference***, on the other hand, refers to a cell by its *fixed* position in the worksheet, for example, the total in cell E10.

A relative cell reference automatically adjusts when a formula is copied. In some calculations, you do *not* want the cell reference to adjust; rather, you want the cell reference to remain the same when the formula is copied.

1 Click cell **F4**, type **=** and then click cell **E4**. Type **/** and then click cell **E10**.

The formula *=E4/E10* indicates that the value in cell E4 will be *divided* by the value in cell E10. Why? Because Ms. Lovrick wants to know the percentage by which each product's Total Retail Value makes up the Total Retail Value for All Products.

Arithmetically, the percentage is computed by dividing the *Total Retail Value* for each product by the *Total Retail Value for All Products*. The result will be a percentage expressed as a decimal.

2 Press Enter. Click cell **F4** and notice that the formula displays in the **Formula Bar**. Then, point to cell **F4** and double-click.

The formula, with the two referenced cells displayed in color and bordered with the same color, displays in the cell. This feature, called the ***range finder***, is useful for verifying formulas because it visually indicates which workbook cells are included in a formula calculation.

3 Press Enter to redisplay the result of the calculation in the cell, and notice that approximately 8% of the total retail value of the inventory is made up of Antenna Signal Boosters.

4 Click cell **F4** again, and then drag the fill handle down through cell **F9**. Compare your screen with Figure 1.45.

Each cell displays an error message—*#DIV/0!* and a green triangle in the upper left corner of each cell indicates that Excel detects an error.

Like a grammar checker, Excel uses rules to check for formula errors and flags errors in this manner. Additionally, the Auto Fill Options button displays, from which you can select formatting options for the copied cells.

Figure 1.45

Auto Fill Options button

Cells F5:F9 display
error message and
green triangles

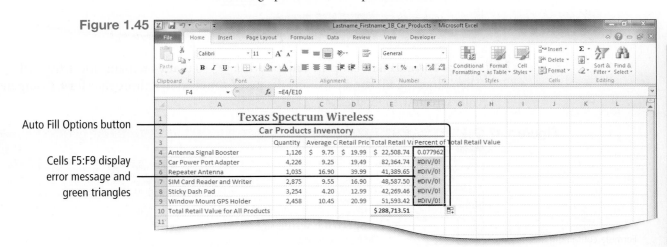

5 Click cell **F5**, and to the left of the cell, point to the **Error Checking** button ◈ to display its ScreenTip—*The formula or function used is dividing by zero or empty cells.*

In this manner, Excel suggests the cause of an error.

6 Look at the **Formula Bar** and examine the formula.

The formula is =*E5/E11*. The cell reference to *E5* is correct, but the cell reference following the division operator (/) is *E11*, and E11 is an *empty* cell.

7 Click cell **F6**, point to the **Error Checking** button ◈, and in the **Formula Bar** examine the formula.

Because the cell references are relative, Excel builds the formulas by increasing the row number for each equation. But in this calculation, the divisor must always be the value in cell E10—the *Total Retail Value for All Products*.

8 Point to cell **F4**, and then double-click to place the insertion point within the cell.

Another Way

Edit the formula so that
it indicates =*E4/E10*

9 Within the cell, use the arrow keys as necessary to position the insertion point to the left of *E10*, and then press F4 . Compare your screen with Figure 1.46.

Dollar signs ($) display, which changes the reference to cell E10 to an absolute cell reference. The use of the dollar sign to denote an absolute reference is not related in any way to whether or not the values you are working with are currency values. It is simply the symbol that Excel uses to denote an absolute cell reference.

Figure 1.46

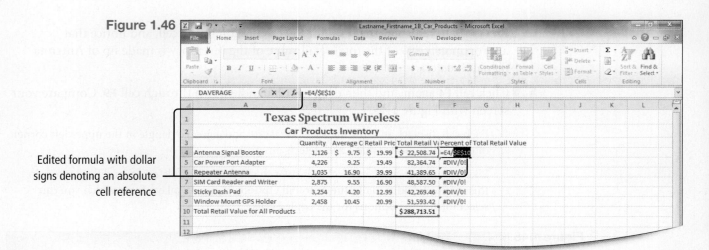

Edited formula with dollar signs denoting an absolute cell reference

10 On the **Formula Bar**, click the **Enter** button ✓ so that **F4** remains the active cell. Then, drag the fill handle to copy the new formula down through cell **F9**. Compare your screen with Figure 1.47.

Figure 1.47

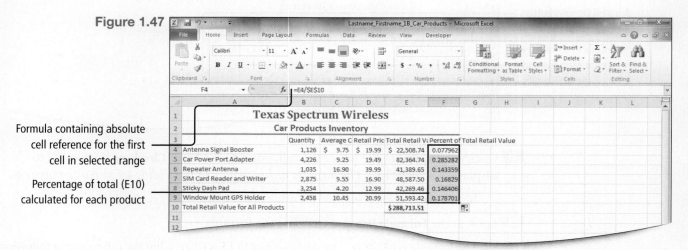

Formula containing absolute cell reference for the first cell in selected range

Percentage of total (E10) calculated for each product

11 Click cell **F5**, examine the formula in the **Formula Bar**, and then examine the formulas for cells **F6**, **F7**, **F8**, and **F9**.

For each formula, the cell reference for the *Total Retail Value* of each product changed relative to its row; however, the value used as the divisor—*Total Retail Value for All Products* in cell F10—remained absolute. Thus, using either relative or absolute cell references, it is easy to duplicate formulas without typing them.

12 **Save** 🖬 your workbook.

More Knowledge | Calculate a Percentage if You Know the Total and the Amount

Using the equation *amount/total = percentage*, you can calculate the percentage by which a part makes up a total—with the percentage formatted as a decimal. For example, if on a test you score 42 points correctly out of 50, your percentage of correct answers is 42/50 = 0.84 or 84%.

Objective 10 | Edit Values in a Worksheet

Excel performs calculations on numbers; that is why you use Excel. If you make changes to the numbers, Excel automatically *re*-calculates. This is one of the most powerful and valuable features of Excel.

Activity 1.21 | Editing Values in a Worksheet

You can edit text and number values directly within a cell or on the Formula Bar.

1 In cell **E10**, notice the column total *$288,713.51*. Then, click cell **B5**, and to change its value type **3546** Watch cell **E5** and press Enter.

> Excel formulas *re-calculate* if you change the value in a cell that is referenced in a formula. It is not necessary to delete the old value in a cell; selecting the cell and typing a new value replaces the old value with your new typing.
>
> The *Total Retail Value* of all *Car Power Port Adapters* items recalculates to *69,111.54* and the total in cell E10 recalculates to *$275,460.31*. Additionally, all of the percentages in column F recalculate.

2 Point to cell **D8**, and then double-click to place the insertion point within the cell. Use the arrow keys to move the insertion point to left or right of *2*, and use either Del or Backspace to delete *2* and then type **1** so that the new Retail Price is *11.99*.

3 Watch cell **E8** and **E10** as you press Enter, and then notice the recalculation of the formulas in those two cells.

> Excel recalculates the value in cell E8 to *39,015.46* and the value in cell E10 to *$272,206.31*. Additionally, all of the percentages in column F recalculate because the *Total Retail Value for All Products* recalculated.

4 Point to cell **A2** so that the ⊕ pointer is positioned slightly to the right of the word *Inventory*, and then double-click to place the insertion point in the cell. Edit the text to add the word **Valuation** pressing Spacebar as necessary, and then press Enter.

5 Click cell **B3**, and then in the **Formula Bar**, click to place the insertion point after the letter *y*. Press Spacebar one time, type **In Stock** and then on the **Formula Bar**, click the **Enter** button ✓. Click **Save** 🖫, and then compare your screen with Figure 1.48.

> Recall that if text is too long to fit in the cell and the cell to the right contains data, the text is truncated—cut off—but the entire value still exists as the underlying value.

Figure 1.48

In Stock added to column title

Valuation added to subtitle

New value in cell B5

New value in cell D8

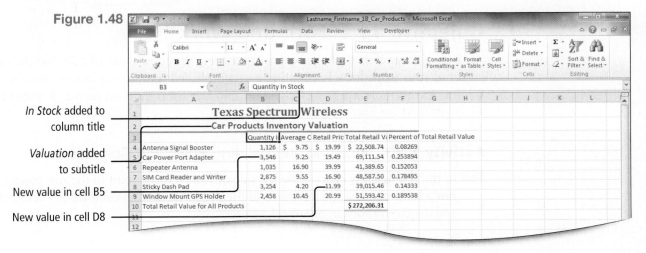

Activity 1.22 │ Formatting Cells with the Percent Style

A percentage is part of a whole expressed in hundredths. For example, 75 cents is the same as 75 percent of one dollar. The Percent Style button formats the selected cell as a percentage rounded to the nearest hundredth.

1 Click cell **F4**, and then in the **Number group**, click the **Percent Style** button ％ .

> Your result is 8%, which is *0.08269* rounded to the nearest hundredth and expressed as a percentage. Percent Style displays the value of a cell as a percentage.

2 Select the range **F4:F9**, right-click over the selection, and then on the Mini toolbar, click the **Percent Style** button ％ , click the **Increase Decimal** button two times, and then click the **Center** button.

> Percent Style may not offer a percentage precise enough to analyze important financial information—adding additional decimal places to a percentage makes data more precise.

3 Click any cell to cancel the selection, **Save** 🖫 your workbook, and then compare your screen with Figure 1.49.

Figure 1.49

F4:F9 formatted with Percent Style and two decimal places

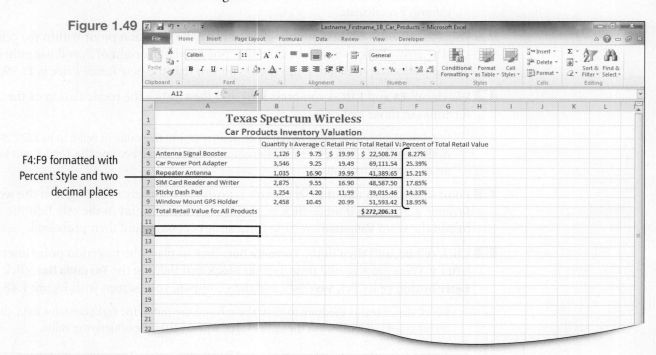

Objective 11 │ Format a Worksheet

Formatting refers to the process of specifying the appearance of cells and the overall layout of your worksheet. Formatting is accomplished through various commands on the Ribbon, for example, applying Cell Styles, and also from shortcut menus, keyboard shortcuts, and the Format Cells dialog box.

Activity 1.23 │ Inserting and Deleting Rows and Columns

1 In the **row heading area** on the left side of your screen, point to the row heading for **row 3** to display the ➡ pointer, and then right-click to simultaneously select the row and display a shortcut menu.

Another Way

Select the row, on the Home tab, in the Cells group, click the Insert button arrow, and then click Insert Sheet Rows. Or, select the row and click the Insert button—the default setting of the button inserts a new sheet row above the selected row.

2 On the displayed shortcut menu, click **Insert** to insert a new **row 3**.

> The rows below the new row 3 move down one row, and the Insert Options button displays. By default, the new row uses the formatting of the row *above*.

3 Click cell **E11**. On the **Formula Bar**, notice that the range changed to sum the new range **E5:E10**. Compare your screen with Figure 1.50.

> If you move formulas by inserting additional rows or columns in your worksheet, Excel automatically adjusts the formulas. Excel adjusted all of the formulas in the worksheet that were affected by inserting this new row.

Figure 1.50

Formula Bar displays the formula in E11

New row 3 inserted

Insert Options button

Cell E11 selected

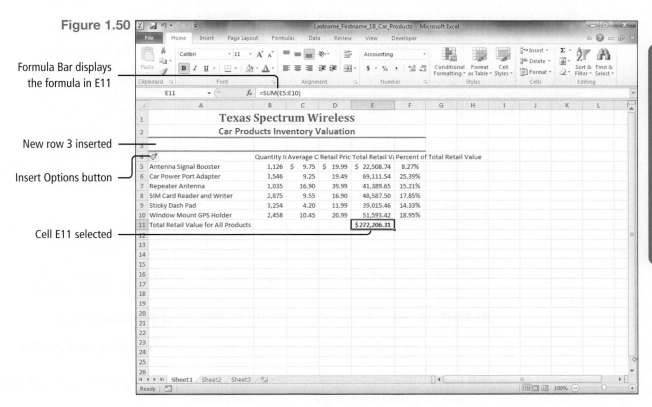

Another Way

Select the column, on the Home tab, in the Cells group, click the Insert button arrow, and then click Insert Sheet Columns. Or, select the column and click the Insert button—the default setting of the button inserts a new sheet column to the right of the selected column.

4 Click cell **A3**, type **As of December 31** and then on the **Formula Bar**, click the **Enter** button ✓ to maintain **A3** as the active cell. **Merge & Center** 🔳 the text across the range **A3:F3**, and then apply the **Heading 2** cell style.

5 In the **column heading area**, point to **column B** to display the ⬇ pointer, right-click, and then click **Insert**.

> By default, the new column uses the formatting of the column to the *left*.

6 Click cell **B4**, type **Warehouse Location** and then press Enter.

7 In cell **B5**, type **Dallas** and then type **Dallas** again in cells **B6** and **B10**. Use AutoComplete to speed your typing by pressing Enter as soon as the AutoComplete suggestion displays. In cells **B7**, **B8**, and **B9**, type **Houston**

8 In the **column heading area**, point to **column D**, right-click, and then click **Delete**.

The remaining columns shift to the left, and Excel adjusts all the formulas in the worksheet accordingly. You can use a similar technique to delete a row in a worksheet.

9 Compare your screen with Figure 1.51, and then **Save** 🖫 your workbook.

Figure 1.51

Text entered and formatted in cell A3

New column B with warehouse locations added

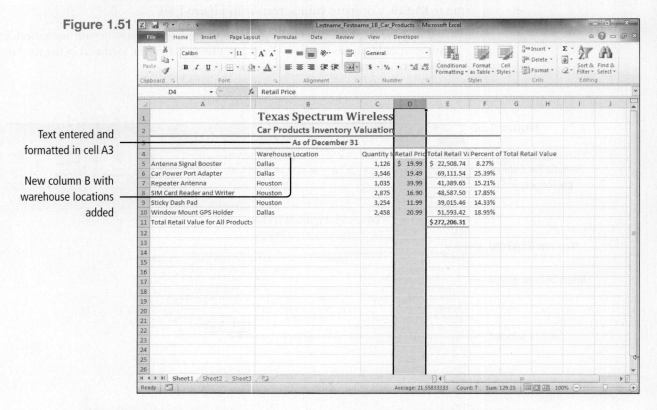

Activity 1.24 | Adjusting Column Widths and Wrapping Text

Use the Wrap Text command to display the contents of a cell on multiple lines.

1 In the **column heading area**, point to the **column B** heading to display the ↓ pointer, and then drag to the right to select **columns B:F**.

2 With the columns selected, in the **column heading area**, point to the right boundary of any of the selected columns to display the ✛ pointer, and then drag to set the width to **90 pixels**.

Use this technique to format multiple columns or rows simultaneously.

3 Select the range **B4:F4** that comprises the column headings, and then on the **Home tab**, in the **Alignment group**, click the **Wrap Text** button 🖹. Notice that the row height adjusts.

4 With the range **B4:F4** still selected, in the **Alignment group**, click the **Center** button ▤ and the **Middle Align** button ▤. With the range **B4:F4** still selected, apply the **Heading 4** cell style.

The Middle Align command aligns text so that it is centered between the top and bottom of the cell.

5 Select the range **B5:B10**, right-click, and then on the shortcut menu, click the **Center** button ☰. Click cell **A11**, and then from the **Cell Styles** gallery, under **Themed Cell Styles**, click **40% - Accent1**. Click any blank cell, and then compare your screen with Figure 1.52.

Figure 1.52

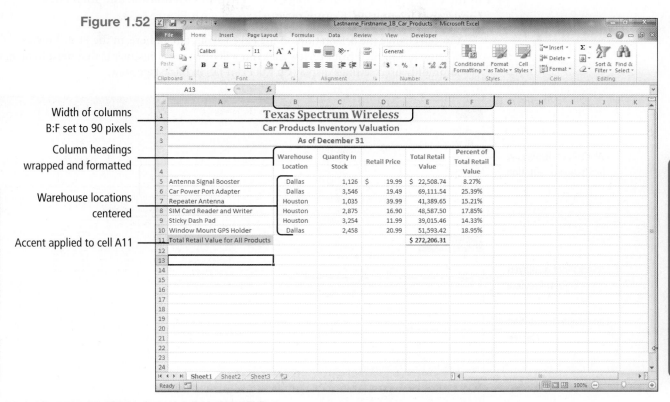

Width of columns B:F set to 90 pixels

Column headings wrapped and formatted

Warehouse locations centered

Accent applied to cell A11

6 Click the **Insert tab**, and then in the **Text group**, click **Header & Footer** to switch to Page Layout view and open the **Header area**.

7 In the **Navigation group**, click the **Go to Footer** button to move to the bottom of the page and open the **Footer area**, and then click just above the word *Footer* to place the insertion point in the **left section** of the **Footer area**.

8 In the **Header & Footer Elements group**, click the **File Name** button to add the name of your file to the footer—&*[File]* displays in the left section of the **Footer area**. Then, click in a cell above the footer to exit the **Footer area** and view your file name.

9 Click the **Page Layout tab**, in the **Page Setup group**, click the **Margins** button, and then at the bottom of the **Margins gallery**, click **Custom Margins**. In the **Page Setup** dialog box, under **Center on page**, select the **Horizontally** check box; click **OK**.

10 In the upper left corner of your screen, click **File** to display **Backstage** view. On the **Info tab**, on the right under the screen thumbnail, click **Properties**, and then click **Show Document Panel**.

11 In the **Author** box, replace the existing text with your firstname and lastname. In the **Subject** box, type your course name and section number. In the **Keywords** box, type **car products, inventory** and then **Close** ☒ the **Document Information Panel**.

12 Press `Ctrl` + `F2` to view the **Print Preview**. At the bottom of the **Print Preview**, click the **Next Page** button ▶, and notice that as currently formatted, the worksheet occupies two pages.

13 In the center panel, under **Settings**, click **Portrait Orientation**, and then click **Landscape Orientation**. Compare your screen with Figure 1.53.

> You can change the orientation on the Page Layout tab, or here, in the Print Preview. Because it is in the Print Preview that you will often see adjustments that need to be made, commonly used settings display on the Print tab in Backstage view.

Figure 1.53

Worksheet displays in landscape orientation

Worksheet displayed in Print Preview

Landscape Orientation selected

Footer with your name

Worksheet occupies one page

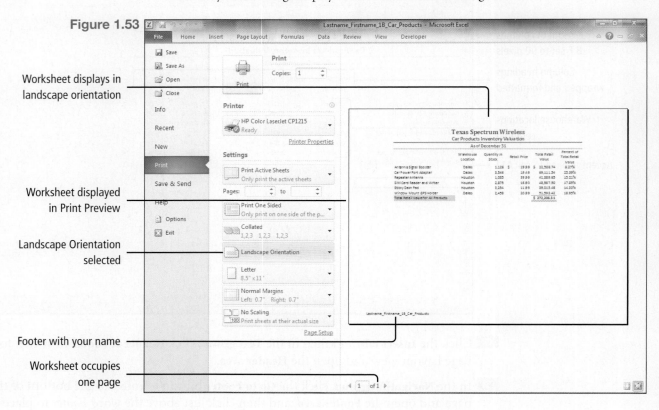

14 Note any additional adjustments or corrections that need to be made, and then on the Ribbon, click **Home** to redisplay your worksheet. In the lower right corner of your screen, on the right side of the status bar, click the **Normal** button 🔳 to return to the Normal view, and then press `Ctrl` + `Home` to return to cell **A1**.

15 Make any necessary corrections. Then, at the bottom of your worksheet, click the **Sheet2 tab** to make it the active worksheet. Hold down `Ctrl`, and then click the **Sheet3 tab**. Release `Ctrl`, and then with both sheets selected (tab background is white), point to either of the selected sheet tabs, right-click, and click **Delete** to delete the unused sheets in the workbook.

16 Save 💾 your workbook.

17 Print or submit your worksheet electronically as directed by your instructor. If required by your instructor, print or create an electronic version of your worksheet with formulas displayed using the instructions in Activity 1.16 in Project 1A.

18 Close your workbook and close Excel.

End **You have completed Project 1B** ————————————————

Content-Based Assessments

Summary

In this chapter, you used Microsoft Excel 2010 to create and analyze data organized into columns and rows and to chart and perform calculations on the data. By organizing your data with Excel, you will be able to make calculations and create visual representations of your data in the form of charts.

Key Terms

Matching

Match each term in the second column with its correct definition in the first column by writing the letter of the term on the blank line in front of the correct definition.

_____ 1. An Excel file that contains one or more worksheets.

_____ 2. Another name for a worksheet.

_____ 3. The intersection of a column and a row.

A Cell

B Cell address

C Cell content

Content-Based Assessments

_____ 4. The labels along the lower border of the Excel window that identify each worksheet.

_____ 5. A vertical group of cells in a worksheet.

_____ 6. A horizontal group of cells in a worksheet.

_____ 7. Anything typed into a cell.

_____ 8. Information such as numbers, text, dates, or times of day that you type into a cell.

_____ 9. Text or numbers in a cell that are not a formula.

_____ 10. An equation that performs mathematical calculations on values in a worksheet.

_____ 11. A constant value consisting of only numbers.

_____ 12. Another name for a cell reference.

_____ 13. Another name for a constant value.

_____ 14. The small black square in the lower right corner of a selected cell.

_____ 15. The graphic representation of data in a worksheet.

D Chart
E Column
F Constant value
G Data
H Fill handle
I Formula
J Number value
K Row
L Sheet tabs
M Spreadsheet
N Value
O Workbook

Multiple Choice

Circle the correct answer.

1. On startup, Excel displays a new blank:
   A. document   **B.** workbook   **C.** grid

2. An Excel window element that displays the value or formula contained in the active cell is the:
   A. name box   **B.** status bar   **C.** formula bar

3. An Excel window element that displays the name of the selected cell, table, chart, or object is the:
   A. name box   **B.** status bar   **C.** formula bar

4. A box in the upper left corner of the worksheet grid that selects all the cells in a worksheet is the:
   A. name box   **B.** select all box   **C.** split box

5. A cell surrounded by a black border and ready to receive data is the:
   A. active cell   **B.** address cell   **C.** reference cell

6. The feature that generates and extends values into adjacent cells based on the values of selected cells is:
   A. AutoComplete   **B.** Auto Fill   **C.** fill handle

7. The default format that Excel applies to numbers is the:
   A. comma format   **B.** accounting format   **C.** general format

8. The data that displays in the Formula Bar is referred to as the:
   A. constant value   **B.** formula   **C.** underlying value

9. The type of cell reference that refers to cells by their fixed position in a worksheet is:
   A. absolute   **B.** relative   **C.** exponentiation

10. Tiny charts embedded in a cell that give a visual trend summary alongside your data are:
    A. embedded charts   **B.** sparklines   **C.** chart styles

Content-Based Assessments

1 Create, Save, and Navigate an Excel Workbook

2 Enter Data in a Worksheet

3 Construct and Copy Formulas and Use the Sum Function

4 Format Cells with Merge & Center and Cell Styles

5 Chart Data to Create a Column Chart and Insert Sparklines

6 Print, Display Formulas, and Close Excel

Skills Review | Project **1C** GPS Sales

In the following Skills Review, you will create a new Excel worksheet with a chart that summarizes the first quarter sales of GPS (Global Positioning System) navigation devices. Your completed worksheet will look similar to Figure 1.54.

Project Files

For Project 1C, you will need the following file:

New blank Excel workbook

You will save your workbook as:

Lastname_Firstname_1C_GPS_Sales

Project Results

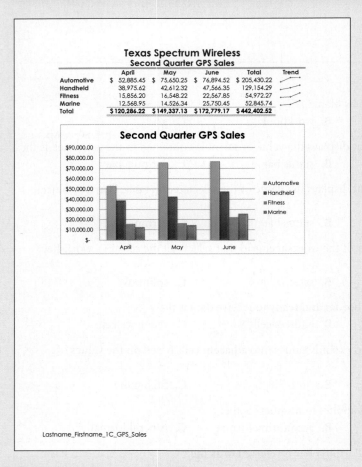

Figure 1.54

(Project 1C GPS Sales continues on the next page)

Content-Based Assessments

Skills Review | Project 1C GPS Sales (continued)

1 **Start** Excel. Click the **File tab** to display **Backstage** view, click **Save As**, and then in the **Save As** dialog box, navigate to your **Excel Chapter 1** folder. In the **File name** box, using your own name, type **Lastname_Firstname_1C_GPS_Sales** and then press [Enter].

a. With cell **A1** as the active cell, type the worksheet title **Texas Spectrum Wireless** and then press [Enter]. In cell **A2**, type the worksheet subtitle **Second Quarter GPS Sales** and then press [Enter].

b. Click in cell **A4**, type **Automotive** and then press [Enter]. In cell **A5**, type **Handheld** and then press [Enter]. In cell **A6**, type **Fitness** and then press [Enter]. In cell **A7**, type **Marine** and then press [Enter]. In cell **A8**, type **Total** and then press [Enter].

c. Click cell **B3**. Type **April** and then in the **Formula Bar**, click the **Enter** button to keep cell **B3** the active cell. With **B3** as the active cell, point to the fill handle in the lower right corner of the selected cell, drag to the right to cell **D3**, and then release the mouse button to enter the text *May* and *June*.

d. Press [Ctrl] + [Home], to make cell **A1** the active cell. In the **column heading area**, point to the vertical line between **column A** and **column B** to display the ⊞ pointer, hold down the left mouse button and drag to the right to increase the column width to **100 pixels**.

e. Point to cell **B3**, and then drag across to select cells **B3** and **C3** and **D3**. With the range **B3:D3** selected, point anywhere over the selected range, right-click, and then on the Mini toolbar, click the **Center** button.

f. Click cell **B4**, type **52885.45** and press [Tab] to make cell **C4** active. Enter the remaining values, as shown in **Table 1**, pressing [Tab] to move across the rows and [Enter] to move down the columns.

2 Click cell **B8** to make it the active cell and type **=**

a. At the insertion point, type **b4** and then type **+** Type **b5** and then type **+b6+b7** Press [Enter]. Your result is *120286.2*.

b. Click in cell **C8**. Type **=** and then click cell **C4**. Type **+** and then click cell **C5**. Repeat this process to complete the formula to add cells **C4** through **C7**, and then press [Enter]. Your result is *149337.1*.

c. Click cell **D8**. On the **Home tab**, in the **Editing group**, click the **Sum** button, and then press [Enter] to construct a formula by using the SUM function. Your result is *172779.2*. You can use any of these methods to add values; the Sum button is the most efficient.

d. In cell **E3** type **Total** and press [Enter]. With cell **E4** as the active cell, hold down [Alt], and then press [=]. On the **Formula Bar**, click the **Enter** button to display the result and keep cell **E4** active.

e. With cell **E4** active, point to the fill handle in the lower right corner of the cell. Drag down through cell **E8**, and then release the mouse button to copy the formula with relative cell references down to sum each row.

3 Click cell **F3**. Type **Trend** and then press [Enter].

a. Select the range **A1:F1**, and then on the **Home tab**, in the **Alignment group**, click the **Merge & Center** button. Select the range **A2:F2**, and then click the **Merge & Center** button.

b. Click cell **A1**. In the **Styles group**, click the **Cell Styles** button. Under **Titles and Headings**, click **Title**. Click cell **A2**, display the **Cell Styles** gallery, and then click **Heading 1**.

c. Select the range **B3:F3**, hold down [Ctrl], and then select the range **A4:A8**. From the **Cell Styles** gallery, click **Heading 4** to apply this cell style to the column and row titles.

d. Select the range **B4:E4**, hold down [Ctrl], and then select the range **B8:E8**. On the **Home tab**, in the **Number group**, click the **Accounting Number Format** button. Select the range **B5:E7**, and then in the **Number group**, click the **Comma Style** button. Select the range **B8:E8**. From the **Styles group**, display the **Cell Styles** gallery, and then under **Titles and Headings**, click **Total**.

Table 1

	April	May	June
Automotive	52885.45	75650.25	76894.52
Handheld	38975.62	42612.32	47566.35
Fitness	15856.20	16548.22	22567.85
Marine	12568.95	14526.34	25750.45

- - - → (Return to Step 2)

(Project 1C GPS Sales continues on the next page)

e. On the Ribbon, click the **Page Layout tab**, and then from the **Themes group**, click the **Themes** button to display the **Themes** gallery. Click the **Austin** theme.

4 Select the range **A3:D7**. Click the **Insert tab**, and then in the **Charts group**, click **Column**. From the gallery of column chart types, under **2-D Column**, click the first chart—**Clustered Column**.

a. On the Quick Access Toolbar, click the **Save** button to be sure that you have saved your work up to this point. Point to the top border of the chart to display the [pointer icon] pointer, and then drag to position the chart inside the upper left corner of cell **A10**.

b. On the **Design tab**, in the **Data group**, click the **Switch Row/Column** button so that the months display on the Horizontal (Category) axis and the types of GPS equipment display in the legend.

c. On the **Design tab**, in the **Chart Layouts group**, click the first layout—**Layout 1**.

d. In the chart, click anywhere in the text *Chart Title* to select the text box. Type **Second Quarter GPS Sales** and then press [Enter].

e. Click anywhere in the chart so that the chart title text box is not selected. On the **Design tab**, in the **Chart Styles group**, click the **More** button. Using the ScreenTips as your guide, locate and click **Style 18**.

f. Point to the lower right corner of the chart to display the [pointer icon] pointer, and then drag down and to the right so that the lower right border of the chart is positioned just inside the lower right corner of cell **F26**.

5 Select the range **B4:D7**. Click the **Insert tab**, and then in the **Sparklines group**, click **Line**. In the **Create Sparklines** dialog box, in the **Location Range** box, type **f4:f7** and then click **OK** to insert the sparklines.

a. On the **Design tab**, in the **Show group**, select the **Markers** check box to display markers in the sparklines.

b. On the **Design tab**, in the **Style group**, click the **More** button, and then in the second row, click the fourth style—**Sparkline Style Accent 4, Darker 25%**.

6 On the **Insert tab**, in the **Text group**, click **Header & Footer** to switch to **Page Layout** view and open the **Header** area.

a. In the **Navigation group**, click the **Go to Footer** button to open the Footer area. Click just above the word *Footer* to place the insertion point in the **left section** of the Footer.

b. In the **Header & Footer Elements group**, click the **File Name** button, and then click in a cell just above the footer to exit the Footer area.

7 On the right side of the status bar, click the **Normal** button to return to Normal view, and then press [Ctrl] + [Home] to make cell **A1** active.

a. Click the **File tab**, and then on the right, click **Properties**. Click **Show Document Panel**, and then in the **Author** box, delete any text and type your firstname and lastname. In the **Subject** box, type your course name and section number, and in the **Keywords** box, type **GPS sales Close** the Document Information Panel.

b. At the bottom of your worksheet, click the **Sheet2** tab. Hold down [Ctrl], and then click the **Sheet3** tab. With both sheets selected, point to either of the selected sheet tabs, right-click, and then click **Delete** to delete the sheets.

c. Click the **Page Layout tab**. In the **Page Setup group**, click the **Margins** button, and then at the bottom of the **Margins** gallery, click **Custom Margins**. In the **Page Setup** dialog box, under **Center on page**, select the **Horizontally** check box.

d. In the lower right corner of the **Page Setup** dialog box, click **OK**. On the **File tab**, click **Print** to view the **Print Preview**. Click the **Home tab** to return to Normal view and if necessary, make any necessary corrections and resize and move your chart so that it is centered under the worksheet.

e. On the Quick Access Toolbar, click the **Save** button to be sure that you have saved your work up to this point.

f. Print or submit your workbook electronically as directed by your instructor. If required by your instructor, print or create an electronic version of your worksheets with formulas displayed by using the instructions in Activity 1.16. **Exit** Excel without saving so that you do not save the changes you made to print formulas.

 You have completed Project 1C ————————

Content-Based Assessments

Apply **1B** skills from these Objectives:

7 Check Spelling in a Worksheet

8 Enter Data by Range

9 Construct Formulas for Mathematical Operations

10 Edit Values in a Worksheet

11 Format a Worksheet

Skills Review | Project **1D** Charger Inventory

In the following Skills Review, you will create a worksheet that summarizes the inventory of cell phone chargers. Your completed worksheet will look similar to Figure 1.55.

Project Files

For Project 1D, you will need the following file:

New blank Excel workbook

You will save your workbook as:

Lastname_Firstname_1D_Charger_Inventory

Project Results

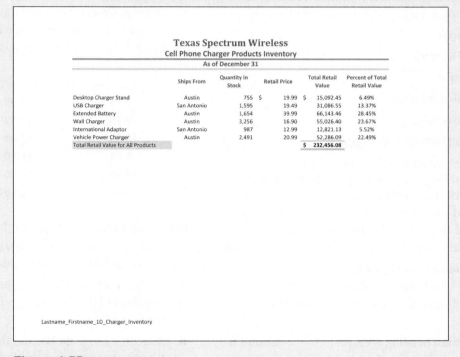

Figure 1.55

(Project 1D Charger Inventory continues on the next page)

Skills Review | Project **1D** Charger Inventory (continued)

1 **Start** Excel and display a new blank workbook. **Save** the workbook in your **Excel Chapter 1** folder, as **Lastname_Firstname_1D_Charger_Inventory** In cell **A1** type **Texas Spectrum Wireless** and in cell **A2** type **Cell Phone Charger Products Inventory**

a. Click cell **B3**, type **Quantity in Stock** and press Tab. In cell **C3** type **Average Cost** and press Tab. In cell **D3**, type **Retail Price** and press Tab. In cell **E3**, type **Total Retail Value** and press Tab. In cell **F3** type **Percent of Total Retail Value** and press Enter.

b. Click cell **A4**, type **Desktop Charger Stand** and press Enter. In the range **A5:A10**, type the remaining row titles as shown, including the misspelled words.

   USB Charger

   Extended Battery

   Wall Charger

   International Adaptor

   Vehicle Powr Charger

   Total Retail Value for All Products

c. Press Ctrl + Home to move to the top of your worksheet. On the **Review tab**, in the **Proofing group**, click the **Spelling** button. Correct *Powr* to **Power** and any other spelling errors you may have made, and then when the message displays, *The spelling check is complete for the entire sheet*, click **OK**.

d. In the **column heading area**, point to the right boundary of **column A** to display the ⊞ pointer, and then drag to the right to widen **column A** to **225** pixels.

e. In the **column heading area**, point to the **column B** heading to display the ⬇ pointer, and then drag to the right to select **columns B:F**. With the columns selected, in the **column heading area**, point to the right boundary of any of the selected columns, and then drag to the right to set the width to **100 pixels**.

f. Select the range **A1:F1**. On the **Home tab**, in the **Alignment group**, click the **Merge & Center** button, and then from the **Cell Styles** gallery, apply the **Title** style. Select the range **A2:F2**. **Merge & Center** the text across the selection, and then from the **Cell Styles** gallery, apply the **Heading 1** style.

2 Select the empty range **B4:D9**. With cell B4 active in the range, type **755** and then press Enter.

a. With cell **B5** active in the range, and pressing Enter after each entry, type the following data in the *Quantity in Stock* column:

   1595

   2654

   3256

   987

   2491

b. With the selected range still active, from the following table, beginning in cell **C4** and pressing Enter after each entry, enter the following data for the **Average Cost** column and then the **Retail Price** column. If you prefer, type without selecting the range first; recall that this is optional.

Average Cost	Retail Price
9.75	19.99
9.25	19.49
16.90	39.99
9.55	16.90
14.20	12.99
10.45	20.99

3 In cell **E4**, type **=b4*d4** and then press Enter to construct a formula that calculates the *Total Retail Value* of the *Desktop Charger Stands* (Quantity × Retail Price).

a. Click cell **E4**, position your pointer over the fill handle, and then drag down through cell **E9** to copy the formula.

b. Select the range **B4:B9**, and then on the **Home tab**, in the **Number group**, click the **Comma Style** button. Then, in the **Number group**, click the **Decrease Decimal** button two times to remove the decimal places from these non-currency values.

c. Click cell **E10**, in the **Editing group**, click the **Sum** button, and then press Enter to calculate the *Total Retail Value for All Products*. Your result is *272446.1*.

d. Select the range **C5:E9** and apply the **Comma Style**. Select the range **C4:E4**, hold down Ctrl, and then click cell **E10**. With the nonadjacent cells selected, apply the **Accounting Number Format**. Click cell **E10**, and then from the **Cell Styles** gallery, apply the **Total** style.

(Project 1D Charger Inventory continues on the next page)

Content-Based Assessments

e. Click cell **F4**, type **=** and then click cell **E4**. Type **/** and then click cell **E10**. Press `F4` to make the reference to cell *E10* absolute, and then on the **Formula Bar**, click the **Enter** button so that **F4** remains the active cell. Drag the fill handle to copy the formula down through cell **F9**.

f. Point to cell **B6**, and then double-click to place the insertion point within the cell. Use the arrow keys to move the insertion point to left or right of *2*, and use either `Del` or `Backspace` to delete 2, and then type **1** and press `Enter` so that the new *Quantity in Stock* is *1654*. Notice the recalculations in the worksheet.

4 Select the range **F4:F9**, right-click over the selection, and then on the Mini toolbar, click the **Percent Style** button. Click the **Increase Decimal** button two times, and then **Center** the selection.

a. In the **row heading area** on the left side of your screen, point to **row 3** to display the `→` pointer, and then right-click to simultaneously select the row and display a shortcut menu. On the displayed shortcut menu, click **Insert** to insert a new **row 3**.

b. Click cell **A3**, type **As of December 31** and then on the **Formula Bar**, click the **Enter** button to keep cell **A3** as the active cell. **Merge & Center** the text across the range **A3:F3**, and then apply the **Heading 2** cell style.

5 In the **column heading area**, point to **column B**. When the `↓` pointer displays, right-click, and then click **Insert** to insert a new column.

a. Click cell **B4**, and type **Ships From** and press `Enter`. In cell **B5**, type **Austin** and then press `Enter`. In cell **B6,** type **San Antonio** and then press `Enter`

b. Using AutoComplete to speed your typing by pressing `Enter` as soon as the AutoComplete suggestion displays, in cells **B7**, **B8**, and **B10** type **Austin** and in cell **B9** type **San Antonio**

c. In the **column heading area**, point to the right boundary of **column B**, and then drag to the left and set the width to **90 pixels**. From the **column heading area**, point to **column D**, right-click, and then click **Delete**.

d. Select the range **B4:F4**, and then on the **Home tab**, in the **Alignment group**, click the **Wrap Text** button, the **Center** button, and the **Middle Align** button. With the range still selected, apply the **Heading 4** cell style.

e. Select the range **B5:B10**, right-click, and then click the **Center** button. Click cell **A11**, and then from the **Cell Styles** gallery, under **Themed Cell Styles**, click **40% - Accent1**.

6 On the **Insert tab**, in the **Text group**, click **Header & Footer**. In the **Navigation group**, click the **Go To Footer** button, and then click just above the word *Footer*. In the **Header & Footer Elements group**, click the **File Name** button to add the name of your file to the footer. Click in a cell just above the footer to exit the **Footer area**, and then return the worksheet to **Normal** view.

a. Press `Ctrl` + `Home` to move the insertion point to cell **A1**. On the **Page Layout tab**, in the **Page Setup group**, click **Orientation**, and then click **Landscape**.

b. In the **Page Setup group**, click the **Margins** button, and then at the bottom of the **Margins gallery**, click **Custom Margins**. In the **Page Setup** dialog box, under **Center on page**, select the **Horizontally** check box, and then click **OK**.

c. Click the **File tab** to display **Backstage** view, and then on the right, click **Properties**. Click **Show Document Panel**, and then in the **Author** box, delete any text and type your firstname and lastname. In the **Subject** box type your course name and section number, in the **Keywords** box type **cell phone chargers** and then **Close** the **Document Information Panel**.

d. Select **Sheet2** and **Sheet3**, and then **Delete** both sheets.

e. **Save** your file and then print or submit your workbook electronically as directed by your instructor. If required by your instructor, print or create an electronic version of your worksheet with formulas displayed by using the instructions in Activity 1.16. **Exit** Excel without saving so that you do not save the changes you made to print formulas.

End **You have completed Project 1D**

Apply **1A** skills from these Objectives:

1 Create, Save, and Navigate an Excel Workbook

2 Enter Data in a Worksheet

3 Construct and Copy Formulas and Use the SUM Function

4 Format Cells with Merge & Center and Cell Styles

5 Chart Data to Create a Column Chart and Insert Sparklines

6 Print, Display Formulas, and Close Excel

Mastering Excel | Project **1E** Hard Drives

In the following Mastering Excel project, you will create a worksheet comparing the sales of different types of external hard drives sold in the second quarter. Your completed worksheet will look similar to Figure 1.56.

Project Files

For Project 1E, you will need the following file:

New blank Excel workbook

You will save your workbook as:

Lastname_Firstname_1E_Hard_Drives

Project Results

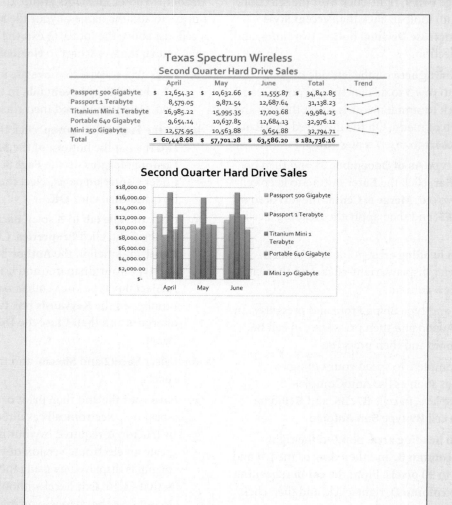

Figure 1.56

(Project 1E Hard Drives continues on the next page)

Content-Based Assessments

Mastering Excel | Project **1E** Hard Drives (continued)

1 **Start** Excel. In cell **A1**, type **Texas Spectrum Wireless** and in cell **A2**, type **Second Quarter Hard Drive Sales** Change the **Theme** to **Module**, and then **Save** the workbook in your **Excel Chapter 1** folder as **Lastname_Firstname_1E_Hard_Drives**

2 In cell **B3**, type **April** and then use the fill handle to enter the months *May* and *June* in the range **C3:D3**. In cell **E3**, type **Total** and in cell **F3**, type **Trend**

3 **Center** the column titles in the range **B3:F3**. **Merge & Center** the title across the range **A1:F1**, and apply the **Title** cell style. **Merge & Center** the subtitle across the range **A2:F2**, and apply the **Heading 1** cell style.

4 Widen **column A** to **170 pixels**, and then in the range **A4:A9**, type the following row titles:

> **Passport 500 Gigabyte**
>
> **Passport 1 Terabyte**
>
> **Titanium Mini 1 Terabyte**
>
> **Portable 640 Gigabyte**
>
> **Mini 250 Gigabyte**
>
> **Total**

5 Widen columns **B:F** to **100 pixels**, and then in the range **B4:D8**, enter the monthly sales figures for each type of hard drive, as shown in **Table 1** at the bottom of the page.

6 In cell **B9**, **Sum** the *April* hard drive sales, and then copy the formula across to cells **C9:D9**. In cell **E4**, **Sum** the *Passport 500 Gigabyte sales*, and then copy the formula down to cells **E5:E9**.

7 Apply the **Heading 4** cell style to the row titles and the column titles. Apply the **Total** cell style to the totals in the range **B9:E9**. Apply the **Accounting Number Format**

to the first row of sales figures and to the total row. Apply the **Comma Style** to the remaining sales figures.

8 To compare the monthly sales of each product visually, select the range that represents the sales figures for the three months, including the month names, and for each product name—do not include any totals in the range. With this data selected, **Insert** a **2-D Clustered Column** chart. Switch the Row/Column data so that the months display on the category axis and the types of hard drives display in the legend.

9 Position the upper left corner of the chart in the approximate center of cell **A11** so that the chart is visually centered below the worksheet, as shown in Figure 1.56. Apply **Chart Style 26**, and then modify the **Chart Layout** by applying **Layout 1**. Change the **Chart Title** to **Second Quarter Hard Drive Sales**

10 In the range **F4:F8**, insert **Line** sparklines that compare the monthly data. Do not include the totals. Show the sparkline **Markers** and apply **Sparkline Style Accent 2, Darker 50%**—in the first row, the second style.

11 Insert a **Footer** with the **File Name** in the **left section**, and then return the worksheet to **Normal** view. Display the **Document Panel**, add your name, your course name and section, and the keywords **hard drives, sales** Delete the unused sheets, and then center the worksheet **Horizontally** on the page. Check your worksheet by previewing it in **Print Preview**, and then make any necessary corrections.

12 **Save** your workbook, and then print or submit electronically as directed. If required by your instructor, print or create an electronic version of your worksheets with formulas displayed by using the instructions in Activity 1.16. **Exit** Excel without saving so that you do not save the changes you made to print formulas.

Table 1

	April	May	June
Passport 500 Gigabyte	12654.32	10632.66	11555.87
Passport 1 Terabyte	8579.05	9871.54	12687.64
Titanium Mini 1 Terabyte	16985.22	15995.35	17003.68
Portable 640 Gigabyte	9654.14	10637.85	12684.13
Mini 250 Gigabyte	12575.95	10563.88	9654.88

(Return to Step 6)

End **You have completed Project 1E**

Content-Based Assessments

Apply 1B skills from these Objectives:

7 Check Spelling in a Worksheet

8 Enter Data by Range

9 Construct Formulas for Mathematical Operations

10 Edit Values in a Worksheet

11 Format a Worksheet

Mastering Excel | Project 1F Camera Accessories

In the following Mastering Excel project, you will create a worksheet that summarizes the sale of digital camera accessories. Your completed worksheet will look similar to Figure 1.57.

Project Files

For Project 1F, you will need the following file:

New blank Excel workbook

You will save your workbook as:

Lastname_Firstname_1F_Camera_Accessories

Project Results

Texas Spectrum Wireless
Digital Camera Accessories Sales

	Quantity Sold	Retail Price	Total Sales	Percent of Total Sales
Small Cloth Gear Bag	254	$ 19.99	$ 5,077.46	10.69%
Large Cloth Gear Bag	182	24.99	4,548.18	9.58%
Lens Cap	351	6.99	2,453.49	5.17%
Lens Hood	125	5.49	686.25	1.44%
Remote Switch	750	22.50	16,875.00	35.53%
Mini Tripod	554	24.99	13,844.46	29.15%
Cleaning Kit	365	10.99	4,011.35	8.45%
Total Sales for All Products			$ 47,496.19	

Month Ending August 31

Lastname_Firstname_1F_Camera_Accessories

Figure 1.57

(Project 1F Camera Accessories continues on the next page)

Content-Based Assessments

Mastering Excel | Project 1F Camera Accessories (continued)

1 **Start** Excel and display a new blank workbook. **Save** the workbook in your **Excel Chapter 1** folder as **Lastname_Firstname_1F_Camera_Accessories** In cell **A1**, type **Texas Spectrum Wireless** In cell **A2**, type **Digital Camera Accessories Sales** and then **Merge & Center** the title and the subtitle across **columns A:F**. Apply the **Title** and **Heading 1** cell styles respectively.

2 Beginning in cell **B3**, type the following column titles: **Product Number** and **Quantity Sold** and **Retail Price** and **Total Sales** and **Percent of Total Sales**

3 Beginning in cell **A4**, type the following row titles, including misspelled words:

> Small Cloth Gear Bag
>
> Large Cloth Gear Bag
>
> Lens Cap
>
> Lens Hood
>
> Remote Switch
>
> Mini Tripod
>
> Cleening Kit
>
> Total Sales for All Products

4 Make cell **A1** the active cell, and then check spelling in your worksheet. Correct *Cleening* to **Cleaning**, and make any other necessary corrections. Widen **column A** to **180 pixels** and **columns B:F** to **90 pixels**.

5 In the range **B4:D10**, type the data shown in **Table 1** at the bottom of the page.

6 In cell **E4**, construct a formula to calculate the *Total Sales* of the *Small Cloth Gear Bags* by multiplying the *Quantity Sold* times the *Retail Price*. Copy the formula down for the remaining products. In cell **E11**, use the **SUM** function to calculate the *Total Sales for All Products*, and then apply the **Total** cell style to the cell.

7 Using absolute cell references as necessary so that you can copy the formula, in cell **F4**, construct a formula to calculate the *Percent of Total Sales* for the first product by dividing the *Total Sales* of the *Small Cloth Gear Bags* by the *Total Sales for All Products*. Copy the formula down for the remaining products. To the computed percentages, apply **Percent Style** with two decimal places, and then **Center** the percentages.

8 Apply the **Comma Style** with no decimal places to the *Quantity Sold* figures. To cells **D4**, **E4**, and **E11** apply the **Accounting Number Format**. To the range **D5:E10**, apply the **Comma Style**.

9 Change the *Retail Price* of the *Mini Tripod* to **24.99** and the *Quantity Sold* of the *Remote Switch* to **750** Delete **column B**, and then **Insert** a new **row 3**. In cell **A3**, type **Month Ending August 31** and then **Merge & Center** the text across the range **A3:E3**. Apply the **Heading 2** cell style. To cell **A12**, apply the **Accent1** cell style. Select the four column titles, apply **Wrap Text**, **Middle Align**, and **Center** formatting, and then apply the **Heading 3** cell style.

10 Insert a **Footer** with the **File Name** in the **left section**, and then return to **Normal** view. Display the **Document Panel**, add your name, your course name and section, and the keywords **digital camera accessories, sales**

11 Delete the unused sheets, and then center the worksheet **Horizontally** on the page. Preview the worksheet in **Print Preview**, and make any necessary corrections.

12 **Save** your workbook, and then print or submit electronically as directed. If required by your instructor, print or create an electronic version of your worksheets with formulas displayed by using the instructions in Activity 1.16. **Exit** Excel without saving so that you do not save the changes you made to print formulas.

Table 1

	Product Number	Quantity Sold	Retail Price
Small Cloth Gear Bag	CGB-3	254	19.99
Large Cloth Gear Bag	CGB-8	182	24.99
Lens Cap	LC-2	351	6.99
Lens Hood	LH-4	125	5.49
Remote Switch	RS-5	677	22.50
Mini Tripod	MTP-6	554	29.99
Cleaning Kit	CK-8	365	10.99

- - - → (Return to Step 6)

End **You have completed Project 1F**

Mastering Excel | Project **1G** Sales Comparison

In the following Mastering Excel project, you will create a new worksheet that compares annual laptop sales by store location. Your completed worksheet will look similar to Figure 1.58.

Project Files

For Project 1G, you will need the following file:

New blank Excel workbook

You will save your workbook as:

Lastname_Firstname_1G_Sales_Comparison

Project Results

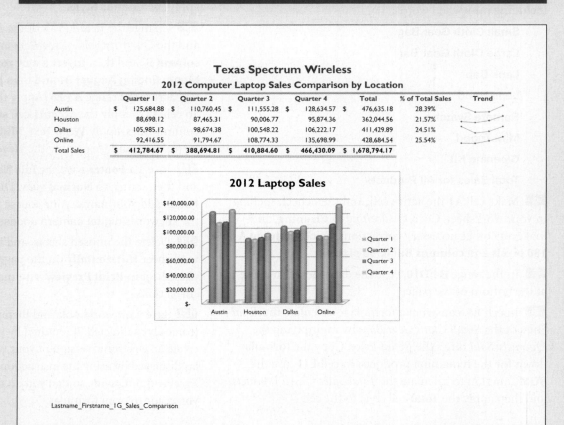

Figure 1.58

(Project 1G Sales Comparison continues on the next page)

Content-Based Assessments

Mastering Excel | Project **1G** Sales Comparison (continued)

1 **Start** Excel. In a new blank workbook, as the worksheet title, in cell **A1**, type **Texas Spectrum Wireless** As the worksheet subtitle, in cell **A2**, type **2012 Computer Laptop Sales Comparison by Location** and then **Save** the workbook in your **Excel Chapter 1** folder as Lastname_Firstname_1G_Sales_Comparison

2 In cell **B3**, type **Quarter 1** and then use the fill handle to enter *Quarter 2*, *Quarter 3*, and *Quarter 4* in the range **C3:E3**. In cell **F3**, type **Total** In cell **G3**, type **% of Total Sales** In cell **H3**, type **Trend**

3 In the range **A4:A7**, type the following row titles: **Austin** and **Houston** and **Online** and **Total Sales**

4 Widen columns **A:H** to **115 pixels**. **Merge & Center** the title across the range **A1:H1**, and then apply the **Title** cell style. **Merge & Center** the subtitle across the range **A2:H2**, and then apply the **Heading 1** cell style. Select the seven column titles, apply **Center** formatting, and then apply the **Heading 4** cell style.

5 In the range **B4:E6**, enter the sales values for each Quarter as shown in **Table 1** at the bottom of the page.

6 **Sum** the *Quarter 1* sales, and then copy the formula across for the remaining Quarters. **Sum** the sales for the *Austin* location, and then copy the formula down through cell **F7**. Apply the **Accounting Number Format** to the first row of sales figures and to the total row, and the **Comma Style** to the remaining sales figures. Format the totals in **row 7** with the **Total** cell style.

7 **Insert** a new **row 6** with the row title **Dallas** and the following sales figures for each quarter: **105985.12** and **98674.38** and **100548.22** and **106222.17** Copy the formula in cell **F5** down to cell **F6** to sum the new row.

8 Using absolute cell references as necessary so that you can copy the formula, in cell **G4** construct a formula to calculate the *Percent of Total Sales* for the first location by dividing the *Total* for the *Austin* location by the *Total Sales* for all Quarters. Copy the formula down for the remaining locations. To the computed percentages, apply

Percent Style with two decimal places, and then **Center** the percentages.

9 Insert **Line** sparklines in the range **H4:H7** that compare the quarterly data. Do not include the totals. Show the sparkline **Markers** and apply the second style in the second row—**Sparkline Style Accent 2, Darker 25%**.

10 **Save** your workbook. To compare the quarterly sales of each location visually, select the range that represents the sales figures for the four quarters, including the quarter names and each location—do not include any totals in the range. With this data selected, **Insert** a **Column**, **Clustered Cylinder** chart.

11 Switch the row/column data so that the locations display on the category axis. Position the top edge of the chart in **row 10** and visually center it below the worksheet data. Apply **Chart Style 26**, and then modify the **Chart Layout** by applying **Layout 1**. Change the **Chart Title** to **2012 Laptop Sales**

12 Deselect the chart. Change the **Orientation** to **Landscape**, center the worksheet **Horizontally** on the page, and then change the **Theme** to **Solstice**. Scale the worksheet so that the **Width** fits to **1 page**. Insert a **Footer** with the **File Name** in the **left section**. Return the worksheet to **Normal** view and make **A1** the active cell so that you can view the top of your worksheet.

13 Display the **Document Panel**, add your name, your course name and section, and the keywords **laptops, sales** Delete the unused sheets, preview your worksheet in **Print Preview**, and then make any necessary corrections.

14 **Save** your workbook, and then print or submit electronically as directed. If required by your instructor, print or create an electronic version of your worksheets with formulas displayed by using the instructions in Activity 1.16. **Exit** Excel without saving so that you do not save the changes you made to print formulas.

Table 1

	Quarter 1	Quarter 2	Quarter 3	Quarter 4
Austin	125684.88	110760.45	111555.28	128634.57
Houston	88698.12	87465.31	90006.77	95874.36
Online	92416.55	91794.67	108774.33	135698.99

- - - ➤ (Return to Step 6)

End **You have completed Project 1G** ——————

GO! Fix It | Project **1H** Team Sales

Project Files

For Project 1H, you will need the following file:

e01H_Team_Sales

You will save your workbook as:

Lastname_Firstname_1H_Team_Sales

In this project, you will edit a worksheet that summarizes sales by each sales team member at the Texas Spectrum Wireless San Antonio location for the month of February. From the student files that accompany this textbook, open the file e01H_Team_Sales, and then save the file in your Excel Chapter 1 folder as **Lastname_Firstname_1H_Team_Sales**

To complete the project, you must find and correct errors in formulas and formatting. View each formula in the Formula Bar and edit as necessary. In addition to errors that you find, you should know:

- There are two spelling errors.

- Worksheet titles should be merged and centered and appropriate cell styles should be applied.

- Appropriate number and accounting format with zero decimals should be applied to the data and text should be wrapped where necessary. Percent style formatting should be applied appropriately where necessary.

- Column headings should be formatted with the Heading 4 style.

- In the chart, the team member names should display on the Horizontal (Category) axis and the week names should display in the legend.

- The chart should include the title **February Team Member Sales**

- The worksheet should be centered horizontally on one page in Landscape orientation. Remove unused sheets.

- A footer should be inserted that includes the file name, and document properties should include the keywords **team sales, San Antonio**

Save your workbook, and then print or submit electronically as directed. If required by your instructor, print or create an electronic version of your worksheets with formulas displayed by using the instructions in Activity 1.16. Exit Excel without saving so that you do not save the changes you made to print formulas.

End **You have completed Project 1H** ———————————

Content-Based Assessments

GO! Make It | Project 1I Printer Sales

Project Files

For Project 1I, you will need the following file:

New blank Excel workbook

You will save your workbook as:

Lastname_Firstname_1I_Printer_Sales

Create the worksheet shown in Figure 1.59. Use the Pushpin theme and change the Orientation to Landscape. Construct formulas in the Total Sold, Total Sales, and Percent of Total Sales columns, and in the Total row. Apply cell styles and number formatting as shown. Use Style 26 for the chart. Insert sparklines for the monthly data using the first style in the second row—Sparkline Style Accent 1, Darker 25%. Add your name, your course name and section, and the keywords **inkjet, printer, sales** to the document properties. Save the file in your Excel Chapter 1 folder as **Lastname_Firstname_1I_Printer_Sales**

Project Results

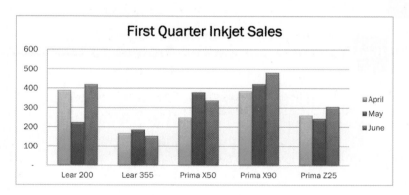

Texas Spectrum Wireless
First Quarter Inkjet Printer Sales

Model	April	May	June	Total Sold	Retail Price	Total Sales	Percent of Total Sales	Trend
Lear 200	390	224	421	1,035	$ 79.99	$ 82,789.65	8.50%	
Lear 355	168	186	153	507	169.99	86,184.93	8.85%	
Prima X50	250	379	339	968	199.99	193,590.32	19.88%	
Prima X90	386	423	482	1,291	249.99	322,737.09	33.15%	
Prima Z25	261	244	307	812	354.99	288,251.88	29.61%	
Total	1,455	1,456	1,702	4,613		$ 973,553.87		

Lastname_Firstname_1I_Printer_Sales

Figure 1.59

Excel | Chapter 1

Content-Based Assessments

GO! Solve It | Project **1J** Warranty Sales

Project Files

For Project 1J, you will need the following file:

e01J_Warranty_Sales

You will save your workbook as:

Lastname_Firstname_1J_Warranty_Sales

Open the file e01J_Warranty_Sales and save it as **Lastname_Firstname_1J_Warranty_Sales** Complete the worksheet by using Auto Fill to enter the Quarter headings, and then calculating *Total Sold, Total Sales, Total For All Products,* and *Percent of Total Sales.* Format the worksheet attractively, and apply appropriate financial formatting. Insert a chart that compares the total number of warranties sold for each item across Quarters, and format the chart to display the information appropriately. Include the file name in the footer, add appropriate document properties, and submit as directed.

		Performance Level		
		Exemplary: You consistently applied the relevant skills	**Proficient:** You sometimes, but not always, applied the relevant skills	**Developing:** You rarely or never applied the relevant skills
Performance Element	Create formulas	All formulas are correct and are efficiently constructed.	Formulas are correct but not always constructed in the most efficient manner.	One or more formulas are missing or incorrect; or only numbers were entered.
	Create a chart	Chart created properly.	Chart was created but incorrect data was selected.	No chart was created.
	Format attractively and appropriately	Formatting is attractive and appropriate.	Adequately formatted but difficult to read or unattractive.	Inadequate or no formatting.

End You have completed Project 1J _____

Content-Based Assessments

Apply a combination of the **1A** and **1B** skills.

GO! Solve It | Project **1K** Service Receipts

Project Files

For Project 1K, you will need the following file:

e01K_Service_Receipts

You will save your workbook as:

Lastname_Firstname_1K_Service_Receipts

Open the file e01K_Service_Receipts and save it as **Lastname_Firstname_1K_Service_Receipts** Complete the worksheet by using Auto Fill to complete the month headings, and then calculating the Total Receipts for each month and for each product. Insert and format appropriate sparklines in the Trend column. Format the worksheet attractively with a title and subtitle, check spelling, adjust column width, and apply appropriate financial formatting. Insert a chart that compares the total sales receipts for each product with the months displaying as the categories, and format the chart attractively. Include the file name in the footer, add appropriate properties, and submit as directed.

		Performance Level		
		Exemplary: You consistently applied the relevant skills	**Proficient:** You sometimes, but not always, applied the relevant skills	**Developing:** You rarely or never applied the relevant skills
Performance Element	Create formulas	All formulas are correct and are efficiently constructed.	Formulas are correct but not always constructed in the most efficient manner.	One or more formulas are missing or incorrect; or only numbers were entered.
	Create a chart	Chart created properly.	Chart was created but incorrect data was selected.	No chart was created.
	Insert and format sparklines	Sparklines inserted and formatted properly.	Sparklines were inserted but incorrect data was selected or sparklines were not formatted.	No sparklines were inserted.
	Format attractively and appropriately	Formatting is attractive and appropriate.	Adequately formatted but difficult to read or unattractive.	Inadequate or no formatting.

End You have completed Project 1K ———————————————————

Outcomes-Based Assessments

Rubric

The following outcomes-based assessments are *open-ended assessments*. That is, there is no specific correct result; your result will depend on your approach to the information provided. Make *Professional Quality* your goal. Use the following scoring rubric to guide you in *how* to approach the problem, and then to evaluate *how well* your approach solves the problem.

The *criteria*—Software Mastery, Content, Format and Layout, and Process—represent the knowledge and skills you have gained that you can apply to solving the problem. The *levels of performance*—Professional Quality, Approaching Professional Quality, or Needs Quality Improvements—help you and your instructor evaluate your result.

	Your completed project is of Professional Quality if you:	Your completed project is Approaching Professional Quality if you:	Your completed project Needs Quality Improvements if you:
1-Software Mastery	Choose and apply the most appropriate skills, tools, and features and identify efficient methods to solve the problem.	Choose and apply some appropriate skills, tools, and features, but not in the most efficient manner.	Choose inappropriate skills, tools, or features, or are inefficient in solving the problem.
2-Content	Construct a solution that is clear and well organized, contains content that is accurate, appropriate to the audience and purpose, and is complete. Provide a solution that contains no errors in spelling, grammar, or style.	Construct a solution in which some components are unclear, poorly organized, inconsistent, or incomplete. Misjudge the needs of the audience. Have some errors in spelling, grammar, or style, but the errors do not detract from comprehension.	Construct a solution that is unclear, incomplete, or poorly organized; contains some inaccurate or inappropriate content; and contains many errors in spelling, grammar, or style. Do not solve the problem.
3-Format and Layout	Format and arrange all elements to communicate information and ideas, clarify function, illustrate relationships, and indicate relative importance.	Apply appropriate format and layout features to some elements, but not others. Overuse features, causing minor distraction.	Apply format and layout that does not communicate information or ideas clearly. Do not use format and layout features to clarify function, illustrate relationships, or indicate relative importance. Use available features excessively, causing distraction.
4-Process	Use an organized approach that integrates planning, development, self-assessment, revision, and reflection.	Demonstrate an organized approach in some areas, but not others; or, use an insufficient process of organization throughout.	Do not use an organized approach to solve the problem.

Apply a combination of the 1A and 1B skills.

GO! Think | Project 1L Phone Plans

Project Files

For Project 1L, you will need the following file:

New blank Excel workbook

You will save your workbook as:

Lastname_Firstname_1L_Phone_Plans

Roslyn Thomas, President of Texas Spectrum Wireless, needs a worksheet that summarizes the following data regarding the first quarter sales of cell phone calling plans that the company is offering for domestic and international calls. Roslyn would like the worksheet to include a calculation of the total sales for each plan and a total of the sales of all of the plans. She would also like to know each plan's percentage of total sales.

	Number Sold	Price
Domestic Standard	2556	29.99
Domestic Premium	3982	49.99
Domestic Platinum	1647	64.99
International Standard	582	85.99
International Premium	365	102.99

Create a worksheet that provides Roslyn with the information needed. Include appropriate worksheet, column, and row titles. Using the formatting skills that you practiced in this chapter, format the worksheet in a manner that is professional and easy to read and understand. Insert a footer with the file name and add appropriate document properties. Save the file as **Lastname_ Firstname_1L_Phone_Plans** and print or submit as directed by your instructor.

End You have completed Project 1L ⸺⸺⸺⸺⸺⸺⸺⸺⸺

Outcomes-Based Assessments

GO! Think | Project **1M** Advertising

Project Files

For Project 1M, you will need the following file:

New blank Excel workbook

You will save your workbook as:

Lastname_Firstname_1M_Advertising

Eliott Verschoren, Vice President of Marketing for Texas Spectrum Wireless, is conducting an analysis of the advertising expenditures at the company's four retail locations based on the following data:

	Quarter 1	Quarter 2	Quarter 3	Quarter 4
Austin	22860	25905	18642	28405
Dallas	18557	17963	22883	25998
Houston	32609	28462	25915	31755
San Antonio	12475	15624	13371	17429

Using this information, create a workbook that includes totals by quarter and by location, sparklines to demonstrate the quarterly trends, and a column chart that compares the quarterly data across locations. Include appropriate worksheet, row, and column titles. Using the formatting skills that you practiced in this chapter, format the worksheet in a manner that is professional and easy to read and understand. Insert a footer with the file name and add appropriate document properties. Save the file as **Lastname_Firstname_1M_Advertising** and print or submit as directed by your instructor.

End **You have completed Project 1M** ————————————————

Outcomes-Based Assessments

You and GO! | Project **1N** Personal Expenses

Project Files

For Project 1N, you will need the following file:

New blank Excel workbook

You will save your workbook as:

Lastname_Firstname_1N_Personal_Expenses

Develop a worksheet that details your personal expenses from the last three months. Some of these expenses might include, but are not limited to, Mortgage, Rent, Utilities, Phone, Food, Entertainment, Tuition, Childcare, Clothing, and Insurance. Include a total for each month and for each category of expense. Insert a column with a formula that calculates the percent that each expense category is of the total expenditures. Format the worksheet by adjusting column widths and wrapping text, and by applying appropriate financial number formatting and cell styles. Insert a column chart that compares your expenses by month and modify the chart layout and style. Insert a footer with the file name and center the worksheet horizontally on the page. Save your file as **Lastname_Firstname_1N_Personal_Expenses** and submit as directed.

End **You have completed Project 1N** —————————

Using Functions, Creating Tables, and Managing Large Workbooks

OUTCOMES
At the end of this chapter you will be able to:

OBJECTIVES
Mastering these objectives will enable you to:

PROJECT 2A
Analyze inventory by applying statistical and logical calculations to data and by sorting and filtering data.

1. Use the SUM, AVERAGE, MEDIAN, MIN, and MAX Functions (p. 117)
2. Move Data, Resolve Error Messages, and Rotate Text (p. 121)
3. Use COUNTIF and IF Functions and Apply Conditional Formatting (p. 123)
4. Use Date & Time Functions and Freeze Panes (p. 128)
5. Create, Sort, and Filter an Excel Table (p. 130)
6. Format and Print a Large Worksheet (p. 133)

PROJECT 2B
Summarize the data on multiple worksheets.

7. Navigate a Workbook and Rename Worksheets (p. 138)
8. Enter Dates, Clear Contents, and Clear Formats (p. 139)
9. Copy and Paste by Using the Paste Options Gallery (p. 143)
10. Edit and Format Multiple Worksheets at the Same Time (p. 144)
11. Create a Summary Sheet with Column Sparklines (p. 150)
12. Format and Print Multiple Worksheets in a Workbook (p. 154)

grafica/Shutterstock

In This Chapter

In this chapter, you will use the Statistical functions to calculate the average of a group of numbers, and use other Logical and Date & Time functions. You will use the counting functions and apply conditional formatting to make data easy to visualize. In this chapter, you will also create a table and analyze the table's data by sorting and filtering the data. You will summarize a workbook that contains multiple worksheets.

The projects in this chapter relate to **Laurales Herbs and Spices**. After ten years as an Executive Chef, Laura Morales started her own business, which offers quality products for cooking, eating, and entertaining in retail stores and online. In addition to herbs and spices, there is a wide variety of condiments, confections, jams, sauces, oils, and vinegars. Later this year, Laura will add a line of tools, cookbooks, and gift baskets. The company name is a combination of Laura's first and last names, and also the name of an order of plants related to cinnamon.

Project 2A Inventory Status Report

Project Activities

In Activities 2.01 through 2.15, you will edit a worksheet for Laura Morales, President, detailing the current inventory of flavor products at the Oakland production facility. Your completed worksheet will look similar to Figure 2.1.

Project Files

For Project 2A, you will need the following file:

e02A_Flavor_Inventory

You will save your workbook as:

Lastname_Firstname_2A_Flavor_Inventory

Project Results

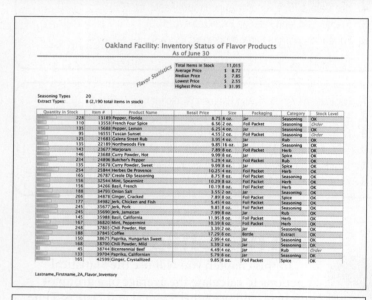

Figure 2.1
Project 2A Flavor Inventory

Objective 1 | Use the SUM, AVERAGE, MEDIAN, MIN, and MAX Functions

A *function* is a predefined formula—a formula that Excel has already built for you—that performs calculations by using specific values in a particular order or structure. *Statistical functions*, which include the AVERAGE, MEDIAN, MIN, and MAX functions, are useful to analyze a group of measurements.

Activity 2.01 | Using the SUM and AVERAGE Functions

Laura has a worksheet with information about the inventory of flavor product types currently in stock at the Oakland facility. In this activity, you will use the SUM and AVERAGE functions to gather information about the product inventory.

1 **Start** Excel. From **Backstage** view, display the **Open** dialog box, and then from the student files that accompany this textbook, locate and open **e02A_Flavor_Inventory**. Click the **File tab** to redisplay **Backstage** view, and then click **Save As**. In the **Save As** dialog box, navigate to the location where you are storing your projects for this chapter.

2 Create a new folder named **Excel Chapter 2** open the new folder, and then in the **File name** box, type **Lastname_Firstname_2A_Flavor_Inventory** Click **Save** or press Enter.

3 Scroll down. Notice that the worksheet contains data related to types of flavor products in inventory, including information about the *Quantity in Stock*, *Item #*, *Product Name*, *Retail Price*, *Size*, *Packaging*, and *Category*.

4 Leave row 3 blank, and then in cell **A4**, type **Total Items in Stock** In cell **A5**, type **Average Price** In cell **A6**, type **Median Price**

5 Click cell **B4**. Click the **Formulas tab**, and then in the **Function Library group**, click the **AutoSum** button. Compare your screen with Figure 2.2.

The *SUM function* that you have used is a predefined formula that adds all the numbers in a selected range of cells. Because it is frequently used, there are several ways to insert the function.

For example, you can insert the function from the Home tab's Editing group, by using the keyboard shortcut Alt + =, from the Function Library group on the Formulas tab, and also from the Math & Trig button in that group.

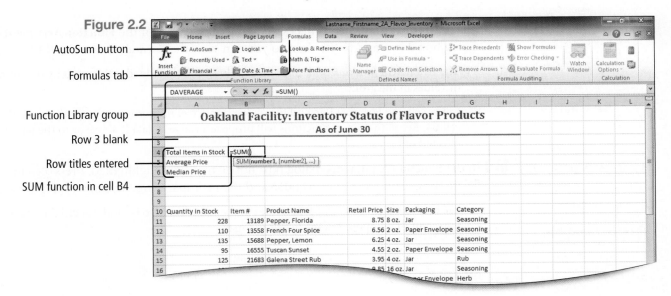

Figure 2.2

- AutoSum button
- Formulas tab
- Function Library group
- Row 3 blank
- Row titles entered
- SUM function in cell B4

6 With the insertion point blinking in the function, select the range **A11:A65**, dragging down as necessary, and then press Enter. Scroll up to view the top of your worksheet, and notice your result in cell **B4**, *11015*.

7 Click cell **B4** and look at the **Formula Bar**: Compare your screen with Figure 2.3.

> *SUM* is the name of the function. The values in parentheses are the ***arguments***—the values that an Excel function uses to perform calculations or operations. In this instance, the argument consists of the values in the range A11:A65.

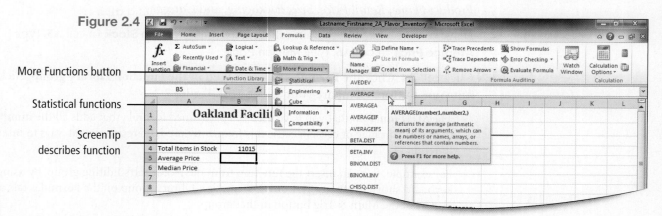

Figure 2.3

Function and arguments display in Formula Bar

Result of SUM function displays in B4

8 Click cell **B5**. In the **Function Library group**, click the **More Functions** button, point to **Statistical**, point to **AVERAGE**, and notice the ScreenTip. Compare your screen with Figure 2.4.

> The ScreenTip describes how the AVERAGE function will compute the calculation.

Figure 2.4

More Functions button

Statistical functions

ScreenTip describes function

9 Click **AVERAGE**, and then if necessary, drag the title bar of the **Function Arguments** dialog box down and to the right so you can view the **Formula Bar** and cell **B5**.

> The ***AVERAGE function*** adds a group of values, and then divides the result by the number of values in the group.

> In the cell, the Formula Bar, and the dialog box, Excel proposes to average the value in cell B4. Recall that Excel functions will propose a range if data is above or to the left of a selected cell.

Another Way

Alternatively, with the existing text selected, select the range D11:D65 and press Enter.

10 In the **Function Arguments** dialog box, notice that *B4* is highlighted. Press Del to delete the existing text, type **d11:d65** and then compare your screen with Figure 2.5.

> Because you want to average the values in the range D11:D65—and not cell B4—you must edit the proposed range in this manner.

Figure 2.5

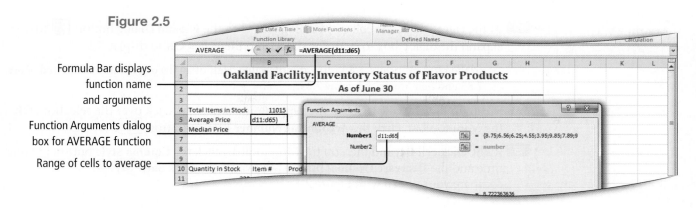

Formula Bar displays function name and arguments

Function Arguments dialog box for AVERAGE function

Range of cells to average

11 In the **Function Arguments** dialog box, click **OK**, and then **Save** 💾.

The result indicates that the average Retail Price of all products is *8.72.*

Activity 2.02 │ Using the MEDIAN Function

The ***MEDIAN function*** is a statistical function that describes a group of data—you may have seen it used to describe the price of houses in a particular geographical area. The MEDIAN function finds the middle value that has as many values above it in the group as are below it. It differs from AVERAGE in that the result is not affected as much by a single value that is greatly different from the others.

1 Click cell **B6**. In the **Function Library group**, click the **More Functions** button, display the list of **Statistical** functions, scroll down as necessary, and then click **MEDIAN**.

2 In the **Function Arguments** dialog box, to the right of the **Number 1** box, click the **Collapse Dialog** button 📇.

The dialog box collapses to a small size with space only for the first argument so you can see more of your data.

3 Select the range **D11:D65**, and then compare your screen with Figure 2.6.

When indicating which cells you want to use in the function's calculation—known as *defining the arguments*—you can either select the values with your mouse or type the range of values, whichever you prefer.

Figure 2.6

	A	B	C	D	E	F	G	H	I	J	K	L
40		95	43625 Orange Peel	8.19	4 oz.	Tin	Seasoning					
41		211	43633 Peppermint	5.65	4 oz.	Bottle	Extract					
42		244	43813 Marjoram	4.45	4 oz.	Jar	Herb					
43		168	44482 Garlic Powder	5.89	6 oz.	Jar	Seasoning					
44		75	44587 Tand	Function Arguments								
45		235	44589 Garli									
46		160	44879 Ging	D11:D65								
47		165	45265 Pickling Spice	6.49	2 oz.	Jar	Spice					
48		100	45688 Nutmeg	7.85	8 oz.	Jar	Spice					
49		265	46532 Oregano	10.19	8 oz.	Jar	Herb					
50		73	49652 Rojo Taco	5.29	4 oz.	Paper Envelope	Seasoning					
51		185	52164 Cloves, Whole	18.70	8 oz.	Jar	Spice					
52		165	53634 Vanilla, Double Strength	16.75	8 oz.	Bottle	Extract					
53		325	54635 Dill Weed	2.65	4 oz.	Paper Envelope	Herb					
54		195	55255 Sea Salt, Pacific	2.55	8 oz.	Tin	Seasoning					
55		312	56853 Peppercorns, Indian	4.59	2 oz.	Jar	Spice					
56		152	64525 Onion Powder	4.85	4 oz.	Jar	Seasoning					
57		215	78655 Garlic Salt	2.58	6 oz.	Jar	Seasoning					
58		540	85655 Peppercorns, Red	3.69	2 oz.	Tin	Spice					
59		225	92258 Vanilla	15.95	4 oz.	Bottle	Extract					
60		368	93157 Almond	7.33	4 oz.	Bottle	Extract					
61		285	93553 Lemon	24.90	6 oz.	Bottle	Extract					
62		126	94236 Cumin	3.55	4 oz.	Paper Envelope	Spice					
63		423	96854 Vanilla	31.95	6 oz.	Bottle	Extract					
64		325	98225 Orange	24.19	6 oz.	Bottle	Extract					
65		211	98655 Cloves, Ground	4.55	6 oz.	Jar	Spice					
66												

Formula Bar displays function and argument

Collapsed dialog box displays selected range

Selected range surrounded by moving border

Excel │ Chapter 2

Another Way

Press Enter to expand the dialog box.

4 At the right end of the collapsed dialog box, click the **Expand Dialog** button ⊡ to expand the dialog box to its original size, and then click **OK** to display *7.85*.

> In the range of prices, 7.85 is the middle value. Half of all flavor products are priced *above* 7.85 and half are priced *below* 7.85.

5 Scroll up to view **row 1**. Select the range **B5:B6** and right-click over the selection. On the Mini toolbar, click the **Accounting Number Format** button $ ·.

6 Right-click cell **B4**, and then on the Mini toolbar, click the **Comma Style** button ’ one time and the **Decrease Decimal** button ⤵ two times. Click **Save** ⊟ and compare your screen with Figure 2.7.

Figure 2.7

Comma Style applied with no decimal places

Accounting Number Format applied

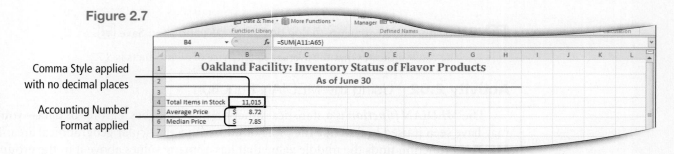

Activity 2.03 | Using the MIN and MAX Functions

The statistical *MIN function* determines the smallest value in a selected range of values. The statistical *MAX function* determines the largest value in a selected range of values.

1 In cell **A7**, type **Lowest Price** and then in cell **A8**, type **Highest Price**

2 Click cell **B7**. On the **Formulas tab**, in the **Function Library group**, click the **More Functions** button, display the list of **Statistical** functions, scroll as necessary, and then click **MIN**.

3 At the right end of the **Number1** box, click the **Collapse Dialog** button ⊞, select the range **D11:D65**, and then click the **Expand Dialog** button ⊡. Click **OK**.

> The lowest Retail Price is *2.55*.

4 Click cell **B8**, and then by using a similar technique, insert the **MAX** function to determine the highest **Retail Price**—*31.95*.

5 Select the range **B7:B8** and apply the **Accounting Number Format** $ ·, click **Save** ⊟, and then compare your screen with Figure 2.8.

Figure 2.8

MIN function calculates lowest price

MAX function calculates highest price

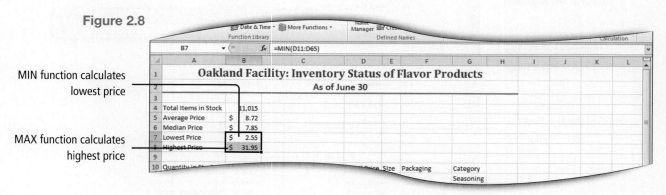

Objective 2 | Move Data, Resolve Error Messages, and Rotate Text

When you move a formula, the cell references within the formula do not change, no matter what type of cell reference you use.

If you move cells into a column that is not wide enough to display number values, Excel will display a message so that you can adjust as necessary.

You can reposition data within a cell at an angle by rotating the text.

Activity 2.04 | Moving Data and Resolving a # # # # # Error Message

1 Select the range **A4:B8**. Point to the right edge of the selected range to display the ⬚ pointer, and then compare your screen with Figure 2.9.

Figure 2.9

Move pointer

Selected range

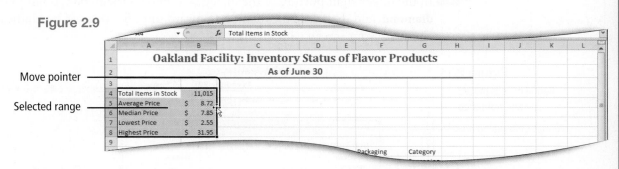

2 Drag the selected range to the right until the ScreenTip displays *D4:E8*, release the mouse button, and then notice that a series of # symbols displays in **column E**. Point to any of the cells that display # symbols, and then compare your screen with Figure 2.10.

Using this technique, cell contents can be moved from one location to another; this is referred to as *drag and drop*.

If a cell width is too narrow to display the entire number, Excel displays the ##### error, because displaying only a portion of a number would be misleading. The underlying values remain unchanged and are displayed in the Formula Bar for the selected cell. An underlying value also displays in the ScreenTip if you point to a cell containing # symbols.

Figure 2.10

ScreenTip indicates underlying value

Range moved to D4:E8

symbols display

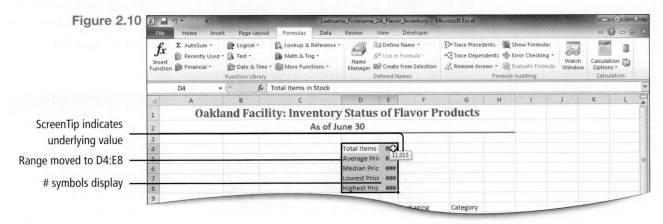

3 Select **column E** and widen it to **50** pixels, and notice that two cells are still not wide enough to display the cell contents.

4 In the **column heading area**, point to the right boundary of **column E** to display the ⊞ pointer. Double-click to AutoFit the column to accommodate the widest entry.

5 Using the same technique, AutoFit **column D** to accommodate the widest text entry.

6 Select the range **D4:E8**. On the **Home tab**, in the **Styles group**, display the **Cell Styles** gallery. Under **Themed Cell Styles**, click **20%-Accent1**. Click **Save** 🖫.

Activity 2.05 │ Rotating Text

Rotated text is useful to draw attention to data on your worksheet.

Another Way
Type the number of degrees directly into the Degrees box or use the spin box arrows to set the number.

1 In cell **C6**, type **Flavor Statistics** Select the range **C4:C8**, right-click over the selection, and then on the shortcut menu, click **Format Cells**. In the **Format Cells** dialog box, click the **Alignment tab**. Under **Text control**, select the **Merge cells** check box.

2 In the upper right portion of the dialog box, under **Orientation**, point to the **red diamond**, and then drag the diamond upward until the **Degrees** box indicates **30**. Compare your screen with Figure 2.11.

Figure 2.11

Range of cells moved and formatted

Format Cells dialog box

Orientation set to 30 degrees

Merge cells selected

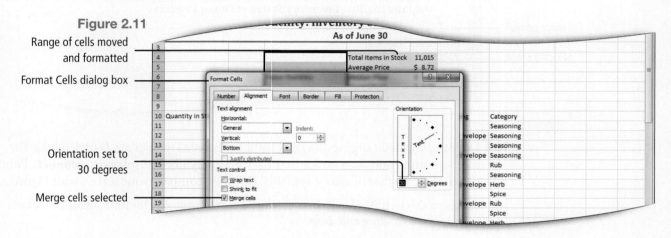

3 In the lower right corner of the **Format Cells** dialog box, click **OK**.

4 With the merged cell still selected, on the **Home tab**, in the **Font group**, change the **Font Size** 11 ▾ to **14**, and then apply **Bold** **B** and **Italic** **I**. Click the **Font Color arrow** **A** ▾, and then in the fourth column, click the first color—**Dark Blue, Text 2**.

5 In the **Alignment group**, apply **Align Text Right** 🖹. Click cell **A1**, **Save** 🖫 your workbook, and then compare your screen with Figure 2.12.

Figure 2.12

Text rotated and formatted

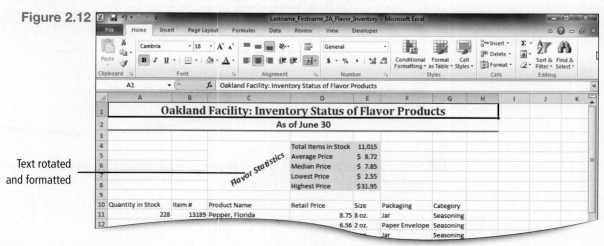

Objective 3 | Use COUNTIF and IF Functions and Apply Conditional Formatting

Recall that statistical functions analyze a group of measurements. Another group of Excel functions, referred to as *logical functions*, test for specific conditions. Logical functions typically use conditional tests to determine whether specified conditions—called *criteria*—are true or false.

Activity 2.06 | Using the COUNTIF Function

The *COUNTIF function* is a statistical function that counts the number of cells within a range that meet the given condition—the criteria that you provide. The COUNTIF function has two arguments—the range of cells to check and the criteria.

The seasonings of Laurales Herbs and Spices will be featured on an upcoming segment of a TV shopping channel. In this activity, you will use the COUNTIF function to determine the number of *seasoning* products currently available in inventory.

1 In the **row heading area**, point to **row 9** and right-click to select the row and display the shortcut menu. Click **Insert**, and then press [F4] two times to repeat the last action and thus insert three blank rows.

> [F4] is useful to repeat commands in Microsoft Office programs. Most commands can be repeated in this manner.

2 From the **row heading area**, select **rows 9:11**. On the **Home tab**, in the **Editing group**, click the **Clear** button ⌫, and then click **Clear Formats** to remove the blue accent color in columns D and E from the new rows.

> When you insert rows or columns, formatting from adjacent rows or columns repeats in the new cells.

3 Click cell **E4**, look at the **Formula Bar**, and then notice that the arguments of the **SUM** function adjusted and refer to the appropriate cells in rows 14:68.

> The referenced range updates to *A14:A68* after you insert the three new rows. In this manner, Excel adjusts the cell references in a formula relative to their new locations.

4 In cell **A10**, type **Seasoning Types:** and then press [Tab].

5 With cell **B10** as the active cell, on the **Formulas tab**, in the **Function Library group**, click the **More Functions** button, and then display the list of **Statistical** functions. Click **COUNTIF**.

> Recall that the COUNTIF function counts the number of cells within a range that meet the given condition.

6 In the **Range** box, click the **Collapse Dialog** button 🔲, select the range **G14:G68**, and then at the right end of the collapsed dialog box, click the **Expand Dialog** button 🔲. Click in the **Criteria** box, type **Seasoning** and then compare your screen with Figure 2.13.

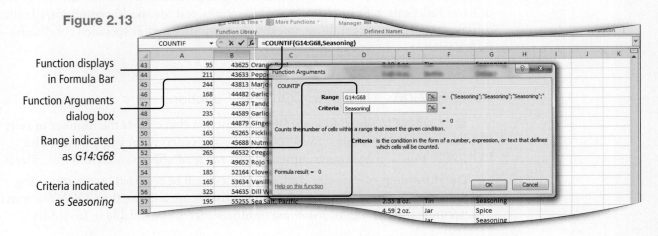

Figure 2.13

- Function displays in Formula Bar
- Function Arguments dialog box
- Range indicated as *G14:G68*
- Criteria indicated as *Seasoning*

7 In the lower right corner of the **Function Arguments** dialog box, click **OK**.

There are *20* different *Seasoning* products available to feature on the TV show.

8 On the **Home tab**, in the **Alignment group**, click **Align Text Left** 📄 to place the result closer to the row title. **Save** 💾 your workbook.

Activity 2.07 | Using the IF Function

A ***logical test*** is any value or expression that you can evaluate as being true or false. The ***IF function*** uses a logical test to check whether a condition is met, and then returns one value if true, and another value if false.

For example, *C14=228* is an expression that can be evaluated as true or false. If the value in cell C14 is equal to 228, the expression is true. If the value in cell C14 is not 228, the expression is false.

In this activity, you will use the IF function to determine the inventory levels and determine if more products should be ordered.

1 Click cell **H13**, type **Stock Level** and then press ⏎.

2 In cell **H14**, on the **Formulas tab**, in the **Function Library group**, click the **Logical** button, and then in the list, click **IF**. Drag the title bar of the **Function Arguments** dialog box up or down to view **row 14** on your screen.

3 With the insertion point in the **Logical_test** box, click cell **A14**, and then type **<125**

This logical test will look at the value in cell A14, which is *228*, and then determine if the number is less than 125. The expression *<125* includes the < ***comparison operator***, which means *less than*. Comparison operators compare values.

4 Examine the table in Figure 2.14 for a list of comparison operator symbols and their definitions.

Comparison Operators

Comparison Operator	Symbol Definition
=	Equal to
>	Greater than
<	Less than
>=	Greater than or equal to
<=	Less than or equal to
<>	Not equal to

Figure 2.14

5 Press Tab to move the insertion point to the **Value_if_true** box, and then type **Order**

> If the result of the logical test is true—the Quantity in Stock is less than 125—cell H14 will display the text *Order* indicating that additional product must be ordered.

6 Click in the **Value_if_false** box, type **OK** and then compare your dialog box with Figure 2.15.

> If the result of the logical test is false—the Quantity in Stock is *not* less than 125—then Excel will display *OK* in the cell.

Figure 2.15

Logical test will determine if value in A14 is less than 125

Value if true (less than 125) will indicate *Order*

Value if false (125 or more) will indicate *OK*

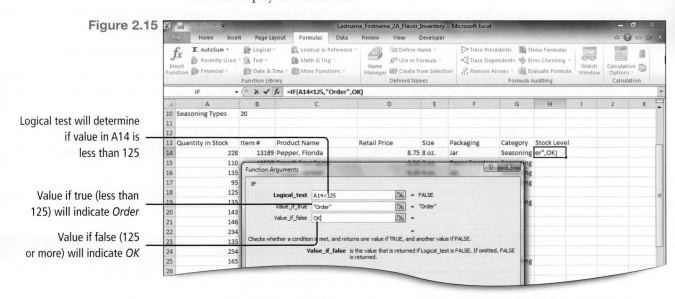

7 Click **OK** to display the result *OK* in cell **H14**.

8 Using the fill handle, copy the function in cell **H14** down through cell **H68**. Then scroll as necessary to view cell **A18**, which indicates *125*. Look at cell **H18** and notice that the **Stock Level** is indicated as *OK*. **Save** your workbook. Compare your screen with Figure 2.16.

> The comparison operator indicated <125 (less than 125) and thus a value of *exactly* 125 is indicated as OK.

Figure 2.16

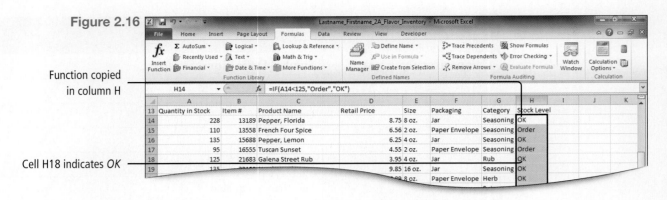

Function copied
in column H

Cell H18 indicates *OK*

Activity 2.08 | Applying Conditional Formatting by Using Highlight Cells Rules and Data Bars

A *conditional format* changes the appearance of a cell based on a condition—a criteria. If the condition is true, the cell is formatted based on that condition; if the condition is false, the cell is *not* formatted. In this activity, you will use conditional formatting as another way to draw attention to the Stock Level of products.

1 Be sure the range **H14:H68** is selected. On the **Home tab**, in the **Styles group**, click the **Conditional Formatting** button. In the list, point to **Highlight Cells Rules**, and then click **Text that Contains**.

2 In the **Text That Contains** dialog box, with the insertion point blinking in the first box, type **Order** and notice that in the selected range, the text *Order* displays with the default format—Light Red Fill with Dark Red Text.

3 In the second box, click the **arrow**, and then in the list, click **Custom Format**.

Here, in the Format Cells dialog box, you can select any combination of formats to apply to the cell if the condition is true. The custom format you specify will be applied to any cell in the selected range if it contains the text *Order*.

4 On the **Font tab**, under **Font style**, click **Bold Italic**. Click the **Color arrow**, and then under **Theme Colors**, in the sixth column, click the first color—**Red, Accent 2**. Click **OK**. Compare your screen with Figure 2.17.

In the range, if the cell meets the condition of containing *Order*, the font color will change to Bold Italic, Red, Accent 2.

Figure 2.17

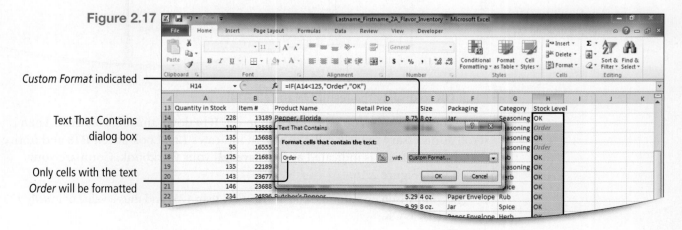

Custom Format indicated

Text That Contains
dialog box

Only cells with the text
Order will be formatted

5 In the **Text That Contains** dialog box, click **OK**.

6 Select the range **A14:A68**. In the **Styles group**, click the **Conditional Formatting** button. Point to **Data Bars**, and then under **Gradient Fill**, click **Orange Data Bar**. Click anywhere to cancel the selection; click 🖫. Compare your screen with Figure 2.18.

> A *data bar* provides a visual cue to the reader about the value of a cell relative to other cells. The length of the data bar represents the value in the cell. A longer bar represents a higher value and a shorter bar represents a lower value. Data bars are useful for identifying higher and lower numbers quickly within a large group of data, such as very high or very low levels of inventory.

Figure 2.18

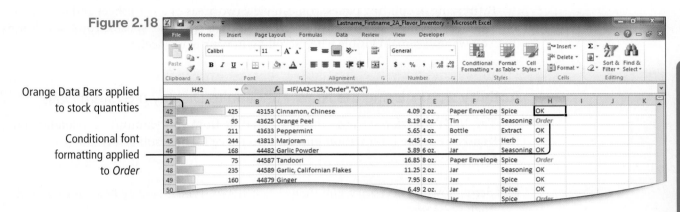

Orange Data Bars applied to stock quantities

Conditional font formatting applied to *Order*

Activity 2.09 | Using Find and Replace

The *Find and Replace* feature searches the cells in a worksheet—or in a selected range—for matches, and then replaces each match with a replacement value of your choice.

Comments from customers on the company's blog indicate that, for dried herbs and seasonings, customers prefer a sealable foil packet rather than a paper envelope. Thus, all products of this type have been repackaged. In this activity, you will replace all occurrences of *Paper Envelope* with *Foil Packet*.

1 Select the range **F14:F68**.

> Restrict the find and replace operation to a specific range in this manner, especially if there is a possibility that the name occurs elsewhere.

2 On the **Home tab**, in the **Editing group**, click the **Find & Select** button, and then click **Replace**.

3 Type **Paper Envelope** to fill in the **Find what** box. In the **Replace with** box, type **Foil Packet** and then compare your screen with Figure 2.19.

Figure 2.19

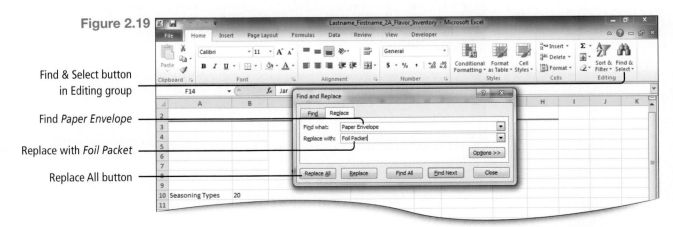

Find & Select button in Editing group

Find *Paper Envelope*

Replace with *Foil Packet*

Replace All button

Excel | Chapter 2

4 Click the **Replace All** button. In the message box, notice that 19 replacements were made, and then click **OK**. In the lower right corner of the **Find and Replace** dialog box, click the **Close** button. Click **Save** 🔲.

Objective 4 | Use Date & Time Functions and Freeze Panes

Excel can obtain the date and time from your computer's calendar and clock and display this information on your worksheet.

By freezing or splitting panes, you can view two areas of a worksheet and lock rows and columns in one area. When you freeze panes, you select the specific rows or columns that you want to remain visible when scrolling in your worksheet.

Activity 2.10 | Using the NOW Function to Display a System Date

The *NOW function* retrieves the date and time from your computer's calendar and clock and inserts the information into the selected cell. The result is formatted as a date and time.

1 Scroll down as necessary, and then click cell **A70**. Type **Edited by Frank Barnes** and then press Enter.

2 With cell **A71** as the active cell, on the **Formulas tab**, in the **Function Library group**, click the **Date & Time** button. In the list of functions, click **NOW**. Compare your screen with Figure 2.20.

Figure 2.20

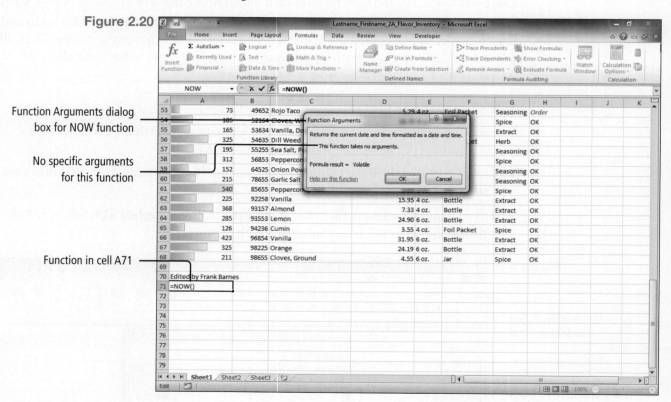

Function Arguments dialog box for NOW function

No specific arguments for this function

Function in cell A71

3 Read the description in the **Function Arguments** dialog box, and notice that this result is *Volatile*.

> The Function Arguments dialog box displays a message indicating that this function does not require an argument. It also states that this function is ***volatile***, meaning the date and time will not remain as entered, but rather the date and time will automatically update each time you open this workbook.

4 In the **Function Arguments** dialog box, click **OK** to close the dialog box to display the current date and time in cell **A71**. **Save** 🔲 your workbook.

More Knowledge | NOW Function Recalculates Each Time a Workbook Opens

The NOW function updates each time the workbook is opened. With the workbook open, you can force the NOW function to update by pressing F9 , for example, to update the time.

Activity 2.11 | Freezing and Unfreezing Panes

In a large worksheet, if you scroll down more than 25 rows or scroll beyond column O (the exact row number and column letter varies, depending on your screen resolution), you will no longer see the top rows or first column of your worksheet where identifying information about the data is usually placed. You will find it easier to work with your data if you can always view the identifying row or column titles.

The ***Freeze Panes*** command enables you to select one or more rows or columns and then freeze (lock) them into place. The locked rows and columns become separate panes. A ***pane*** is a portion of a worksheet window bounded by and separated from other portions by vertical or horizontal bars.

1 Press Ctrl + Home to make cell **A1** the active cell. Scroll down until **row 40** displays at the top of your Excel window, and notice that all of the identifying information in the column titles is out of view.

2 Press Ctrl + Home again, and then from the **row heading area**, select **row 14**. Click the **View tab**, and then in the **Window group**, click the **Freeze Panes** button. In the list, click **Freeze Panes**. Click any cell to deselect the row, and then notice that a line displays along the upper border of **row 14**.

> By selecting row 14, the rows above—rows 1 - 13—are frozen in place and will not move as you scroll down.

3 Watch the row numbers below **row 13**, and then begin to scroll down to bring **row 40** into view again. Notice that rows 1:13 are frozen in place. Compare your screen with Figure 2.21.

> The remaining rows of data continue to scroll. Use this feature when you have long or wide worksheets.

Figure 2.21

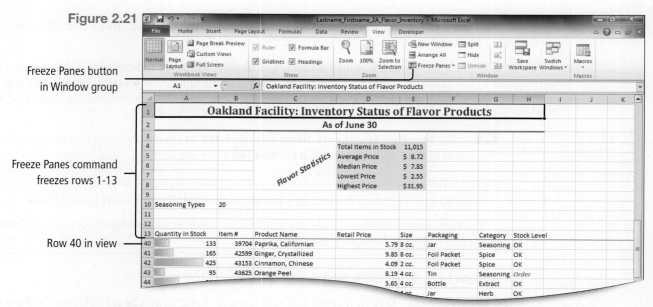

Freeze Panes button in Window group

Freeze Panes command freezes rows 1-13

Row 40 in view

4 In the **Window group**, click the **Freeze Panes** button, and then click **Unfreeze Panes** to unlock all rows and columns. **Save** 💾 your workbook.

> **More Knowledge** | Freeze Columns or Freeze both Rows and Columns
>
> You can freeze columns that you want to remain in view on the left. Select the column to the right of the column(s) that you want to remain in view while scrolling to the right, and then click the Freeze Panes command. You can also use the command to freeze both rows and columns; click a *cell* to freeze the rows *above* the cell and the columns to the *left* of the cell.

Objective 5 | Create, Sort, and Filter an Excel Table

To analyze a group of related data, you can convert a range of cells to an *Excel table*. An Excel table is a series of rows and columns that contains related data that is managed independently from the data in other rows and columns in the worksheet.

Activity 2.12 | Creating an Excel Table

1 Be sure that you have applied the Unfreeze Panes command—no rows on your worksheet are locked. Then, click any cell in the data below row 13.

> **Another Way**
>
> Select the range of cells that make up the table, including the header row, and then click the Table button.

2 Click the **Insert tab**. In the **Tables group**, click the **Table** button. In the **Create Table** dialog box, if necessary, click to select the **My table has headers** check box, and then compare your screen with Figure 2.22.

The column titles in row 13 will form the table headers. By clicking in a range of contiguous data, Excel will suggest the range as the data for the table. You can adjust the range if necessary.

Figure 2.22

Moving border surrounds range

Column titles will form table headers

Create Table dialog box

Range of data selected

Check box selected

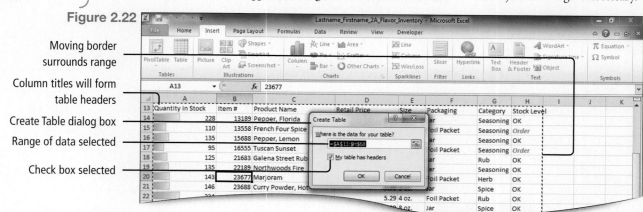

3 Click **OK**. With the range still selected, on the Ribbon notice that the **Table Tools** are active.

4 On the **Design tab**, in the **Table Styles group**, click the **More** button ⊡, and then under **Light**, locate and click **Table Style Light 16**.

5 Press Ctrl + Home. Click **Save** 🖫, and then compare your screen with Figure 2.23.

Sorting and filtering arrows display in the table's header row.

Figure 2.23

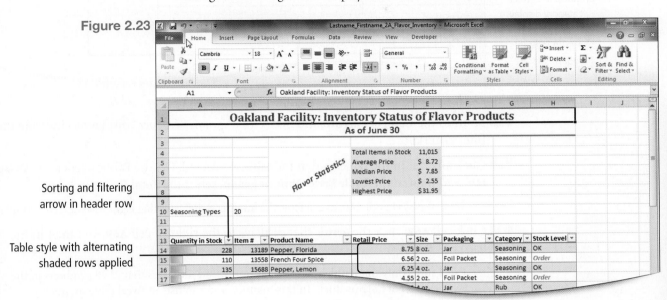

Sorting and filtering arrow in header row

Table style with alternating shaded rows applied

Activity 2.13 | Sorting and Filtering an Excel Table

You can *sort* tables—arrange all the data in a specific order—in ascending or descending order. You can *filter* tables—display only a portion of the data based on matching a specific value—to show only the data that meets the criteria that you specify.

1 In the header row of the table, click the **Retail Price arrow**, and then on the menu, click **Sort Smallest to Largest**. Next to the arrow, notice the small **up arrow** indicating an ascending (smallest to largest) sort.

The rows in the table are sorted from the lowest retail price to highest retail price.

2 In the table's header row, click the **Category arrow**. On the menu, click **Sort A to Z**. Next to the arrow, notice the small **up arrow** indicating an ascending (A to Z) sort.

The rows in the table are sorted alphabetically by Category.

3 Click the **Category arrow** again, and then sort from **Z to A**.

The rows in the table are sorted in reverse alphabetic order by Category name, and the small arrow points downward, indicating a descending (Z to A) sort.

4 Click the **Category arrow** again. On the menu, click the **(Select All)** check box to clear all the check boxes. Click to select only the **Extract** check box, and then click **OK**. Compare your screen with Figure 2.24.

Only the rows containing *Extract* in the Category column display—the remaining rows are hidden from view. A small funnel—the filter icon—indicates that a filter is applied to the data in the table. Additionally, the row numbers display in blue to indicate that some rows are hidden from view. A filter hides entire rows in the worksheet.

Figure 2.24

Funnel indicates
filter applied

Blue row numbers indicate
some rows hidden

Only products in *Extract*
category display

ScreenTip indicates
Equals "Extract"

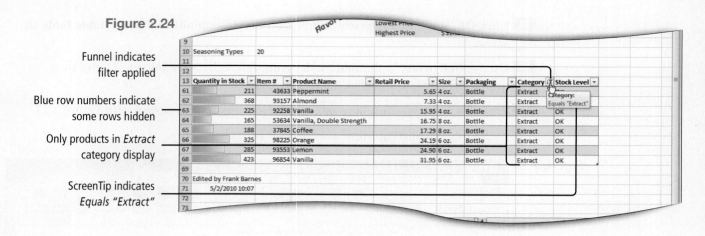

5 Point to the **Category arrow**, and notice that *Equals "Extract"* displays to indicate the filter criteria.

6 Click any cell in the table so that the table is selected. On the Ribbon, click the **Design tab**, and then in the **Table Style Options group**, select the **Total Row** check box.

Total displays in cell A69. In cell H69, the number *8* indicates that eight rows currently display.

7 Click cell **A69**, click the **arrow** that displays to the right of cell **A69**, and then in the list, click **Sum**.

Excel sums only the visible rows in Column A, and indicates that 2190 products in the Extract category are in stock. In this manner, you can use an Excel table to quickly find information about a group of data.

8 Click cell **A11**, type **Extract Types:** and press [Tab]. In cell **B11**, type **8 (2,190 total items in stock)** and then press [Enter].

9 In the table header row, click the **Category arrow**, and then on the menu, click **Clear Filter From "Category"**.

All the rows in the table redisplay. The Z to A sort on Category remains in effect.

10 Click the **Packaging arrow**, click the (**Select All**) check box to clear all the check boxes, and then click to select the **Foil Packet** check box. Click **OK**.

11 Click the **Category arrow**, click the (**Select All**) check box to clear all the check boxes, and then click the **Herb** check box. Click **OK**, and then compare your screen with Figure 2.25.

By applying multiple filters, Laura can quickly determine that seven items in the Herb category are packaged in foil packets with a total of 1,346 such items in stock.

Figure 2.25

Seven items in *Herb*
category are packaged
in *Foil Packets*

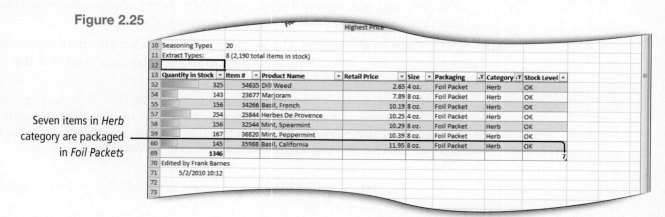

12 Click the **Category arrow**, and then click **Clear Filter From "Category"**. Use the same technique to remove the filter from the **Packaging** column.

13 In the table header row, click the **Item# arrow**, and then click **Sort Smallest to Largest**, which will apply an ascending sort to the data using the *Item#* column. **Save** 💾 your workbook.

Activity 2.14 | Converting a Table to a Range of Data

When you are finished answering questions about the data in a table by sorting, filtering, and totaling, you can convert the table into a normal range. Doing so is useful if you want to use the feature only to apply an attractive Table Style to a range of cells. For example, you can insert a table, apply a Table Style, and then convert the table to a normal range of data but keep the formatting.

> **Another Way**
>
> With any table cell selected, right-click, point to Table, and then click Convert to Range.

1 Click anywhere in the table to activate the table and display the **Table Tools** on the Ribbon. On the **Design tab**, in the **Table Style Options group**, click the **Total Row** check box to clear the check mark and remove the Total row from the table.

2 On the **Design tab**, in the **Tools group**, click the **Convert to Range** button. In the message box, click **Yes**. Click **Save** 💾, and then compare your screen with Figure 2.26.

Figure 2.26

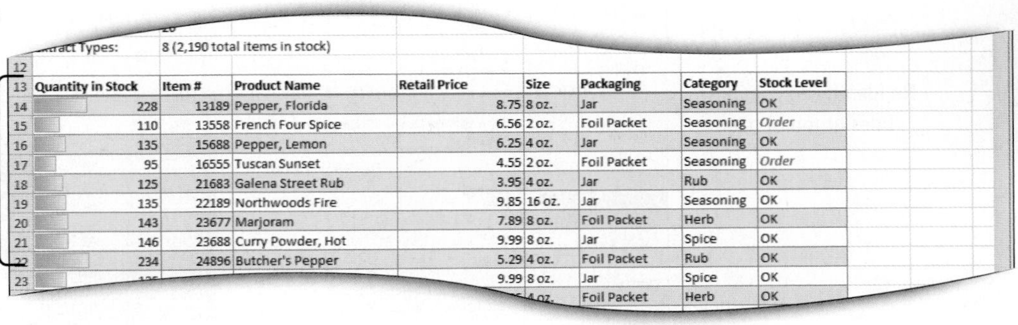

Table converted to a normal range, color and shading formats remain

Quantity in Stock	Item #	Product Name	Retail Price	Size	Packaging	Category	Stock Level
		tract Types:	8 (2,190 total items in stock)				
228	13189	Pepper, Florida	8.75	8 oz.	Jar	Seasoning	OK
110	13558	French Four Spice	6.56	2 oz.	Foil Packet	Seasoning	*Order*
135	15688	Pepper, Lemon	6.25	4 oz.	Jar	Seasoning	OK
95	16555	Tuscan Sunset	4.55	2 oz.	Foil Packet	Seasoning	*Order*
125	21683	Galena Street Rub	3.95	4 oz.	Jar	Rub	OK
135	22189	Northwoods Fire	9.85	16 oz.	Jar	Seasoning	OK
143	23677	Marjoram	7.89	8 oz.	Foil Packet	Herb	OK
146	23688	Curry Powder, Hot	9.99	8 oz.	Jar	Spice	OK
234	24896	Butcher's Pepper	5.29	4 oz.	Foil Packet	Rub	OK
			9.99	8 oz.	Jar	Spice	OK
				4 oz.	Foil Packet	Herb	OK

Objective 6 | Format and Print a Large Worksheet

A worksheet might be too wide, too long—or both—to print on a single page. Use Excel's *Print Titles* and *Scale to Fit* commands to create pages that are attractive and easy to read.

The Print Titles command enables you to specify rows and columns to repeat on each printed page. Scale to Fit commands enable you to stretch or shrink the width, height, or both, of printed output to fit a maximum number of pages.

Activity 2.15 | Printing Titles and Scaling to Fit

1 Press Ctrl + Home to display the top of your worksheet. Select the range **A13:H13**. On the **Home tab**, from the **Styles group**, apply the **Heading 4** cell style, and then apply **Center** ≡.

2 On the **Insert tab**, in the **Text group**, click **Header & Footer**. In the **Navigation group**, click the **Go to Footer** button, and then click just above the word *Footer*.

3 In the **Header & Footer Elements group**, click the **File Name** button to add the name of your file to the footer—&[File] displays. Then, click in a cell just above the footer to exit the Footer and view your file name.

4 Delete the unused sheets **Sheet2** and **Sheet3**. On the right edge of the status bar, click the **Normal** button 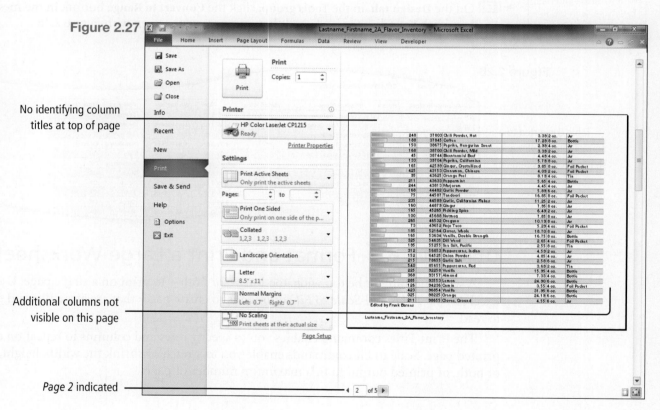, and then press [Ctrl] + [Home] to display the top of your worksheet.

> Dotted lines indicate where the pages would break if printed as currently formatted; these dotted lines display when you switch from Page Layout view to Normal view.

5 On the **Page Layout tab**, in the **Themes group**, click the **Themes** button, and then click **Concourse**.

6 In the **Page Setup group**, click **Margins**, and then at the bottom, click **Custom Margins**. In the **Page Setup** dialog box, under **Center on page**, select the **Horizontally** check box, and then click **OK**.

7 In the **Page Setup group**, click **Orientation**, and then click **Landscape**. Press [Ctrl] + [F2] to display the **Print Preview**. At the bottom of the **Print Preview**, click the **Next Page** button [▶]. Compare your screen with Figure 2.27.

> As currently formatted, the worksheet will print on five pages, and the columns will span multiple pages. Additionally, after Page 1, no column titles are visible to identify the data in the columns.

Figure 2.27

No identifying column titles at top of page

Additional columns not visible on this page

Page 2 indicated

8 Click **Next Page** ▶ two times to display **Page 4**, and notice that two columns move to an additional page.

9 On the Ribbon, click **Page Layout** to redisplay the worksheet. In the **Page Setup group**, click the **Print Titles** button. Under **Print titles**, click in the **Rows to repeat at top** box, and then at the right, click the **Collapse Dialog** button 🔳.

10 From the **row heading area**, select **row 13**, and then click the **Expand Dialog** button 🔲. Click **OK** to print the column titles in row 13 at the top of every page.

Adding the titles on each page increases the number of pages to 6.

Another Way

With the worksheet displayed, on the Page Layout tab, in the Scale to Fit group, click the Width button arrow, and then click 1 page.

11 Press `Ctrl` + `F2` to display the **Print Preview**. In the center panel, at the bottom of the **Settings group**, click the **Scaling** button, and then on the displayed list, point to **Fit All Columns on One Page**. Compare your screen with Figure 2.28.

This action will shrink the width of the printed output to fit all the columns on one page. You can make adjustments like this on the Page Layout tab, or here, in the Print Preview.

Figure 2.28

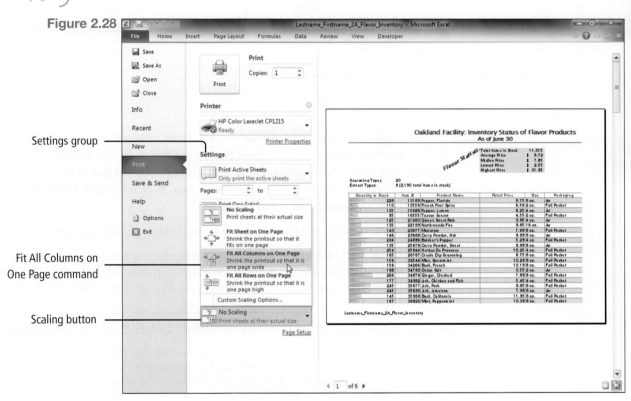

Settings group
Fit All Columns on One Page command
Scaling button

12 Click **Fit All Columns on One Page**. Notice in the **Print Preview** that all the columns display on one page.

13 At the bottom of the **Print Preview**, click the **Next Page** button ▶ one time. Notice that the output will now print on two pages and that the column titles display at the top of **Page 2**. Compare your screen with Figure 2.29.

Figure 2.29

Column titles display
on Page 2

Page 2 of 2 indicated

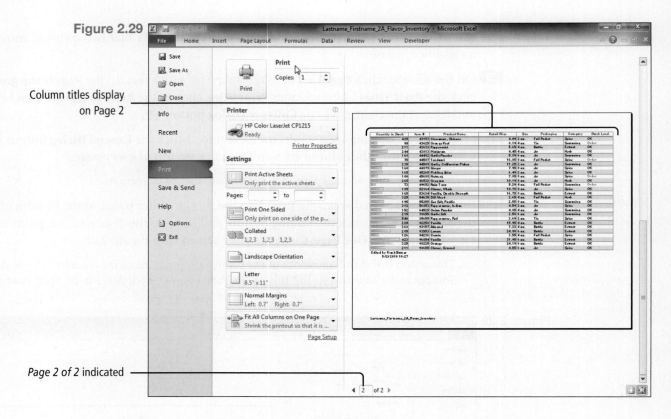

14 In **Backstage** view, click the **Info tab**. On the right, under the document thumbnail, click **Properties**, and then click **Show Document Panel**. In the **Author** box, replace the existing text with your firstname and lastname. In the **Subject** box, type your course name and section number. In the **Keywords** box, type **inventory, Oakland** and then **Close** ⊠ the **Document Information Panel**.

15 **Save** your workbook, and then print or submit electronically as directed.

16 If required by your instructor, print or create an electronic version of your worksheets with formulas displayed by using the instructions in Activity 1.16, and then **Close** ⊠ Excel without saving so that you do not save the changes you made to print formulas.

More Knowledge | Scaling for Data that is Slightly Larger than the Printed Page

If your data is just a little too large to fit on a printed page, you can scale the worksheet to make it fit. Scaling reduces both the width and height of the printed data to a percentage of its original size or by the number of pages that you specify. To adjust the printed output to a percentage of its actual size, for example to 80%, on the Page Layout tab, in the Scale to Fit group, click the Scale arrows to select a percentage.

End **You have completed Project 2A** —————————

Project 2B Weekly Sales Summary

Project Activities

In Activities 2.16 through 2.26, you will edit an existing workbook for Laura Morales. The workbook summarizes the online and in-store sales of products during a one-week period in July. The worksheets of your completed workbook will look similar to Figure 2.30.

Project Files

For Project 2B, you will need the following file:

e02B_Weekly_Sales

You will save your workbook as:

Lastname_Firstname_2B_Weekly_Sales

Project Results

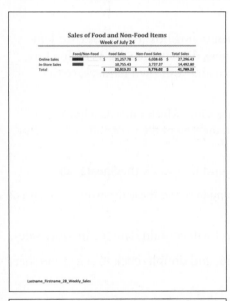

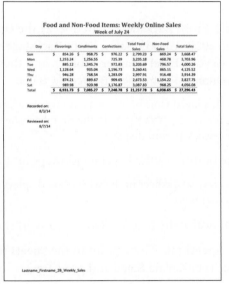

Figure 2.30
Project 2B Weekly Sales

Objective 7 | Navigate a Workbook and Rename Worksheets

Use multiple worksheets in a workbook to organize data in a logical arrangement. When you have more than one worksheet in a workbook, you can *navigate* (move) among worksheets by clicking the *sheet tabs*. Sheet tabs identify each worksheet in a workbook and are located along the lower left edge of the workbook window. When you have more worksheets in the workbook than can be displayed in the sheet tab area, use the four sheet tab scrolling buttons to move sheet tabs into and out of view.

Activity 2.16 | Navigating Among Worksheets, Renaming Worksheets, and Changing the Tab Color of Worksheets

Excel names the first worksheet in a workbook *Sheet1* and each additional worksheet in order—*Sheet2*, *Sheet3*, and so on. Most Excel users rename the worksheets with meaningful names. In this activity, you will navigate among worksheets, rename worksheets, and change the tab color of sheet tabs.

> **Another Way**
>
> Press [Ctrl] + [F12] to display the Open dialog box. Press [F12] to display the Save As dialog box.

1 **Start** Excel. From **Backstage** view, display the **Open** dialog box. From your student files, open **e02B_Weekly_Sales**. From **Backstage** view, display the **Save As** dialog box, navigate to your **Excel Chapter 2** folder, and then using your own name, save the file as **Lastname_Firstname_2B_Weekly_Sales**

In the displayed workbook, there are two worksheets into which some data has already been entered. For example, on the first worksheet, the days of the week and sales data for the one-week period displays.

2 Along the bottom of the Excel window, point to and then click the **Sheet2 tab**.

The second worksheet in the workbook displays and becomes the active worksheet. *Sheet2* displays in bold.

3 In cell **A1**, notice the text *In-Store*—this worksheet will contain data for in-store sales.

4 Click the **Sheet1 tab**. Then, point to the **Sheet1 tab**, and double-click to select the sheet tab name. Type **Online Sales** and press [Enter].

The first worksheet becomes the active worksheet, and the sheet tab displays *Online Sales*.

5 Point to the **Sheet2 tab**, right-click, and then from the shortcut menu, click **Rename**. Type **In-Store Sales** and press [Enter]. Compare your screen with Figure 2.31.

You can use either of these methods to rename a sheet tab.

Figure 2.31

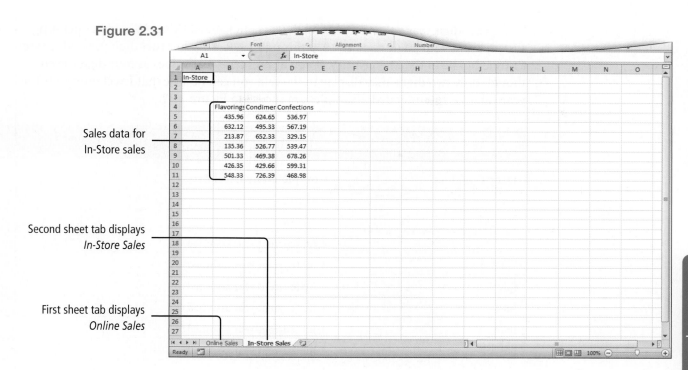

Sales data for
In-Store sales

Second sheet tab displays
In-Store Sales

First sheet tab displays
Online Sales

Excel | Chapter 2

Another Way

Alternatively, on the
Home tab, in the Cells
group, click the Format
button, and then on the
displayed list, point to
Tab Color.

6 Point to the **In-Store Sales sheet tab** and right-click. On the shortcut menu, point to **Tab Color**, and then in the last column, click the first color—**Orange, Accent 6**.

7 Using the technique you just practiced, change the tab color of the **Online Sales sheet tab** to **Aqua, Accent 5**—in the next to last column, the first color. **Save** your workbook.

Objective 8 | Enter Dates, Clear Contents, and Clear Formats

Dates represent a type of value that you can enter in a cell. When you enter a date, Excel assigns a serial value—a number—to the date. This makes it possible to treat dates like other numbers. For example, if two cells contain dates, you can find the number of days between the two dates by subtracting the older date from the more recent date.

Activity 2.17 | Entering and Formatting Dates

In this activity, you will examine the various ways that Excel can format dates in a cell. Date values entered in any of the following formats will be recognized by Excel as a date:

Format	Example
m/d/yy	7/4/12
d-mmm	4-Jul
d-mmm-yy	4-Jul-12
mmm-yy	Jul-12

On your keyboard, - (the hyphen key) and / (the forward slash key) function identically in any of these formats and can be used interchangeably. You can abbreviate the month name to three characters or spell it out. You can enter the year as two digits, four digits, or even leave it off. When left off, the current year is assumed but does not display in the cell.

A two-digit year value of 30 through 99 is interpreted by the Windows operating system as the four-digit years of 1930 through 1999. All other two-digit year values are assumed to be in the 21st century. If you always type year values as four digits, even though only two digits may display in the cell, you can be sure that Excel interprets the year value as you intended. Examples are shown in Figure 2.32.

How Excel Interprets Dates

Date Typed As:	Completed by Excel As:
7/4/12	7/4/2012
7-4-98	7/4/1998
7/4	4-Jul (current year assumed)
7-4	4-Jul (current year assumed)
July 4	4-Jul (current year assumed)
Jul 4	4-Jul (current year assumed)
Jul/4	4-Jul (current year assumed)
Jul-4	4-Jul (current year assumed)
July 4, 1998	4-Jul-98
July 2012	Jul-12 (first day of month assumed)
July 1998	Jul-98 (first day of month assumed)

Figure 2.32

1 On the **Online Sales** sheet, click cell **A16** and notice that the cell indicates *8/3* (August 3). In the **Formula Bar**, notice that the full date of August 3, 2014 displays in the format *8/3/2014*.

2 With cell **A16** selected, on the **Home tab**, in the **Number group**, click the **Number Format arrow**. At the bottom of the menu, click **More Number Formats** to display the **Number tab** of the **Format Cells** dialog box.

Under Category, *Date* is selected, and under Type, *3/14* is selected. Cell A16 uses this format type; that is, only the month and day display in the cell.

3 In the displayed dialog box, under **Type**, click several other date types and watch the **Sample** area to see how applying the selected date format would format your cell. When you are finished, click the **3/14/01** type, and then compare your screen with Figure 2.33.

Figure 2.33

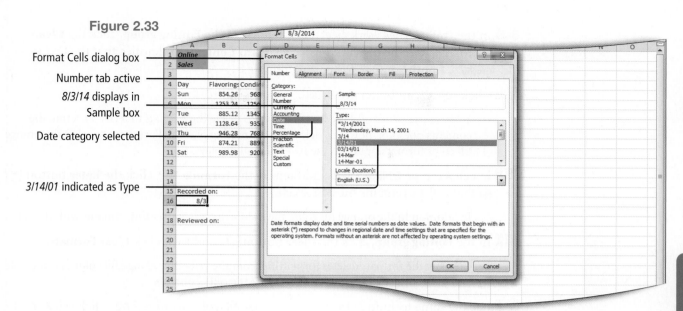

Format Cells dialog box

Number tab active

8/3/14 displays in Sample box

Date category selected

3/14/01 indicated as Type

---

4 At the bottom of the dialog box, click **OK**. Click cell **A19**, type **8-7-14** and then press Enter.

Cell A19 has no special date formatting applied, and thus displays in the default date format *8/7/2014*.

> **Alert!** | **The Date Does Not Display as 8/7/2014?**
>
> Settings in your Windows operating system determine the default format for dates. If your result is different, it is likely that the formatting of the default date was adjusted on the computer at which you are working.

---

5 Click cell **A19** again. Hold down Ctrl and press ; (semicolon) on your keyboard. Press Enter to confirm the entry.

Excel enters the current date, obtained from your computer's internal calendar, in the selected cell using the default date format. Ctrl + ; is a quick method to enter the current date.

6 Click cell **A19** again, type **8/7/14** and then press Enter.

Because the year *14* is less than 30, Excel assumes a 21st century date and changes *14* to *2014* to complete the four-digit year. Typing *98* would result in *1998*. For two-digit years that you type that are between 30 and 99, Excel assumes a 20th century date.

7 Click cell **A16**, and then on the **Home tab**, in the **Clipboard group**, click the **Format Painter** button. Click cell **A19**, and notice that the date format from cell **A16** is copied to cell **A19**. **Save** your workbook.

Activity 2.18 | Clearing Cell Contents and Formats

A cell has *contents*—a value or a formula—and a cell may also have one or more *formats* applied, for example bold and italic font styles, fill color, font color, and so on. You can choose to clear—delete—the *contents* of a cell, the *formatting* of a cell, or both.

Clearing the contents of a cell deletes the value or formula typed there, but it does *not* clear formatting applied to a cell. In this activity, you will clear the contents of a cell and then clear the formatting of a cell that contains a date to see its underlying content.

1 In the **Online Sales** worksheet, click cell **A1**. In the **Editing group**, click the **Clear** button ⊘. On the displayed list, click **Clear Contents** and notice that the text is cleared, but the orange formatting remains.

2 Click cell **A2**, and then press Del.

You can use either of these two methods to delete the *contents* of a cell. Deleting the contents does not, however, delete the formatting of the cell; you can see that the orange fill color format applied to the two cells still displays.

3 In cell **A1**, type **Online Sales** and then on the **Formula Bar**, click the **Enter** button ✓ so that cell **A1** remains the active cell.

In addition to the orange fill color, the bold italic text formatting remains with the cell.

4 In the **Editing group**, click the **Clear** button ⊘, and then click **Clear Formats**.

Clearing the formats deletes formatting from the cell—the orange fill color and the bold and italic font styles—but does not delete the cell's contents.

5 Use the same technique to clear the orange fill color from cell **A2**. Click cell **A16**, click the **Clear** button ⊘, and then click **Clear Formats**. In the **Number group**, notice that *General* displays as the number format of the cell.

The box in the Number group indicates the current Number format of the selected cell. Clearing the date formatting from the cell displays the date's serial number. The date, August 3, 2014, is stored as a serial number that indicates the number of days since January 1, 1900. This date is the 41,854th day since the reference date of January 1, 1900.

6 On the Quick Access Toolbar, click the **Undo** button ↺ to restore the date format. **Save** 💾 your workbook, and then compare your screen with Figure 2.34.

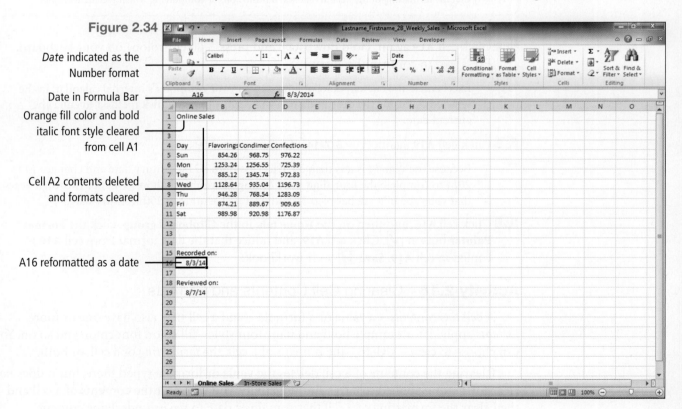

Figure 2.34

Date indicated as the Number format

Date in Formula Bar

Orange fill color and bold italic font style cleared from cell A1

Cell A2 contents deleted and formats cleared

A16 reformatted as a date

Objective 9 | Copy and Paste by Using the Paste Options Gallery

Data in cells can be copied to other cells in the same worksheet, to other sheets in the same workbook, or to sheets in another workbook. The action of placing cell contents that have been copied or moved to the Office Clipboard into another location is called *paste*.

Activity 2.19 | Copying and Pasting by Using the Paste Options Gallery

Recall that the Office Clipboard is a temporary storage area maintained by your Windows operating system. When you select one or more cells, and then perform the Copy command or the Cut command, the selected data is placed on the Office Clipboard. From the Office Clipboard storage area, the data is available for pasting into other cells, other worksheets, other workbooks, and even into other Office programs. When you paste, the *Paste Options gallery* displays, which includes Live Preview to preview the Paste formatting that you want.

1 With the **Online Sales** worksheet active, select the range **A4:A19**.

A range of cells identical to this one is required for the *In-Store Sales* worksheet.

Another Way

Use the keyboard shortcut for Copy, which is Ctrl + C; or click the Copy button in the Clipboard group on the Home tab.

2 Right-click over the selection, and then click **Copy** to place a copy of the cells on the Office Clipboard. Notice that the copied cells display a moving border.

3 At the bottom of the workbook window, click the **In-Store Sales sheet tab** to make it the active worksheet. Point to cell **A4**, right-click, and then on the shortcut menu, under **Paste Options**, *point* to the first button—**Paste**. Compare your screen with Figure 2.35.

Live Preview displays how the copied cells will be placed in the worksheet if you click the Paste button. In this manner, you can experiment with different paste options, and then be sure you are selecting the paste operation that you want. When pasting a range of cells, you need only point to or select the cell in the upper left corner of the *paste area*—the target destination for data that has been cut or copied using the Office Clipboard.

Figure 2.35

Paste Options (6 option buttons)

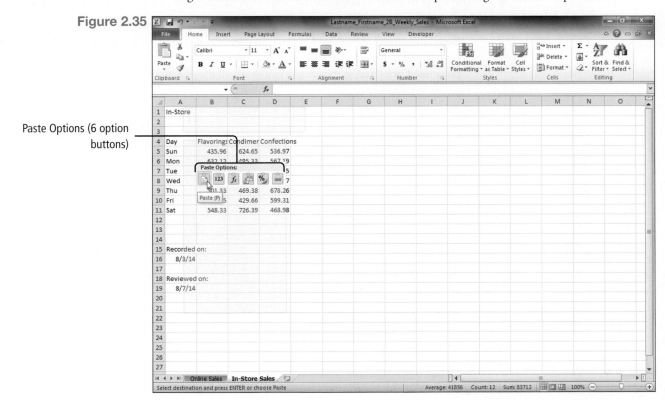

4 Click the first button, **Paste**. In the status bar, notice that the message still displays, indicating that your selected range remains available on the Office Clipboard.

5 Display the **Online Sales** worksheet. Press Esc to cancel the moving border. **Save** 🖫 your workbook.

The status bar no longer displays the message.

Note | Pressing Enter to Complete a Paste Action

If you want to paste the same text more than one time, click the Paste button so that the copied text remains available on the Office Clipboard. Otherwise, you can press Enter to complete the Paste command.

Objective 10 | Edit and Format Multiple Worksheets at the Same Time

You can enter or edit data on several worksheets at the same time by selecting and grouping multiple worksheets. Data that you enter or edit on the active sheet is reflected in all selected sheets. If you apply color to the sheet tabs, the name of the sheet tab will be underlined in the color you selected. If the sheet tab displays with a background color, you know the sheet is not selected.

Activity 2.20 | Grouping Worksheets for Editing

In this activity, you will group the two worksheets, and then format both worksheets at the same time.

1 With the **Online Sales** sheet active, press Ctrl + Home to make cell **A1** the active cell. Point to the **Online Sales sheet tab**, right-click, and then from the shortcut menu, click **Select All Sheets**.

2 At the top of your screen, notice that *[Group]* displays in the title bar. Compare your screen with Figure 2.36.

Both worksheets are selected, as indicated by *[Group]* in the title bar and the sheet tab names underlined in the selected tab color. Data that you enter or edit on the active sheet will also be entered or edited in the same manner on all the selected sheets in the same cells.

Figure 2.36

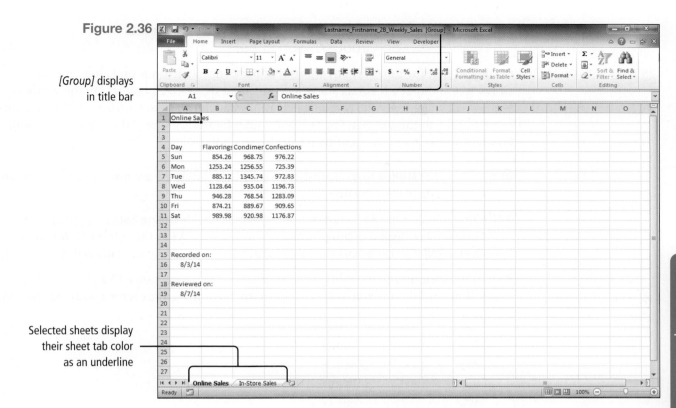

[Group] displays
in title bar

Selected sheets display
their sheet tab color
as an underline

3 Select **columns A:G**, and then set their width to **85 pixels**.

4 Click cell **A2**, type **Week of July 24** and then on the **Formula Bar**, click the **Enter** button ✓ to keep cell **A2** as the active cell. **Merge & Center** 🔳 the text across the range **A2:G2**, and then apply the **Heading 1** cell style.

5 Click cell **E4**, type **Total Food Sales** and then press Tab. In cell **F4**, type **Non-Food Sales** and then press Tab. In cell **G4**, type **Total Sales** and then press Enter.

6 Select the range **A4:G4**, and then apply the **Heading 3** cell style. In the **Alignment group**, click the **Center** ≣, **Middle Align** ≣, and **Wrap Text** 🔳 buttons. **Save** 🔳 your workbook.

Another Way

Right-click any sheet tab, and then click Ungroup Sheets.

7 Display the **In-Store Sales** worksheet to cancel the grouping, and then compare your screen with Figure 2.37.

As soon as you select a single sheet, the grouping of the sheets is canceled and *[Group]* no longer displays in the title bar. Because the sheets were grouped, the same new text and formatting was applied to both sheets. In this manner, you can make the same changes to all the sheets in a workbook at one time.

Figure 2.37

[Group] no longer displays
in title bar

In-Store Sales sheet active

Subtitle entered

Formatting applied to
column widths and
column titles

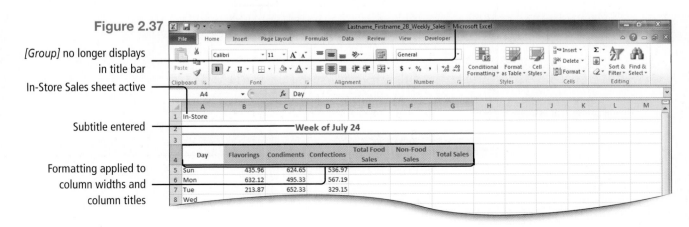

Activity 2.21 | Formatting and Constructing Formulas on Grouped Worksheets

Recall that formulas are equations that perform calculations on values in your worksheet and that a formula starts with an equal sign (=). Operators are the symbols with which you specify the type of calculation that you want to perform on the elements of a formula. In this activity, you will enter sales figures for Non-Food items from both Online and In-Store sales, and then calculate the total sales.

1 Display the **Online Sales** worksheet. Verify that the sheets are not grouped—*[Group]* does *not* display in the title bar.

2 Click cell **A1**, type **Food and Non-Food Items: Weekly Online Sales** and then on the **Formula Bar**, click the **Enter** button ☑ to keep cell **A1** as the active cell. **Merge & Center** ☒ the text across the range **A1:G1**, and then apply the **Title** cell style.

3 In the column titled *Non-Food Sales*, click cell **F5**, in the range **F5:F11**, type the following data for Non-Food Sales, and then compare your screen with Figure 2.38.

	Non-Food Sales
Sun	869.24
Mon	468.78
Tue	796.57
Wed	865.11
Thu	916.48
Fri	1154.22
Sat	968.25

Figure 2.38

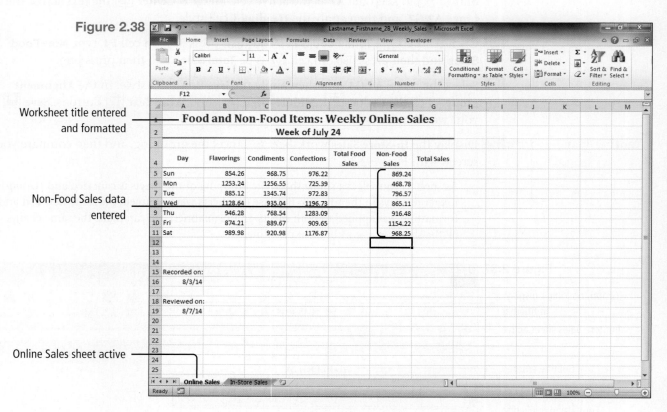

Worksheet title entered and formatted

Non-Food Sales data entered

Online Sales sheet active

4 Display the **In-Store Sales** sheet. In cell **A1**, replace *In-Store* by typing **Food and Non-Food Items: Weekly In-Store Sales** and then on the **Formula Bar**, click the **Enter** button ✓ to keep cell **A1** as the active cell. **Merge & Center** ☰ the text across the range **A1:G1**, and then apply the **Title** cell style.

5 In the column titled *Non-Food Sales*, click cell **F5**, in the range **F5:F11**, type the following data for Non-Food Sales, and then compare your screen with Figure 2.39.

	Non-Food Sales
Sun	**569.34**
Mon	**426.44**
Tue	**636.57**
Wed	**721.69**
Thu	**359.12**
Fri	**587.99**
Sat	**436.22**

Figure 2.39

Worksheet title entered and formatted for In-Store Sales sheet

Non-Food Sales data entered

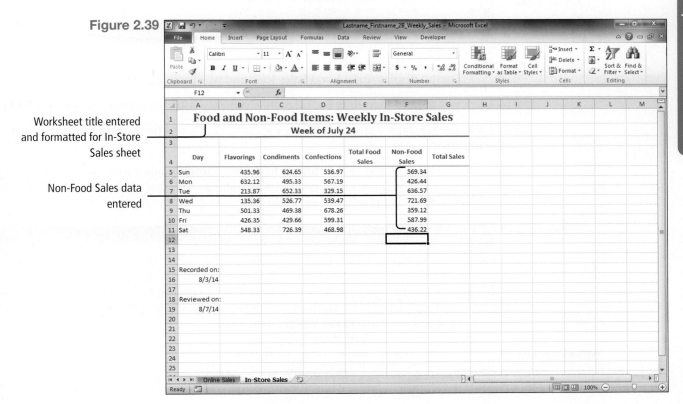

6 **Save** 🖫 your workbook. Right-click the **Online Sales sheet tab**, and then from the shortcut menu, click **Select All Sheets**.

> The first worksheet becomes the active sheet, and the worksheets are grouped. *[Group]* displays in the title bar, and the sheet tabs are underlined in the tab color to indicate they are selected as part of the group. Recall that when grouped, any action that you perform on the active worksheet is *also* performed on any other selected worksheets.

7 With the sheets *grouped* and the **Online Sales** sheet active, click cell **E5**. On the **Home tab**, in the **Editing group**, click the **Sum** button Σ. Compare your screen with Figure 2.40.

> Recall that when you enter the SUM function, Excel looks first above and then left for a proposed range of cells to sum.

Figure 2.40

[Group] indicates the worksheets are grouped

SUM function in cell

Proposed range of cells to sum surrounded by moving border

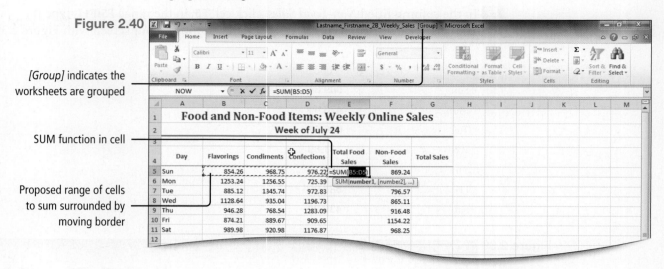

8 Press Enter to display Total Food Sales for Sunday, which is *2799.23*.

9 Click cell **E5**, and then drag the fill handle down to copy the formula through cell **E11**.

10 Click cell **G5**, type = click cell **E5**, type + click cell **F5**, and then compare your screen with Figure 2.41.

> Using the point-and-click technique to construct this formula is only one of several techniques you can use. Alternatively, you could use any other method to enter the SUM function to add the values in these two cells.

Figure 2.41

Formula in cell G5

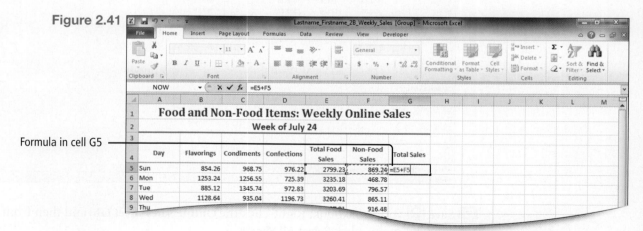

11 Press Enter to display the result *3668.47*, and then copy the formula down through cell **G11**.

12 In cell **A12**, type **Total** and then select the range **B5:G12**, which is all of the sales data and the empty cells at the bottom of each column of sales data.

13 With the range **B5:G12** selected, hold down Alt and press = to enter the **SUM** function in each empty cell.

> Selecting a range in this manner will place the Sum function in the empty cells at the bottom of each column.

14 Select the range **A5:A12**, and then apply the **Heading 4** cell style.

15 To apply financial formatting to the worksheets, select the range **B5:G5**, hold down Ctrl, and then select the range **B12:G12**. With the nonadjacent ranges selected, apply the **Accounting Number Format** $ ▾.

16 Select the range **B6:G11** and apply **Comma Style** , . Select the range **B12:G12** and apply the **Total** cell style.

17 Press Ctrl + Home to move to the top of the worksheet; compare your screen with Figure 2.42.

Figure 2.42

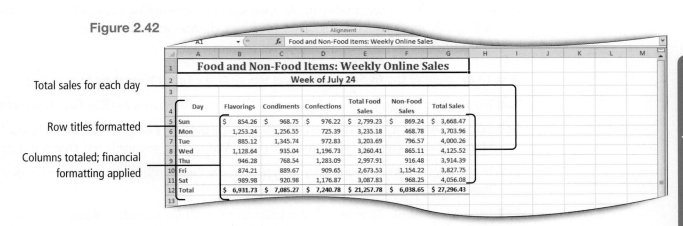

Total sales for each day

Row titles formatted

Columns totaled; financial formatting applied

18 Click the **In-Store Sales sheet tab** to cancel the grouping and display the second worksheet. Click **Save** 🖫, and then compare your screen with Figure 2.43.

> With your worksheets grouped, the calculations on the first worksheet were also performed on the second worksheet.

Figure 2.43

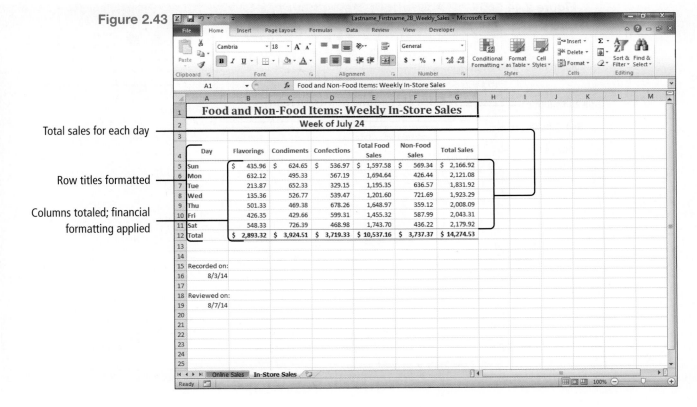

Total sales for each day

Row titles formatted

Columns totaled; financial formatting applied

Objective 11 | Create a Summary Sheet with Column Sparklines

A *summary sheet* is a worksheet where totals from other worksheets are displayed and summarized. Recall that sparklines are tiny charts within a single cell that show a data trend.

Activity 2.22 | Constructing Formulas that Refer to Cells in Another Worksheet

In this activity, you will insert a new worksheet in which you will place the totals from the Online Sales worksheet and the In-Store Sales worksheet. You will construct formulas in the Summary worksheet to display the total sales for both online sales and in-store sales that will update the Summary worksheet whenever changes are made to the other worksheet totals.

1 To the right of the **In-Store Sales** sheet tab, click the **Insert Worksheet** button.

2 Rename the new worksheet tab **Summary** Change the **Tab Color** to **Olive Green, Accent 3**.

3 Widen **columns A:E** to **110** pixels. In cell **A1**, type **Sales of Food and Non-Food Items** Merge & Center the title across the range **A1:E1**, and then apply the **Title** cell style.

4 In cell **A2**, type **Week of July 24** and then **Merge & Center** across **A2:E2**; apply the **Heading 1** cell style.

5 Leave **row 3** blank. To form column titles, in cell **B4**, type **Food/Non-Food** and press Tab. In cell **C4**, type **Food Sales** and press Tab. In cell **D4**, type **Non-Food Sales** and press Tab. In cell **E5**, type **Total Sales** Press Enter. Select the range **B4:E4**. Apply the **Heading 3** cell style and **Center**.

6 To form row titles, in cell **A5**, type **Online Sales** In cell **A6**, type **In-Store Sales** and then compare your screen with Figure 2.44.

Figure 2.44

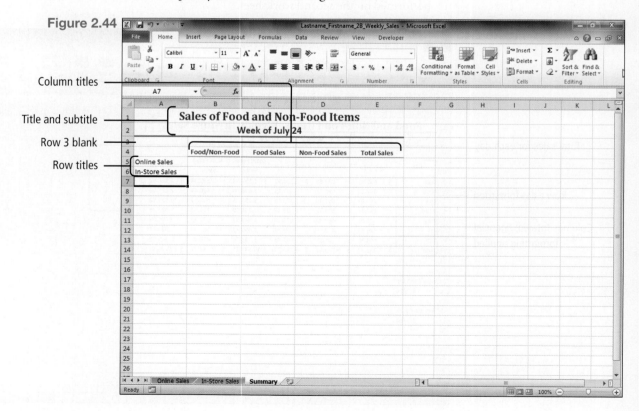

Column titles
Title and subtitle
Row 3 blank
Row titles

7 Click cell **C5**. Type = Click the **Online Sales sheet tab**. On the **Online Sales** worksheet, click cell **E12**, and then press Enter to redisplay the **Summary** worksheet and insert the total **Food Sales** amount of *$21,257.78*.

8 Click cell **C5** to select it again. Look at the **Formula Bar**, and notice that instead of a value, the cell contains a formula that is equal to the value in another cell in another worksheet. Compare your screen with Figure 2.45.

> The value in this cell is equal to the value in cell E12 of the *Online Sales* worksheet. The Accounting Number Format applied to the referenced cell is carried over. By using a formula of this type, changes in cell E12 on the *Online Sales* worksheet will be automatically updated in this *Summary* worksheet.

Figure 2.45

Formula Bar indicates
formula referring to cell in
another worksheet

Total Food Sales from
Online Sales worksheet

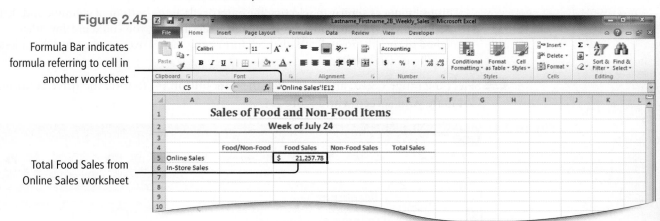

9 Click cell **D5**. Type = and then click the **Online Sales sheet tab**. Click cell **F12**, and then press Enter to redisplay the **Summary** worksheet and insert the total **Non-Food Sales** amount of *$6,038.65*.

10 By using the techniques you just practiced, in cells **C6** and **D6** insert the total **Food Sales** and **Non-Food Sales** data from the **In-Store Sales** worksheet. Click **Save**, and then compare your screen with Figure 2.46.

Figure 2.46

Totals from other
worksheets

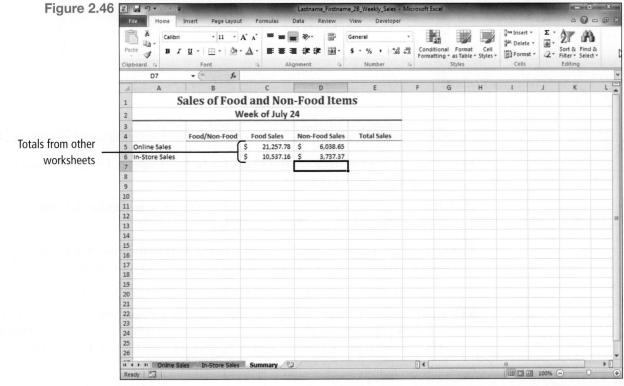

Activity 2.23 | Changing Values in a Detail Worksheet
to Update a Summary Worksheet

The formulas in cells C5:D6 display the totals from the other two worksheets. Changes made to any of the other two worksheets—sometimes referred to as *detail sheets* because the details of the information are contained there—that affect their totals will display on this Summary worksheet. In this manner, the Summary worksheet accurately displays the current totals from the other worksheets.

1 In cell **A7**, type **Total** Select the range **C5:E6**, and then click the **Sum** button Σ to total the two rows.

> This technique is similar to selecting the empty cells at the bottom of columns and then inserting the SUM function for each column. Alternatively, you could use any other method to sum the rows. Recall that cell formatting carries over to adjacent cells unless two cells are left blank.

2 Select the range **C5:E7**, and then click the **Sum** button Σ to total the three columns. Compare your screen with Figure 2.47.

Figure 2.47

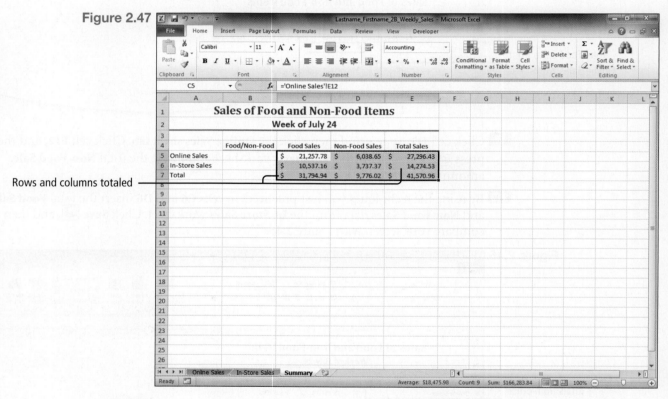

Rows and columns totaled

3 In cell **C6**, notice that total **Food Sales** for **In-Store Sales** is *$10,537.16*, and in cell **C7**, notice the total of *$31,794.94*.

4 Display the **In-Store Sales** worksheet, click cell **B8**, type **353.63** and then press Enter. Notice that the formulas in the worksheet recalculate.

5 Display the **Summary** worksheet, and notice that in the **Food Sales** column, both the total for the *In-Store Sales* location and the *Total* also recalculated.

> In this manner, a Summary sheet recalculates any changes made in the other worksheets.

6 Select the range **C6:E6** and change the format to **Comma Style**. Select the range **C7:E7**, and then apply the **Total** cell style. Select the range **A5:A7** and apply the **Heading 4** cell style. **Save** your workbook. Click cell **A1**, and then compare your screen with Figure 2.48.

Figure 2.48

Total style applied to C7:E7

Comma Style applied to C6:E6

Heading 4 cell style applied to row titles

Food sales recalculates to *$32,013.21*

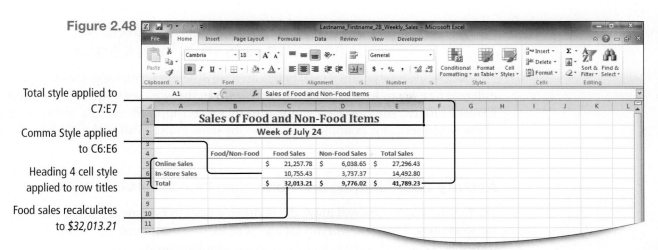

Activity 2.24 | Inserting Sparklines

In this activity, you will insert column sparklines to visualize the ratio of Food to Non-Food sales for both Online and In-Store.

1 Click cell **B5**. On the **Insert tab**, in the **Sparklines group**, click **Column**. In the **Create Sparklines** dialog box, with the insertion point blinking in the **Data Range** box, select the range **C5:D5**. Compare your screen with Figure 2.49.

Figure 2.49

Range C5:D5 selected

Create Sparklines dialog box

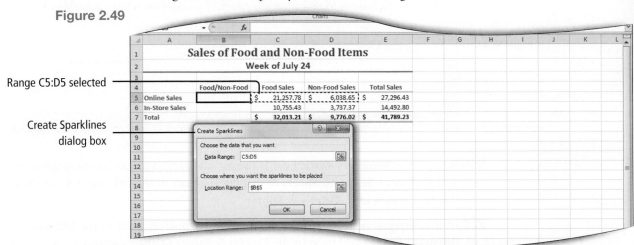

2 Click **OK**. Click cell **B6**, and then **Insert** a **Column Sparkline** for the range **C6:D6**. In the **Style group**, apply **Sparkline Style Accent 2, Darker 25%**—in the second row, the second style. Press Ctrl + Home, click **Save** 💾, and then compare your screen with Figure 2.50.

You can see, at a glance, that for both Online and In-Store sales, Food sales are much greater than Non-Food sales.

Figure 2.50

Column sparklines compare sales of Food to Non-Food in both Online and In-Store

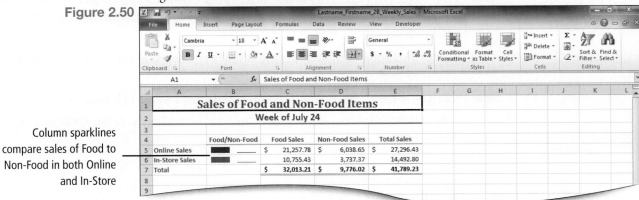

Objective 12 | Format and Print Multiple Worksheets in a Workbook

Each worksheet within a workbook can have different formatting, for example different headers or footers. If all the worksheets in the workbook will have the same header or footer, you can select all the worksheets and apply formatting common to all of the worksheets; for example, you can set the same footer in all of the worksheets.

Activity 2.25 | Moving and Formatting Worksheets in a Workbook

In this activity, you will move the Summary sheet to become the first worksheet in the workbook. Then you will format and prepare your workbook for printing. The three worksheets containing data can be formatted simultaneously.

1 Point to the **Summary sheet tab**, hold down the left mouse button to display a small black triangle—a caret—and then notice that a small paper icon attaches to the mouse pointer.

2 Drag to the left until the caret and mouse pointer are to the left of the **Online Sales sheet tab**, as shown in Figure 2.51, and then release the left mouse button.

Use this technique to rearrange the order of worksheets within a workbook.

Figure 2.51

Caret moved to the left; mouse pointer with paper icon attached

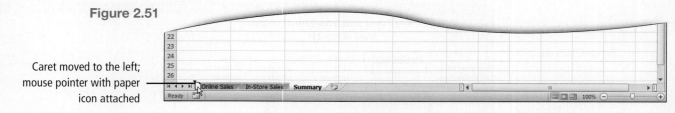

3 Be sure the **Summary** worksheet is the active sheet, point to its sheet tab, right-click, and then click **Select All Sheets** to display *[Group]* in the title bar. On the **Insert tab**, in the **Text group**, click **Header & Footer**.

4 In the **Navigation group**, click the **Go to Footer** button, click in the **left section** above the word *Footer*, and then in the **Header & Footer Elements group**, click the **File Name** button.

5 Click in a cell above the footer to deselect the **Footer area**. On the **Page Layout tab**, in the **Page Setup group**, click the **Margins** button, and then at the bottom of the **Margins** gallery, click **Custom Margins**.

6 In the displayed **Page Setup** dialog box, under **Center on page**, select the **Horizontally** check box. Click **OK**, and then on the status bar, click the **Normal** button ▦ to return to Normal view.

After displaying worksheets in Page Layout View, dotted lines indicate the page breaks in Normal view.

7 Press [Ctrl] + [Home]; verify that *[Group]* still displays in the title bar.

By selecting all sheets, you can apply the same formatting to all the worksheets at the same time.

8 Display **Backstage** view, show the **Document Panel**, type your firstname and lastname in the Author box, and then type your course name and section number in the **Subject** box. As the **Keywords** type **weekly sales, online, in-store** and then **Close** ☒ the **Document Information Panel**.

9 Press Ctrl + F2 ; compare your screen with Figure 2.52.

> By grouping, you can view all sheets in Print Preview. If you do not see *1 of 3* at the bottom of the Preview, click the Home tab, select all the sheets again, and then redisplay Print Preview.

Figure 2.52

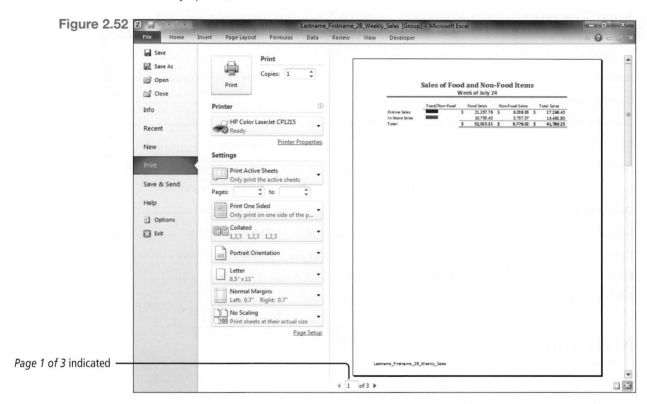

Page 1 of 3 indicated

10 At the bottom of the **Print Preview**, click the **Next Page** ▶ button as necessary and take a moment to view each page of your workbook.

Activity 2.26 | Printing All the Worksheets in a Workbook

1 In **Backstage** view, click the **Save** button to save your workbook before printing. To submit your workbook electronically, follow the instructions provided by your instructor. To print your workbook, continue to Step 2.

2 Display **Backstage** view, click the **Print tab**, verify that the worksheets in your workbook are still grouped—*[Group]* displays in the title bar—and then in the center panel, in the **Print group**, click the **Print** button.

3 If required, print or create an electronic version of your worksheets with formulas displayed by using the instructions in Activity 1.16, and then **Close** ☒ Excel without saving so that you do not save the changes you made to print formulas.

End You have completed Project 2B —————

Content-Based Assessments

Summary

In this chapter, you used the Statistical, Logical, and Date & Time functions from the Function Library. You created a table and analyzed the table's data by sorting and filtering. You also created a workbook with multiple worksheets, and then summarized all the worksheets on a summary worksheet.

Key Terms

Matching

Match each term in the second column with its correct definition in the first column by writing the letter of the term on the blank line in front of the correct definition.

_____ 1. A predefined formula that performs calculations by using specific values in a particular order or structure.

_____ 2. Excel functions such as AVERAGE that are useful to analyze a group of measurements.

_____ 3. A predefined formula that adds all the numbers in a selected range.

_____ 4. A function that adds a group of values, and then divides the result by the number of values in the group.

_____ 5. A function that finds the middle value that has as many values above it in the group as are below it.

_____ 6. A function that determines the smallest value in a range.

_____ 7. A function that determines the largest value in a range.

_____ 8. The action of moving a selection by dragging it to a new location.

_____ 9. A group of functions that tests for specific conditions, and which typically use conditional tests to determine whether specified conditions are true or false.

_____ 10. Conditions that you specify in a logical function.

_____ 11. A statistical function that counts the number of cells within a range that meet the given condition and which has two arguments—the range of cells to check and the criteria.

_____ 12. Any value or expression that can be evaluated as being true or false.

A AVERAGE function

B Comparison operators

C Conditional format

D COUNTIF function

E Criteria

F Drag and drop

G Function

H IF function

I Logical functions

J Logical test

K MAX function

L MEDIAN function

M MIN function

N Statistical functions

O SUM function

Content-Based Assessments

_____ 13. A function that uses a logical test to check whether a condition is met, and then returns one value if true, and another value if false.

_____ 14. Symbols that evaluate each value to determine if it is the same (=), greater than (>), less than (<), or in between a range of values as specified by the criteria.

_____ 15. A format that changes the appearance of a cell based on a condition.

Multiple Choice

Circle the correct answer.

1. A shaded bar that provides a visual cue about the value of a cell relative to other cells is a:
   A. data bar   **B.** detail bar   **C.** filter

2. The function that retrieves and then displays the date and time from your computer is the:
   A. DATE function   **B.** NOW function   **C.** CALENDAR function

3. The command that enables you to select one or more rows or columns and lock them into place is:
   A. drag and drop   **B.** scale to fit   **C.** freeze panes

4. A series of rows and columns with related data that is managed independently from other data is a:
   A. table   **B.** pane   **C.** detail sheet

5. The process of arranging data in a specific order based on the value in each field is called:
   A. filtering   **B.** sorting   **C.** scaling

6. The process of displaying only a portion of the data based on matching a specific value to show only the data that meets the criteria that you specify is called:
   A. filtering   **B.** sorting   **C.** scaling

7. The Excel command that enables you to specify rows and columns to repeat on each printed page is:
   A. navigate   **B.** print titles   **C.** conditional format

8. The labels along the lower border of the workbook window that identify each worksheet are the:
   A. data bars   **B.** sheet tabs   **C.** detail sheets

9. A worksheet where totals from other worksheets are displayed and summarized is a:
   A. summary sheet   **B.** detail sheet   **C.** table

10. The worksheets that contain the details of the information summarized on a summary sheet are called:
    A. summary sheets   **B.** detail sheets   **C.** tables

Content-Based Assessments

Apply **2A** skills from these Objectives:

1 Use the SUM, AVERAGE, MEDIAN, MIN, and MAX Functions

2 Move Data, Resolve Error Messages, and Rotate Text

3 Use COUNTIF and IF Functions and Apply Conditional Formatting

4 Use Date & Time Functions and Freeze Panes

5 Create, Sort, and Filter an Excel Table

6 Format and Print a Large Worksheet

Skills Review | Project **2C** Sauces Inventory

In the following Skills Review, you will edit a worksheet for Laura Morales, President, detailing the current inventory of sauces at the Portland facility. Your completed workbook will look similar to Figure 2.53.

Project Files

For Project 2C, you will need the following file:

e02C_Sauces_Inventory

You will save your workbook as:

Lastname_Firstname_2C_Sauces_Inventory

Project Results

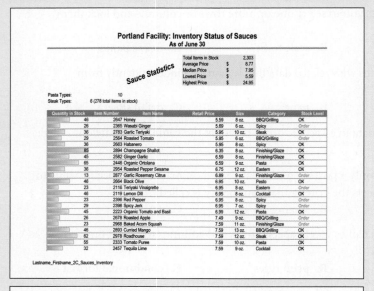

Figure 2.53

(Project 2C Sauces Inventory continues on the next page)

Content-Based Assessments

1 **Start** Excel. From your student files, locate and open **e02C_Sauces_Inventory**. From **Backstage** view, display the **Save As** dialog box, navigate to your **Excel Chapter 2** folder, and then save the workbook as **Lastname_ Firstname_2C_Sauces_Inventory**

a. Click cell **B4**. Click the **Formulas tab**, and then in the **Function Library group**, click the **AutoSum** button. Select the range **A14:A68**, and then press Enter.

b. With cell **B5** active, in the **Function Library group**, click the **More Functions** button. Point to **Statistical**, click **AVERAGE**, and then in the **Number1** box, type **d14:d68** Click **OK**.

c. Click cell **B6**. In the **Function Library group**, click the **More Functions** button, point to **Statistical**, and then click **MEDIAN**. In the **Function Arguments** dialog box, to the right of the **Number1** box, click the **Collapse Dialog** button. Select the range **D14:D68**, click the **Expand Dialog** button, and then click **OK**.

d. Click cell **B7**, and then by using a similar technique to insert a statistical function, insert the **MIN** function to determine the lowest **Retail Price**. Click cell **B8**, and then insert the **MAX** function to determine the highest **Retail Price**.

2 Right-click cell **B4**. On the Mini toolbar, click the **Comma Style** button, and then click the **Decrease Decimal** button two times. Select the range **B5:B8**, and apply the **Accounting Number Format**.

a. Select the range **A4:B8**. Point to the right edge of the selected range to display the ⌖ pointer. Drag the selected range to the right until the ScreenTip displays *D4:E8*, and then release the mouse button.

b. With the range **D4:E8** selected, on the **Home tab**, in the **Styles group**, display the **Cell Styles** gallery, and then under **Themed Cell Styles**, click **20% - Accent1**.

c. In cell **C6**, type **Sauce Statistics** Select the range **C4:C8**, right-click over the selection, and then click **Format Cells**. In the **Format Cells** dialog box, click the **Alignment tab**. Under **Text control**, select the **Merge cells** check box.

d. In the upper right portion of the dialog box, under **Orientation**, point to the **red diamond**, and then drag the diamond upward until the **Degrees** box indicates *20*. Click **OK**.

e. With the merged cell still selected, on the **Home tab**, in the **Font group**, change the **Font Size** to **18**, and then apply **Bold** and **Italic**. Click the **Font Color**

button arrow, and then in the fourth column, click the first color—**Dark Blue, Text 2**.

3 Click cell **B10**. On the **Formulas tab**, in the **Function Library group**, click the **More Functions** button, and then display the list of **Statistical** functions. Click **COUNTIF**.

a. At the right edge of the **Range** box, click the **Collapse Dialog** button, select the range **F14:F68**, and then press Enter. Click in the **Criteria** box, type **Pasta** and then click **OK** to calculate the number of *Pasta* types.

b. Click cell **G14**. On the **Formulas tab**, in the **Function Library group**, click the **Logical** button, and then in the list, click **IF**. If necessary, drag the title bar of the **Function Arguments** dialog box up so that you can view **row 14** on your screen.

c. With the insertion point in the **Logical_test** box, click cell **A14**, and then type **<30** Press Tab to move the insertion point to the **Value_if_true** box, and then type **Order** Press Tab to move the insertion point to the **Value_if_false** box, type **OK** and then click **OK**. Using the fill handle, copy the function in cell **G14** down through cell **G68**.

4 With the range **G14:G68** selected, on the **Home tab**, in the **Styles group**, click the **Conditional Formatting** button. In the list, point to **Highlight Cells Rules**, and then click **Text that Contains**.

a. In the **Text That Contains** dialog box, with the insertion point blinking in the first box, type **Order** and then in the second box, click the **arrow**. In the list, click **Custom Format**.

b. In the **Format Cells** dialog box, on the **Font tab**, under **Font style**, click **Bold Italic**. Click the **Color arrow**, and then under **Theme Colors**, in the sixth column, click the first color—**Red, Accent 2**. In the lower right corner of the **Format Cells** dialog box, click **OK**. In the **Text That Contains** dialog box, click **OK** to apply the font color, bold, and italic to the cells that contain the word *Order*.

c. Select the range **A14:A68**. In the **Styles group**, click the **Conditional Formatting** button. In the list, point to **Data Bars**, and then under **Gradient Fill**, click **Orange Data Bar**. Click anywhere to cancel the selection.

d. Select the range **F14:F68**. On the **Home tab**, in the **Editing group**, click the **Find & Select** button, and then click **Replace**. In the **Find and Replace** dialog box, in the **Find what** box, type **Hot** and then in the

(Project 2C Sauces Inventory continues on the next page)

Replace with box type **Spicy** Click the **Replace All** button and then click **OK**. In the lower right corner of the **Find and Replace** dialog box, click the **Close** button.

e. Scroll down as necessary, and then click cell **A70**. Type **Edited by Michelle Albright** and then press [Enter]. With cell **A71** as the active cell, on the **Formulas tab**, in the **Function Library group**, click the **Date & Time** button. In the list of functions, click **NOW**, and then click **OK** to enter the current date and time.

5 Select the range **A13:G68**. Click the **Insert tab**, and then in the **Tables group**, click the **Table** button. In the **Create Table** dialog box, if necessary, select the My table has headers check box, and then click **OK**. On the **Design tab**, in the **Table Styles group**, click the **More** button, and then under **Light**, locate and click **Table Style Light 9**.

a. In the header row of the table, click the **Retail Price arrow**, and then from the menu, click **Sort Smallest to Largest**. Click the **Category arrow**. On the menu, click the **(Select All)** check box to clear all the check boxes. Scroll as necessary and then click to select only the **Steak** check box. Click **OK**.

b. On the **Design tab**, in the **Table Style Options group**, select the **Total Row** check box. Click cell **A69**, click the **arrow** that displays to the right of cell **A69**, and then in the list, click **Sum**. In cell **B11**, type the result **6 (278 total items in stock)** and then press [Enter].

c. In the header row of the table, click the **Category arrow** and then click **Clear Filter From "Category"** to redisplay all of the data. Click anywhere in the table. Click the **Design tab**, in the **Table Style Options group**, clear the **Total Row** check box, and

then in the **Tools group**, click the **Convert to Range** button. Click **Yes**.

d. On the **Page Layout tab**, in the **Themes group**, click the **Themes** button, and then click **Horizon**.

6 On the **Page Layout tab**, click the **Margins** button, and then click **Custom Margins**. On the **Margins tab**, under **Center on page**, select the **Horizontally** check box. Click **OK**. On the **Page Layout tab**, in the **Scale to Fit group**, click the **Width button arrow**, and then click **1 page**.

a. In the **Page Setup group**, click the **Print Titles** button. Under **Print titles**, click in the **Rows to repeat at top** box, and then to the right, click the **Collapse Dialog** button. From the **row heading area**, select **row 13**, and then click the **Expand Dialog** button. Click **OK**.

b. On the **Insert tab**, in the **Text group**, click the **Header & Footer** button. Insert the **File Name** in the **left section** of the footer. Return to **Normal** view, make cell **A1** the active cell, and then delete the unused sheets.

c. Display the **Document Panel**, and then add your name, your course name and section, and the keywords **inventory, Portland** Close the **Document Information Panel**.

d. **Save** your workbook. Print or submit electronically as directed by your instructor. If required by your instructor, print or create an electronic version of your worksheets with formulas displayed by using the instructions in Activity 1.16, and then **Close** Excel without saving so that you do not save the changes you made to print formulas.

End **You have completed Project 2C** —————————

Content-Based Assessments

Apply **2B** skills from these Objectives:

7 Navigate a Workbook and Rename Worksheets

8 Enter Dates, Clear Contents, and Clear Formats

9 Copy and Paste by Using the Paste Options Gallery

10 Edit and Format Multiple Worksheets at the Same Time

11 Create a Summary Sheet with Column Sparklines

12 Format and Print Multiple Worksheets in a Workbook

Skills Review | Project **2D** February Sales

In the following Skills Review, you will edit a workbook that summarizes in-store and online sales in the California and Oregon retail locations. Your completed workbook will look similar to Figure 2.54.

Project Files

For Project 2D, you will need the following file:

e02D_February_Sales

You will save your workbook as:

Lastname_Firstname_2D_February_Sales

Project Results

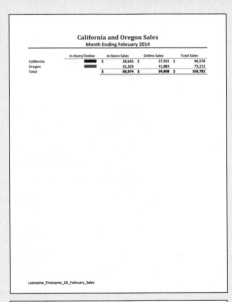

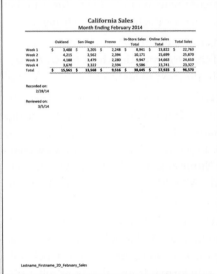

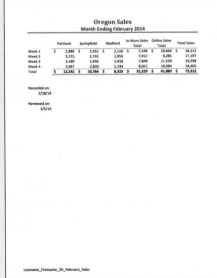

Figure 2.54

(Project 2D February Sales continues on the next page)

Content-Based Assessments

1 **Start** Excel. From your student files, locate and open **e02D_February_Sales**. Click the **File tab**, click **Save As**, navigate to your **Excel Chapter 2** folder, and then using your own name, save the file as **Lastname_Firstname_2D_February_Sales**

a. Point to the **Sheet1 tab**, and then double-click to select the sheet tab name. Type **California Sales** and then press Enter.

b. Point to the **Sheet2 tab**, right-click, and then from the shortcut menu, click **Rename**. Type **Oregon Sales** and press Enter.

c. Point to the **California Sales sheet tab** and right-click. On the shortcut menu, point to **Tab Color**, and then in the last column, click the first color—**Orange, Accent 6**.

d. Using the technique you just practiced, change the tab color of the **Oregon Sales sheet tab** to **Aqua, Accent 5**—in the next to last column, the first color.

e. Click the **California Sales sheet tab**, and then click cell **A13**. On the **Home tab**, in the **Number group**, click the **Number Format arrow**. From the bottom of the displayed menu, click **More Number Formats** to display the **Number tab** of the **Format Cells** dialog box. Click the **3/14/01** type, and then at the bottom of the dialog box, click **OK**.

f. Click cell **A16**, type **3/5/14** and then press Enter. Click cell **A13**, and then on the **Home tab**, in the **Clipboard group**, click the **Format Painter** button. Click cell **A16** to copy the date format from cell **A13** to cell **A16**.

g. Click cell **A1**. In the **Editing group**, click the **Clear** button. From the displayed list, click **Clear Formats**.

h. Select the range **A4:A16**. On the **Home tab**, in the **Clipboard group**, click the **Copy** button. At the bottom of the workbook window, click the **Oregon Sales sheet tab** to make it the active worksheet. Right-click cell **A4**, and then under **Paste Options**, click the first button—**Paste**. Display the **California Sales** sheet. Press Esc to cancel the moving border.

2 With the **California Sales** sheet active, press Ctrl + Home to make cell **A1** the active cell. Point to the sheet tab, right-click, and then on the shortcut menu, click **Select All Sheets**. Verify that *[Group]* displays in the title bar.

a. **Merge & Center** the text in cell A1 across the range **A1:G1**, and then apply the **Title** cell style. Select **columns A:G**, and then set their widths to **85 pixels**.

b. Click cell **A2**, type **Month Ending February 2014** and then on the **Formula Bar**, click the **Enter** button to keep cell **A2** as the active cell. **Merge & Center** the text across the range **A2:G2**, and then apply the **Heading 1** cell style.

c. Select the range **B4:G4**, and then apply the **Heading 3** cell style. In the **Alignment group**, click the **Center**, **Middle Align**, and **Wrap Text** buttons.

d. With the sheets still *grouped* and the **California Sales** sheet active, click cell **E5**. On the **Home tab**, in the **Editing group**, click the **Sum** button, and then press Enter. Click cell **E5**, and then drag the fill handle down to copy the formula through cell **E8**.

e. Click cell **G5**, type **=** click cell **E5**, type **+** click cell **F5**, and then press Enter. Copy the formula down through cell **G8**. In cell **A9**, type **Total** Select the range **B5:G9**, and then press Alt + = to enter the SUM function for all the columns. Select the range **A5:A9**, and then apply the **Heading 4** cell style.

f. Select the range **B5:G5**, hold down Ctrl, and then select the range **B9:G9**. Apply the **Accounting Number Format** and decrease the decimal places to zero. Select the range **B6:G8**, and then apply **Comma Style** with zero decimal places. Select the range **B9:G9** and apply the **Total** cell style.

3 Click the **Oregon Sales sheet tab** to cancel the grouping and display the second worksheet.

a. To the right of the **Oregon Sales** sheet tab, click the **Insert Worksheet** button. Rename the new worksheet tab **Summary** and then change the **Tab Color** to **Olive Green, Accent 3**—in the seventh column, the first color.

b. Widen **columns A:E** to **125** pixels. In cell **A1**, type **California and Oregon Sales** and then **Merge & Center** the title across the range **A1:E1**. Apply the **Title** cell style. In cell **A2**, type **Month Ending February 2014** and then **Merge & Center** the text across the range **A2:E2**. Apply the **Heading 1** cell style. In cell **A5**, type **California** and in cell **A6**, type **Oregon**

c. In cell **B4**, type **In-Store/Online** and press Tab. In cell **C4**, type **In-Store Sales** and press Tab. In cell **D4**, type **Online Sales** and press Tab. In cell **E4**, type **Total Sales** Select the range **B4:E4**, apply the **Heading 3** cell style, and then **Center** these column titles.

(Project 2D February Sales continues on the next page)

Content-Based Assessments

d. Click cell **C5**. Type **=** and then click the **California Sales sheet tab**. In the **California Sales** worksheet, click cell **E9**, and then press ⏎. Click cell **D5**. Type **=** and then click the **California Sales sheet tab**. Click cell **F9**, and then press ⏎.

e. By using the techniques you just practiced, in cells **C6** and **D6**, insert the total **In-Store Sales** and **Online Sales** data from the **Oregon Sales** worksheet.

f. Select the range **C5:E6**, and then click the **Sum** button to total the two rows. In cell **A7**, type **Total** and then select the range **C5:E7**. Click the **Sum** button to total the three columns. Select the nonadjacent ranges **C5:E5** and **C7:E7**, and then apply **Accounting Number Format** with zero decimal places. Select the range **C6:E6**, and then apply **Comma Style** with zero decimal places. Select the range **C7:E7**, and then apply the **Total** cell style. Select the range **A5:A7** and apply the **Heading 4** cell style.

g. Click cell **B5**. On the **Insert tab**, in the **Sparklines group**, click **Column**. In the **Create Sparklines** dialog box, with the insertion point blinking in the **Data Range** box, select the range **C5:D5** and then click **OK**.

h. Click cell **B6**, and then **Insert** a **Column Sparkline** for the range **C6:D6**. In the **Style group**, apply the second style in the second row—**Sparkline Style Accent 2, Darker 25%** to this sparkline.

4 Point to the **Summary sheet tab**, hold down the left mouse button to display a small black triangle, and drag to the left until the triangle and mouse pointer are

to the left of the **California Sales sheet tab**, and then release the left mouse button.

a. Be sure the **Summary** worksheet is the active sheet, point to its sheet tab, right-click, and then click **Select All Sheets** to display *[Group]* in the title bar. On the **Insert tab**, in the **Text group**, click the **Header & Footer** button. Display the **Footer** area, and then in the **left section**, insert the **File Name**. Center the worksheets **Horizontally** on the page, return to **Normal** view, and make cell **A1** active.

b. Display the **Document Panel**, and then add your name, your course name and section, and the keywords **February sales Close** the **Document Information Panel**.

c. **Save** your workbook. To submit your workbook electronically, follow the instructions provided by your instructor. To print your workbook, continue to Step d.

d. Display **Backstage** view, verify that the worksheets in your workbook are still grouped—*[Group]* displays in the title bar—and then on the left click **Print**. Under **Settings**, verify that **Print Active Sheets** displays. At the top of the screen, verify that the **Number of Copies** is **1**. Click the **Print** button.

e. If required by your instructor, print or create an electronic version of your worksheets with formulas displayed by using the instructions in Activity 1.16, and then **Close** Excel without saving so that you do not save the changes you made to print formulas.

End **You have completed Project 2D**

Content-Based Assessments

Apply 2A skills from these Objectives:

1. Use the SUM, AVERAGE, MEDIAN, MIN, and MAX Functions
2. Move Data, Resolve Error Messages, and Rotate Text
3. Use COUNTIF and IF Functions and Apply Conditional Formatting
4. Use Date & Time Functions and Freeze Panes
5. Create, Sort, and Filter an Excel Table
6. Format and Print a Large Worksheet

Mastering Excel | Project 2E Desserts

In the following Mastery project, you will edit a worksheet for Laura Morales, President, detailing the current inventory of desserts produced at the San Diego facility. Your completed worksheet will look similar to Figure 2.55.

Project Files

For Project 2E, you will need the following file:

e02E_Desserts

You will save your workbook as:

Lastname_Firstname_2E_Desserts

Project Results

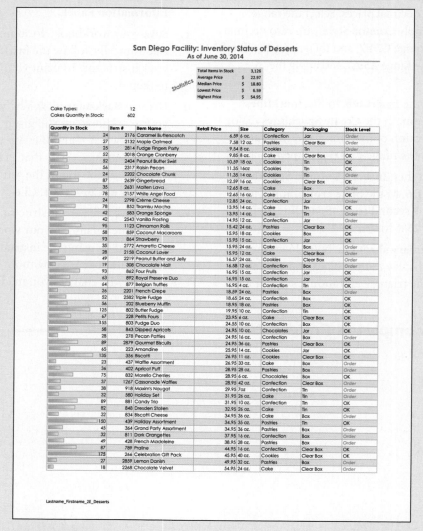

Figure 2.55

(Project 2E Desserts continues on the next page)

Content-Based Assessments

Mastering Excel | Project 2E Desserts (continued)

1 **Start** Excel, from your student files, locate and open **e02E_Desserts**, and then **Save** the file in your **Excel Chapter 2** folder as **Lastname_Firstname_2E_Desserts**

2 In cell **B4**, calculate the **Total Items in Stock** by summing the **Quantity in Stock** data, and then apply **Comma Style** with zero decimal places to the result. In each cell in the range **B5:B8**, insert formulas to calculate the Average, Median, Lowest, and Highest retail prices, and then apply the **Accounting Number Format** to each result.

3 Move the range **A4:B8** to the range **D4:E8**, and then apply the **20% - Accent1** cell style. Widen **column D** to **130 pixels**. In cell **C6**, type **Statistics** select the range **C4:C8**, and then from the **Format Cells** dialog box, merge the selected cells. Change the text **Orientation** to **25 Degrees**, and then apply **Bold** and **Italic**. Change the **Font Size** to **14** and the **Font Color** to **Pink, Accent 1, Darker 25%**. Apply **Middle Align** and **Align Text Right**.

4 In cell **B10**, use the **COUNTIF** function to count the number of **Cake** items. In the **Packaging** column, **Replace All** occurrences of **Cellophane** with **Clear Box**

5 In cell **H14**, enter an **IF** function to determine the items that must be ordered. If the **Quantity in Stock** is less than **50** the **Value_if_true** is **Order** Otherwise the **Value_if_false** is **OK** Fill the formula down through cell **H65**. Apply **Conditional Formatting** to the **Stock Level** column so that cells that contain the text *Order* are formatted with **Bold Italic** and with a **Color** of **Blue, Accent 5**. Apply conditional formatting

to the **Quantity in Stock** column by applying a **Gradient Fill Orange Data Bar**.

6 Format the range **A13:H65** as a **Table** with headers, and apply the **Table Style Light 16** style. Sort the table from smallest to largest by **Retail Price**, and then filter on the **Category** column to display the **Cake** types. Display a **Total Row** in the table and then in cell **A66**, **Sum** the **Quantity in Stock** for the **Cake** items. Type the result in cell **B11**, and apply appropriate number formatting. Click in the table, and then on the **Design tab**, remove the total row from the table. Clear the **Category** filter and convert the table to a range.

7 Change the theme to **Composite**. Display the footer area, and insert the **File Name** in the **left section**. Center the worksheet **Horizontally**, and then use the **Scale to Fit** option to change the **Width** to **1 page**. Return to **Normal** view and make cell **A1** the active cell. In **Backstage** view, display the **Print Preview**, and then make any necessary corrections.

8 Add your name, your course name and section, and the keywords **desserts inventory, San Diego** to the Document Panel. **Save**, and then print or submit electronically as directed. If required by your instructor, print or create an electronic version of your worksheets with formulas displayed by using the instructions in Activity 1.16, and then **Close** Excel without saving so that you do not save the changes you made to print formulas.

End **You have completed Project 2E** _____

Content-Based Assessments

Apply **2B** skills from these Objectives:

- **7** Navigate a Workbook and Rename Worksheets
- **8** Enter Dates, Clear Contents, and Clear Formats
- **9** Copy and Paste by Using the Paste Options Gallery
- **10** Edit and Format Multiple Worksheets at the Same Time
- **11** Create a Summary Sheet with Column Sparklines
- **12** Format and Print Multiple Worksheets in a Workbook

Mastering Excel | Project **2F** Compensation

In the following Mastery project, you will edit a workbook that summarizes the Laurales Herb and Spices salesperson compensation for the month of November. Your completed worksheet will look similar to Figure 2.56.

Project Files

For Project 2F, you will need the following file:

> e02F_Compensation

You will save your workbook as:

> Lastname_Firstname_2F_Compensation

Project Results

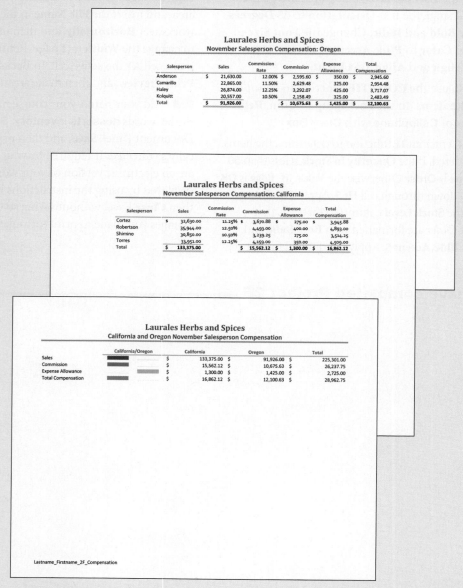

Figure 2.56

(Project 2F Compensation continues on the next page)

Content-Based Assessments

Mastering Excel | Project 2F Compensation (continued)

1 **Start** Excel, from your student files, open **e02F_ Compensation**, and then save the file in your **Excel Chapter 2** folder as **Lastname_Firstname_2F_ Compensation**

2 Rename **Sheet1** as **California** and change the **Tab Color** to **Green, Accent 1**. Rename **Sheet2** as **Oregon** and change the **Tab Color** to **Gold, Accent 3**.

3 Click the **California sheet tab** to make it the active sheet, and then group the worksheets. In cell **A1**, type **Laurales Herbs and Spices** and then **Merge & Center** the text across the range **A1:F1**. Apply the **Title** cell style. **Merge & Center** the text in cell **A2** across the range **A2:F2**, and then apply the **Heading 1** cell style.

4 With the sheets still grouped, in cell **D5** calculate **Commission** for *Cortez* by multiplying the **Sales** by the **Commission Rate**. Copy the formula down through cell **D8**. In cell **F5**, calculate **Total Compensation** by summing the **Commission** and **Expense Allowance** for *Cortez*. Copy the formula down through the cell **F8**.

5 In **row 9**, sum the **Sales**, **Commission**, **Expense Allowance**, and **Total Compensation** columns. Apply the **Accounting Number Format** with two decimal places to the appropriate cells in **row 5** and **row 9** (do not include the percentages). Apply the **Comma Style** with two decimal places to the appropriate cells in **rows 6:8** (do not include the percentages). Apply the **Total** cell style to the appropriate cells in the Total row.

6 Insert a new worksheet. Change the sheet name to **Summary** and then change the **Tab Color** to **Periwinkle, Accent 5**. Widen **columns A:E** to **165** pixels, and then move the **Summary** sheet so that it is the first sheet in the workbook. In cell **A1**, type **Laurales Herbs and Spices** **Merge & Center** the title across the range **A1:E1**, and then apply the **Title** cell style. In cell **A2**, type **California and Oregon November Salesperson Compensation** and then **Merge & Center** the text across the range **A2:E2**. Apply the **Heading 1** cell style.

7 In the range **A5:A8**, type the following row titles and then apply the **Heading 4** cell style:

Sales

Commission

Expense Allowance

Total Compensation

8 In the range **B4:E4**, type the following column titles, and then **Center** and apply the **Heading 3** cell style.

California/Oregon

California

Oregon

Total

9 In cell **C5**, enter a formula that references cell **B9** in the **California** worksheet so that the total sales for California displays in **C5**. Create similar formulas to enter the total **Commission**, **Expense Allowance** and **Total Compensation** for California in the range **C6:C8**. Using the same technique, enter formulas in the range **D5:D8** so that the **Oregon** totals display.

10 Sum the **Sales**, **Commission**, **Expense Allowance**, and **Total Compensation** rows.

11 In cell **B5**, insert a **Column Sparkline** for the range **C5:D5**. In cells **B6**, **B7**, and **B8**, insert **Column** sparklines for the appropriate ranges to compare California totals with Oregon totals. To the sparkline in **B6**, apply the second style in the third row—**Sparkline Style Accent 2, (no dark or light)**. In **B7** apply the third style in the third row—**Sparkline Style Accent 3, (no dark or light)**. In **B8** apply the fourth style in the third row—**Sparkline Style Accent 4, (no dark or light)**.

12 **Group** the three worksheets, and then insert a footer in the left section with the **File Name**. Center the worksheets **Horizontally** on the page, and then change the **Orientation** to **Landscape**. Return the document to **Normal** view.

13 Display the **Document Panel**. Add your name, your course name and section, and the keywords **November sales Save** your workbook, and then print or submit electronically as directed. If required by your instructor, print or create an electronic version of your worksheets with formulas displayed by using the instructions in Activity 1.16, and then **Close** Excel without saving so that you do not save the changes you made to print formulas.

End **You have completed Project 2F**

Content-Based Assessments

Apply **2A** and **2B** skills from these Objectives:

1. Use the SUM, AVERAGE, MEDIAN, MIN, and MAX Functions
2. Move Data, Resolve Error Messages, and Rotate Text
3. Use COUNTIF and IF Functions and Apply Conditional Formatting
4. Use Date & Time Functions and Freeze Panes
5. Create, Sort, and Filter an Excel Table
6. Format and Print a Large Worksheet
7. Navigate a Workbook and Rename Worksheets
8. Enter Dates, Clear Contents, and Clear Formats
9. Copy and Paste by Using the Paste Options Gallery
10. Edit and Format Multiple Worksheets at the Same Time
11. Create a Summary Sheet with Column Sparklines
12. Format and Print Multiple Worksheets in a Workbook

Mastering Excel | Project **2G** Inventory Summary

In the following Mastery project, you will edit a worksheet that summarizes the inventory status at the Petaluma production facility. Your completed workbook will look similar to Figure 2.57.

Project Files

For Project 2G, you will need the following file:

e02G_Inventory_Summary

You will save your workbook as:

Lastname_Firstname_2G_Inventory_Summary

Project Results

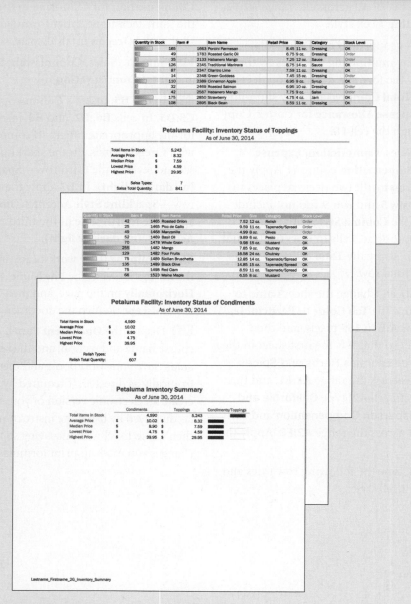

Figure 2.57

(Project 2G Inventory Summary continues on the next page)

Content-Based Assessments

1 **Start** Excel. From your student files, open **e02G_Inventory_Summary**. Save the file in your **Excel Chapter 2** folder as **Lastname_Firstname_2G_Inventory_Summary**

2 Rename **Sheet1** as **Condiments** and **Sheet2** as **Toppings** Make the following calculations in each of the two worksheets *without* grouping the sheets:

- In cell **B4**, enter a formula to sum the **Quantity in Stock** data, and then apply **Comma Style** with zero decimal places to the result.

- In cells **B5:B8**, enter formulas to calculate the Average, Median, Lowest, and Highest retail prices, and then apply the **Accounting Number Format**.

3 In each of the two worksheets, make the following calculations *without* grouping the sheets:

- In cell **B10**, enter a COUNTIF function to determine how many different types of **Relish** products are in stock on the **Condiments** sheet and how many different types of **Salsa** products are in stock on the **Toppings** worksheet.

- In cell **G15**, enter an **IF** function to determine the items that must be ordered. If the **Quantity in Stock** is less than **50** the **Value_if_true** is **Order** Otherwise the **Value_if_false** is **OK** Fill the formula down through all the rows.

- Apply **Conditional Formatting** to the **Stock Level** column so that cells that contain the text *Order* are formatted with **Bold Italic** with a **Font Color** of **Gold, Accent 1, Darker 25%**. Apply **Gradient Fill Green Data Bars** to the **Quantity in Stock** column.

4 In the **Condiments** sheet, format the range **A14:G64** as a table with headers and apply **Table Style Medium 2**. Insert a **Total Row**, filter by **Category** for **Relish**, and then **Sum** the **Quantity in Stock** column. Record the result in cell **B11**.

5 Select the table, clear the filter, **Sort** the table on the **Item #** column from **Smallest to Largest**, remove the **Total Row**, and then convert the table to a range. On the **Page Layout tab**, set **Print Titles** so that **row 14** repeats at the top of each page.

6 In the **Toppings** sheet, format the range **A14:G61** as a table with headers and apply **Table Style Light 16**. Insert a **Total Row**, filter by **Category** for **Salsa**, and then **Sum** the **Quantity in Stock** column. Record the result in cell **B11**.

7 Select the table, clear the filter, **Sort** the table on the **Item #** column from **Smallest to Largest**, remove the **Total Row**, and then convert the table to a range.

8 On the **Page Layout tab**, set **Print Titles** so that **row 14** repeats at the top of each page, and then **Save** your workbook. **Group** the two worksheets. **Center** the worksheets **Horizontally**, and then use the **Scale to Fit** option to change the **Width** to **1 page**.

9 Insert a new worksheet. Change the sheet name to **Summary** and then widen **columns A:D** to **170** pixels. Move the **Summary** sheet so that it is the first sheet in the workbook. In cell **A1**, type **Petaluma Inventory Summary** **Merge & Center** the title across the range **A1:D1**, and then apply the **Title** cell style. In cell **A2**, type **As of June 30, 2014** and then **Merge & Center** the text across the range **A2:D2**. Apply the **Heading 1** cell style.

10 On the **Condiments sheet**, **Copy** the range **A4:A8**. Display the **Summary sheet** and **Paste** the selection to cell **A5**. Apply the **Heading 4** cell style to the selection. In the **Summary sheet**, in cell **B4**, type **Condiments** In cell **C4**, type **Toppings** and in cell **D4**, type **Condiments/Toppings Center** the column titles, and then apply the **Heading 3** cell style.

11 In cell **B5**, enter a formula that references cell **B4** in the **Condiments sheet** so that the **Condiments Total Items in Stock** displays in **B5**. Create similar formulas to enter the **Average Price**, **Median Price**, **Lowest Price**, and **Highest Price** from the **Condiments sheet** into the **Summary** sheet in the range **B6:B9**.

12 Enter formulas in the range **C5:C9** that reference the appropriate cells in the **Toppings** worksheet. To the range **B5:C5**, apply **Comma Style** with zero decimal places. In cells **D5, D6, D7, D8,** and **D9**, insert **Column** sparklines using the values in the *Condiments* and *Toppings* columns. Format each sparkline using the first five Sparkline styles in the first row.

13 Center the **Summary** worksheet **Horizontally** and change the **Orientation** to **Landscape**. **Group** the worksheets and insert a footer in the left section with the **File Name**. In **Normal** view, make cell **A1** the active cell. Display the **Document Panel**. Add your name, your course name and section, and the keywords **Petaluma inventory**

14 **Save** your workbook, and then print or submit electronically as directed. If required by your instructor, print or create an electronic version of your worksheets with formulas displayed by using the instructions in Activity 1.16, and then **Close** Excel without saving so that you do not save the changes you made to print formulas.

End **You have completed Project 2G**

Apply a combination of the 2A and 2B skills.

GO! Fix It | Project **2H** Confections

Project Files

For Project 2H, you will need the following file:

e02H_Confections

You will save your workbook as:

Lastname_Firstname_2H_Confections

In this project, you will correct a worksheet that contains the confection inventory for the month of June at the Laurales Herb and Spices Petaluma production facility. From the student files that accompany this textbook, open the file e02H_Confections, and then save the file in your chapter folder as **Lastname_Firstname_2H_Confections**

To complete the project, you must find and correct errors in formulas and formatting. View each formula in cells B4:B8 and edit as necessary. In addition to errors that you find, you should know:

- The table should be sorted smallest to largest by Item #.
- New stock should be ordered when the Quantity in Stock is less than 50, and the word *Order* should be formatted with bold, italic, in font color Red, Accent 3.
- The table should be converted to a range.
- Gradient fill red data bars should be applied to the Quantity in Stock column.

Insert the file name in the left section of the footer, center the worksheet horizontally, and repeat the table column titles on each page. Edit the document properties with your name, course and section, and the keywords **Petaluma, confections** Save your file, and then print or submit your worksheet electronically as directed by your instructor. If required by your instructor, print or create an electronic version of your worksheets with formulas displayed by using the instructions in Activity 1.16, and then Close Excel without saving so that you do not save the changes you made to print formulas.

End **You have completed Project 2H** ——————————————

Content-Based Assessments

Apply a combination of the **2A** and **2B** skills.

GO! Make It | Project 2I Salary Summary

Project Files

For Project 2I, you will need the following file:

e02I_Salary_Summary

You will save your workbook as:

Lastname_Firstname_2I_Salary_Summary

Open e02I_Salary_Summary and save the file in your Excel Chapter 2 folder as **Lastname_ Firstname_2I_Salary_Summary** Edit the worksheet as shown in Figure 2.58. To calculate Commission for each salesperson, multiply the Sales by the Commission Rate, using absolute cell references as necessary. To determine the Bonus, construct an IF function where the Logical Test determines if Sales are greater than 21,500, the Value_if_true is 500, and the Value_if_false is 0. Calculate Total Compensation by adding the Commission and the Bonus for each salesperson. Determine the Sales and Compensation totals, averages, medians, and highest and lowest amounts. Insert a table, apply Table Medium Style 16, sort the table as shown in Figure 2.58, apply cell styles and number formatting as indicated, and convert the table to a range. Insert a footer with the file name in the left section, center the worksheet horizontally, and add your name, your course name and section, and the keywords **commission, sales** to the document properties. Print or submit electronically as directed by your instructor.

Project Results

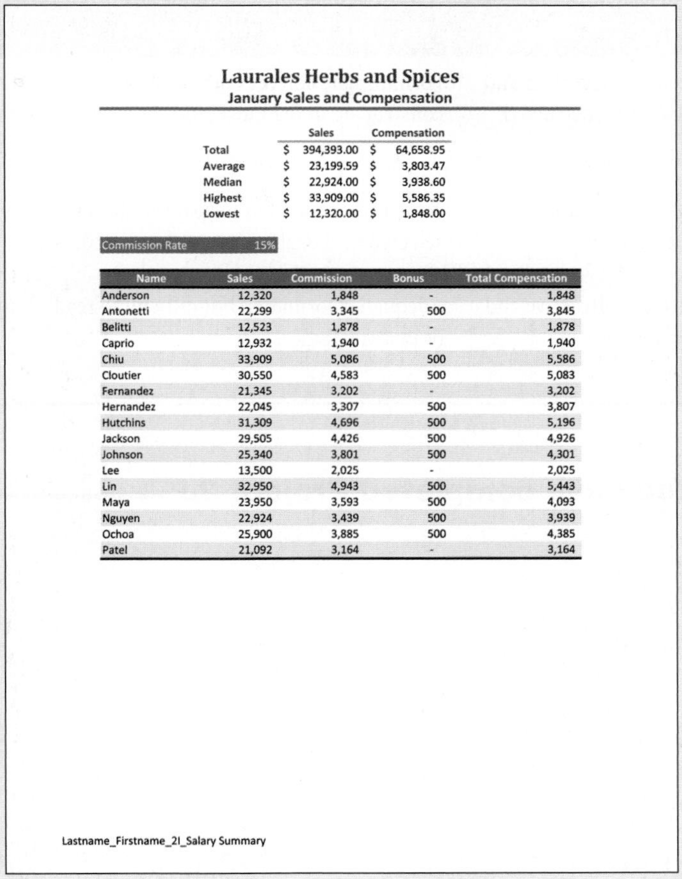

Laurales Herbs and Spices
January Sales and Compensation

	Sales	Compensation
Total	$ 394,393.00	$ 64,658.95
Average	$ 23,199.59	$ 3,803.47
Median	$ 22,924.00	$ 3,938.60
Highest	$ 33,909.00	$ 5,586.35
Lowest	$ 12,320.00	$ 1,848.00

Commission Rate	15%

Name	Sales	Commission	Bonus	Total Compensation
Anderson	12,320	1,848	-	1,848
Antonetti	22,299	3,345	500	3,845
Belitti	12,523	1,878	-	1,878
Caprio	12,932	1,940	-	1,940
Chiu	33,909	5,086	500	5,586
Cloutier	30,550	4,583	500	5,083
Fernandez	21,345	3,202	-	3,202
Hernandez	22,045	3,307	500	3,807
Hutchins	31,309	4,696	500	5,196
Jackson	29,505	4,426	500	4,926
Johnson	25,340	3,801	500	4,301
Lee	13,500	2,025	-	2,025
Lin	32,950	4,943	500	5,443
Maya	23,950	3,593	500	4,093
Nguyen	22,924	3,439	500	3,939
Ochoa	25,900	3,885	500	4,385
Patel	21,092	3,164	-	3,164

Lastname_Firstname_2I_Salary Summary

Figure 2.58

End You have completed Project 2I

Content-Based Assessments

GO! Solve It | Project **2J** Toppings

Project Files

For Project 2J, you will need the following file:

e02J_Toppings

You will save your workbook as:

Lastname_Firstname_2J_Toppings

Open the file e02J_Toppings and save it as **Lastname_Firstname_2J_Toppings** Complete the worksheet by entering appropriate formulas in cells B5 and B6. In the Stock Level column, enter an IF function that determines whether the quantity in stock is greater than 65. If the Quantity in Stock is greater than 65, then the Stock Level should display the text **OK** Otherwise the Stock Level should display the text **Order** Insert a Table with a total row and apply an attractive table style. Sort the table by Item #, calculate the values for B7 and B8, and then clear all filters and remove the total row from the table. Convert the table to a range. Format the worksheet attractively, and apply appropriate Data Bars to the Quantity in Stock column and conditional formatting to the Stock Level column so that items that need to be ordered are easily identified. Include the file name in the footer, add appropriate properties, and submit as directed.

Performance Element		Performance Level		
		Exemplary: You consistently applied the relevant skills	**Proficient:** You sometimes, but not always, applied the relevant skills	**Developing:** You rarely or never applied the relevant skills
	Create formulas	All formulas are correct and are efficiently constructed.	Formulas are correct but not always constructed in the most efficient manner.	One or more formulas are missing or incorrect; or only numbers were entered.
	Insert and format a table	Table was created and formatted properly.	Table was created but incorrect data was selected or the table was not formatted.	No table was created.
	Format worksheet data attractively and appropriately	Formatting is attractive and appropriate.	Adequately formatted but difficult to read or unattractive.	Inadequate or no formatting.

End You have completed Project 2J

Content-Based Assessments

Apply a combination of the **2A** and **2B** skills.

GO! Solve It | Project **2K** First Quarter Summary

Project Files

For Project 2K, you will need the following file:

e02K_First_Quarter

You will save your workbook as:

Lastname_Firstname_2K_First_Quarter

Open the file e02K_First_Quarter and save it as **Lastname_Firstname_2K_First_Quarter** This workbook contains two worksheets; one that includes California sales data by product and one that includes Oregon sales data by product. Complete the two worksheets by calculating totals by product and by month. Then calculate the Percent of Total by dividing the Product Total by the Monthly Total, using absolute cell references as necessary. Format the worksheets attractively with a title and subtitle, and apply appropriate financial formatting. Insert a new worksheet that summarizes the monthly totals by state. Enter the months as the column titles and the states as the row titles. Include a Product Total column and a column for sparklines titled **Jan./Feb./March** Format the Summary worksheet attractively with a title and subtitle, insert column sparklines that compare the months, and apply appropriate financial formatting. Include the file name in the footer, add appropriate document properties, and submit as directed.

Performance Element	Performance Level		
	Exemplary: You consistently applied the relevant skills	**Proficient:** You sometimes, but not always, applied the relevant skills	**Developing:** You rarely or never applied the relevant skills
Create formulas	All formulas are correct and are efficiently constructed.	Formulas are correct but not always constructed in the most efficient manner.	One or more formulas are missing or incorrect; or only numbers were entered.
Create Summary worksheet	Summary worksheet created properly.	Summary worksheet was created but the data, sparklines, or formulas were incorrect.	No Summary worksheet was created.
Format attractively and appropriately	Formatting is attractive and appropriate.	Adequately formatted but difficult to read or unattractive.	Inadequate or no formatting.

End You have completed Project 2K ————————

Outcomes-Based Assessments

Rubric

The following outcomes-based assessments are *open-ended assessments*. That is, there is no specific correct result; your result will depend on your approach to the information provided. Make *Professional Quality* your goal. Use the following scoring rubric to guide you in *how* to approach the problem, and then to evaluate *how well* your approach solves the problem.

The *criteria*—Software Mastery, Content, Format and Layout, and Process—represent the knowledge and skills you have gained that you can apply to solving the problem. The *levels of performance*—Professional Quality, Approaching Professional Quality, or Needs Quality Improvements—help you and your instructor evaluate your result.

	Your completed project is of Professional Quality if you:	Your completed project is Approaching Professional Quality if you:	Your completed project Needs Quality Improvements if you:
1-Software Mastery	Choose and apply the most appropriate skills, tools, and features and identify efficient methods to solve the problem.	Choose and apply some appropriate skills, tools, and features, but not in the most efficient manner.	Choose inappropriate skills, tools, or features, or are inefficient in solving the problem.
2-Content	Construct a solution that is clear and well organized, contains content that is accurate, appropriate to the audience and purpose, and is complete. Provide a solution that contains no errors in spelling, grammar, or style.	Construct a solution in which some components are unclear, poorly organized, inconsistent, or incomplete. Misjudge the needs of the audience. Have some errors in spelling, grammar, or style, but the errors do not detract from comprehension.	Construct a solution that is unclear, incomplete, or poorly organized; contains some inaccurate or inappropriate content; and contains many errors in spelling, grammar, or style. Do not solve the problem.
3-Format and Layout	Format and arrange all elements to communicate information and ideas, clarify function, illustrate relationships, and indicate relative importance.	Apply appropriate format and layout features to some elements, but not others. Overuse features, causing minor distraction.	Apply format and layout that does not communicate information or ideas clearly. Do not use format and layout features to clarify function, illustrate relationships, or indicate relative importance. Use available features excessively, causing distraction.
4-Process	Use an organized approach that integrates planning, development, self-assessment, revision, and reflection.	Demonstrate an organized approach in some areas, but not others; or, use an insufficient process of organization throughout.	Do not use an organized approach to solve the problem.

Outcomes-Based Assessments

Apply a combination of the **2A** and **2B** skills.

GO! Think | Project **2L** Seasonings

Project Files

For Project 2L, you will need the following file:

    e02L_Seasonings

You will save your workbook as:

    Lastname_Firstname_2L_Seasonings

Laura Morales, President of Laurales Herbs and Spices, has requested a worksheet that summarizes the seasonings inventory data for the month of March. Laura would like the worksheet to include the total Quantity in Stock and Number of Items for each category of items and she would like the items to be sorted from lowest to highest retail price.

Edit the workbook to provide Laura with the information requested. Format the worksheet titles and data and include an appropriately formatted table so that the worksheet is professional and easy to read and understand. Insert a footer with the file name and add appropriate document properties. Save the file as **Lastname_Firstname_2L_Seasonings** and print or submit as directed by your instructor.

 You have completed Project 2L ———————————————

Apply a combination of the **2A** and **2B** skills.

GO! Think | Project **2M** Expense Summary

Project Files

For Project 2M, you will need the following file:

    e02M_Expense_Summary

You will save your workbook as:

    Lastname_Firstname_2M_Expense_Summary

Sara Lopez, Director of the San Diego production facility, has requested a summary analysis of the administrative expenses the facility incurred in the last fiscal year. Open e02M_Expense_Summary and then complete the calculation in the four worksheets containing the quarterly data. Summarize the information in a new worksheet that includes formulas referencing the totals for each expense category for each quarter. Sum the expenses to display the yearly expense by quarter and expense category. Format the worksheets in a manner that is professional and easy to read and understand. Insert a footer with the file name and add appropriate document properties. Save the file as **Lastname_Firstname_2M_Expense_Summary** and print or submit as directed by your instructor.

End You have completed Project 2M ———————————————

Outcomes-Based Assessments

You and GO! | Project **2N** Annual Expenses

Project Files

For Project 2N, you will need the following file:

New blank Excel workbook

You will save your workbook as:

Lastname_Firstname_2N_Annual_Expenses

Develop a workbook that details the expenses you expect to incur during the current year. Create four worksheets, one for each quarter of the year and enter your expenses by month. For example, the Quarter 1 sheet will contain expense information for January, February, and March. Some of these expenses might include, but are not limited to, Mortgage, Rent, Utilities, Phone, Food, Entertainment, Tuition, Childcare, Clothing, and Insurance. Include monthly and quarterly totals for each category of expense. Insert a worksheet that summarizes the total expenses for each quarter. Format the worksheet by adjusting column width and wrapping text, and by applying appropriate financial number formatting and cell styles. Insert a footer with the file name and center the worksheet horizontally on the page. Save your file as **Lastname_Firstname_2N_Annual_Expenses** and submit as directed.

End **You have completed Project 2N** ⎯⎯⎯⎯⎯⎯⎯⎯⎯⎯⎯⎯⎯⎯⎯⎯⎯

Analyzing Data with Pie Charts, Line Charts, and What-If Analysis Tools

OUTCOMES

At the end of this chapter you will be able to:

OBJECTIVES

Mastering these objectives will enable you to:

PROJECT 3A
Present budget data in a pie chart.

1. Chart Data with a Pie Chart (p. 179)
2. Format a Pie Chart (p. 182)
3. Edit a Workbook and Update a Chart (p. 188)
4. Use Goal Seek to Perform What-If Analysis (p. 189)

PROJECT 3B
Make projections using what-if analysis and present projections in a line chart.

5. Design a Worksheet for What-If Analysis (p. 195)
6. Answer What-If Questions by Changing Values in a Worksheet (p. 202)
7. Chart Data with a Line Chart (p. 205)

iofoto/Shutterstock

In This Chapter

In this chapter, you will work with two different types of commonly used charts that make it easy to visualize data. You will create a pie chart in a separate chart sheet to show how the parts of a budget contribute to a total budget. You will also practice using parentheses in a formula, calculate the percentage rate of an increase, answer what-if questions, and then chart data in a line chart to show the flow of data over time. In this chapter you will also practice formatting the axes in a line chart.

The projects in this chapter relate to **The City of Orange Blossom Beach**, a coastal city located between Fort Lauderdale and Miami. The city's access to major transportation provides both residents and businesses an opportunity to compete in the global marketplace. Each year the city welcomes a large number of tourists who enjoy the warm climate and beautiful beaches, and who embark on cruises from this major cruise port. The city encourages best environmental practices and partners with cities in other countries to promote sound government at the local level.

Project 3A Budget Pie Chart

Project Activities

In Activities 3.01 through 3.11, you will edit a worksheet for Lila Darius, City Manager, that projects expenses from the city's general fund for the next fiscal year, and then present the data in a pie chart. Your completed worksheet will look similar to Figure 3.1.

Project Files

For Project 3A, you will need the following file:

e03A_Fund_Expenses

You will save your workbook as:

Lastname_Firstname_3A_Fund_Expenses

Project Results

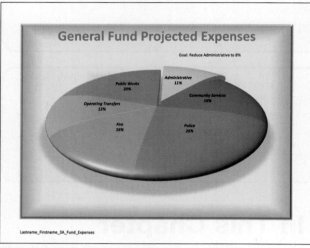

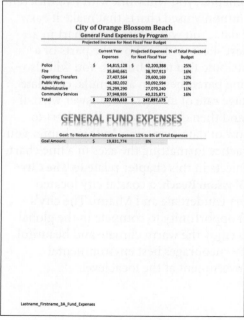

Figure 3.1
Project 3A Fund Expenses

Objective 1 | Chart Data with a Pie Chart

A *pie chart* shows the relationship of each part to a whole. The size of each pie slice is equal to its value compared to the total value of all the slices. The pie chart style charts data that is arranged in a single column or single row, and shows the size of items in a single data series proportional to the sum of the items. Whereas a column or bar chart can have two or more data series in the chart, a pie chart can have only one data series.

Consider using a pie chart when you have only one data series to plot, you do not have more than seven categories, and the categories represent parts of a total value.

Activity 3.01 | Creating a Pie Chart and a Chart Sheet

A *fund* is a sum of money set aside for a specific purpose. In a municipal government like the City of Orange Blossom Beach, the *general fund* is money set aside for the normal operating activities of the city, such as police, fire, and administering the everyday functions of the city.

1 **Start** Excel. From the student files that accompany this textbook, open **e03A_Fund_ Expenses**. From **Backstage view**, display the **Save As** dialog box. Navigate to the location where you are storing projects for this chapter.

2 Create a new folder named **Excel Chapter 3** and open the new folder. In the **File name** box, type **Lastname_Firstname_3A_Fund_Expenses** Click **Save** or press Enter.

> The worksheet indicates the expenses for the current year and the projected expenses for the next fiscal year.

3 Click cell **D5**, and then type = to begin a formula.

4 Click cell **C5**, which is the first value that is part of the total Projected Expenses, to insert it into the formula. Type **/** to indicate division, and then click cell **C11**, which is the total Projected Expenses.

> Recall that to determine the percentage by which a value makes up a total, you must divide the value by the total. The result will be a percentage expressed as a decimal.

5 Press F4 to make the reference to the value in cell **C11** absolute, which will enable you to copy the formula. Compare your screen with Figure 3.2.

> Recall that an *absolute cell reference* refers to a cell by its fixed position in the worksheet. The reference to cell C5 is a *relative cell reference*, because when you copy the formula, you want the reference to change *relative* to its row.

> Recall also that dollar signs display to indicate that a cell reference is absolute.

Figure 3.2

Formula Bar displays formula

Cell C5 bordered in blue indicating it is part of an active formula

Reference to cell C11 with $ signs to indicate an absolute cell reference

Cell C11 selected as part of active formula

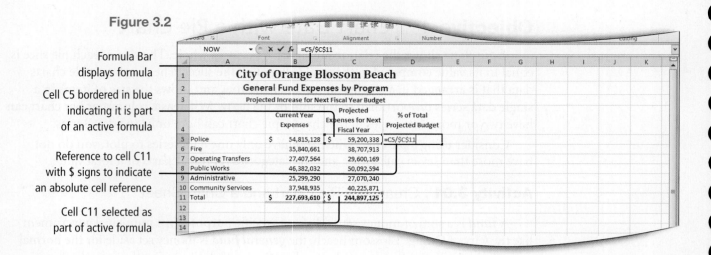

6 On the **Formula Bar**, click the **Enter** button ☑ to confirm the entry and to keep cell **D5** the active cell. Copy the formula down through cell **D10**, and then compare your screen with Figure 3.3.

Figure 3.3

Auto Fill Options button displays

Percentages, expressed as decimals

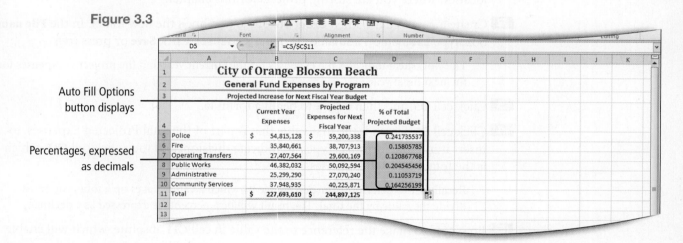

7 With the range **D5:D10** still selected, right-click over the selection, and then on the Mini toolbar, click the **Percent Style** button % and the **Center** 🗏 button. Click cell **A1** to cancel the selection, and then **Save** 🖫 your workbook. Compare your screen with Figure 3.4.

Figure 3.4

Percent of Total for each program calculated, expressed as percentages

8 Select the range **A5:A10**, hold down Ctrl, and then select the range **C5:C10** to select the nonadjacent ranges with the program names and the projected expense for each program.

> To create a pie chart, you must select two ranges. One range contains the labels for each slice of the pie chart, and the other range contains the values that add up to a total. The two ranges must have the same number of cells and the range with the values should *not* include the cell with the total.
>
> The program names (Police, Fire, and so on) are the category names and will identify the slices of the pie chart. Each projected expense is a ***data point***—a value that originates in a worksheet cell and that is represented in a chart by a ***data marker***. In a pie chart, each pie slice is a data marker. Together, the data points form the ***data series***—related data points represented by data markers—and determine the size of each pie slice.

9 With the nonadjacent ranges selected, click the **Insert tab**, and then in the **Charts group**, click **Pie**. Under **3-D Pie**, click the first chart—**Pie in 3-D**—to create the chart on your worksheet.

10 On the **Design tab**, at the right end of the Ribbon in the **Location group**, click the **Move Chart** button. In the **Move Chart** dialog box, click the **New sheet** option button.

11 In the **New sheet** box, replace the highlighted text *Chart1* by typing **Projected Expenses Chart** and then click **OK** to display the chart on a separate worksheet in your workbook. Compare your screen with Figure 3.5.

> The pie chart displays on a separate new sheet in your workbook, and a ***legend*** identifies the pie slices. Recall that a legend is a chart element that identifies the patterns or colors assigned to the categories in the chart.
>
> A ***chart sheet*** is a workbook sheet that contains only a chart; it is useful when you want to view a chart separately from the worksheet data. The sheet tab indicates *Projected Expenses Chart*.

Figure 3.5

Chart Tools active

Move Chart button on Design tab

Chart displays on a separate new worksheet

Legend identifies pie slices

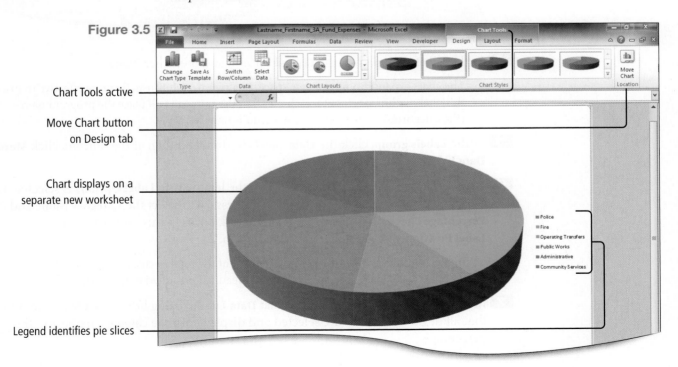

Objective 2 | Format a Pie Chart

Activity 3.02 | Applying Percentages to Labels in a Pie Chart

In your worksheet, for each expense, you calculated the percent of the total in column D. These percentages can also be calculated by the Chart feature and added to the pie slices as labels.

1 On the Ribbon under **Chart Tools**, click the **Layout tab**, and then in the **Labels group**, click the **Chart Title** button. On the displayed list, click **Above Chart**.

2 With the **Chart Title** box selected, watch the **Formula Bar** as you type **General Fund Projected Expenses** and then press Enter to create the new chart title in the box.

3 Point to the chart title text, right-click to display the Mini toolbar, and then change the **Font Size** to **36** and change the **Font Color** [A ▾] to **Olive Green, Accent 1, Darker 25%**—in the fifth column, the fifth color. Compare your screen with Figure 3.6.

Figure 3.6

Text displays in Formula Bar as you type

New chart title text entered and formatted

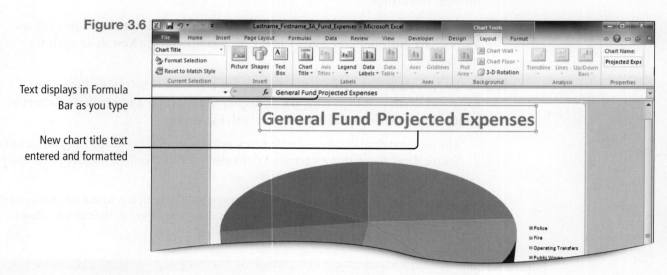

4 In the **Labels group**, click the **Legend** button, and then click **None**.

The chart expands to fill the new space. In a pie chart, it is usually more effective to place the labels within, or close to, each pie slice. Because you will place the program names (the categories) on the pie slices, a legend is unnecessary.

5 In the **Labels group**, click the **Data Labels** button, and then at the bottom, click **More Data Label Options**.

6 In the **Format Data Labels** dialog box, on the left, be sure **Label Options** is selected. On the right, under **Label Contains**, click as necessary to select the **Category Name** and **Percentage** check boxes. *Clear* any other check boxes in this group. Under **Label Position**, click the **Center** option button.

In the worksheet, you calculated the percent of the total in column D. Here, the percentage will be calculated by the Chart feature and added to the chart as a label.

7 In the lower right corner of the **Format Data Labels** dialog box, click **Close**, and notice that all of the data labels are selected and display both the category name and the percentage.

8 Point to any of the selected labels, right-click to display the Mini toolbar, and then change the **Font Size** to **11**, apply **Bold** B, and apply **Italic** I.

9 **Save** 🖫 your workbook. Press Esc to deselect the labels, and then compare your screen with Figure 3.7.

Figure 3.7

Data labels on pie slices replace legend; labels include category name and percentage; data labels centered in slice, 11 pt font, bold and italic

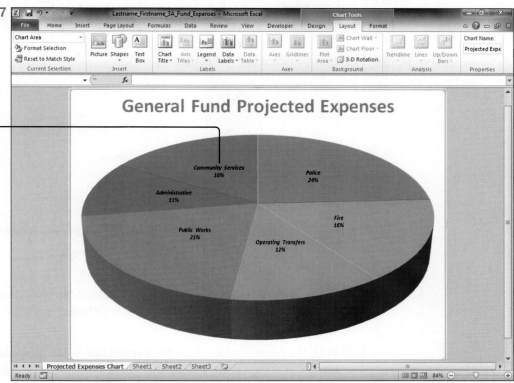

Activity 3.03 | Formatting a Pie Chart with 3-D

3-D, which is short for *three-dimensional*, refers to an image that appears to have all three spatial dimensions—length, width, and depth.

1 Click in any pie slice outside of the label to select the entire pie; notice that selection handles display on the outside corners of each slice.

2 Click the **Format tab**. In the **Shape Styles group**, click the **Shape Effects** button, point to **Bevel**, and then at the bottom of the gallery, click **3-D Options**.

3 In the **Format Data Series** dialog box, on the right, under **Bevel**, click the **Top** button. In the displayed gallery, under **Bevel**, point to the first button to display the ScreenTip *Circle*. Click the **Circle** button. Then click the **Bottom** button, and apply the **Circle** bevel.

Bevel is a shape effect that uses shading and shadows to make the edges of a shape appear to be curved or angled.

4 In the four **Width** and **Height** spin boxes, type **512 pt** and then compare your screen with Figure 3.8.

Figure 3.8

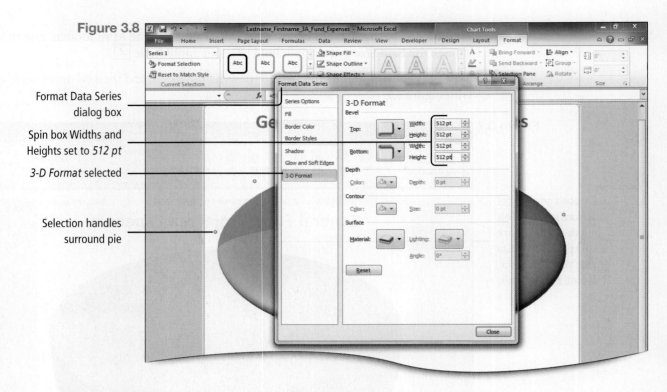

Format Data Series
dialog box

Spin box Widths and
Heights set to *512 pt*

3-D Format selected

Selection handles
surround pie

5. In the lower portion of the dialog box, under **Surface**, click the **Material** button. Under **Standard**, click the third button—**Plastic**. In the lower right corner, click **Close**.

6. With the pie still selected, on the **Format tab**, in the **Shape Styles group**, click **Shape Effects**, and then point to **Shadow**. At the bottom of the displayed gallery, scroll if necessary, and then under **Perspective**, click the third button, which displays the ScreenTip *Below* to display a shadow below the pie chart. Click **Save**.

Activity 3.04 | Rotating a Pie Chart

The order in which the data series in pie charts are plotted in Excel is determined by the order of the data on the worksheet. To gain a different view of the chart, you can rotate the chart within the 360 degrees of the circle of the pie shape to present a different visual perspective of the chart.

1. Notice the position of the **Fire** and **Police** slices in the chart. Then, with the pie chart still selected—sizing handles surround the pie—point anywhere in the pie and right-click. On the displayed shortcut menu, click **Format Data Series**.

Another Way

Drag the slider to 100.

2. In the **Format Data Series** dialog box, on the left, be sure **Series Options** is selected. On the right, under **Angle of first slice**, click in the box and type **100** to rotate the chart 100 degrees to the right.

3. Close the **Format Data Series** dialog box. Click **Save**, and then compare your screen with Figure 3.9.

Rotating the chart can provide a better perspective to the chart. Here, rotating the chart in this manner emphasizes that the Fire and Police programs represent a significant portion of the total expenses.

Figure 3.9

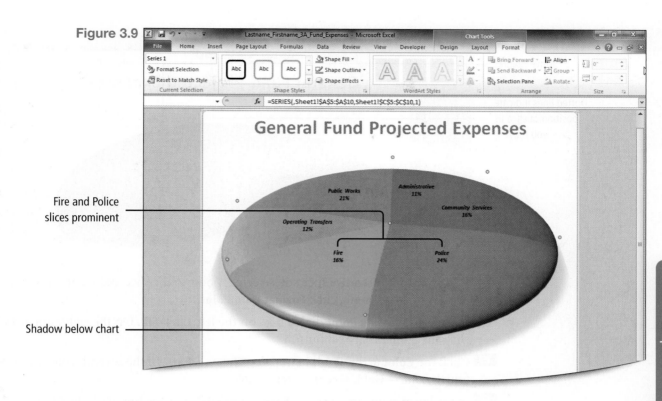

Fire and Police
slices prominent

Shadow below chart

Activity 3.05 | Exploding and Coloring a Pie Slice

You can pull out—*explode*—one or more slices of a pie chart to emphasize a specific slice or slices. Additionally, there is a different chart type you can select if you want *all* the slices to explode and emphasize all the individual slices of a pie chart—the exploded pie or exploded pie in 3-D chart type. The exploded pie chart type displays the contribution of *each* value to the total, while at the same time emphasizing individual values.

1 Press Esc to deselect all chart elements. Click any slice to select the entire pie, and then click the **Administrative** slice to select only that slice. Compare your screen with Figure 3.10.

Figure 3.10

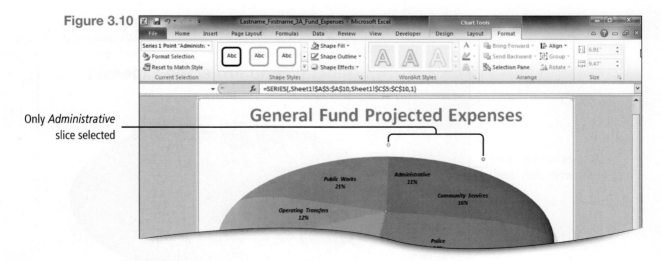

Only *Administrative*
slice selected

2 Point to the **Administrative** slice to display the pointer, and then drag the slice slightly upward and away from the center of the pie, as shown in Figure 3.11, and then release the mouse button.

Figure 3.11

Move pointer

Dotted lines indicate position of slice as you move it

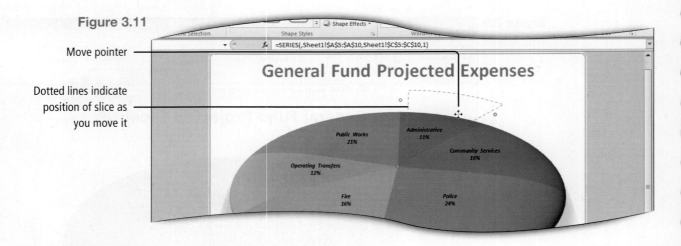

General Fund Projected Expenses

Public Works 21%

Administrative 11%

Community Services 16%

Operating Transfers 12%

Fire 16%

Police 24%

3 With the **Administrative** slice still selected, point to the slice and right-click, and then on the shortcut menu, click **Format Data Point**.

4 In the **Format Data Point** dialog box, on the left, click **Fill**. On the right, under **Fill**, click the **Solid fill** option button.

5 Click the **Color arrow**, and then under **Theme Colors**, in the seventh column, click the fourth color—**Gold, Accent 3, Lighter 40%**.

6 In the lower right corner of the **Format Data Point** dialog box, click the **Close** button.

Activity 3.06 | Formatting the Chart Area

The entire chart and all of its elements comprise the ***chart area***.

1 Point to the white area just inside the border of the chart to display the ScreenTip *Chart Area*. Click one time.

2 On the **Format tab**, in the **Shape Styles group**, click the **Shape Effects** button, point to **Bevel**, and then under **Bevel**, in the second row, click the third bevel—**Convex**.

3 Press Esc to deselect the chart element and view this effect—a convex beveled frame around your entire chart—and then compare your screen with Figure 3.12.

Figure 3.12

Convex beveled frame surrounds chart sheet

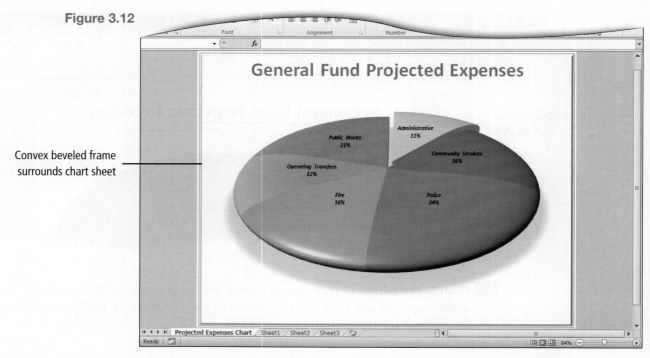

General Fund Projected Expenses

Public Works 21%

Administrative 11%

Community Services 16%

Operating Transfers 12%

Fire 16%

Police 24%

Projected Expenses Chart | Sheet1 | Sheet2 | Sheet3

Ready

4 Point slightly inside the border of the chart to display the ScreenTip *Chart Area*, right-click, and then on the shortcut menu, click **Format Chart Area**.

5 In the **Format Chart Area** dialog box, on the left, be sure that **Fill** is selected. On the right, under **Fill**, click the **Gradient fill** option button.

6 Click the **Preset colors** arrow, and then in the second row, click the last preset, **Fog**. Click the **Type arrow**, and then click **Path**. Click the **Close** button.

7 Compare your screen with Figure 3.13, and then **Save** your workbook.

Figure 3.13

Chart area formatted
with *Fog* gradient

Bevel effect added
to chart area

Border indicates that
the chart is selected

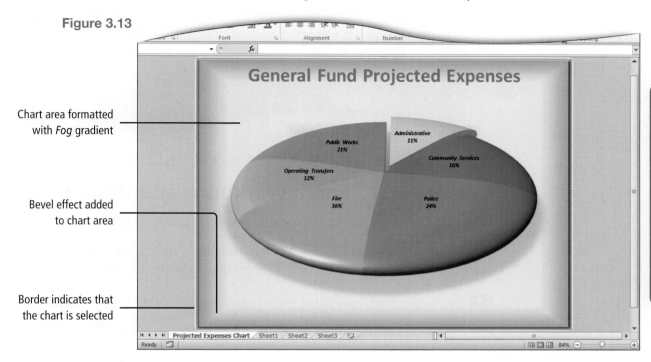

Activity 3.07 | Inserting a Text Box in a Chart

A *text box* is a movable, resizable container for text or graphics.

1 With the Chart Area still selected, click the **Layout tab**, and then in the **Insert group**, click the **Text Box** button, and then move the pointer into the chart area.

2 Position the displayed ↧ pointer under the *c* in *Projected* and about midway between the title and the pie—above the *Administrative* slice. Hold down the left mouse button, and then drag down and to the right approximately as shown in Figure 3.14; your text box need not be precise.

Figure 3.14

Text Box button

Text box drawn

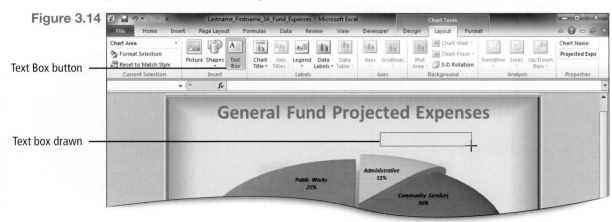

3 With the insertion point blinking inside the text box, type **Goal: Reduce Administrative to 8%** Press [Esc] or click outside the chart area to deselect the chart element, and then compare your screen with Figure 3.15.

Figure 3.15

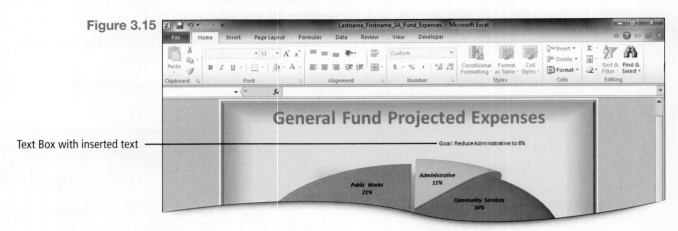

Text Box with inserted text ———————————— Goal: Reduce Administrative to 8%

General Fund Projected Expenses

Public Works 21% Administrative 11% Community Services 16%

4 If necessary, select and then adjust or move your text box. **Save** 💾 your workbook.

Objective 3 | Edit a Workbook and Update a Chart

Activity 3.08 | Editing a Workbook and Updating a Chart

If you edit the data in your worksheet, the chart data markers—in this instance the pie slices—will adjust automatically to accurately represent the new values.

1 On the pie chart, notice that *Police* represents 24% of the total projected expenses.

2 In the sheet tab area at the bottom of the workbook, click the **Sheet1 tab** to redisplay the worksheet.

> **Another Way**
> Double-click the cell to position the insertion point in the cell and edit.

3 Click cell **C5**, and then in **Formula Bar**, change *59,200,338* to **62,200,388**

4 Press [Enter], and notice that the total in cell **C11** recalculates to *$247,897,175* and the percentages in **column D** also recalculate.

5 Display the **Projected Expenses Chart** sheet. Notice that the pie slices adjust to show the recalculation—*Police* is now *25%* of the projected expenses. Click **Save** 💾, and then compare your screen with Figure 3.16.

Figure 3.16

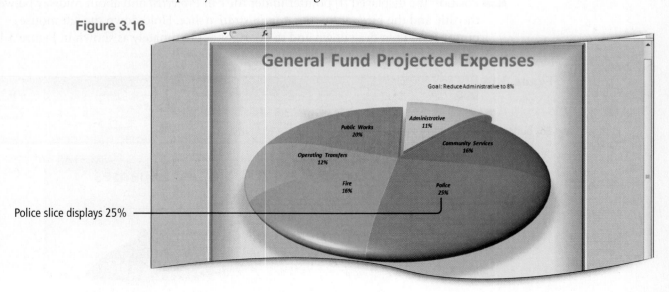

General Fund Projected Expenses

Goal: Reduce Administrative to 8%

Public Works 20% Administrative 11% Community Services 16% Operating Transfers 12% Fire 16% Police 25%

Police slice displays 25% ——————————

Activity 3.09 | Inserting WordArt in a Worksheet

WordArt is a gallery of text styles with which you can create decorative effects, such as shadowed or mirrored text. In an Excel worksheet, WordArt can be effective if you plan to display your worksheet in a PowerPoint presentation, or if readers will be viewing the worksheet data online.

1 In the sheet tab area at the bottom of the workbook, click the **Sheet1 tab** to redisplay the worksheet. Click the **Insert tab**, and then in the **Text group**, click the **WordArt** button.

2 In the WordArt gallery, in the last row, click the last style—**Fill – Olive Green, Accent 1, Metal Bevel, Reflection**.

The WordArt indicating *YOUR TEXT HERE* displays in the worksheet.

3 With the WordArt selected, type **general fund expenses** and then point anywhere on the dashed border surrounding the WordArt object. Click the dashed border one time to change it to a solid border, indicating that all of the text is selected.

4 On the **Home tab**, in the **Font group**, change the **Font Size** to **28**.

5 Point to the WordArt border to display the ⊹ pointer, and then drag to position the upper left corner of the WordArt approximately as shown in Figure 3.17. If necessary, hold down Ctrl and press any of the arrow keys on your keyboard to move the WordArt object into position in small increments. Click any cell to deselect the WordArt, and then click **Save** 💾.

Figure 3.17

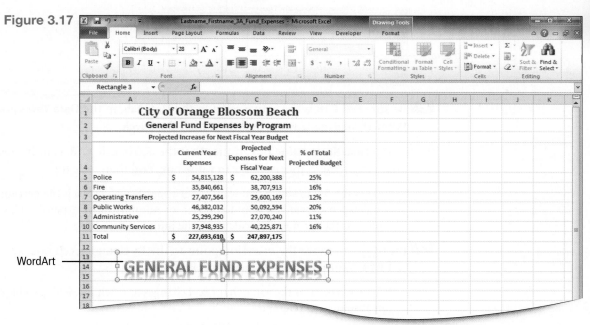

WordArt

Objective 4 | Use Goal Seek to Perform What-If Analysis

Activity 3.10 | Using Goal Seek to Perform What-If Analysis

The process of changing the values in cells to see how those changes affect the outcome of formulas in your worksheet is referred to as *what-if analysis*. A what-if analysis tool that is included with Excel is *Goal Seek*, which finds the input needed in one cell to arrive at the desired result in another cell.

1 In cell **A17**, type **Goal: To Reduce Administrative Expenses from 11% to 8% of Total Expenses** Merge and center the text across the range **A17:D17**, and then apply the **Heading 3** Cell Style.

2 In cell **A18**, type **Goal Amount:** and press Enter.

3 Select the range **C9:D9**, right-click over the selection, and then click **Copy**. Point to cell **B18**, right-click, and then under **Paste Options**, click the **Paste** button.

4 Press Esc to cancel the moving border, click cell **C18**, and then compare your screen with Figure 3.18.

Figure 3.18

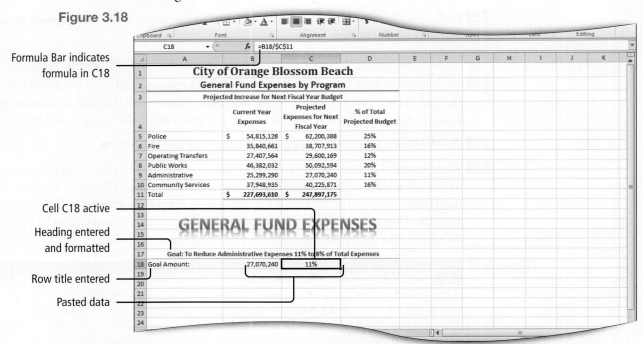

Formula Bar indicates formula in C18

Cell C18 active

Heading entered and formatted

Row title entered

Pasted data

5 Be sure cell **C18** is the active cell. On the **Data tab**, in the **Data Tools group**, click the **What-If Analysis** button, and then click **Goal Seek**.

6 In the **Goal Seek** dialog box, notice that the active cell, **C18**, is indicated in the **Set cell** box. Press Tab to move to the **To value** box, and then type **8%**

C18 is the cell in which you want to set a specific value; 8% is the percentage of the total expenses that you want to budget for Administrative expenses. The Set cell box contains the formula that calculates the information you seek.

7 Press Tab to move the insertion point to the **By changing cell** box, and then click cell **B18**. Compare your screen with Figure 3.19.

Cell B18 contains the value that Excel changes to reach the goal. Excel formats this cell as an absolute cell reference.

Figure 3.19

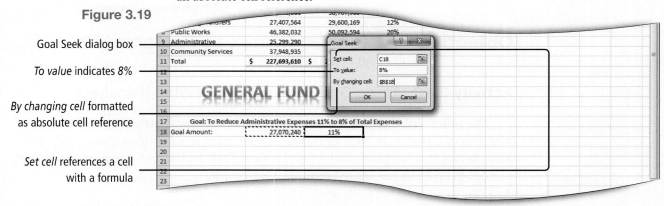

Goal Seek dialog box

To value indicates 8%

By changing cell formatted as absolute cell reference

Set cell references a cell with a formula

8 Click **OK**. In the displayed **Goal Seek Status** dialog box, click **OK**.

9 Select the range **A18:C18**. From the **Home tab**, display the **Cell Styles** gallery. Under **Themed Cell Styles**, apply **20% - Accent3**. Click cell **B18**, and then from the **Cell Styles** gallery, at the bottom of the gallery under **Number Format**, apply the **Currency [0]** cell style.

10 Press Ctrl + Home, click **Save** 🖫 , and then compare your screen with Figure 3.20.

> Excel calculates that the City must budget for *$19,831,774* in Administrative expenses in order for this item to become 8% of the total projected budget.

Figure 3.20

Goal of *$19,831,774*

Accent shading applied

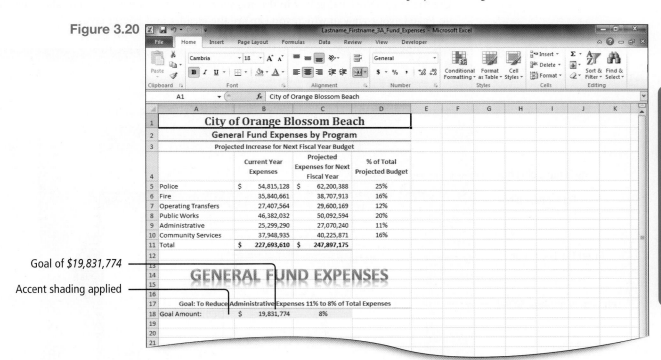

Activity 3.11 | Preparing and Printing a Workbook with a Chart Sheet

Another Way

Right-click the sheet tab, click Rename, type, and press Enter.

1 With your worksheet displayed, in the sheet tab area, double-click *Sheet1* to select the text, and then type **Projected Expenses Data** and press Enter.

2 Select **Sheet2** and **Sheet3**, right-click over the selected tabs, and then click **Delete** to delete the unused sheets.

3 On the **Insert tab**, click **Header & Footer**. In the **Navigation group**, click the **Go to Footer** button, click in the **left section** above the word *Footer*, and then in the **Header & Footer Elements group**, click the **File Name** button.

4 Click in a cell above the footer to deselect the **Footer area** and view your file name. On the **Page Layout tab**, in the **Page Setup group**, click the **Margins** button, and then at the bottom click **Custom Margins**.

5 In the displayed **Page Setup** dialog box, under **Center on page**, select the **Horizontally** check box. Click **OK**, and then on the status bar, click the **Normal** button 🔲 to return to Normal view.

> Recall that after displaying worksheets in Page Layout View, dotted lines display to indicate the page breaks when you return to Normal view.

6 Press Ctrl + Home to move to the top of the worksheet.

7 Click the **Projected Expenses Chart** sheet tab to display the chart sheet. On the **Insert tab**, in the **Text group**, click **Header & Footer** to display the **Header/Footer tab** of the **Page Setup** dialog box.

8 In the center of the **Page Setup** dialog box, click **Custom Footer**. With the insertion point blinking in the **Left section**, in the row of buttons in the middle of the dialog box, locate and click the **Insert File Name** button 📄. Compare your screen with Figure 3.21.

> Use the Page Setup dialog box in this manner to insert a footer on a chart sheet, which has no Page Layout view in which you can see the Header and Footer areas.

Figure 3.21

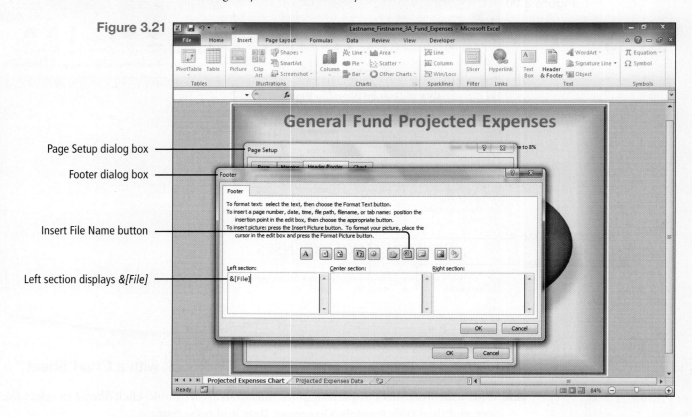

Page Setup dialog box

Footer dialog box

Insert File Name button

Left section displays *&[File]*

9 Click **OK** two times. Display **Backstage** view, on the right under the thumbnail, click **Properties**, and then click **Show Document Panel**. In the **Author** box, replace the existing text with your firstname and lastname. In the **Subject** box, type your course name and section number. In the **Keywords** box type **general fund, expenses, pie chart** and then **Close** ☒ the **Document Information Panel**.

10 Right-click either of the sheet tabs, and then click **Select All Sheets**. Verify that *[Group]* displays in the title bar.

> Recall that by selecting all sheets, you can view all of the workbook pages in Print Preview.

11 Press Ctrl + F2 to display the **Print Preview**. Examine the first page, and then at the bottom of the **Print Preview**, click the **Next Page** ▶ button to view the second page of your workbook.

> **Note | Printing a Chart Sheet Uses More Toner**
>
> Printing a chart that displays on a chart sheet will use more toner or ink than a small chart that is part of a worksheet. If you are printing your work, check with your instructor to verify whether or not you should print the chart sheet.

12 Click **Save** to redisplay the workbook. Print or submit electronically as directed by your instructor.

13 If you are directed to submit printed formulas, refer to Activity 1.16 in Project 1A to do so.

14 If you printed your formulas, be sure to redisplay the worksheet by clicking the Show Formulas button to turn it off. **Close** the workbook. If you are prompted to save changes, click **No** so that you do not save the changes to the worksheet that you used for printing formulas. **Close** Excel.

> **More Knowledge | Setting the Default Number of Sheets in a New Workbook**
>
> By default, the number of new worksheets in a new workbook is three, but you can change this default number. From Backstage view, display the Excel Options dialog box, click the General tab, and then under When creating new workbooks, change the number in the Include this many sheets box.

End **You have completed Project 3A** ———————————————

Project 3B Growth Projection with Line Chart

Project Activities

In Activities 3.12 through 3.19, you will assist Lila Darius, City Manager, in creating a worksheet to estimate future population growth based on three possible growth rates. You will also create a line chart to display past population growth. Your resulting worksheet and chart will look similar to Figure 3.22.

Project Files

For Project 3B, you will need the following files:

> e03B_Population_Growth
> e03B_Beach

You will save your workbook as:

> Lastname_Firstname_3B_Population_Growth

Project Results

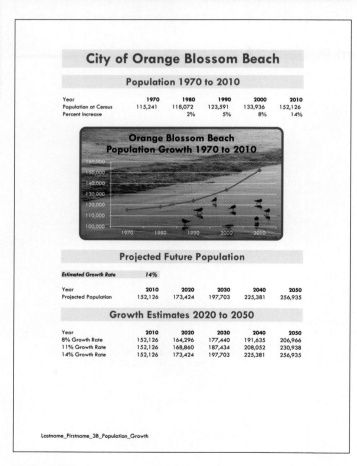

Figure 3.22
Project 3B Population Growth

Objective 5 | Design a Worksheet for What-If Analysis

Excel recalculates; if you change the value in a cell referenced in a formula, Excel automatically recalculates the result of the formula. Thus, you can change cell values to see *what* would happen *if* you tried different values. Recall that this process of changing the values in cells to see how those changes affect the outcome of formulas in your worksheet is referred to as what-if analysis.

Activity 3.12 | Using Parentheses in a Formula to Calculate a Percentage Rate of Increase

Ms. Darius has the city's population figures for the past five 10-year census periods. In each 10-year census period, the population has increased. In this activity, you will construct a formula to calculate the *percentage rate of increase*—the percent by which one number increases over another number—for each 10-year census period since 1970. From this information, future population growth can be estimated.

1 **Start** Excel. From your student files, open the file **e03B_Population_Growth**. From **Backstage** view, display the **Save As** dialog box. Navigate to your **Excel Chapter 3** folder, in the **File name** box, name the file **Lastname_Firstname_3B_Population_Growth** and then click **Save** or press [Enter].

2 Leave **row 4** blank, and then click cell **A5**. Type **Year** and then press [Tab]. In cell **B5**, type **1970** and then press [Tab].

3 In cell **C5**, type **1980** and then press [Tab]. Select the range **B5:C5**, and then drag the fill handle to the right through cell **F5** to extend the series to 2010.

> By establishing a pattern of 10-year intervals with the first two cells, you can use the fill handle to continue the series. The AutoFill feature will do this for any pattern that you establish with two or more cells.

4 With the range **B5:F5** still selected, right-click over the selection, and then on the Mini toolbar, click **Bold** [B]. Compare your screen with Figure 3.23.

Figure 3.23

AutoFill used to fill 10-year periods to create column titles

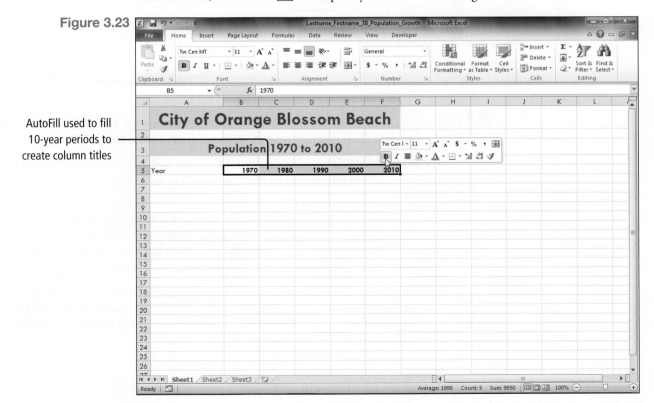

5 In cell **A6**, type **Population at Census** and press ⏎. In cell **A7**, type **Percent Increase** and press ⏎.

6 Click cell **B6**, and then beginning in cell **B6**, and pressing ⇥ to move across the row, enter the following values for the population in the years listed:

1970	1980	1990	2000	2010
115241	**118072**	**123591**	**133936**	**152126**

7 Select the range **B6:F6**, right-click, on the Mini toolbar, click **Comma Style** ⟨ ʼ ⟩, and then click **Decrease Decimal** ⟨⁰⁰⟩ two times.

8 Click cell **C7**. Being sure to include the parentheses, type **=(c6-b6)/b6** and then on the **Formula Bar**, click the **Enter** button ✔ to keep cell **C7** active; your result is *0.02456591* (or *0.02*). Compare your screen with Figure 3.24.

> Recall that as you type, a list of Excel functions that begin with the letter *C* and *B* may briefly display. This is ***Formula AutoComplete***, an Excel feature which, after typing an = (equal sign) and the beginning letter or letters of a function name, displays a list of function names that match the typed letter(s). In this instance, the letters represent cell references, *not* the beginning of a function name.

Figure 3.24

Formula Bar displays formula

Formula result in cell C7 (yours may display *0.02*)

Values entered for population, Comma Style with no decimals applied

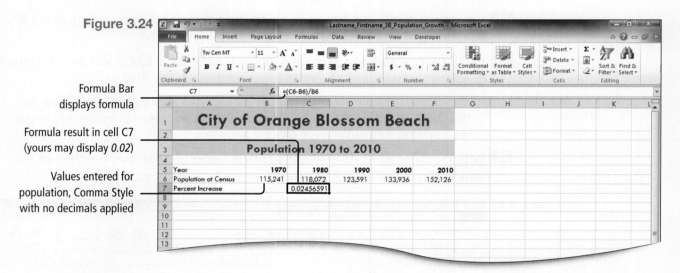

9 With cell **C7** active, on the **Home tab**, in the **Number group**, click the **Percent Style** button ⟨%⟩, and then examine the formula in the **Formula Bar**.

> The mathematical formula ***rate = amount of increase/base*** is used to calculated the percentage rate of population increase from 1970 to 1980. The formula is applied as follows:

> First, determine the *amount of increase* by subtracting the ***base***—the starting point represented by the 1970 population—from the 1980 population. Thus, the *amount of increase* = 118,072 – 115,241 or 2,831. Between 1970 and 1980, the population increased by 2,831 people. In the formula, this calculation is represented by *C6-B6*.

> Second, calculate the *rate*—what the amount of increase (2,831) represents as a percentage of the base (1970's population of 115,241). Determine this by dividing the amount of increase (2,831) by the base (115,241). Thus, 2,831 divided by 115,241 is equal to 0.02456591 or, when formatted as a percent, 2%.

10 In the **Formula Bar**, locate the parentheses enclosing *C6-B6*.

Excel follows a set of mathematical rules called the ***order of operations***, which has four basic parts:

- Expressions within parentheses are processed first.
- Exponentiation, if present, is performed before multiplication and division.
- Multiplication and division are performed before addition and subtraction.
- Consecutive operators with the same level of precedence are calculated from left to right.

11 Click cell **D7**, type = and then by typing, or using a combination of typing and clicking cells to reference them, construct a formula similar to the one in cell **C7** to calculate the rate of increase in population from 1980 to 1990. Compare your screen with Figure 3.25.

Recall that the first step is to determine the *amount of increase*—1990 population minus 1980 population—and then to write the calculation so that Excel performs this operation first; that is, place it in parentheses.

The second step is to divide the result of the calculation in parentheses by the *base*—the population for 1980.

Figure 3.25

Formula to calculate percent increase from 1980 to 1990

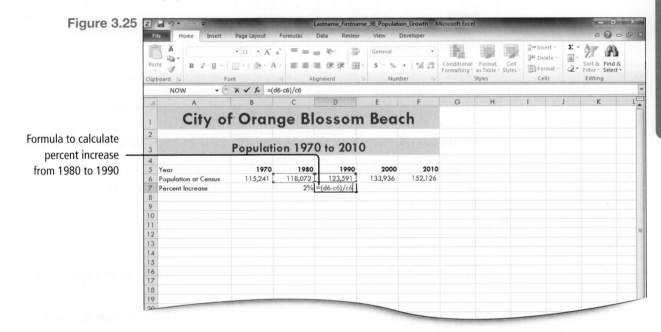

12 Press Enter; your result is *0.04674267* (or *0.05*). Format cell **D7** with the **Percent Style** %.

Your result is *5%*; Excel rounds up or down to format percentages.

13 With cell **D7** selected, drag the fill handle to the right through cell **F7**. Click any empty cell to cancel the selection, **Save** 🖫 your workbook, and then compare your screen with Figure 3.26.

Because this formula uses relative cell references—that is, for each year, the formula is the same but the values used are relative to the formula's location—you can copy the formula in this manner. For example, the result for 1990 uses the 1980 population as the base, the result for 2000 uses the 1990 population as the base, and the result for 2010 uses the 2000 population as the base.

The formula results show the percent of increase for each 10-year period between 1970 and 2010. You can see that in each 10-year period, the population has grown as much as 14%—from 2000 to 2010—and as little as 2%—from 1970 to 1980.

Figure 3.26

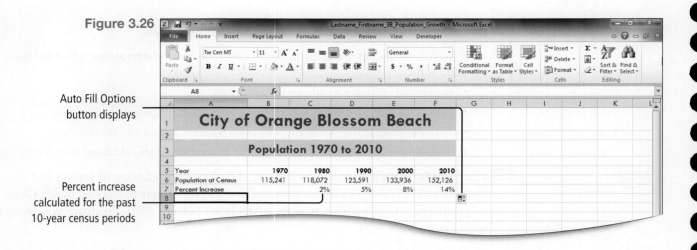

Auto Fill Options button displays

Percent increase calculated for the past 10-year census periods

---

More Knowledge | Use of Parentheses in a Formula

When writing a formula in Excel, use parentheses to communicate the order in which the operations should occur. For example, to average three test scores of 100, 50, and 90 that you scored on three different tests, you would add the test scores and then divide by the number of test scores in the list. If you write this formula as =100+50+90/3, the result would be 180, because Excel would first divide 90 by 3 and then add 100+50+30. Excel would do so because the order of operations states that multiplication and division are calculated *before* addition and subtraction.

The correct way to write this formula is =(100+50+90)/3. Excel will add the three values, and then divide the result by 3, or 240/3 resulting in a correct average of 80. Parentheses play an important role in ensuring that you get the correct result in your formulas.

Activity 3.13 | Using Format Painter and Formatting as You Type

You can format numbers as you type them. When you type numbers in a format that Excel recognizes, Excel automatically applies that format to the cell. Recall that once applied, cell formats remain with the cell, even if the cell contents are deleted. In this activity, you will format cells by typing the numbers with percent signs and use Format Painter to copy text (non-numeric) formats.

1 Leave **row 8** blank, and then click cell **A9**. Type **Projected Future Population** and then press Enter.

Another Way

On the Home tab, in the Clipboard group, click the Format Painter button.

2 Point to cell **A3**, right-click, on the Mini toolbar click the **Format Painter** button , and then click cell **A9**.

> The format of cell A3 is *painted*—applied to—cell A9, including the merging and centering of the text across the range A9:F9.

3 Leave **row 10** blank, and then click cell **A11**, type **Estimated Growth Rate** and then press Enter.

4 Leave **row 12** blank, and then click cell **A13**. Type **Year** and then in cell **A14**, type **Projected Population**

5 In cell **B13**, type **2010** and then press Tab. In cell **C13**, type **2020** and then press Tab.

6 Select the range **B13:C13**, and then drag the fill handle through cell **F13** to extend the pattern of years to *2050*. Apply **Bold B** to the selected range. Compare your screen with Figure 3.27.

Figure 3.27

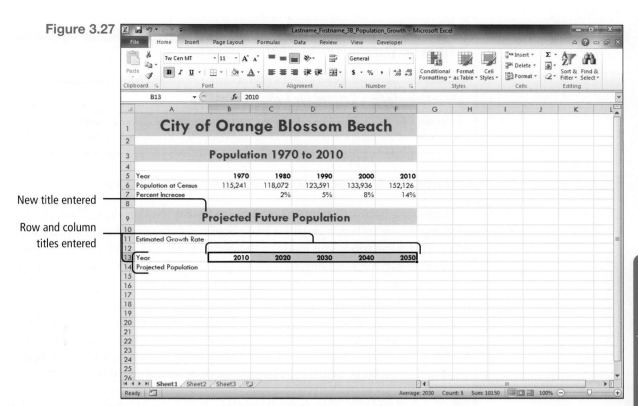

New title entered

Row and column
titles entered

7 Click cell **B14**, and then on the **Home tab**, in the **Number group**, notice that the **Number Format** box indicates *General*. Then, being sure to type the comma, type **152,126**

8 On the **Formula Bar**, click the **Enter** button ☑ to keep the cell active, and then in the **Number group**, notice that the format changed to *Number*.

9 Press `Del`, and then in the **Number group**, notice that the *Number* format is still indicated.

> Recall that deleting the contents of a cell does not delete the cell's formatting.

10 *Without* typing a comma, in cell **B14**, type **152126** and then press `Enter`.

> The comma displays even though you did not type it. When you type a number and include a formatting symbol such as a comma or dollar sign, Excel applies the format to the cell. Thus, if you delete the contents of the cell and type in the cell again, the format you established remains applied to the cell. This is referred to as *format as you type*.

11 Examine the format of the value in cell **B14**, and then compare it to the format in cell **B6** where you used the **Comma Style** button to format the cell. Notice that the number in cell **B14** is flush with the right edge of the cell, but the number in cell **B6** leaves a small amount of space on the right edge.

> When you type commas as you enter numbers, Excel applies the *Number* format, which does *not* leave a space at the right of the number for a closing parenthesis in the event of a negative number. This is different from the format that is applied when you use the *Comma Style* button on the Ribbon or Mini toolbar, as you did for the numbers entered in row 6. Recall that the Comma Style format applied from either the Ribbon or the Mini toolbar leaves space on the right for a closing parenthesis in the event of a negative number.

12 In cell **B11**, type **8%** Select the range **A11:B11**, and then from the Mini toolbar, apply **Bold** B and **Italic** I. **Save** 🖫 your workbook.

> **More Knowledge | Percentage Calculations**
>
> When you type a percentage into a cell—for example *8%*—the percentage format, without decimal points, displays in both the cell and the Formula Bar. Excel will, however, use the decimal value of *0.08* for actual calculations.

Activity 3.14 | Calculating a Value After an Increase

A growing population results in increased use of city services. Thus, city planners in Orange Blossom Beach must estimate how much the population will increase in the future. The calculations you made in the previous activity show that the population has increased at varying rates during each 10-year period from 1970 to 2010, ranging from a low of 2% to a high of 14% per 10-year census period.

Population data from the state and surrounding areas suggests that future growth will trend close to that of the recent past. To plan for the future, Ms. Darius wants to prepare three forecasts of the city's population based on the percentage increases in 2000, in 2010, and for a percentage increase halfway between the two; that is, for 8%, 11%, and 14%. In this activity, you will calculate the population that would result from an 8% increase.

1 Click cell **C14**. Type **=b14*(100%+b11)** and then on the **Formula Bar**, click the **Enter** ✔ button to display a result of *164296.08*. Compare your screen with Figure 3.28.

> This formula calculates what the population will be in the year 2020 assuming an increase of 8% over 2010's population. Use the mathematical formula *value after increase = base ×percent for new value* to calculate a value after an increase as follows:
>
> First, establish the *percent for new value*. The *percent for new value = base percent + percent of increase*. The *base percent* of 100% represents the base population and the *percent of increase* in this instance is 8%. Thus, the population will equal 100% of the base year plus 8% of the base year. This can be expressed as 108% or 1.08. In this formula, you will use 100% + the rate in cell B11, which is 8%, to equal 108%.
>
> Second, enter a reference to the cell that contains the *base*—the population in 2010. The base value resides in cell B14—*152,126*.
>
> Third, calculate the *value after increase*. Because in each future 10-year period the increase will be based on 8%—an absolute value located in cell B11—this cell reference can be formatted as absolute by typing dollar signs.

Figure 3.28

Formula includes absolute reference to cell B11

Formula result

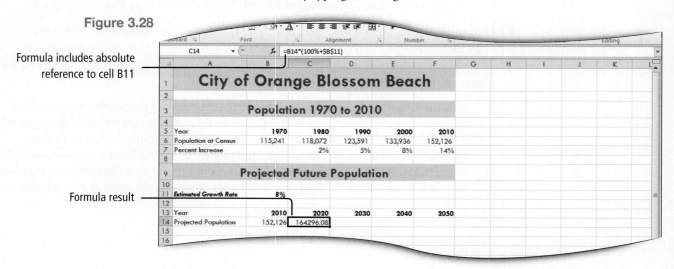

2 With cell **C14** as the active cell, drag the fill handle to copy the formula to the range **D14:F14**.

3 Point to cell **B14**, right-click, click the **Format Painter** ✍ button, and then select the range **C14:F14**. Click an empty cell to cancel the selection, click **Save** 🖫 and then compare your screen with Figure 3.29.

> This formula uses a relative cell address—B14—for the *base*; the population in the previous 10-year period is used in each of the formulas in cells D14:F14 as the *base* value. Because the reference to the *percent of increase* in cell B11 is an absolute reference, each *value after increase* is calculated with the value from cell B11.
>
> The population projected for 2020—*164,296*—is an increase of 8% over the population in 2010. The projected population in 2030—*177,440*—is an increase of 8% over the population in 2020 and so on.

Figure 3.29

Each value represents an 8% increase over the previous base year

Projection calculated using an 8% growth rate

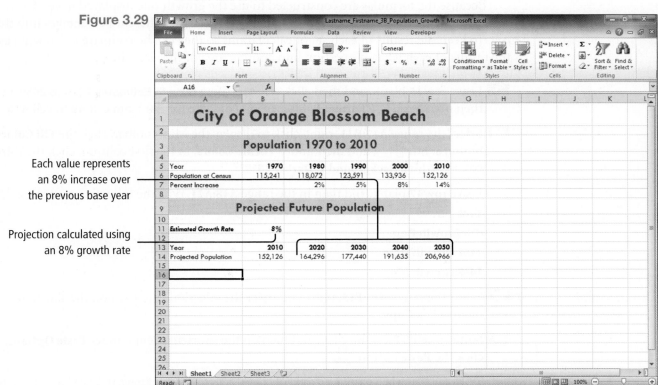

More Knowledge | **Percent Increase or Decrease**

The basic formula for calculating an increase or decrease can be done in two parts. First determine the percent by which the base value will be increased or decreased, and then add or subtract the results to the base. The formula can be simplified by using (1+amount of increase) or (1–amount of decrease), where 1, rather than 100%, represents the whole. Thus, the formula used in Step 1 of Activity 3.14 could also be written =b14*(1+b11), or =(b14*b11)+b14.

Objective 6 | Answer What-If Questions by Changing Values in a Worksheet

If a formula depends on the value in a cell, you can see what effect it will have if you change the value in that cell. Then, you can copy the value computed by the formula and paste it into another part of the worksheet where you can be compare it to other values.

Activity 3.15 | Answering What-If Questions and Using Paste Special

A growth rate of 8% in each 10-year period will result in a population of almost 207,000 people by 2050. The city planners will likely ask: *What if* the population grows at the highest rate (14%)? *What if* the population grows at a rate that is halfway between the 2000 and 2010 rates (11%)?

Because the formulas are constructed to use the growth rate displayed in cell B11, Ms. Darius can answer these questions quickly by entering different percentages into that cell. To keep the results of each set of calculations so they can be compared, you will paste the results of each what-if question into another area of the worksheet.

1 Leave **row 15** blank, and then click cell **A16**. Type **Growth Estimates 2020 to 2050** and then press Enter. Use **Format Painter** to copy the format from cell **A9** to cell **A16**.

2 Select the range **A11:B11**, right-click to display the Mini toolbar, click the **Fill Color button arrow**, and then under **Theme Colors**, in the first column, click the third color—**White, Background 1, Darker 15%**.

3 Leave **row 17** blank, and then in the range **A18:A21**, type the following row titles:

Year

8% Growth Rate

11% Growth Rate

14% Growth Rate

Another Way
Press Ctrl + C; or, on the Home tab, in the Clipboard group, click the Copy button.

4 Select the range **B13:F13**, right-click over the selection, and then on the shortcut menu, click **Copy**.

5 Point to cell **B18**, right-click, and then on the shortcut menu, under **Paste Options**, click the **Paste** button.

Recall that when pasting a group of copied cells to a target range, you need only point to or select the first cell of the range.

6 Select and **Copy** the range **B14:F14**, and then **Paste** it beginning in cell **B19**.

7 Click cell **C19**. On the **Formula Bar**, notice that the *formula* was pasted into the cell, as shown in Figure 3.30.

> This is *not* the desired result. The actual *calculated values*—not the formulas—are needed in the range.

Figure 3.30

Formula Bar indicates copied formula

Fill color applied to range A11:B11

Formulas copied

Row titles entered

Status bar indicates that Clipboard is still active

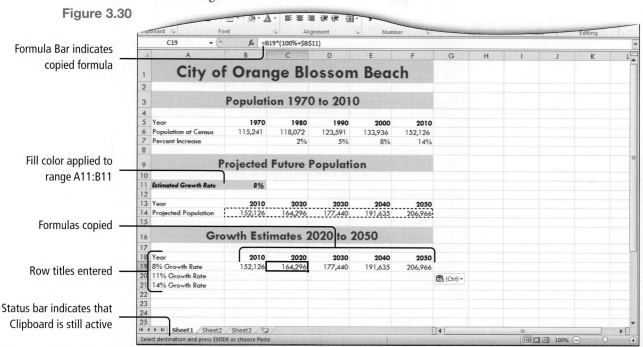

8 On the Quick Access Toolbar, click the **Undo** button. With the range **B14:F14** still copied to the Clipboard—as indicated by the message in the status bar and the moving border—point to cell **B19**, and then right-click to display the shortcut menu.

9 Under **Paste Options**, point to **Paste Special** to display another gallery, and then under **Paste Values**, point to the **Values & Number Formatting** button to display the ScreenTip as shown in Figure 3.31.

> The ScreenTip *Values & Number Formatting (A)* indicates that you can paste the *calculated values* that result from the calculation of formulas along with the formatting applied to the copied cells. *(A)* is the keyboard shortcut for this command.

Figure 3.31

Gallery of Paste Special buttons

Values & Number Formatting ScreenTip

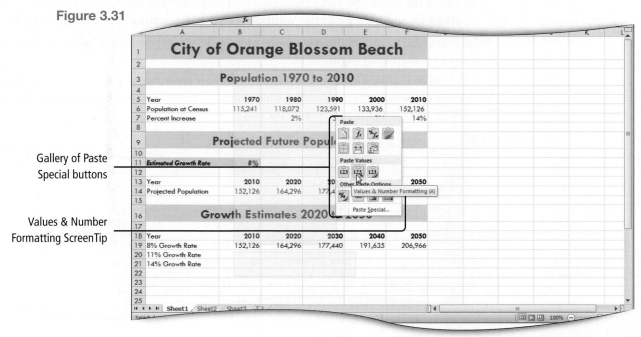

10 Click the **Values & Number Formatting** button 🔢, click cell **C19** and notice on the **Formula Bar** that the cell contains a *value*, not a formula. Press (Esc) to cancel the moving border. Compare your screen with Figure 3.32.

The calculated estimates based on an 8% growth rate are pasted along with their formatting.

Figure 3.32

Formula Bar indicates the value

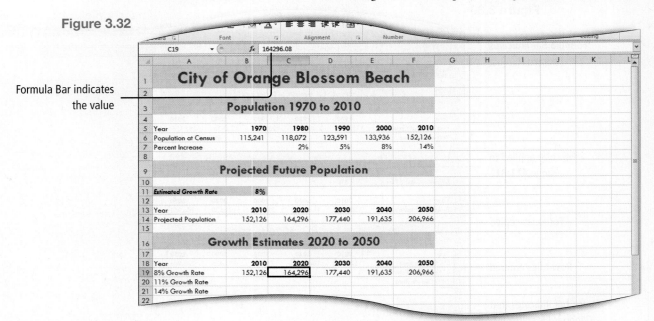

11 Click cell **B11**. Type **11** and then watch the values in **C14:F14** *recalculate* as, on the **Formula Bar**, you click the **Enter** button ✓.

The value *11%* is halfway between 8% and 14%—the growth rates from the two most recent 10-year periods.

12 Select and **Copy** the new values in the range **B14:F14**. Point to cell **B20**, right-click, and then on the shortcut menu, point to **Paste Special**. Under **Paste Values**, click the **Values & Number Formatting** button 🔢.

13 In cell **B11**, change the percentage by typing **14** and then press (Enter). Notice that the projected values in **C14:F14** recalculate.

14 Using the skills you just practiced, select and copy the recalculated values in the range **B14:F14**, and then paste the **Values & Number Formatting** to the range **B21:F21**.

15 Press (Esc) to cancel the moving border, click cell **A1**, click **Save** 💾, and then compare your screen with Figure 3.33.

With this information, Ms. Darius can answer several what-if questions about the future population of the city and provide a range of population estimates based on the rates of growth over the past 10-year periods.

Figure 3.33

Values copied for each what-if question

Objective 7 | Chart Data with a Line Chart

A *line chart* displays trends over time. Time is displayed along the bottom axis and the data point values connect with a line. The curve and direction of the line makes trends obvious to the reader.

Whereas the columns in a column chart and the pie slices in a pie chart emphasize the distinct values of each data point, the line in a line chart emphasizes the flow from one data point value to the next.

Activity 3.16 | Inserting Multiple Rows and Creating a Line Chart

So that city council members can see how the population has increased over the past five census periods, in this activity, you will chart the actual population figures from 1970 to 2010 in a line chart.

1 In the **row header area**, point to **row 8** to display the → pointer, and then drag down to select **rows 8:24**. Right-click over the selection, and then click **Insert** to insert the same number of blank rows as you selected. Compare your screen with Figure 3.34.

Use this technique to insert multiple rows quickly.

Figure 3.34

New blank rows inserted

Insert Options button

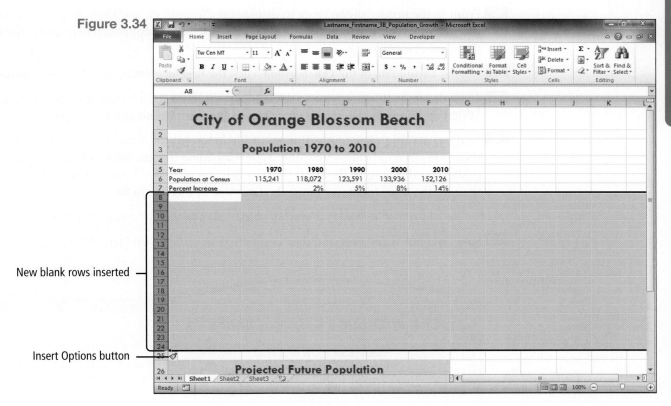

2 Near **row 25**, click the **Insert Options** button, and then click the **Clear Formatting** option button to clear any formatting from these rows.

You will use this blank area in which to position your line chart.

3 Select the range **A6:F6**. On the **Insert tab**, in the **Charts group**, click the **Line** button.

4 In the displayed gallery of line charts, in the second row, point to the first chart type to display the ScreenTip *Line with Markers*. Compare your screen with Figure 3.35.

Figure 3.35

Line button in Charts group

Line with Markers chart type

Data selected for charting

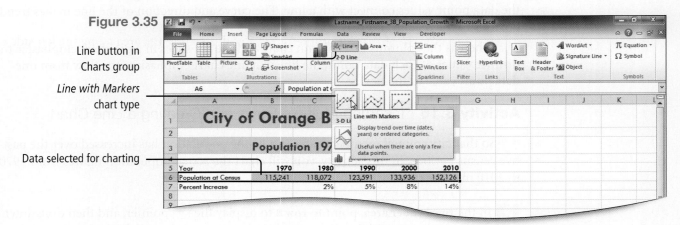

5 Click the **Line with Markers** chart type to create the chart as an embedded chart in the worksheet.

6 Point to the border of the chart to display the 🖑 pointer, and then drag the chart so that its upper left corner is positioned in cell **A9**, aligned approximately under the *t* in the word *Percent* above.

7 On the **Layout tab**, in the **Labels group**, click the **Legend** button, and then click **None**.

8 Click the chart title one time to select it and display a solid border around the title. Watch the **Formula Bar** as you type **Orange Blossom Beach** and then press Enter.

9 In the chart title, click to position the insertion point following the *h* in *Beach*, and then press Enter to begin a new line. Type **Population Growth 1970 to 2010** Click the dashed border around the chart title to change it to a solid border, right-click, and then on the Mini toolbar, change the **Font Size** of the title to **20**.

Recall that a solid border around an object indicates that the entire object is selected.

10 **Save** 🖫 your workbook, and then compare your screen with Figure 3.36.

Figure 3.36

Line with Markers chart inserted, upper left corner aligned in cell A9

Chart title on two lines, 20 pt font size

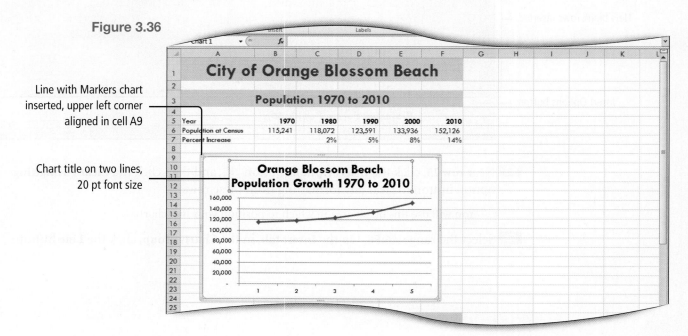

Activity 3.17 | Formatting Axes in a Line Chart

An *axis* is a line that serves as a frame of reference for measurement; it borders the chart *plot area*. The plot area is the area bounded by the axes, including all the data series. Recall that the area along the bottom of a chart that identifies the categories of data is referred to as the *category axis* or the *x-axis*. Recall also that the area along the left side of a chart that shows the range of numbers for the data points is referred to as the *value axis* or the *y-axis*.

In this activity, you will change the category axis to include the names of the 10-year census periods and adjust the numeric scale of the value axis.

Another Way

At the bottom of the chart, point to any of the numbers 1 through 5 to display the ScreenTip *Horizontal (Category) Axis*. Right-click, and then from the shortcut menu, click Select Data.

1 Be sure the chart is still selected—a pale frame surrounds the chart area. Click the **Design tab**, and then in the **Data group**, click the **Select Data** button.

2 On the right side of the displayed **Select Data Source** dialog box, under **Horizontal (Category) Axis Labels**, locate the **Edit** button, as shown in Figure 3.37.

Figure 3.37

Select Data Source dialog box

Edit button to edit labels on the category axis

Category axis requires labels to identify each 10-year period

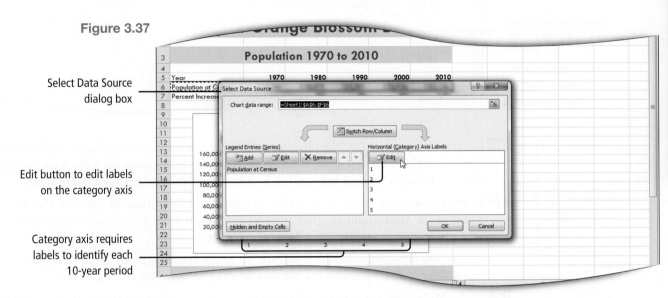

3 In the right column, click the **Edit** button. If necessary, drag the title bar of the **Axis Labels** dialog box to the right of the chart so that it is not blocking your view of the data, and then select the years in the range **B5:F5**. Compare your screen with Figure 3.38.

Figure 3.38

Range of years surrounded by moving border

Axis Labels dialog box

Range indicated with absolute references

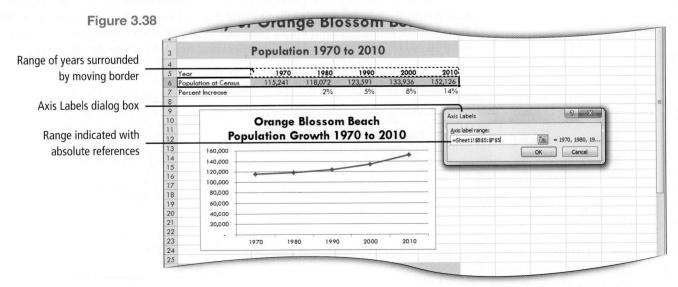

4 In the **Axis Labels** dialog box, click **OK**, and notice that in the right column of the **Select Data Source** dialog box, the years display as the category labels. Click **OK** to close the **Select Data Source** dialog box. Compare your screen with Figure 3.39.

Figure 3.39

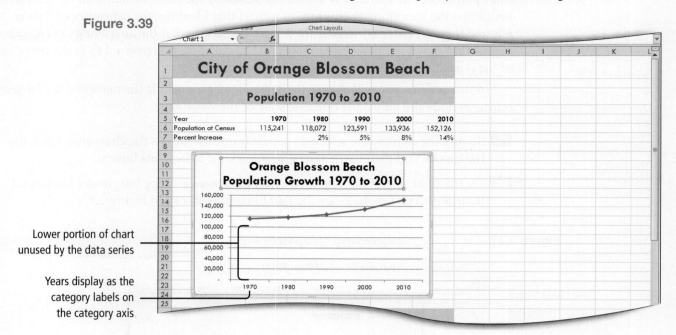

Lower portion of chart unused by the data series

Years display as the category labels on the category axis

Another Way

On the left side of the chart, point to any of the numbers to display the ScreenTip *Vertical (Value) Axis*, and then right-click. From the shortcut menu, click Format Axis.

5 On the chart, notice that the blue line—the data series—does not display in the lower portion of the chart. Then, on the **Layout tab**, in the **Axes group**, click the **Axes** button. Point to **Primary Vertical Axis**, and then click **More Primary Vertical Axis Options**.

6 In the **Format Axis** dialog box, on the left, be sure **Axis Options** is selected. On the right, in the **Minimum** row, click the **Fixed** option button. In the box to the right, select the existing text *0.0*, and then type **100000**

> Because none of the population figures are under 100,000, changing the Minimum number to 100,000 will enable the data series to occupy more of the plot area.

7 In the **Major unit** row, click the **Fixed** option button, select the text in the box to the right *20000.0*, and then type **10000** In the lower right corner, click **Close**. **Save** 💾 your workbook, and then compare your screen with Figure 3.40.

> The *Major unit* value determines the spacing between *tick marks* and thus between the gridlines in the plot area. Tick marks are the short lines that display on an axis at regular intervals. By default, Excel started the values at zero and increased in increments of 20,000. By setting the Minimum value on the value axis to 100,000 and changing the Major unit from 20,000 to 10,000, the line chart shows a clearer trend in the population growth.

Figure 3.40

Gridlines

Value axis still selected

Tick marks on value axis

Values increase in increments of 10,000 (Major unit)

Values begin with 100,000 (Minimum)

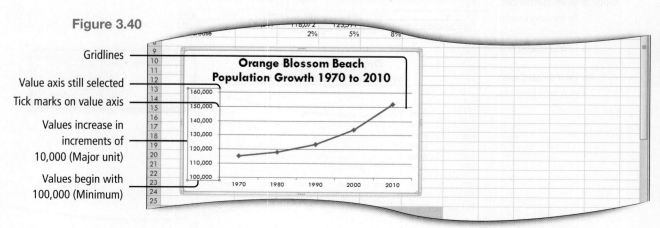

Activity 3.18 | Formatting the Chart and Plot Areas

An Excel chart has two background elements—the plot area and the chart area—which, by default display a single fill color. To add visual appeal to a chart, you can insert a graphic image as the background.

When formatting chart elements, there are several ways to display the dialog boxes that you need. You can right-click the area you want to format and choose a command on the shortcut menu. In this activity, you will use the Chart Elements box in the Current Selection group on the Format tab of the Ribbon, which is convenient if you are changing the format of a variety of chart elements.

1 Click the **Format tab**, and then in the **Current Selection group**, point to the small arrow to the right of the first item in the group to display the ScreenTip *Chart Elements*. Compare your screen with Figure 3.41.

From the **Chart Elements box**, you can select a chart element so that you can format it.

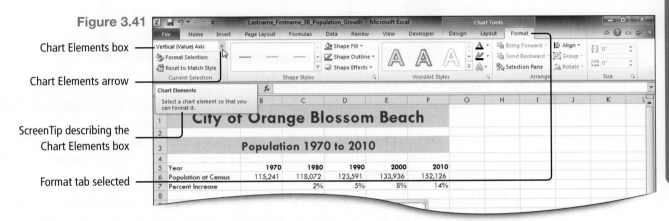

Figure 3.41

Chart Elements box

Chart Elements arrow

ScreenTip describing the Chart Elements box

Format tab selected

2 Click the **Chart Elements arrow**, and then from the displayed list, click **Chart Area**. Directly below the **Chart Elements** box, click the **Format Selection** button.

The Format Chart Area dialog box displays. Use this technique to select the chart element that you want to format, and then click the Format Selection button to display the appropriate dialog box.

3 In the **Format Chart Area** dialog box, on the left, be sure that **Fill** is selected.

4 On the right, under **Fill**, click the **Picture or texture fill** option button, and then under **Insert from**, click the **File** button. In the **Insert Picture** dialog box, navigate to your student files, and then insert the picture **e03B_Beach**. Leave the dialog box open, and then compare your screen with Figure 3.42.

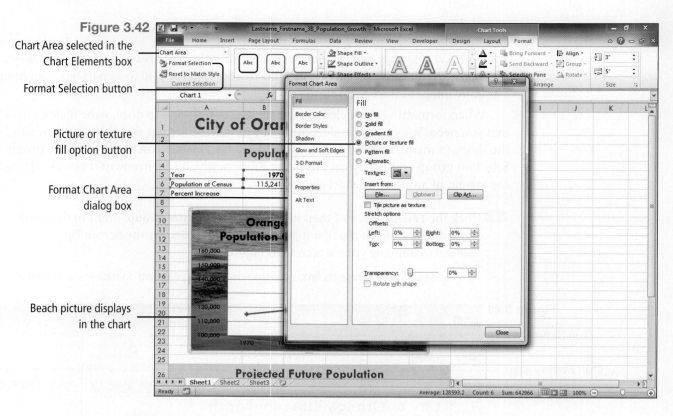

Figure 3.42

Chart Area selected in the Chart Elements box

Format Selection button

Picture or texture fill option button

Format Chart Area dialog box

Beach picture displays in the chart

5 In the **Format Chart Area** dialog box, on the left, click **Border Color**, on the right click the **Solid line** option button, click the **Color arrow**, and then under **Theme Colors**, in the fourth column, click the first color—**Dark Teal, Text 2**.

6 On the left, click **Border Styles**. On the right, select the text in the **Width** box and type **4 pt** At the bottom select the **Rounded corners** check box, and then **Close** the dialog box.

A 4 pt teal border with rounded corners frames the chart.

7 In the **Current Selection group**, click the **Chart Elements arrow**, on the list click **Plot Area**, and then click the **Format Selection** button.

8 In the **Format Plot Area** dialog box, on the left, be sure that **Fill** is selected, and then on the right, click the **No fill** option button. **Close** the dialog box.

The fill is removed from the plot area so that the picture is visible as the background.

9 Click the **Chart Elements arrow**, on the list click **Vertical (Value) Axis**, and then click the **Format Selection** button.

10 In the **Format Axis** dialog box, on the left click **Line Color**, on the right click the **Solid line** option button, click the **Color arrow**, and then click the first color—**White, Background 1**. Compare your screen with Figure 3.43.

The vertical line with tick marks displays in white.

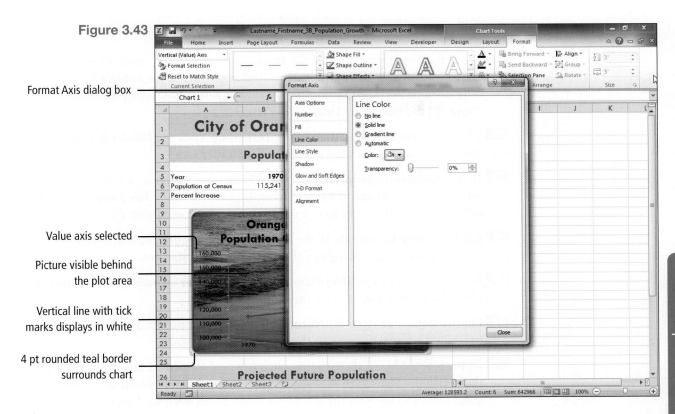

Figure 3.43

Format Axis dialog box

Value axis selected

Picture visible behind the plot area

Vertical line with tick marks displays in white

4 pt rounded teal border surrounds chart

11 **Close** the dialog box. From the **Chart Elements** box, select the **Vertical (Value) Axis Major Gridlines**, and then click **Format Selection**. Change the **Line Color** to a **Solid line**, and then apply the **White, Background 1** color. **Close** the dialog box.

12 From the **Chart Elements** list, select the **Horizontal (Category) Axis**, and then click **Format Selection**. In the **Format Axis** dialog box, change the **Line Color** to a **Solid line**, and then apply the **White, Background 1** color. **Close** the dialog box.

13 Point to any of the numbers on the vertical value axis, right-click, and then on the Mini toolbar, change the **Font Color** to **White, Background 1**. Point to any of the years on the horizontal category axis, right-click, and then change the **Font Color** to **White, Background 1**.

> For basic text-formatting changes—for example changing the size, font, style, or font color—you must leave the Chart Tools on the Ribbon and use commands from the Home tab or the Mini toolbar.

14 Click any cell to deselect the chart, press Ctrl + Home to move to the top of your worksheet, click **Save**, and then compare your screen with Figure 3.44.

Figure 3.44

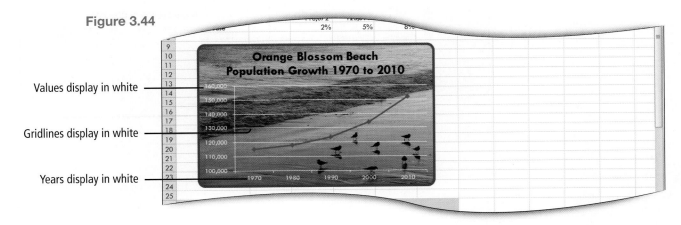

Values display in white

Gridlines display in white

Years display in white

Activity 3.19 │ Preparing and Printing Your Worksheet

1 From **Backstage** view, display the **Document Panel**. In the **Author** box, replace the existing text with your firstname and lastname. In the **Subject** box, type your course name and section number. In the **Keywords** box, type **population** and then **Close** ⏺ the **Document Information Panel**.

2 Click the **Insert tab**, and then in the **Text group**, click the **Header & Footer** button to switch to **Page Layout View** and open the **Header area**.

3 In the **Navigation group**, click the **Go to Footer** button, click just above the word *Footer*, and then in the **Header & Footer Elements group**, click the **File Name** button. Click in a cell just above the footer to exit the **Footer area** and view your file name.

4 Click the **Page Layout tab**. In the **Page Setup group**, click the **Margins** button, and then at the bottom of the **Margins** gallery, click **Custom Margins**.

5 In the displayed **Page Setup** dialog box, under **Center on page**, select the **Horizontally** check box. Click **OK** to close the dialog box.

6 On the status bar, click the **Normal** button ▦ to return to Normal view, and then press `Ctrl` + `Home` to move to the top of your worksheet.

7 At the lower edge of the window, click to select the **Sheet2 tab**, hold down `Ctrl`, and then click the **Sheet3 tab** to select the two unused sheets. Right-click over the selected sheet tabs, and then on the displayed shortcut menu, click **Delete**.

8 **Save** 🖫 your workbook before printing or submitting. Press `Ctrl` + `F2` to display the **Print Preview** to check your worksheet. Compare your screen with Figure 3.45.

Figure 3.45

Completed worksheet in Print Preview

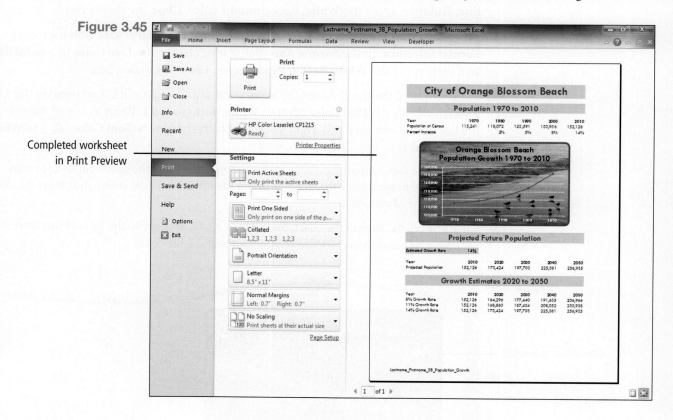

9 If necessary, return to the worksheet to make any necessary adjustments or corrections, and then **Save**.

10 Print or submit electronically as directed. If you are directed to submit printed formulas, refer to Activity 1.16 to do so.

11 If you printed your formulas, be sure to redisplay the worksheet by clicking the Show Formulas button to turn it off. From **Backstage** view, click **Close**. If the dialog box displays asking if you want to save changes, click **No** so that you do *not* save the changes you made for printing formulas. **Close** Excel.

End **You have completed Project 3B**

Content-Based Assessments

Summary

In this chapter, you created a pie chart to show how the parts of a budget contribute to a total budget. Then you formatted the pie chart attractively and used Goal Seek. You also practiced using parentheses in a formula, calculating the percentage rate of an increase, answering what-if questions, and charting data in a line chart to show the flow of data over time.

Key Terms

Matching

Match each term in the second column with its correct definition in the first column by writing the letter of the term on the blank line in front of the correct definition.

_____ 1. A chart that shows the relationship of each part to a whole.

_____ 2. The term used to describe money set aside for the normal operating activities of a government entity such as a city.

_____ 3. In a formula, the address of a cell based on the relative position of the cell that contains the formula and the cell referred to.

_____ 4. A column, bar, area, dot, pie slice, or other symbol in a chart that represents a single data point.

_____ 5. A workbook sheet that contains only a chart.

_____ 6. A shape effect that uses shading and shadows to make the edges of a shape appear to be curved or angled.

_____ 7. The entire chart and all of its elements.

_____ 8. The process of changing the values in cells to see how those changes affect the outcome of formulas in a worksheet.

_____ 9. The mathematical formula to calculate a rate of increase.

A Axis

B Bevel

C Category axis

D Chart area

E Chart sheet

F Data marker

G Format as you type

H General Fund

I Order of operations

J Pie chart

K Rate=amount of increase/base

L Relative cell reference

M Tick marks

N Value axis

O What-if analysis

Content-Based Assessments

_____ 10. The mathematical rules for performing multiple calculations within a formula.

_____ 11. The Excel feature by which a cell takes on the formatting of the number typed into the cell.

_____ 12. A line that serves as a frame of reference for measurement and that borders the chart plot area.

_____ 13. The area along the bottom of a chart that identifies the categories of data; also referred to as the x-axis.

_____ 14. A numerical scale on the left side of a chart that shows the range of numbers for the data points; also referred to as the y-axis.

_____ 15. The short lines that display on an axis at regular intervals.

Multiple Choice

Circle the correct answer.

1. A sum of money set aside for a specific purpose is a:
   A. value axis   B. fund   C. rate

2. A cell reference that refers to a cell by its fixed position in a worksheet is referred to as being:
   A. absolute   B. relative   C. mixed

3. A value that originates in a worksheet cell and that is represented in a chart by a data marker is a data:
   A. point   B. cell   C. axis

4. Related data points represented by data markers are referred to as the data:
   A. slices   B. set   C. series

5. The action of pulling out a pie slice from a pie chart is called:
   A. extract   B. explode   C. plot

6. A gallery of text styles with which you can create decorative effects, such as shadowed or mirrored text is:
   A. WordArt   B. shape effects   C. text fill

7. The percent by which one number increases over another number is the percentage rate of:
   A. decrease   B. change   C. increase

8. A chart type that displays trends over time is a:
   A. pie chart   B. line chart   C. column chart

9. The area bounded by the axes of a chart, including all the data series, is the:
   A. chart area   B. plot area   C. axis area

10. The x-axis is also known as the:
    A. category axis   B. value axis   C. data axis

Content-Based Assessments

Apply **3A** skills from these Objectives:

1. Chart Data with a Pie Chart
2. Format a Pie Chart
3. Edit a Workbook and Update a Chart
4. Use Goal Seek to Perform What-If Analysis

Skills Review | Project **3C** Fund Revenue

In the following Skills Review, you will edit a worksheet for Jennifer Carson, City Finance Manager, which details the City general fund revenue. Your completed worksheets will look similar to Figure 3.46.

Project Files

For Project 3C, you will need the following file:

e03C_Fund_Revenue

You will save your workbook as:

Lastname_Firstname_3C_Fund_Revenue

Project Results

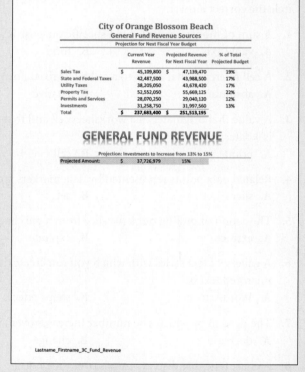

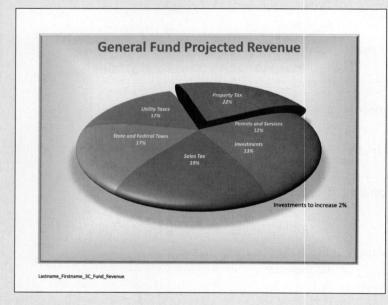

Figure 3.46

(Project 3C Fund Revenue continues on the next page)

Content-Based Assessments

Skills Review | Project 3C Fund Revenue (continued)

1 **Start** Excel. From your student files, open the file e03C_Fund_Revenue. **Save** the file in your **Excel Chapter 3** folder as **Lastname_Firstname_3C_Fund_Revenue**

  a. Click cell **D5**, and then type = to begin a formula. Click cell **C5**, type / and then click cell **C11**. Press F4 to make the reference to the value in cell **C11** absolute. On the **Formula Bar**, click the **Enter** button, and then fill the formula down through cell **D10**.

  b. With the range **D5:D10** selected, right-click over the selection, and then on Mini toolbar, click the **Percent Style** button and the **Center** button.

2 Select the nonadjacent ranges **A5:A10** and **C5:C10** to select the revenue names and the projected revenue. Click the **Insert tab**, and then in the **Charts group**, click **Pie**. Under **3-D Pie**, click the first chart—**Pie in 3-D**.

  a. On the **Design tab**, in the **Location group**, click the **Move Chart** button. In the **Move Chart** dialog box, click the **New sheet** option button. In the **New sheet** box, replace the highlighted text *Chart1* by typing **Projected Revenue Chart** and then click **OK**.

  b. On the **Layout tab**, in the **Labels group**, click the **Chart Title** button, and then click **Above Chart**. With the **Chart Title** box selected, type **General Fund Projected Revenue** and then press Enter to create the new chart title.

  c. Point to the chart title text, and then right-click to display the Mini toolbar. Change the **Font Size** to **32** and change the **Font Color** to **Blue-Gray, Text 2**— in the fourth column, the first color.

  d. Click in a white area of the chart to deselect the chart title. On the **Layout tab**, in the **Labels group**, click the **Legend** button, and then click **None**.

  e. In the **Labels group**, click the **Data Labels** button, and then click **More Data Label Options**. In the **Format Data Labels** dialog box, on the left, be sure **Label Options** is selected. On the right, under **Label Contains**, click as necessary to select the **Category Name** and **Percentage** check boxes. *Clear* any other check boxes in this group. Under **Label Position**, click the **Center** option button. Click **Close**.

  f. Point to any of the selected labels, right-click to display the Mini toolbar, and then change the **Font Size** to **12**, the **Font Color** to **White, Background 1, Darker 5%**, and then apply **Bold** and **Italic**.

3 3. Click in any pie slice outside of the label to select the entire pie. Click the **Format tab**, and then in the **Shape**

Styles group, click the **Shape Effects** button. Point to **Bevel**, and then at the bottom of the gallery, click **3-D Options**.

  a. In the **Format Data Series** dialog box, on the right, under **Bevel**, click the **Top** button. In the gallery, under **Bevel**, in the first row, click the first button— **Circle**. Then click the **Bottom** button, and apply the **Circle** bevel. In the four **Width** and **Height** spin boxes, type **512**

  b. In the lower portion of the dialog box, under **Surface**, click the **Material** button. Under **Standard**, click the third button—**Plastic**. In the lower right corner, click the **Close** button.

  c. On the **Format tab**, in the **Shape Styles group**, click **Shape Effects**, and then point to **Shadow**. Under **Perspective**, click the third button—**Below**.

  d. With the pie chart still selected, point anywhere in the pie and right-click. On the displayed shortcut menu, click **Format Data Series**. In the **Format Data Series** dialog box, on the left, be sure **Series Options** is selected. On the right, click in the box under **Angle of first slice**, change *0* to type **150** to move the largest slice—*Property Tax*—to the top of the pie. Click **Close**.

  e. Click in the area outside of the chart sheet to deselect all chart elements. Then, on the pie chart, click the outer edge of the **Property Tax** slice one time to select the pie chart, and then click the **Property Tax** slice again to select only that slice.

  f. Point to the **Property Tax** slice, and then explode the slice by dragging it slightly away from the center of the pie.

  g. With the **Property Tax** slice still selected, point to the slice and right-click. On the shortcut menu, click **Format Data Point**. In the displayed **Format Data Point** dialog box, on the left, click **Fill**. On the right, under **Fill**, click the **Solid fill** option button. Click the **Color arrow**, and then under **Theme Colors**, in the sixth column, click the fifth color—**Dark Yellow, Accent 2, Darker 25%**. Click **Close**.

4 Point to the white area just inside the border of the chart to display the ScreenTip **Chart Area**, and then click one time.

  a. On the **Format tab**, in the **Shape Styles group**, click the **Shape Effects** button, point to **Bevel**, and then under **Bevel**, in the second row, click the third bevel—**Convex**.

  b. With the chart area still selected, right-click in a white area at the outer edge of the chart, and then

(Project 3C Fund Revenue continues on the next page)

on the shortcut menu, click **Format Chart Area**. In the **Format Chart Area** dialog box, on the left, be sure that **Fill** is selected. On the right, under **Fill**, click the **Gradient fill** option button. Click the **Preset colors** arrow, and then in the third row, click the fourth preset, **Parchment**. Click the **Type arrow**, and then click **Path**. Click the **Close** button.

c. Click the **Layout tab**, and then in the **Insert group**, click the **Text Box** button. Position the pointer near the lower corner of the *Investments* slice. Hold down the left mouse button, and then drag down and to the right so that the text box extends to the end of the chart area and is approximately one-half inch high. With the insertion point blinking inside the text box, type **Investments to increase 2%** Select the text and then on the Mini toolbar, change the **Font Size** to **12**. If necessary, use the sizing handles to widen the text box so that the text displays on one line.

5 In the sheet tab area at the bottom of the workbook, click the **Sheet1 tab** to redisplay the worksheet.

a. Click the **Insert tab**, and then in the **Text group**, click the **WordArt** button.

b. In the **WordArt** gallery, in the last row, click the last style—**Fill – Red, Accent 1, Metal Bevel, Reflection**. Type **general fund revenue** and then point anywhere on the dashed border surrounding the WordArt object. Click the dashed border one time to change it to a solid border, indicating that all of the text is selected. Right-click the border to display the Mini toolbar, and then change the **Font Size** to **28**.

c. Drag to position the upper left corner of the WordArt in cell **A13**, centered below the worksheet.

6 In cell **A17**, type **Projection: Investments to Increase from 13% to 15%** and then **Merge & Center** the text across the range **A17:D17**. Apply the **Heading 3** cell style.

a. In cell **A18**, type **Projected Amount:** and press Enter. Select the range **C10:D10**, right-click over the selection, and then click **Copy**. Point to cell **B18**, right-click, and then under **Paste Options**, click the **Paste** button. Press Esc to cancel the moving border.

b. Click cell **C18**. On the **Data tab**, in the **Data Tools group**, click the **What-If Analysis** button, and then click **Goal Seek**. In the **Goal Seek** dialog box, press Tab to move to the **To value** box, and then type **15%**

c. Press Tab to move the insertion point to the **By changing cell** box, and then click cell **B18**. Click

OK. In the displayed **Goal Seek Status** dialog box, click **OK**.

d. Select the range **A18:C18**. From the **Home tab**, display the **Cell Styles** gallery. Under **Themed Cell Styles**, apply **40% - Accent3**. Click cell **B18**, and then from the **Cell Styles** gallery, apply the **Currency [0]** cell style.

7 With your worksheet displayed, in the sheet tab area, double-click *Sheet1* to select the text, and then type **Projected Revenue Data** and press Enter.

a. On the **Insert tab**, in the **Text group**, click **Header & Footer**. In the **Navigation group**, click the **Go to Footer** button, click in the **left section** above the word *Footer*, and then in the **Header & Footer Elements group**, click the **File Name** button. Click in a cell above the footer to deselect the **Footer area** and view your file name.

b. On the **Page Layout tab**, in the **Page Setup group**, click the **Margins** button, and then at the bottom of the **Margins gallery**, click **Custom Margins**. In the **Page Setup** dialog box, under **Center on page**, select the **Horizontally** check box. Click **OK**, and then on the status bar, click the **Normal** button. Press Ctrl + Home to move to the top of your worksheet.

c. Click the **Projected Revenue Chart** sheet tab to display the chart sheet. On the **Insert tab**, click **Header & Footer**. In the center of the **Page Setup** dialog box, click **Custom Footer**. With the insertion point blinking in the **Left section**, in the row of buttons in the middle of the dialog box, locate and click the **Insert File Name** button. Click **OK** two times.

d. Right-click either of the sheet tabs, and then click **Select All Sheets**. From **Backstage** view, show the **Document Panel**. In the **Author** box, replace the existing text with your firstname and lastname. In the **Subject** box, type your course name and section number. In the **Keywords** box type **general fund, projected revenue** **Close** the **Document Information Panel**.

e. With the two sheets still grouped, press Ctrl + F2 to display the **Print Preview**, and then view the two pages of your workbook.

f. **Save** your workbook. Print or submit electronically as directed by your instructor. If required by your instructor, print or create an electronic version of your worksheets with formulas displayed by using the instructions in Activity 1.16, and then **Close** Excel without saving so that you do not save the changes you made to print formulas.

End You have completed Project 3C

Skills Review | Project **3D** Revenue Projection

In the following Skills Review, you will edit a worksheet for Jennifer Carson, City Finance Manager, which forecasts the permit revenue that the City of Orange Blossom Beach expects to collect in the next five years. Your completed worksheet will look similar to Figure 3.47.

Project Files

For Project 3D, you will need the following files:

> e03D_Revenue_Projection
> e03D_Shoreline

You will save your workbook as:

> Lastname_Firstname_3D_Revenue_Projection

Project Results

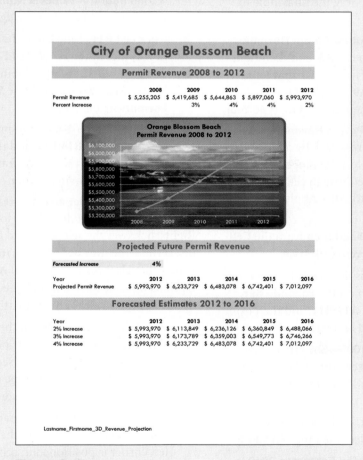

Figure 3.47

(Project 3D Revenue Projection continues on the next page)

Skills Review | Project 3D Revenue Projection (continued)

1 **Start** Excel. From your student files, open the file **e03D_Revenue_Projection**. **Save** the file in your **Excel Chapter 3** folder with the file name **Lastname_Firstname_3D_Revenue_Projection**

a. Click cell **C7**. Being sure to include the parentheses, type **=(c6-b6)/b6** and then on the **Formula Bar**, click the **Enter** button. In the **Number group**, click the **Percent Style** button.

b. Click cell **D7**, type **=** and then by typing, or using a combination of typing and clicking cells to reference them, construct a formula similar to the one in cell **C7** to calculate the rate of increase in population from 2009 to 2010. Format cell **D7** with the **Percent Style**. With cell **D7** selected, drag the fill handle to the right through cell **F7**.

c. In cell **A9**, type **Projected Future Permit Revenue** and then press [Enter]. Point to cell **A3**, and then right-click. On the Mini toolbar, click the **Format Painter** button, and then click cell **A9**. In cell **A11**, type **Forecasted Increase** and then in cell **A13**, type **Year**

d. In cell **A14**, type **Projected Permit Revenue** and then in cell **B13**, type **2012** and press [Tab]. In cell **C13**, type **2013** and then press [Tab]. Select the range **B13:C13**, and then drag the fill handle through cell **F13** to extend the pattern of years to *2016*. Apply **Bold** to the selection.

e. Click cell **B14**, type **5993970** and then from the **Cell Styles** gallery, apply the **Currency [0]** style.

f. In cell **B11**, type **2%** which is the percent of increase from 2011 to 2012, and then on the **Formula Bar**, click **Enter**. Select the range **A11:B11**, and then from the Mini toolbar, apply **Bold** and **Italic**.

2 Click cell **C14**. Type **=b14*(100%+b11)** and then on the **Formula Bar**, click the **Enter** button. With cell **C14** as the active cell, drag the fill handle to copy the formula to the range **D14:F14**.

a. Point to cell **B14**, right-click, click the **Format Painter** button, and then select the range **C14:F14**.

b. Click cell **A16**. Type **Forecasted Estimates 2012 to 2016** and then press [Enter]. Use **Format Painter** to copy the format from cell **A9** to cell **A16**.

c. Select the range **A11:B11**, right-click to display the Mini toolbar, click the **Fill Color button arrow**, and then under **Theme Colors**, in the first column, click the third color—**White, Background 1, Darker 15%**.

d. In the range **A18:A21**, type the following row titles:

Year

2% Increase

3% Increase

4% Increase

3 Select the range **B13:F13**, right-click over the selection, and then on the shortcut menu, click **Copy**. **Paste** the selection to the range **B18:F18**.

a. Select the range **B14:F14**, right-click over the selection, and then on the shortcut menu, click **Copy**. Point to **B19**, right-click, and then from the shortcut menu, point to **Paste Special**. Under **Paste Values**, click the second button—**Values & Number Formatting**. Press [Esc] to cancel the moving border,

b. Click cell **B11**. Type **3** and then press [Enter]. **Copy** the new values in the range **B14:F14**. Point to cell **B20** and right-click, and then point to **Paste Special**. Under **Paste Values**, click the **Values & Number Formatting** button.

c. In cell **B11**, type **4** and then press [Enter]. Select and copy the range **B14:F14**, and then paste the values and number formats to the range **B21:F21**. Press [Esc] to cancel the moving border.

4 In the **row header area**, point to **row 8** to display the [→] pointer, and then drag down to select **rows 8:24**. Right-click over the selection, and then click **Insert** to insert the same number of blank rows as you selected. Under the selection area near cell **A25**, click the **Insert Options** button, and then click the **Clear Formatting** option button to clear any formatting from these rows.

a. Select the range **A6:F6**. On the **Insert tab**, in the **Charts group**, click the **Line** button. In the displayed gallery of line charts, in the second row, click the **Line with Markers** chart type to create the chart as an embedded chart in the worksheet.

b. Point to the border of the chart to display the [⬚] pointer, and then drag the chart so that its upper left corner is positioned in cell **A9**, aligned approximately under the *r* in the word *Increase* above.

c. On the **Layout tab**, in the **Labels group**, click the **Legend** button, and then click **None**. Click the chart title one time to select it. Type **Orange Blossom Beach** and then press [Enter].

(Project 3D Revenue Projection continues on the next page)

Content-Based Assessments

Skills Review | Project 3D Revenue Projection (continued)

d. In the chart title, click to position the insertion point following the *h* in *Beach*, and then press Enter to begin a new line. Type **Permit Revenue 2008 to 2012** Click the dashed border around the chart title to change it to a solid border, right-click the solid border, and then on the Mini toolbar, change the **Font Size** of the title to **14**.

5 With the chart selected, click the **Design tab**, and then in the **Data group**, click the **Select Data** button. On the right side of the **Select Data Source** dialog box, under **Horizontal (Category) Axis Labels**, in the right column, click the **Edit** button. If necessary, drag the title bar of the Axis Labels dialog box to the right of the chart so that it is not blocking your view of the data, and then select the years in the range **B5:F5**. Click **OK** two times to enter the years as the category labels.

a. On the **Layout tab**, in the **Axes group**, click the **Axes** button. Point to **Primary Vertical Axis**, and then click **More Primary Vertical Axis Options**. In the **Format Axis** dialog box, on the left, be sure **Axis Options** is selected. On the right, in the **Minimum** row, click the **Fixed** option button. In the box to the right, select the existing text, and then type **5200000**

b. In the **Major unit** row, click the **Fixed** option button, select the value *200000.0* in the box to the right, and then type **100000** In the lower right corner, click **Close**.

c. Click the **Format tab**, and then in the **Current Selection group**, click the **Chart Elements arrow**. From the displayed list, click **Chart Area**. Directly below the **Chart Elements** box, click the **Format Selection** button.

d. In the **Format Chart Area** dialog box, on the left, be sure that **Fill** is selected. On the right, under **Fill**, click the **Picture or texture fill** option button, and then under **Insert from**, click the **File** button. In the **Insert Picture** dialog box, navigate to your student files, and then insert the picture **e03D_Shoreline**. In the **Format Chart Area** dialog box, on the left, click **Border Color**. On the right click the **Solid line** option button, and then click the **Color arrow**. Under **Theme Colors**, in the fourth column, click the first color—**Brown, Text 2**.

e. On the left, click **Border Styles**. On the right, select the text in the **Width** box and type **4** Select the **Rounded corners** check box, and then **Close** the dialog box.

6 In the **Current Selection group**, click the **Chart Elements arrow**, on the list click **Plot Area**, and then click the **Format Selection** button. In the **Format Plot Area** dialog box, on the left, be sure that **Fill** is selected, and then on the right, click the **No fill** option button. **Close** the dialog box.

a. Click the **Chart Elements arrow**, on the list click **Vertical (Value) Axis**, and then click the **Format Selection** button. In the **Format Axis** dialog box, on the left, click **Line Color**. On the right, click the **Solid line** option button, click the **Color arrow**, and then click the first color—**White, Background 1**. **Close** the dialog box.

b. From the **Chart Elements** box, select the **Vertical (Value) Axis Major Gridlines**, and then click **Format Selection**. Change the **Line Color** to a **Solid line**, and then apply the **White, Background 1** color. **Close** the dialog box.

c. From the **Chart Elements** box, select the **Horizontal (Category) Axis**, and then click **Format Selection**. Change the **Line Color** to a **Solid line**, and then apply the **White, Background 1** color. **Close** the dialog box.

d. Point to any of the numbers on the **vertical value axis**, right-click, and then on the Mini toolbar, change the **Font Color** to **White, Background 1**. Point to any of the years on the **horizontal category axis**, right-click, and then change the **Font Color** to **White, Background 1**.

e. Click any cell to deselect the chart. Insert a **Header & Footer** with the **file name** in the **left section** of the footer, and then center the worksheet **Horizontally** on the page. Return to **Normal** view, and press Ctrl + Home. From **Backstage** view, show the **Document Panel**. In the **Author** box, replace the existing text with your firstname and lastname. In the **Subject** box, type your course name and section number. In the **Keywords** box type **permit revenue, forecast** **Close** the **Document Information Panel**.

f. **Save** your workbook. Print or submit electronically as directed by your instructor. If required by your instructor, print or create an electronic version of your worksheet with formulas displayed by using the instructions in Activity 1.16, and then **Close** Excel without saving so that you do not save the changes you made to print formulas.

End You have completed Project 3D

Excel | Chapter 3

Content-Based Assessments

Mastering Excel | Project **3E** Investments

In the following project, you will you will edit a worksheet for Jennifer Carson, City Finance Manager, that summarizes the investment portfolio of the City of Orange Blossom Beach. Your completed worksheets will look similar to Figure 3.48.

Project Files

For Project 3E, you will need the following file:

e03E_Investments

You will save your workbook as:

Lastname_Firstname_3E_Investments

Project Results

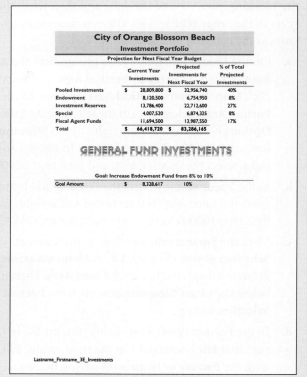

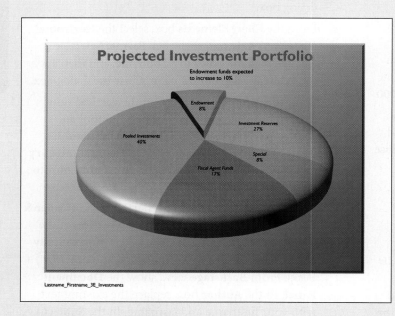

Figure 3.48

(Project 3E Investments continues on the next page)

Content-Based Assessments

Mastering Excel | Project 3E Investments (continued)

1 **Start** Excel. From your student files, locate and open **e03E_Investments**. **Save** the file in your **Excel Chapter 3** folder as **Lastname_Firstname_3E_Investments**

2 In cells **B10** and **C10**, enter formulas to calculate totals for each column. Then, in cell **D5**, enter a formula to calculate the % of Total Projected Investments for Pooled Investments by dividing the **Projected Investments for Next Fiscal Year** for the **Pooled Investments** by the **Total Projected Investments for Next Fiscal Year**. Use absolute cell references as necessary, format the result in **Percent Style**, and **Center** the percentage. Fill the formula down through cell **D9**.

3 Select the nonadjacent ranges **A5:A9** and **C5:C9**, and then insert a **Pie in 3-D** chart. Move the chart to a **New sheet** named **Projected Investment Chart** Insert a **Chart Title** above the chart with the text **Projected Investment Portfolio** Change the chart title **Font Size** to **32** and change the **Font Color** to **Brown, Accent 6**—in the last column, the first color.

4 Remove the **Legend** from the chart, and then add **Data Labels** formatted so that only the **Category Name** and **Percentage** display positioned in the **Center**. Change the data labels **Font Size** to **11**, and then apply **Italic**.

5 Select the entire pie, display the **Shape Effects** gallery, point to **Bevel**, and then at the bottom of the gallery, click **3-D Options**. Change the **Top** and **Bottom** options to the last **Bevel** type—**Art Deco**. Set the **Top Width** and **Height** boxes to **256** and then set the **Bottom Width** and **Height** boxes to **0** Change the **Material** to the third **Standard** type—**Plastic**.

6 With the pie chart selected, display the shortcut menu, and then click **Format Data Series**. Change the **Angle of first slice** to **200** to move the *Endowment* slice to the top of the pie. Select the **Endowment** slice, and then explode the slice slightly.

7 Change the **Fill Color** of the **Pooled Investments** slice to **Gray-50%, Accent 1, Lighter 40%**. Format the **Chart Area** by applying a **Convex Bevel**. To the **Chart Area**, apply the **Moss, Preset Gradient fill**. In the **Angle** box, type **45** and then **Close** the **Format Chart Area** dialog box.

8 **Insert** a **Text Box** positioned approximately halfway between the *Endowment* pie slice and the *v* in the word *Investment* in the title. In the text box, type **Endowment funds expected to increase to 10%** Select the text and then on the Mini toolbar, change the **Font Size** to **12**. Size the text box as necessary so that the text displays on two lines as shown in Figure 3.48.

9 Display **Sheet1** and rename the sheet as **Projected Investment Data** Insert a **WordArt**—in the fifth row, insert the last WordArt style—**Fill – Gray-50%, Accent 1, Plastic Bevel, Reflection**. Type **General Fund Investments** and then change the **Font Size** to **20**. Drag to position the upper left corner of the WordArt in cell **A12**, centered below the worksheet.

10 In cell **A16**, type **Goal: Increase Endowment Fund from 8% to 10%** and then **Merge & Center** the text across the range **A16:D16**. Apply the **Heading 3** cell style. In cell **A17**, type **Goal Amount**

11 **Copy** the range **C6:D6** to cell **B17**. Click cell **C17**, and then use **Goal Seek** to determine the projected amount of endowment funds in cell **B17** if the value in **C17** is **10%**.

12 Select the range **A17:C17**, and then apply the **20% - Accent2** cell style. In **B17**, from the **Cell Styles** gallery, apply the **Currency [0]** cell style.

13 Insert a **Header & Footer** with the file name in the **left section** of the footer. In Page Layout view, check that the WordArt is centered under the worksheet data. Center the worksheet **Horizontally** on the page, and then return to **Normal** view. Display the **Projected Investment Chart** sheet and insert a **Custom Footer** with the file name in the **Left section**.

14 Group the sheets, and then display the **Document Panel**. Add your name, your course name and section, and the keywords **investment portfolio**

15 **Save** your workbook. Print or submit electronically as directed by your instructor. If required by your instructor, print or create an electronic version of your worksheets with formulas displayed by using the instructions in Activity 1.16, and then **Close** Excel without saving so that you do not save the changes you made to print formulas.

End **You have completed Project 3E** ————

Apply **3B** skills from
these Objectives:

5 Design a Worksheet
for What-If Analysis

6 Answer What-If
Questions by
Changing Values in
a Worksheet

7 Chart Data with a
Line Chart

Mastering Excel | Project **3F** Benefit Analysis

In the following project, you will edit a worksheet that Jeffrey Lovins, Human Resources Director,
will use to prepare a five-year forecast of the annual cost of city employee benefits per employee.
Your completed worksheet will look similar to Figure 3.49.

Project Files

For Project 3F, you will need the following file:

e03F_Benefit_Analysis

You will save your workbook as:

Lastname_Firstname_3F_Benefit Analysis

Project Results

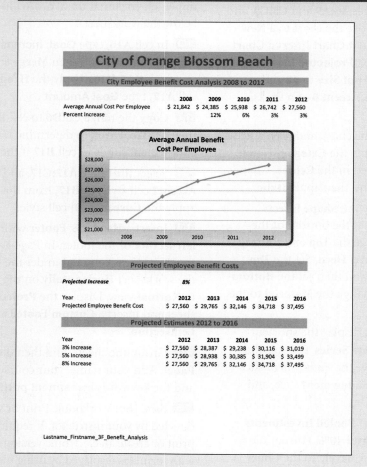

Figure 3.49

(Project 3F Benefit Analysis continues on the next page)

Content-Based Assessments

1 **Start** Excel. From your student files, open the file **e03F_Benefit_Analysis**. **Save** the file in your **Excel Chapter 3** folder as **Firstname_Lastname_3F_Benefit_Analysis**

2 In cell **C7**, construct a formula to calculate the percent of increase in employee annual benefit costs from 2008 to 2009. Format the result with the **Percent Style** and then fill the formula through cell **F7**.

3 In cell **A9**, type **Projected Employee Benefit Costs** and then use **Format Painter** to copy the formatting from cell **A3** to cell **A9**. In cell **A11**, type **Projected Increase** and then in cell **A13**, type **Year** In cell **A14**, type **Projected Employee Benefit Cost** and then in the range **B13:F13**, use the fill handle to enter the years 2012 through 2016. Apply **Bold** to the years. In cell **B14**, type **27560** and then from the **Cell Styles** gallery, apply the **Currency [0]** format. In cell **B11**, type **3%** which is the percent of increase from 2011 to 2012. To the range **A11:B11**, apply **Bold** and **Italic**.

4 In cell **C14**, construct a formula to calculate the annual cost of employee benefits for the year 2013 after the projected increase of 3% is applied. Fill the formula through cell **F14**, and then use **Format Painter** to copy the formatting from cell **B14** to the range **C14:F14**.

5 In cell **A16**, type **Projected Estimates 2012 to 2016** and then use **Format Painter** to copy the format from cell **A9** to cell **A16**. In cells **A18:A21**, type the following row titles:

> **Year**
> **3% Increase**
> **5% Increase**
> **8% Increase**

6 **Copy** the range **B13:F13**, and then **Paste** the selection to **B18:F18**. Copy the range **B14:F14** and then paste the

Values & Number Formatting to the range **B19:F19**. Complete the Projected Estimates section of the worksheet by changing the *Projected Increase* in **B11** to **5%** and then to **8%** copying and pasting the **Values & Number Formatting** to the appropriate ranges in the worksheet.

7 Select **rows 8:24**, and then **Insert** the same number of blank rows as you selected. **Clear Formatting** from the inserted rows. By using the data in **A5:F6**, insert a **Line with Markers** chart in the worksheet. Move the chart so that its upper left corner is positioned in cell **A9** and centered under the data above. Remove the **Legend**, and then replace the existing chart title with the two-line title **Average Annual Benefit Cost Per Employee** The text *Cost per Employee* should display on the second line. Change the title **Font Size** to **14**.

8 Format the **Primary Vertical Axis** so that the **Minimum** is **21000** and the **Major unit** is **1000** Format the **Chart Area** with a **Gradient fill** by applying the third **Preset color** in the third row—**Wheat**. Change the **Border Color** by applying a **Solid line—Orange, Accent 1, Darker 50%**. Change the **Width** of the border to **4** and apply the **Rounded corners** option.

9 Deselect the chart, and then insert a **Header & Footer** with the file name in the **left section** of the footer; center the worksheet **Horizontally** on the page. In the **Document Panel**, add your name, your course name and section, and the keywords **employee benefits, forecast**

10 **Save** your workbook. Print or submit electronically as directed by your instructor. If required by your instructor, print or create an electronic version of your worksheets with formulas displayed by using the instructions in Activity 1.16, and then **Close** Excel without saving so that you do not save the changes you made to print formulas.

End **You have completed Project 3F**

Apply **3A** and **3B** skills from these Objectives:

1. Chart Data with a Pie Chart
2. Format a Pie Chart
3. Edit a Workbook and Update a Chart
4. Use Goal Seek to Perform What-If Analysis
5. Design a Worksheet for What-If Analysis
6. Answer What-If Questions by Changing Values in a Worksheet
7. Chart Data with a Line Chart

Mastering Excel | Project **3G** Operations Analysis

In the following project, you will you will edit a workbook for Jennifer Carson, City Finance Manager, that summarizes the operations costs for the Public Works Department. Your completed worksheets will look similar to Figure 3.50.

Project Files

For Project 3G, you will need the following file:

e03G_Operations_Analysis

You will save your workbook as:

Lastname_Firstname_3G_Operations_Analysis

Project Results

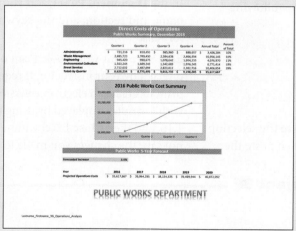

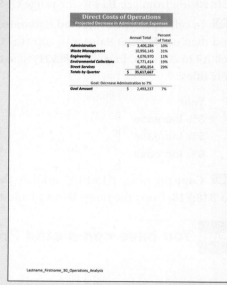

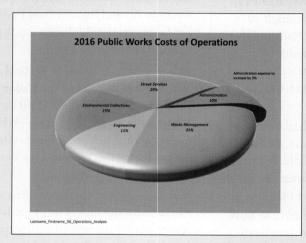

Figure 3.50

(Project 3G Operations Analysis continues on the next page)

Content-Based Assessments

Mastering Excel | Project 3G Operations Analysis (continued)

1 **Start** Excel. From your student files, open **e03G_Operations_Analysis**. **Save** the file as in your **Excel Chapter 3** folder as **Lastname_Firstname_3G_Operations_Analysis**

2 In the **Public Works** sheet, calculate totals in the ranges **F5:F9** and **B10:F10**. In cell **G5**, construct a formula to calculate the **Percent of Total** by dividing the **Annual Total** for **Administration** in cell **F5** by the **Annual Total** for all quarters in cell **F10**. Use absolute cell references as necessary, format the result in **Percent Style**, and then **Center**. Fill the formula down through cell **G9**.

3 Select the nonadjacent ranges **A5:A9** and **F5:F9**, and then insert a **Pie in 3-D** chart. Move the chart to a **New sheet** with the name **Public Works Summary Chart** Insert a **Chart Title** above the chart with the text **2016 Public Works Costs of Operations** and then change the **Font Size** to **28**.

4 Remove the **Legend** from the chart and then add **Data Labels** formatted so that only the **Category Name** and **Percentage** displays positioned in the **Center**. Change the data labels **Font Size** to **12**, and apply **Bold** and **Italic**.

5 Select the chart, and then modify the pie chart **Shape Effects** by changing the **Bevel**, **3-D Options**. Change the **Top** and **Bottom** options to the first **Bevel** type—**Circle**. Set the **Top Width** and **Height** boxes to **256 pt** and then set the **Bottom Width** and **Height** boxes to **50 pt** Change the **Material** to the fourth **Standard Effect** type—**Metal**.

6 In the displayed **Format Data Series** dialog box, on the left, click **Series Options**, and then change the **Angle of first** slice to **50** Explode the **Administration** slice slightly away from the pie. Format the **Chart Area** with a **Solid fill**—**Aqua, Accent 2**—in the sixth column, the first color.

7 Insert a **Text Box** positioned outside the upper corner of the **Administration** pie slice extending to the edge of the chart area and that is about one-half inch in height. In the text box, type **Administration expense to increase by 3%** Change the **Font Size** to **10.5**. Size the text box so that the text displays on two lines. On this chart sheet, insert a **Custom Footer** with the file name in the **left section**.

8 In the **Public Works** sheet, using the data in the nonadjacent ranges **B4:E4** and **B10:E10**, insert a **Line with Markers** chart in the worksheet. Move the chart so that its upper left corner is positioned in cell **A12**, aligned approximately under the *t* in the word *Collections* above.

Remove the **Legend** and then add a **Chart Title** above the chart with the text **2016 Public Works Cost Summary** Edit the **Primary Vertical Axis** so that the **Minimum** is **Fixed** at **8600000** and the **Major unit** is **Fixed** at **200000** Format the **Chart Area** with a **Solid fill** by applying **Aqua, Accent 2, Lighter 40%**—in the sixth column, the fourth color.

9 In cell **B35**, type **35617667** and then apply the **Currency [0]** cell style. In cell **C35**, construct a formula to calculate the **Projected Operations Costs** after the forecasted increase is applied. Fill the formula through cell **F35**, and then use **Format Painter** to copy the formatting from cell **B35** to the range **C35:F35**.

10 Insert a **WordArt** using the last style—**Fill - Brown, Accent 1, Metal Bevel, Reflection** Type **Public Works Department** and then change the **Font Size** to **32**. Drag to position the WordArt in cell **A38**, centered below the worksheet.

11 Change the **Orientation** to **Landscape**, and then use the **Scale to Fit** options to fit the **Height** to **1 page**. Insert a **Header & Footer** with the **file name** in the left area of the footer. In **Page Layout** view, check and adjust if necessary the visual centering of the chart and the WordArt. Center the worksheet **Horizontally** on the page, and then return to **Normal** view.

12 Display the **Projected Decrease sheet**. In cell **C5**, calculate the **Percent of Total** by dividing the *Administration Annual Total* by the *Totals by Quarter*, using absolute cell references as necessary. Apply **Percent Style** and then fill the formula from **C5:C9**.

13 **Copy** cell **B5**, and then use **Paste Special** to paste the **Values & Number Formatting** to cell **B13**. **Copy** and **Paste** cell **C5** to **C13**. With cell **C13** selected, use **Goal Seek** to determine the goal amount of administration expenses in cell **B13** if the value in **C13** is set to **7%**

14 On the **Projected Decrease** sheet, insert a **Header & Footer** with the file name in the **left section** of the footer, and then center the worksheet **Horizontally** on the page. Show the **Document Panel**. Add your name, your course name and section, and the keywords **public works**

15 **Save** your workbook. Print or submit electronically as directed by your instructor. If required by your instructor, print or create an electronic version of your worksheets with formulas displayed by using the instructions in Activity 1.16, and then **Close** Excel without saving so that you do not save the changes you made to print formulas.

End **You have completed Project 3G**

GO! Fix It | Project **3H** Recreation

Project Files

For Project 3H, you will need the following file:

e03H_Recreation

You will save your workbook as:

Lastname_Firstname_3H_Recreation

In this project, you will correct a worksheet that contains the annual enrollment of residents in city-sponsored recreation programs. From the student files that accompany this textbook, open the file e03H_Recreation, and then save the file in your chapter folder as **Lastname_Firstname_3H_Recreation**

To complete the project, you must find and correct errors in formulas and formatting. View each formula in the worksheet and edit as necessary. Review the format and title of the pie chart and make corrections and formatting changes as necessary. In addition to errors that you find, you should know:

- The pie chart data should include the Age Group and the Total columns.
- The Chart Area should include a blue solid fill background and the title font color should be white.
- The pie chart should be in a separate worksheet named **Enrollment Analysis Chart**

Add a footer to both sheets, and add your name, your course name and section, and the keywords **Parks and Recreation, enrollment** to the document properties. Save your file and then print or submit your worksheet electronically as directed by your instructor. If required by your instructor, print or create an electronic version of your worksheets with formulas displayed by using the instructions in Activity 1.16, and then close Excel without saving so that you do not save the changes you made to print formulas.

End You have completed Project 3H ———————————————————

Content-Based Assessments

GO! Make It | Project 3I Tax Projection

Project Files

For Project 3I, you will need the following file:

New blank Excel workbook

You will save your workbook as:

Lastname_Firstname_3I_Tax_Projection

Start a new blank Excel workbook and create the worksheet shown in Figure 3.51. In the range C7:F7, calculate the rate of increase from the previous year. In the range C31:F31, calculate the projected property tax for each year based on the forecasted increase. Complete the worksheet by entering in the range B36:F38, the projected property tax revenue for each year based on 2%, 3%, and 4% increases. Insert the chart as shown, using the 2010 through 2014 Property Tax Revenue data. Fill the chart area with the Daybreak gradient fill and change the chart title font size to 14. Scale the width to fit to one page, and then add your name, your course name and section, and the keywords **property tax** to the document properties. Save the file in your Excel Chapter 3 folder as **Lastname_Firstname_3I_Tax_Projection** and then print or submit electronically as directed by your instructor.

Project Results

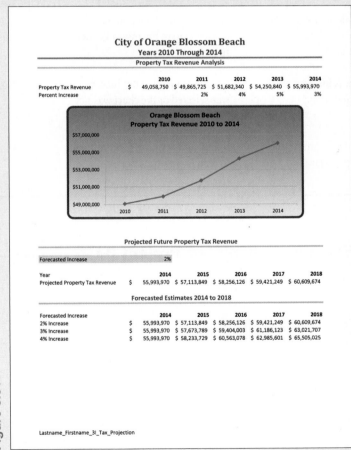

Figure 3.51

End **You have completed Project 3I**

Content-Based Assessments

GO! Solve It | Project 3J Staffing

Project Files

For Project 3J, you will need the following file:

  e03J_Staffing

You will save your workbook as:

  Lastname_Firstname_3J_Staffing

Open the file e03J_Staffing and save it as **Lastname_Firstname_3J_Staffing** Complete the worksheet by calculating totals and the % of Total Employees. Format the worksheet attractively including appropriate number formatting. Insert a pie chart in a separate sheet that illustrates the Two-Year Projection staffing levels by department and use the techniques that you practiced in this chapter to format the chart so that it is attractive and easy to understand. Change the angle of the first slice so that the Public Safety slice displays below the title. Then, insert a text box that indicates that the increase in Public Safety staffing is contingent upon City Council approval. Include the file name in the footer, add appropriate properties, save and submit as directed.

	Performance Level		
	Exemplary: You consistently applied the relevant skills	Proficient: You sometimes, but not always, applied the relevant skills	Developing: You rarely or never applied the relevant skills
Create formulas	All formulas are correct and are efficiently constructed.	Formulas are correct but not always constructed in the most efficient manner.	One or more formulas are missing or incorrect; or only numbers were entered.
Chart inserted and formatted	Chart was inserted and formatted properly.	Chart was inserted but incorrect data was selected or the chart was not formatted.	No chart was inserted.
Format attractively and appropriately	Formatting is attractive and appropriate.	Adequately formatted but difficult to read or unattractive.	Inadequate or no formatting.

(Performance Criteria)

End You have completed Project 3J

Content-Based Assessments

Apply a combination of
the **3A** and **3B** skills.

GO! Solve It | Project **3K** Water Usage

Project Files

For Project 3K, you will need the following file:

New blank Excel workbook
e03K_Beach

You will save your workbook as:

Lastname_Firstname_3K_Water_Usage

The City of Orange Blossom Beach is a growing community and the City Council has requested an analysis of future resource needs. In this project, you will create a worksheet for the Department of Water and Power that lists residential water usage over the past ten years and that forecasts the amount of water that city residents will use in the next ten years. Create a worksheet with the following data:

	2008	2010	2012	2014	2016
Water Use in Acre Feet	62500	68903	73905	76044	80342

Calculate the percent increase for the years 2010 to 2016. Below the Percent Increase, insert a line chart that illustrates the city's water usage from 2008 to 2016. Below the chart, add a section to the worksheet to calculate the projected water usage for the years 2016 to 2024 in two-year increments based on a 4% annual increase. The 2016 amount is 80,342. Format the chart and worksheet attractively with a title and subtitle, and apply appropriate formatting. If you choose to format the chart area with a picture, you can use e03K_Beach located with your student files. Include the file name in the footer and enter appropriate document properties. Save the workbook as **Lastname_Firstname_3K_Water_Usage** and submit it as directed.

		Performance Level		
		Exemplary: You consistently applied the relevant skills	**Proficient:** You sometimes, but not always, applied the relevant skills	**Developing:** You rarely or never applied the relevant skills
Performance Criteria	**Create formulas**	All formulas are correct and are efficiently constructed.	Formulas are correct but not always constructed in the most efficient manner.	One or more formulas are missing or incorrect or only numbers were entered.
	Insert and format line chart	Line chart created correctly and is attractively formatted.	Line chart was created but the data was incorrect or the chart was not appropriately formatted.	No line chart was created.
	Format attractively and appropriately	Formatting is attractive and appropriate.	Adequately formatted but difficult to read or unattractive.	Inadequate or no formatting.

End You have completed Project 3K

Outcomes-Based Assessments

Rubric

The following outcomes-based assessments are *open-ended assessments*. That is, there is no specific correct result; your result will depend on your approach to the information provided. Make *Professional Quality* your goal. Use the following scoring rubric to guide you in *how* to approach the problem, and then to evaluate *how well* your approach solves the problem.

The *criteria*—Software Mastery, Content, Format and Layout, and Process—represent the knowledge and skills you have gained that you can apply to solving the problem. The *levels of performance*—Professional Quality, Approaching Professional Quality, or Needs Quality Improvements—help you and your instructor evaluate your result.

	Your completed project is of Professional Quality if you:	Your completed project is Approaching Professional Quality if you:	Your completed project Needs Quality Improvements if you:
1-Software Mastery	Choose and apply the most appropriate skills, tools, and features and identify efficient methods to solve the problem.	Choose and apply some appropriate skills, tools, and features, but not in the most efficient manner.	Choose inappropriate skills, tools, or features, or are inefficient in solving the problem.
2-Content	Construct a solution that is clear and well organized, contains content that is accurate, appropriate to the audience and purpose, and is complete. Provide a solution that contains no errors in spelling, grammar, or style.	Construct a solution in which some components are unclear, poorly organized, inconsistent, or incomplete. Misjudge the needs of the audience. Have some errors in spelling, grammar, or style, but the errors do not detract from comprehension.	Construct a solution that is unclear, incomplete, or poorly organized; contains some inaccurate or inappropriate content; and contains many errors in spelling, grammar, or style. Do not solve the problem.
3-Format and Layout	Format and arrange all elements to communicate information and ideas, clarify function, illustrate relationships, and indicate relative importance.	Apply appropriate format and layout features to some elements, but not others. Overuse features, causing minor distraction.	Apply format and layout that does not communicate information or ideas clearly. Do not use format and layout features to clarify function, illustrate relationships, or indicate relative importance. Use available features excessively, causing distraction.
4-Process	Use an organized approach that integrates planning, development, self-assessment, revision, and reflection.	Demonstrate an organized approach in some areas, but not others; or, use an insufficient process of organization throughout.	Do not use an organized approach to solve the problem.

Outcomes-Based Assessments

Apply a combination of the 3A and 3B skills.

GO! Think | Project 3L School Enrollment

Project Files

For Project 3L, you will need the following file:

New blank Excel workbook

You will save your workbook as:

Lastname_Firstname_3L_School_Enrollment

Marcus Chavez, the Superintendent of Schools for the City of Orange Blossom Beach, has requested an enrollment analysis of students in the city public elementary schools in order to plan school boundary modifications resulting in more balanced enrollments. Enrollments in district elementary schools for the past two years are as follows:

School	2014 Enrollment	2015 Enrollment
Orange Blossom	795	824
Kittridge	832	952
Glenmeade	524	480
Hidden Trails	961	953
Beach Side	477	495
Sunnyvale	515	502

Create a workbook to provide Marcus with the enrollment information for each school and the total district enrollment. Insert a column to calculate the percent change from 2014 to 2015. Note that some of the results will be negative numbers. Format the percentages with two decimal places. Insert a pie chart in its own sheet that illustrates the 2015 enrollment figures for each school and format the chart attractively. Format the worksheet so that it is professional and easy to read and understand. Insert a footer with the file name and add appropriate document properties. Save the file as **Lastname_Firstname_3L_School_Enrollment** and print or submit as directed by your instructor.

End You have completed Project 3L ——————————————

Outcomes-Based Assessments

GO! Think | Project **3M** Park Acreage

Project Files

For Project 3M, you will need the following files:

>   **New blank Excel workbook**
>   **e03M_Park**

You will save your workbook as:

>   **Lastname_Firstname_3M_Park_Acreage**

The City of Orange Blossom Beach wants to maintain a high ratio of parkland to residents and has established a goal of maintaining a minimum of 50 parkland acres per 1,000 residents. The following table contains the park acreage and the population, in thousands, since 1980. Start a new blank Excel workbook and then enter appropriate titles. Then, enter the following data in the worksheet and calculate the *Acres per 1,000 residents* by dividing the Park acreage by the Population in thousands.

	1980	1990	2000	2010
Population in thousands	118.4	123.9	133.5	152.6
Park acreage	5,800	6,340	8,490	9,200
Acres per 1,000 residents				

Create a line chart that displays the Park Acres Per 1,000 Residents for each year. Format the chart professionally and insert the picture e03M_Park from your student files in the chart fill area. Below the chart, create a new section titled **Park Acreage Analysis** and then copy and paste the Years and the Park acreage values to the new section. Calculate the *Percent increase* from the previous ten years for the 1990, 2000, and 2010 years. Below the Park Acreage Analysis section, create a new worksheet section titled **Park Acreage Forecast** and then enter the following values.

	2010	2020	2030	2040
Population in thousands	152.6	173.2	197.7	225.3
Park acreage necessary				
Percent increase				

Calculate the *Park acreage necessary* to reach the city's goal by multiplying the Population in thousands by 50. Then calculate the *Percent increase* from the previous ten years for the 2020, 2030, and 2040 years. Use techniques that you practiced in this chapter to format the worksheet professionally. Insert a footer with the file name and add appropriate document properties. Save the file as **Lastname_Firstname_3M_Park_Acreage** and print or submit as directed by your instructor.

End **You have completed Project 3M** ──────────────

Apply a combination of the **3A** and **3B** skills.

You and GO! | Project **3N** Expense Analysis

Project Files

For Project 3N, you will need the following file:

New blank Excel workbook

You will save your workbook as:

Lastname_Firstname_3N_Expense_Analysis

Develop a worksheet that details the expenses you have incurred during the past two months and list the expenses for each month in separate columns. Calculate totals for each column and then add a column in which you can calculate the percent change from one month to the next. Insert and format a pie chart that illustrates the expenses that you incurred in the most recent month. After reviewing the pie chart, determine a category of expense in which you might be overspending, and then pull that slice out of the pie and insert a text box indicating how you might save money on that expense. Insert a footer with the file name and center the worksheet horizontally on the page. Save your file as **Lastname_Firstname_3N_Expense_Analysis** and submit as directed.

End **You have completed Project 3N** _____

Business Running Case

Razvan CHIRNOAGA/Shutterstock

This project relates to **Front Range Action Sports**, which is one of the country's largest retailers of sports gear and outdoor recreation merchandise. The company has large retail stores in Colorado, Washington, Oregon, California, and New Mexico, in addition to a growing online business. Major merchandise categories include fishing, camping, rock climbing, winter sports, action sports, water sports, team sports, racquet sports, fitness, golf, apparel, and footwear.

In this project, you will apply the skills you practiced from the Objectives in Excel Chapters 1 through 3. You will develop a workbook for Frank Osei, the Vice President of Finance, that contains year-end sales and inventory summary information. In the first two worksheets, you will summarize and chart net sales. In the next three worksheets, you will detail the ending inventory of the two largest company-owned production facilities in Seattle and Denver. Mr. Osei is particularly interested in data regarding the new line of ski equipment stocked at these two locations. In the last worksheet, you will summarize and chart annual expenses. Your completed worksheets will look similar to Figure 1.1.

Project Files

For Project BRC1, you will need the following files:

    eBRC1_Annual_Report
    eBRC1_Skiing

You will save your workbook as:

Lastname_Firstname_BRC1_Annual_Report

Project Results

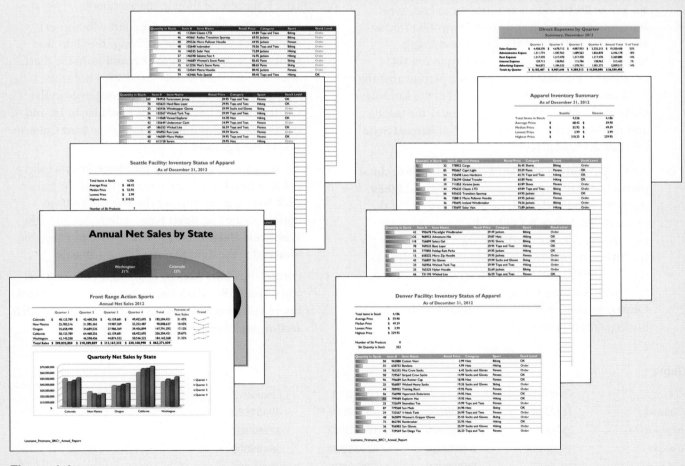

Figure 1.1

Business Running Case

Front Range Action Sports

1 **Start** Excel. From the student files that accompany this textbook, locate and open **eBRC1_Annual_Report**. In the location where you are storing your projects, create a new folder named **Front_Range_Action_Sports** or navigate to this folder if you have already created it. **Save** the new workbook as **Lastname_Firstname_BRC1_Annual_Report**

a. Familiarize yourself with the workbook by clicking each sheet tab, and then display the **Net Sales** worksheet. Click cell **B3**, and then use the fill handle to enter *Quarter 2, Quarter 3,* and *Quarter 4* in the range **C3:E3**. In the range **C4:E8**, enter the sales data for Quarter 2, Quarter 3, and Quarter 4 shown in **Table 1** at the bottom of the page.

b. Adjust the width of columns **B:F** to **125** pixels. Adjust the width of columns **G:H** to **100** pixels. In cell **F3**, type **Total** and then in the range **F4:F8**, calculate the annual total sales for each state. In the range **B9:F9**, calculate totals. In cell **G3**, type **Percent of Net Sales** and apply **Wrap Text** formatting to this cell. In cell **H3**, type **Trend** Using absolute cell references as necessary, in cell **G4**, construct a formula to calculate the percent that the *Colorado Total* is of the *Total Sales*. Fill the formula down through the range **G5:G8**. **Center** the results and then format the percentages with **Percent Style** and **two decimal places**.

c. Apply **Accounting Number Format** with **no decimal places** to the nonadjacent ranges **B4:F4** and **B9:F9**. Apply **Comma Style** with **no decimal** places to the range **B5:F8**. **Merge & Center** the two worksheet titles across columns **A:H**, and then to cell **A1**, apply the **Title** style and to cell **A2**, apply the **Heading 1** style. Apply the **Total** style to the range **B9:F9** and apply the **Heading 4** style to the range **B3:H3**. **Center** the column headings in **B3:H3** both horizontally and vertically.

d. In the range **H4:H8**, insert **Line** sparklines to represent the trend of each state across the four quarters. Add **Markers** and apply **Sparkline Style Accent 2 (no dark or light)**.

e. Select the range **A3:E8**, and then insert a **3-D Clustered Column** chart. Align the upper left corner of the chart inside the upper left corner of cell **A11**, and then size the chart so that its lower right corner is slightly inside cell **H24**. Apply chart **Style 26** and chart **Layout 1**. Replace the chart title text with **Quarterly Net Sales by State** Insert the file name in the **left section** of the footer, set the orientation to **Landscape**, and center the worksheet horizontally. Return to **Normal** view.

2 To show the percent that each state contributes to the total sales, select the nonadjacent ranges that represent the state names and state totals. Insert a **Pie in 3-D** chart and move the chart to a **New sheet**. Name the sheet **Net Sales by State** and then move the sheet so that it is the second sheet in the workbook.

a. Insert a **Chart Title** above the chart with the text **Annual Net Sales by State** Change the chart title **Font Size** to **36**. Remove the **Legend** from the chart, and then add **Data Labels** that display only the **Category Name** and **Percentage** positioned in the **Center**. Change the data labels **Font Size** to **14**, and then apply **Bold** and **Italic**. Change the **Font Color** to **White, Background 1**.

b. Select the entire pie, display the **Shape Effects** gallery, point to **Bevel**, and then at the bottom of the gallery, click **3-D Options**. Change the **Top** and **Bottom** options to the first **Bevel** type—**Circle**. Set all of the **Width** and **Height** boxes to **512** and then change the **Material** to the third **Standard** type—**Plastic**.

c. Format the **Chart Area** by applying a **Convex Bevel** and a **Solid fill—Dark Green, Accent 4, Lighter 60%**. Insert a **Custom Footer** with the **File Name** in the **left section**, and then **Save** the workbook.

Table 1

	Quarter 1	Quarter 2	Quarter 3	Quarter 4
Colorado	48123789	42468256	45159681	49452695
New Mexico	25783516	21985365	19987269	22252487
Oregon	35658498	34689526	37986369	39456899
California	58123789	64468256	65159681	68452695
Washington	42143258	46598456	44874332	50546222

---► (Return to Step 1-b)

(Business Running Case: Front Range Action Sports continues on the next page)

Business Running Case

3 Display the **Seattle Inventory** worksheet, and then in cell **B4**, construct a formula to calculate the *Total Items in Stock* by summing the **Quantity in Stock** column. Format the result with **Comma Style** and **no decimal places**.

a. In cell **B5**, construct a formula to calculate the average of the **Retail Price** column. In the range **B6:B8**, construct similar formulas to calculate the median, lowest, and highest retail prices. Format the results in **B5:B8** with **Accounting Number Format**. In cell **B10**, use the **COUNTIF** function to count the number of **Skiing** items that the Seattle location stocks.

b. In cell **G14**, enter an **IF** function to determine the items that must be ordered. If the **Quantity in Stock** is less than **50** then **Value_if_true** is **Order** Otherwise the **Value_if_false** is **OK** Fill the formula down through cell **G87**. Apply **Conditional Formatting** to the **Stock Level** column so that cells that contain the text *Order* are formatted with **Bold Italic** and with a **Font Color** of **Orange, Accent 1**. Apply **Orange Gradient Fill Data Bars** to the **Quantity in Stock** column.

c. Insert a table with headers using the range **A13:G87**. Apply **Table Style Light 11**. **Sort** the table from smallest to largest on the **Retail Price** column, and then filter the table on the **Sport** column to display the **Skiing** types. Display a **Total Row** in the table, and then in cell **A88**, **Sum** the **Quantity in Stock** for the **Skiing** items. Type the result in cell **B11**. Remove the total row from the table, clear the **Sport** filter so that all of the data displays, and then convert the table to a range.

d. Change the **Print Titles** option so that **row 13** prints at the top of each page. Insert the file name in the **left section** of the footer, set the orientation to **Landscape**, and center the worksheet horizontally. Return to **Normal** view.

4 Display the **Denver Inventory** worksheet, and then in cell **B4**, construct a formula to calculate the *Total Items in Stock* by summing the **Quantity in Stock** column. Format the result with **Comma Style** and **no decimal places**.

a. In the range **B5:B8**, use the appropriate statistical functions to calculate the price data. Format the results with **Accounting Number Format**. In cell **B10**, use the **COUNTIF** function to count the number of **Skiing** items that the Denver location stocks.

b. In cell **G14**, enter an **IF** function to determine the items that must be ordered. If the **Quantity in Stock** is less than **50 Value_if_true** is **Order** Otherwise the **Value_if_false** is **OK** Fill the formula down through cell **G87**. Apply **Conditional Formatting** to the **Stock Level** column so that cells that contain the text *Order* are formatted with **Bold Italic** and with a **Font Color** of **Dark Blue, Accent 3**. Apply **Light Blue Gradient Fill Data Bars** to the **Quantity in Stock** column.

c. Create a table with headers using the range **A13:G87**. Apply **Table Style Light 9**. **Sort** the table from smallest to largest on the **Retail Price** column, and then filter the table on the **Sport** column to display the **Skiing** types. Display a **Total Row** in the table and then in cell **A88**, **Sum** the **Quantity in Stock** for the **Skiing** items. Type the result in cell **B11**. Remove the total row from the table, clear the **Sport** filter so that all of the data displays, and then convert the table to a range.

d. Change the **Print Titles** option so that **row 13** prints at the top of each page. Insert the file name in the **left section** of the footer, set the orientation to **Landscape**, and center the worksheet horizontally. Return to **Normal** view.

e. Display the **Inventory Summary** sheet. In cell **B5**, enter a formula that references cell **B4** in the **Seattle Inventory** sheet so that the Seattle *Total Items in Stock* displays in **B5**. Create similar formulas to enter the **Average Price**, **Median Price, Lowest Price,** and **Highest Price** in the range **B6:B9**. Enter similar formulas in the range **C5:C9** so that the **Denver** totals display. Be sure the range **B6:C9** is formatted with **Accounting Number Format**. Insert the file name in the **left section** of the footer, set the orientation to **Portrait**, and center the worksheet horizontally. Return to **Normal** view. **Save** the workbook.

5 Display the **Annual Expenses** worksheet. Construct formulas to calculate the *Totals by Quarter* in the range **B10:E10** and the *Annual Totals* in the range **F5:F10**.

a. Using absolute cell references as necessary, in cell **G5**, construct a formula to calculate the *% of Total* by dividing the **Sales Expense Annual Total** by the **Annual Totals by Quarter**. Apply **Percent Style**, fill the formula down through the range **G6:G9**, and **Center** the percentages.

(Business Running Case: Front Range Action Sports continues on the next page)

Business Running Case

Front Range Action Sports (continued)

b. Apply appropriate financial formatting to the data using no decimal places, and apply the **Total** cell style to the *Totals by Quarter*. **Center** the column headings and apply the **Heading 4** cell style.

c. **Merge & Center** the worksheet title and subtitle across columns **A:G**, and then to cell **A1**, apply the **Title** style and to cell **A2**, apply the **Heading 1** style. To the range **A1:A2**, apply a **Fill Color** using **Dark Blue, Accent 3, Lighter 60%**.

d. Using the data in the nonadjacent ranges **B4:E4** and **B10:E10**, insert a **Line with Markers** chart. Position the upper left corner of the chart slightly inside cell **B12** and resize the chart so that the lower right corner is inside cell **F25**. Remove the **Legend** and then add a **Chart Title** above the chart with the text **2012 Direct Expenses**

e. Apply chart **Style 13**, and then format the **Chart Area** with the picture **eBRC1_Skiing** from your student files. Format the **Plot Area** by changing the **Fill** option to **No fill**. Edit the **Vertical (Value) Axis** so that the **Minimum** is **8000000** and the **Major unit** is **1000000**

6 Use **Format Painter** to copy the formatting from cell **A2** to **A27**. In cell **B32**, enter a formula that references the value in cell **F10**.

a. Using absolute cell references as necessary, in cell **C32**, construct a formula to calculate the projected expenses for 2013 after the *Forecasted increase* in cell **B29** is applied. Fill the formula through cell **F32**. If necessary, use Format Painter to copy the format in cell B32 to the remaining cells in the row.

b. On the **Page Layout tab**, in the **Scale to Fit group**, set both the **Width** and **Height** to scale to **1 page**. Insert the file name in the **left section** of the footer, set the orientation to **Landscape**, and center the worksheet horizontally. Return to **Normal** view. Display the **Document Properties**. Add your name, your course name and section, and the keywords **annual report**

c. **Save** your workbook. Select all the sheets, and then display and check the Print Preview. There are a total of 10 pages. Print or submit electronically as directed. If required by your instructor, print or create an electronic version of your worksheets with formulas displayed by using the instructions in Activity 1.16, and then **Close** Excel without saving so that you do not save the changes you made to print formulas.

End **You have completed Business Running Case 1** ————

Glossary

3-D The shortened term for *three-dimensional*, which refers to an image that appears to have all three spatial dimensions—length, width, and depth.

Absolute cell reference A cell reference that refers to cells by their fixed position in a worksheet; an absolute cell reference remains the same when the formula is copied.

Accounting Number Format The Excel number format that applies a thousand comma separator where appropriate, inserts a fixed U.S. Dollar sign aligned at the left edge of the cell, applies two decimal places, and leaves a small amount of space at the right edge of the cell to accommodate a parenthesis for negative numbers.

Active cell The cell, surrounded by a black border, ready to receive data or be affected by the next Excel command.

Address bar The bar at the top of a folder window with which you can navigate to a different folder or library, or go back to a previous one.

Alignment The placement of paragraph text relative to the left and right margins.

All Programs An area of the Start menu that displays all the available programs on your computer system.

Application Another term for a program.

Arguments The values that an Excel function uses to perform calculations or operations.

Arithmetic operators The symbols +, −, *, /, %, and ^ used to denote addition, subtraction (or negation), multiplication, division, percentage, and exponentiation in an Excel formula.

Auto Fill An Excel feature that generates and extends values into adjacent cells based on the values of selected cells.

AutoComplete (Excel) A feature that speeds your typing and lessens the likelihood of errors; if the first few characters you type in a cell match an existing entry in the column, Excel fills in the remaining characters for you.

AutoFit An Excel feature that adjusts the width of a column to fit the cell content of the widest cell in the column.

AutoPlay A Windows feature that displays when you insert a CD, a DVD, or other removable device, and which lets you choose which program to use to start different kinds of media, such as music CDs, or CDs and DVDs containing photos.

AutoSum Another name for the *SUM* function.

AVERAGE function An Excel function that adds a group of values, and then divides the result by the number of values in the group.

Axis A line that serves as a frame of reference for measurement and which borders the chart plot area.

Back and Forward buttons Buttons at the top of a folder window that work in conjunction with the address bar to change folders by going backward or forward one folder at a time.

Backstage tabs The area along the left side of Backstage view with tabs to display various pages of commands.

Backstage view A centralized space for file management tasks; for example, opening, saving, printing, publishing, or sharing a file. A navigation pane displays along the left side with tabs that group file-related tasks together.

Base The starting point; used in calculating the rate of increase, which is the amount of increase divided by the base.

Bevel A shape effect that uses shading and shadows to make the edges of a shape appear to be curved or angled.

Category axis The area along the bottom of a chart that identifies the categories of data; also referred to as the *x-axis*.

Category labels The labels that display along the bottom of a chart to identify the categories of data; Excel uses the row titles as the category names.

Cell The intersection of a column and a row.

Cell address Another name for a *cell reference*.

Cell content Anything typed into a cell.

Cell reference The identification of a specific cell by its intersecting column letter and row number.

Cell style A defined set of formatting characteristics, such as font, font size, font color, cell borders, and cell shading.

Center alignment The alignment of text or objects that is centered horizontally between the left and right margin.

Chart (Excel) The graphic representation of data in a worksheet; data presented as a chart is usually easier to understand than a table of numbers.

Chart area The entire chart and all of its elements.

Chart Elements box The box in the Chart Tools tabs from which you can select a chart element so that you can format it.

Chart layout The combination of chart elements that can be displayed in a chart such as a title, legend, labels for the columns, and the table of charted cells.

Chart Layouts gallery A group of predesigned chart layouts that you can apply to an Excel chart.

Chart sheet A workbook sheet that contains only a chart.

Chart style The overall visual look of a chart in terms of its graphic effects, colors, and backgrounds; for example, you can have flat or beveled columns, colors that solid or transparent, and backgrounds that are dark or light.

Chart Styles gallery A group of predesigned chart styles that you can apply to an Excel chart.

Chart types Various chart formats used in a way that is meaningful to the reader; common examples are column charts, pie charts, and line charts.

Click The action of pressing the left button on your mouse pointing device one time.

Column A vertical group of cells in a worksheet.

Column chart A chart in which the data is arranged in columns and which is useful for showing data changes over a period of time or for illustrating comparisons among items.

Column heading The letter that displays at the top of a vertical group of cells in a worksheet; beginning with the first letter of the alphabet, a unique letter or combination of letters identifies each column.

Comma Style The Excel number format that inserts thousand comma separators where appropriate and applies two decimal places; Comma Style also leaves space at the right to accommodate a parenthesis when negative numbers are present.

Command An instruction to a computer program that causes an action to be carried out.

Common dialog boxes The set of dialog boxes that includes Open, Save, and Save As, which are provided by the Windows programming interface, and which display and operate in all of the Office programs in the same manner.

Comparison operator Symbols that evaluate each value to determine if it is the same (=), greater than (>), less than (<), or in between a range of values as specified by the criteria.

Compressed file A file that has been reduced in size and thus takes up less storage space and can be transferred to other computers quickly.

Conditional format A format that changes the appearance of a cell—for example, by adding cell shading or font color—based on a condition; if the condition is true, the cell is formatted based on that condition, and if the condition is false, the cell is *not* formatted.

Constant value Numbers, text, dates, or times of day that you type into a cell.

Context sensitive A command associated with activities in which you are engaged; often activated by right-clicking a screen item.

Context sensitive command A command associated with activities in which you are engaged.

Contextual tabs Tabs that are added to the Ribbon automatically when a specific object, such as a picture, is selected, and that contain commands relevant to the selected object.

Copy A command that duplicates a selection and places it on the Clipboard.

COUNTIF function A statistical function that counts the number of cells within a range that meet the given condition and that has two arguments—the range of cells to check and the criteria.

Criteria (Excel) Conditions that you specify in a logical function.

Cut A command that removes a selection and places it on the Clipboard.

Data (Excel) Text or numbers in a cell.

Data bar A cell format consisting of a shaded bar that provides a visual cue to the reader about the value of a cell relative to other cells; the length of the bar represents the value in the cell—a longer bar represents a higher value and a shorter bar represents s lower value.

Data marker A column, bar, area, dot, pie slice, or other symbol in a chart that represents a single data point; related data points form a data series.

Data point A value that originates in a worksheet cell and that is represented in a chart by a data marker.

Data series Related data points represented by data markers; each data series has a unique color or pattern represented in the chart legend.

Default The term that refers to the current selection or setting that is automatically used by a computer program unless you specify otherwise.

Deselect The action of canceling the selection of an object or block of text by clicking outside of the selection.

Desktop In Windows, the opening screen that simulates your work area.

Detail sheets The worksheets that contain the details of the information summarized on a summary sheet.

Details pane The area at the bottom of a folder window that displays the most common file properties.

Dialog box A small window that contains options for completing a task.

Dialog Box Launcher A small icon that displays to the right of some group names on the Ribbon, and which opens a related dialog box or task pane providing additional options and commands related to that group.

Displayed value The data that displays in a cell.

Document properties Details about a file that describe or identify it, including the title, author name, subject, and keywords that identify the document's topic or contents; also known as *metadata*.

Double-click The action of clicking the left mouse button two times in rapid succession.

Drag The action of holding down the left mouse button while moving your mouse.

Drag and drop The action of moving a selection by dragging it to a new location.

Edit The actions of making changes to text or graphics in an Office file.

Ellipsis A set of three dots indicating incompleteness; when following a command name, indicates that a dialog box will display.

Enhanced ScreenTip A ScreenTip that displays more descriptive text than a normal ScreenTip.

Excel table A series of rows and columns that contains related data that is managed independently from the data in other rows and columns in the worksheet.

Expand Formula Bar button An Excel window element with which you can increase the height of the Formula Bar to display lengthy cell content.

Expand horizontal scroll bar button An Excel window element with which you can increase the width of the horizontal scroll bar.

Explode The action of pulling out one or more pie slices from a pie chart for emphasis.

Extract To decompress, or pull out, files from a compressed form.

File A collection of information stored on a computer under a single name, for example a Word document or a PowerPoint presentation.

File list In a folder window, the area on the right that displays the contents of the current folder or library.

Fill The inside color of an object.

Fill handle The small black square in the lower right corner of a selected cell.

Filter The process of displaying only a portion of the data based on matching a specific value to show only the data that meets the criteria that you specify.

Find and replace (Excel) A command that searches the cells in a worksheet—or in a selected range—for matches and then replaces each match with a replacement value of your choice.

Folder A container in which you store files.

Folder window In Windows, a window that displays the contents of the current folder, library, or device, and contains helpful parts so that you can navigate.

Font A set of characters with the same design and shape.

Font styles Formatting emphasis such as bold, italic, and underline.

Footer A reserved area for text or graphics that displays at the bottom of each page in a document.

Format (Excel) Changing the appearance of cells and worksheet elements to make a worksheet attractive and easy to read.

Format as you type The Excel feature by which a cell takes on the formatting of the number typed into the cell.

Format Painter An Office feature that copies formatting from one selection of text to another.

Formatting The process of establishing the overall appearance of text, graphics, and pages in an Office file—for example, in a Word document.

Formatting marks Characters that display on the screen, but do not print, indicating where the Enter key, the Spacebar, and the Tab key were pressed; also called *nonprinting characters*.

Formula AutoComplete An Excel feature which, after typing an = (equal sign) and the beginning letter or letters of a function name, displays a list of function names that match the typed letter(s).

Formula An equation that performs mathematical calculations on values in a worksheet.

Formula Bar An element in the Excel window that displays the value or formula contained in the active cell; here you can also enter or edit values or formulas.

Freeze Panes A command that enables you to select one or more rows or columns and freeze (lock) them into place; the locked rows and columns become separate panes.

Function A predefined formula—a formula that Excel has already built for you—that performs calculations by using specific values in a particular order or structure.

Fund A sum of money set aside for a specific purpose.

Gallery An Office feature that displays a list of potential results instead of just the command name.

General format The default format that Excel applies to numbers; this format has no specific characteristics—whatever you type in the cell will display, with the exception that trailing zeros to the right of a decimal point will not display.

General fund The term used to describe money set aside for the normal operating activities of a government entity such as a city.

Goal Seek A what-if analysis tool that finds the input needed in one cell to arrive at the desired result in another cell.

Groups On the Office Ribbon, the sets of related commands that you might need for a specific type of task.

Header A reserved area for text or graphics that displays at the top of each page in a document.

Horizontal window split box (Excel) An Excel window element with which you can split the worksheet into two horizontal views of the same worksheet.

Icons Pictures that represent a program, a file, a folder, or some other object.

IF function A function that uses a logical test to check whether a condition is met, and then returns one value if true, and another value if false.

Info tab The tab in Backstage view that displays information about the current file.

Insert Worksheet button Located on the row of sheet tabs, a sheet tab that, when clicked, inserts an additional worksheet into the workbook.

Insertion point A blinking vertical line that indicates where text or graphics will be inserted.

Keyboard shortcut A combination of two or more keyboard keys, used to perform a task that would otherwise require a mouse.

KeyTips The letter that displays on a command in the Ribbon and that indicates the key you can press to activate the command when keyboard control of the Ribbon is activated.

Labels Another name for a text value, and which usually provides information about number values.

Landscape orientation A page orientation in which the paper is wider than it is tall.

Left alignment (Excel) The cell format in which characters align at the left edge of the cell; this is the default for text entries and is an example of formatting information stored in a cell.

Legend A chart element that identifies the patterns or colors that are assigned to the categories in the chart.

Lettered column headings The area along the top edge of a worksheet that identifies each column with a unique letter or combination of letters.

Library In Windows, a collection of items, such as files and folders, assembled from various locations that might be on your computer, an external hard drive, removable media, or someone else's computer.

Line chart A chart type that is useful to display trends over time; time displays along the bottom axis and the data point values are connected with a line.

Live Preview A technology that shows the result of applying an editing or formatting change as you point to possible results—*before* you actually apply it.

Location Any disk drive, folder, or other place in which you can store files and folders.

Logical functions A group of functions that test for specific conditions and that typically use conditional tests to determine whether specified conditions are true or false.

Logical test Any value or expression that can be evaluated as being true or false.

Major unit The value in a chart's value axis that determines the spacing between tick marks and between the gridlines in the plot area.

MAX function An Excel function that determines the largest value in a selected range of values.

MEDIAN function An Excel function that finds the middle value that has as many values above it in the group as are below it; it differs from AVERAGE in that the result is not affected as much by a single value that is greatly different from the others.

Merge & Center A command that joins selected cells in an Excel worksheet into one larger cell and centers the contents in the new cell.

Metadata Details about a file that describe or identify it, including the title, author name, subject, and keywords that identify the document's topic or contents; also known as *document properties*.

Microsoft Access A database program, with which you can collect, track, and report data.

Microsoft Communicator An Office program that brings together multiple modes of communication, including instant messaging, video conferencing, telephony, application sharing, and file transfer.

Microsoft Excel A spreadsheet program, with which you calculate and analyze numbers and create charts.

Microsoft InfoPath An Office program that enables you to create forms and gather data.

Microsoft Office 2010 A Microsoft suite of products that includes programs, servers, and services for individuals, small organizations, and large enterprises to perform specific tasks.

Microsoft OneNote An Office program with which you can manage notes that you make at meetings or in classes.

Microsoft Outlook An Office program with which you can manage e-mail and organizational activities.

Microsoft PowerPoint A presentation program, with which you can communicate information with high-impact graphics.

Microsoft Publisher An Office program with which you can create desktop publishing documents such as brochures.

Microsoft SharePoint Workspace An Office program that enables you to share information with others in a team environment.

Microsoft Word A word processing program, also referred to as an authoring program, with which you create and share documents by using its writing tools.

MIN function An Excel function that determines the smallest value in a selected range of values.

Mini toolbar A small toolbar containing frequently used formatting commands that displays as a result of selecting text or objects.

Name Box An element of the Excel window that displays the name of the selected cell, table, chart, or object.

Navigate The process of exploring within the organizing structure of Windows.

Navigate (Excel) The process of moving within a worksheet or workbook.

Navigation pane (Windows) In a folder window, the area on the left in which you can navigate to, open, and display favorites, libraries, folders, saved searches, and an expandable list of drives.

Nonprinting characters Characters that display on the screen, but do not print, indicating where the Enter key, the Spacebar, and the Tab key were pressed; also called *formatting marks*.

Normal view (Excel) A screen view that maximizes the number of cells visible on your screen and keeps the column letters and row numbers close to the columns and rows.

NOW function An Excel function that retrieves the date and time from your computer's calendar and clock and inserts the information into the selected cell.

Number format A specific way in which Excel displays numbers in a cell.

Number values Constant values consisting of only numbers.

Numbered row headings The area along the left edge of a worksheet that identifies each row with a unique number.

Office Clipboard A temporary storage area that holds text or graphics that you select and then cut or copy.

Operators The symbols with which you can specify the type of calculation you want to perform in an Excel formula.

Option button A round button that allows you to make one choice among two or more options.

Options dialog box A dialog box within each Office application where you can select program settings and other options and preferences.

Order of operations The mathematical rules for performing multiple calculations within a formula.

Page Layout view A screen view in which you can use the rulers to measure the width and height of data, set margins for printing, hide or display the numbered row headings and the lettered column headings, and change the page orientation; this view is useful for preparing your worksheet for printing.

Pane (Excel) A portion of a worksheet window bounded by and separated from other portions by vertical and horizontal bars.

Paragraph symbol The symbol ¶ that represents a paragraph.

Paste The action of placing text or objects that have been copied or moved from one location to another location.

Paste area The target destination for data that has been cut or copied using the Office Clipboard.

Paste Options gallery (Excel) A gallery of buttons that provides a Live Preview of all the Paste options available in the current context.

PDF (Portable Document Format) file A file format that creates an image that preserves the look of your file, but that cannot be easily changed; a popular format for sending documents electronically, because the document will display on most computers.

Percent for new value = base percent + percent of increase The formula for calculating a percentage by which a value increases by adding the base percentage—usually 100%—to the percent increase.

Percentage rate of increase The percent by which one number increases over another number.

Picture element A point of light measured in dots per square inch on a screen; 64 pixels equals 8.43 characters, which is the average number of digits that will fit in a cell in an Excel worksheet using the default font.

Pie chart A chart that shows the relationship of each part to a whole.

Pixel The abbreviated name for a *picture element*.

Plot area The area bounded by the axes of a chart, including all the data series.

Point The action of moving your mouse pointer over something on your screen.

Point and click method The technique of constructing a formula by pointing to and then clicking cells; this method is convenient when the referenced cells are not adjacent to one another.

Pointer Any symbol that displays on your screen in response to moving your mouse.

Points A measurement of the size of a font; there are 72 points in an inch, with 10-12 points being the most commonly used font size.

Portrait orientation A page orientation in which the paper is taller than it is wide.

Preview pane button In a folder window, the button on the toolbar with which you can display a preview of the contents of a file without opening it in a program.

Print Preview A view of a document as it will appear when you print it.

Print Titles An Excel command that enables you to specify rows and columns to repeat on each printed page.

Program A set of instructions that a computer uses to perform a specific task, such as word processing, accounting, or data management; also called an *application*.

Program-level control buttons In an Office program, the buttons on the right edge of the title bar that minimize, restore, or close the program.

Protected view A security feature in Office 2010 that protects your computer from malicious files by opening them in a restricted environment until you enable them; you might encounter this feature if you open a file from an e-mail or download files from the Internet.

Pt. The abbreviation for *point*; for example when referring to a font size.

Quick Access Toolbar In an Office program, the small row of buttons in the upper left corner of the screen from which you can perform frequently used commands.

Quick Commands The commands Save, Save As, Open, and Close that display at the top of the navigation pane in Backstage view.

Range Two or more selected cells on a worksheet that are adjacent or nonadjacent; because the range is treated as a single unit, you can make the same changes or combination of changes to more than one cell at a time.

Range finder An Excel feature that outlines cells in color to indicate which cells are used in a formula; useful for verifying which cells are referenced in a formula.

Rate = amount of increase/base The mathematical formula to calculate a rate of increase.

Read-Only A property assigned to a file that prevents the file from being modified or deleted; it indicates that you cannot save any changes to the displayed document unless you first save it with a new name.

Relative cell reference In a formula, the address of a cell based on the relative position of the cell that contains the formula and the cell referred to.

Ribbon The user interface in Office 2010 that groups the commands for performing related tasks on tabs across the upper portion of the program window.

Ribbon tabs The tabs on the Office Ribbon that display the names of the task-oriented groups of commands.

Right-click The action of clicking the right mouse button one time.

Rounding A procedure in which you determine which digit at the right of the number will be the last digit displayed and then increase it by one if the next digit to its right is 5, 6, 7, 8, or 9.

Row A horizontal group of cells in a worksheet.

Row heading The numbers along the left side of an Excel worksheet that designate the row numbers.

Sans serif A font design with no lines or extensions on the ends of characters.

Scale to Fit Excel commands that enable you to stretch or shrink the width, height, or both, of printed output to fit a maximum number of pages.

Scaling (Excel) The process of shrinking the width and/or height of printed output to fit a maximum number of pages.

ScreenTip A small box that that displays useful information when you perform various mouse actions such as pointing to screen elements or dragging.

Scroll bar A vertical or horizontal bar in a window or a pane to assist in bringing an area into view, and which contains a scroll box and scroll arrows.

Scroll box The box in the vertical and horizontal scroll bars that can be dragged to reposition the contents of a window or pane on the screen.

Search box In a folder window, the box in which you can type a word or a phrase to look for an item in the current folder or library.

Select To highlight, by dragging with your mouse, areas of text or data or graphics, so that the selection can be edited, formatted, copied, or moved.

Select All box A box in the upper left corner of the worksheet grid that, when clicked, selects all the cells in a worksheet.

Series A group of things that come one after another in succession; for example, January, February, March, and so on.

Serif font A font design that includes small line extensions on the ends of the letters to guide the eye in reading from left to right.

Sheet tab scrolling buttons Buttons to the left of the sheet tabs used to display Excel sheet tabs that are not in view; used when there are more sheet tabs than will display in the space provided.

Sheet tabs The labels along the lower border of the Excel window that identify each worksheet.

Shortcut menu A menu that displays commands and options relevant to the selected text or object.

Sort The process of arranging data in a specific order based on the value in each field.

Sparkline A tiny chart in the background of a cell that gives a visual trend summary alongside your data; makes a pattern more obvious.

Split button A button divided into two parts and in which clicking the main part of the button performs a command and clicking the arrow opens a menu with choices.

Spreadsheet Another name for a *worksheet*.

Start button The button on the Windows taskbar that displays the Start menu.

Start menu The Windows menu that provides a list of choices and is the main gateway to your computer's programs, folders, and settings.

Statistical functions Excel functions, including the AVERAGE, MEDIAN, MIN, and MAX functions, which are useful to analyze a group of measurements.

Status bar (Excel) The area along the lower edge of the Excel window that displays, on the left side, the current cell mode, page number, and worksheet information; on the right side, when numerical data is selected, common calculations such as Sum and Average display.

Status bar The area along the lower edge of an Office program window that displays file information on the left and buttons to control how the window looks on the right.

Subfolder A folder within a folder.

SUM function A predefined formula that adds all the numbers in a selected range of cells.

Summary sheet A worksheet where totals from other worksheets are displayed and summarized.

Tabs On the Office Ribbon, the name of each activity area in the Office Ribbon.

Tags Custom file properties that you create to help find and organize your own files.

Task pane A window within a Microsoft Office application in which you can enter options for completing a command.

Text box A movable resizable container for text or graphics.

Text values Constant values consisting of only text, and which usually provides information about number values; also referred to as *labels*.

Theme A predesigned set of colors, fonts, lines, and fill effects that look good together and that can be applied to your entire document or to specific items.

Tick marks The short lines that display on an axis at regular intervals.

Title bar The bar at the top edge of the program window that indicates the name of the current file and the program name.

Toggle button A button that can be turned on by clicking it once, and then turned off by clicking it again.

Toolbar In a folder window, a row of buttons with which you can perform common tasks, such as changing the view of your files and folders or burning files to a CD.

Triple-click The action of clicking the left mouse button three times in rapid succession.

Trusted Documents A security feature in Office 2010 that remembers which files you have already enabled; you might encounter this feature if you open a file from an e-mail or download files from the Internet.

Underlying formula The formula entered in a cell and visible only on the Formula Bar.

Underlying value The data that displays in the Formula Bar.

USB flash drive A small data storage device that plugs into a computer USB port.

Value Another name for a *constant value*.

Value after increase = base x percent for new value The formula for calculating the value after an increase by multiplying the original value—the base—by the percent for new value (see the *Percent for new value* formula).

Value axis A numerical scale on the left side of a chart that shows the range of numbers for the data points; also referred to as the *y-axis*.

Vertical window split box (Excel) A small box on the vertical scroll bar with which you can split the window into two vertical views of the same worksheet.

Views button In a folder window, a toolbar button with which you can choose how to view the contents of the current location.

Volatile A term used to describe an Excel function that is subject to change each time the workbook is reopened; for example the NOW function updates itself to the current date and time each time the workbook is opened.

What-if analysis The process of changing the values in cells to see how those changes affect the outcome of formulas in a worksheet.

Window A rectangular area on a computer screen in which programs and content appear, and which can be moved, resized, minimized, or closed.

Windows Explorer The program that displays the files and folders on your computer, and which is at work anytime you are viewing the contents of files and folders in a window.

Windows taskbar The area along the lower edge of the Windows desktop that contains the Start button and an area to display buttons for open programs.

WordArt A gallery of text styles with which you can create decorative effects, such as shadowed or mirrored text.

Workbook An Excel file that contains one or more worksheets.

Workbook-level buttons Buttons at the far right of the Ribbon tabs that minimize or restore a displayed workbook.

Worksheet The primary document that you use in Excel to work with and store data, and which is formatted as a pattern of uniformly spaced horizontal and vertical lines.

x-axis Another name for the horizontal *(category) axis*.

y-axis Another name for the vertical *(value) axis*.

Zoom The action of increasing or decreasing the viewing area on the screen.

Index

SINGLE PC LICENSE AGREEMENT AND LIMITED WARRANTY